# Whillans's Tax Tables



## Finance (No 2) Act 2017 Edit.

Edited by

Claire Hayes CTA

Shilpa Veerappa ATT

Tolley®

**Members of the LexisNexis Group worldwide**

| | |
|---|---|
| United Kingdom | RELX (UK) Limited trading as LexisNexis, 1–3 Strand, London WC2N 5JR |
| Australia | Reed International Books Australia Pty Ltd trading as LexisNexis, Chatswood, New South Wales |
| Austria | LexisNexis Verlag ARD Orac GmbH & Co KG, Vienna |
| Benelux | LexisNexis Benelux, Amsterdam |
| Canada | LexisNexis Canada, Markham, Ontario |
| China | LexisNexis China, Beijing and Shanghai |
| France | LexisNexis SA, Paris |
| Germany | LexisNexis GmbH, Dusseldorf |
| Hong Kong | LexisNexis Hong Kong, Hong Kong |
| India | LexisNexis India, New Delhi |
| Italy | Giuffrè Editore, Milan |
| Japan | LexisNexis Japan, Tokyo |
| Malaysia | Malayan Law Journal Sdn Bhd, Kuala Lumpur |
| New Zealand | LexisNexis NZ Ltd, Wellington |
| Singapore | LexisNexis Singapore, Singapore |
| South Africa | LexisNexis Butterworths, Durban |
| USA | LexisNexis, Dayton, Ohio |

First published in 1948



Published by LexisNexis
This is a Tolley title


A CIP Catalogue record for this book is available from the British Library.

ISBN for this volume: 9781474304306

Printed and bound by CPI Group (UK) Ltd, Croydon, CR0 4YY

**Visit LexisNexis at www.lexisnexis.co.uk**

# Foreword

The Finance (No 2) Act 2017 Edition of Whillans's Tax Tables is a concise, quick and easy reference book containing rates, allowances and other useful information across all the main taxes, updated to reflect FA 2017, F(No 2)A 2017 and other changes since the Budget edition. Note that, at the time of writing, the Finance (No 2) Act 2017 had not completed its passage through Parliament. The content included here in this Whillans's edition is complete up to 23 October 2017.

As anticipated, the provisions mentioned in the Budget edition which were withdrawn from the March 2017 Finance Bill before enactment were reinstated in the September 2017 Finance Bill.

The Budget for setting the 2018–19 rates will be on 22 November 2017.

Chris Jones

Chairman, Tolley

# Disclaimer

While every care has been taken to ensure the accuracy of this work, no responsibility for loss or damage occasioned to any person acting or refraining from action as a result of any statement in it can be accepted by the authors, editor or publisher.

# Administration

## Bank base rates

| *Period* | *Rate* |
|---|---|
| **from 4 August 2016** | **0.25%** |
| 5 March 2009–3 August 2016 | 0.50% |
| 5 February 2009–4 March 2009 | 1.00% |
| 8 January 2009–4 February 2009 | 1.50% |

## Due dates for tax

### Capital gains tax

*Generally*

Normally 31 January following end of year of assessment. (TMA 1970 s 59B)

*Non-resident CGT disposals*

30 days after the date of completion of sale if not registered for self-assessment. (TMA 1970 s 59AA)

(See also *Extended due dates* under **Income tax**, see p 2.)

### Corporation tax

Must be paid electronically for tax due on or after 1 April 2011.

*Generally* (TMA 1970 s 59D)

9 months and 1 day after end of accounting period.

*Instalments for larger companies* (TMA 1970 s 59E; SI 1998/3175)

A 'large company' is any company responsible for paying the bank levy, and one whose augmented profits (see p 65) for the accounting period exceed £1.5m, divided by 1 plus the number of any active 51% group companies (before 1 April 2015, associated companies). A company is not a large company in respect of an accounting period if its total liability for that period is not more than £10,000, or if its profits for an accounting period are £10m or less and it was not a large company in the 12 months preceding that accounting period. For most large companies (those with no ring fence profits) the amount of each instalment for a 12 month accounting period will be one quarter of its total liability. The amount of each instalment for any accounting period longer than 3 months but shorter than 12 months is calculated using the formula 3 x CTI/n where CTI is the amount of a company's total liability for that accounting period, and n is the number of months in the accounting period. The due dates of instalments are as follows:

- 1st instalment: 6 months and 13 days from start of accounting period (or date of final instalment if earlier);
- 2nd instalment: 3 months after 1st instalment, if length of accounting period allows;
- 3rd instalment: 3 months after 2nd instalment, if length of accounting period allows;
- Final instalment: 3 months and 14 days from end of accounting period.

From 1 April 2019 revised payment dates in the third, sixth, ninth and twelfth months of their accounting period will apply to companies with annual taxable profits of £20 million or more. The £20 million threshold will be divided by the number of companies in the group.

*Close companies: tax on loans or benefits to participators*

9 months and 1 day after the end of the accounting period. To be included in instalment payments for large companies (see above) (TMA 1970 s 59E(11)).

## Income tax

*Payments on account* (TMA 1970 s 59A; SSCBA 1992 ss 11A, 16; SI 1996/1654)

A payment on account is required where a taxpayer was assessed to income tax in the immediately preceding year to an amount exceeding the amount of tax deducted at source in respect of that year (subject to a de minimis limit, see below).

The payment on account (which includes Class 4 NIC) is made in 2 equal instalments due on:

(a) 31 January during the year of assessment, and
(b) 31 July in the following year of assessment.

No payments on account are required where either:

(a) the aggregate of the liability (including Class 4 NIC) for the preceding year (net of tax deducted at source) is less than £1,000; or
(b) more than 80% of the taxpayer's income tax and Class 4 NIC liability for the preceding year was met by tax deducted at source (including PAYE).

Note that payments on account are not required for Class 2 NIC.

*Final payment* (TMA 1970 s 59B, Sch 3ZA)

Balance of income tax due for a year of assessment (after deducting payments on account, tax deducted at source and (before 2016–17) credits in respect of dividends, etc) is due on:

31 January following end of year of assessment (TMA 1970 s 59B(4)).

From 2015–16 Class 2 NIC is also due through the self-assessment system no later than 31 January following end of year of assessment.

*Extended due dates:*

(a) If a taxpayer has given notice of liability within 6 months of the end of the year of assessment , but a notice to make a return is not given until after 31 October following the end of the year of assessment, the due date is 3 months after the notice is given (TMA 1970 s 59B(3)).
(b) If tax is payable as a result of a taxpayer's notice of amendment, an HMRC notice of correction or an HMRC notice of closure following enquiry, in each case given less than 30 days before the due date (or the extended due date at (a) above), the due date is on or before the day following the end of a 30-day period beginning on the day on which the notice is given (TMA 1970 s 59B(5), Sch 3ZA).
(c) If an assessment other than a self-assessment or simple assessment is made, tax payable under the assessment is due on the day following the end of a 30-day period beginning on the day on which notice of the assessment is given (TMA 1970 s 59B(6)).

The extensions under (b) and (c) do *not* alter the due date for *interest purposes* (see p 4).

*Final tax payable under simple assessment:*

(a) If a taxpayer is given notice of the simple assessment after 31 October following the end of the year of assessment, the due date is 3 months after the notice is given (TMA 1970 s 59BA(4)).
(b) In any other case, due date is no later than 31 January following end of year of assessment (TMA 1970 s 59BA(5)).

**Harmonised interest regime** see p 4.
**Interest on overdue tax** see p 5.
**Interest on overpaid tax** see p 6.
**Penalties** see p 13.
**Remission of tax** see p 7.

## Inheritance tax

(IHTA 1984 s 226)

*Chargeable transfers other than on death, made between:*

| | | |
|---|---|---|
| 6 April and 30 September | – | 30 April in next year. |
| 1 October and 5 April | – | 6 months after end of month in which chargeable transfer is made. |

*Relevant property settlements periodic and exit charges*

– 6 months after end of month in which chargeable event occurs. (For chargeable events before 6 April 2014, tax is payable as for chargeable transfers other than on death, see above).

*Chargeable events following conditional exemption for heritage etc property and charge on disposal of trees or underwood before the second death:*

– 6 months after end of month in which chargeable event occurs.

*Transfers on death:*

| | | |
|---|---|---|
| Earlier of | (*a*) | 6 months after end of month in which death occurs, and |
| | (*b*) | delivery of account by personal representatives. |

*Tax or extra tax becoming payable on death:*

Chargeable transfers and potentially exempt transfers within 7 years of death.

– 6 months after end of month in which death occurs.

## PAYE and NIC

(SSCBA 1992 ss 11A, 15; SI 2001/1004; SI 2003/2682)

| | |
|---|---|
| Employer's tax and Class 1 NIC payable under PAYE | In-year payments – 14 days after end of tax month or quarter to which it relates (extended to 17 days where payments are made by electronic means).<br>Final payment for tax year – 19 April following deduction year (extended to 22 April where payments are made by electronic means). |
| Class 1A NIC | 19 July following year in which contributions due (extended to 22 July where payments are made by electronic means). |
| PAYE settlement agreement and Class 1B NIC | 19 October following year to which agreement relates (extended to 22 October where payments are made by electronic means). |
| Class 2 NIC | For 2015–16 onwards contributions based on an annual liability are due through the self-assessment system no later than 31 January following the tax year[1]. Previously due in 2 instalments on 31 January and 31 July. From April 2014 HMRC could collect outstanding Class 2 by an adjustment to PAYE codes. |
| Class 4 NIC | See under income tax on p 2. |

1 Those who do not pay through self-assessment will be sent a bill by HMRC. Voluntary payments may still be made. Class 2 will be abolished from April 2018, see p 117.

## Paying HMRC

HMRC have a number of bank accounts. The respective accounts to which payments should be made from UK bank accounts for the main taxes are as follows:

| Tax | Account name | Sort code | Account number |
|---|---|---|---|
| Self-assessment/ capital gains tax | HMRC Shipley | 08 32 10 | 12001020 |
| Self-assessment/ capital gains tax | HMRC Cumbernauld | 08 32 10 | 12001039 |
| Corporation tax | HMRC Shipley | 08 32 10 | 12001020 |
| Corporation tax | HMRC Cumbernauld | 08 32 10 | 12001039 |
| PAYE/ Class 1/ Class 1A NIC | HMRC Cumbernauld | 08 32 10 | 12001039 |
| Class 2 NIC[1] | HMRC NICO | 08 32 20 | 12001004 |

1 If taxpayer does not pay through self-assessment.

2 Where both Shipley and Cumbernauld can apply and a taxpayer does not know which accounts office he normally pays, generally he should send payment to Cumbernauld. For details of other taxes see the list of taxes at www.gov.uk/dealing-with-hmrc/paying-hmrc.

# Harmonised interest regime

(FA 2009 ss 101–104, Schs 53–54A; SI 2011/701; SI 2011/2391; SI 2013/280; SI 2013/2472; SI 2014/992; SI 2014/3269; SI 2015/974)

A harmonised interest regime is being phased in for all taxes and duties and currently applies to:

— income and capital gains tax self-assessment amounts including penalties from 31 October 2011,
— CIS late return penalties from 6 October 2011,
— tax agent dishonest conduct penalties from 1 April 2013,
— annual tax on enveloped dwellings and penalties from 1 October 2013,
— PAYE and CIS in-year amounts for 2014–15 onwards from 6 April 2014 (although from 6 October 2014 for in-year late filing penalties for employers with 50 or more employees, 6 March 2015 for in-year late filing penalties for employers with fewer than 50 employees, and 6 April 2015 for in-year late payment penalties),
— stamp duty reserve tax and penalties from 1 January 2015,
— diverted profits tax and penalties from 1 April 2015,
— Class 2 NIC from 6 April 2015.

For amounts outstanding immediately prior to 31 October 2011, the previous legislation for income and capital gains tax self-assessment (TMA 1970 s 86, TA 1988 s 824 and TCGA 1992 s 283) had effect up to and including 30 October 2011 (see below and p 5), and the new legislation applies thereafter.

For annual PAYE payments such as Classes 1A and 1B NIC HMRC will continue to charge interest on any amount which remains unpaid after the due date.

Appointed Day Orders will be made in due course to align the treatment of interest and penalties for inheritance tax purposes with other taxes (F(No 2)A 2015 s 15).

The measure provides for differential interest charged and paid by HMRC to be based around the Bank of England base rate. The current late payment rate is:

| Late payment interest | *Rate* |
|---|---|
| **from 23 August 2016** | **2.75%** |
| 29 September 2009–22 August 2016 | 3.00% |

The current repayment rate is:

| Repayment interest | *Rate* |
|---|---|
| **from 29 September 2009** | **0.50%** |

Late payment interest runs from the start date to the date of payment. The start date is generally the date on which the amount becomes due and payable, but special rules apply as follows:

Where an amount is due as a result of—

(a) an amendment or correction to an assessment or self-assessment; or
(b) an HMRC assessment in place of, or in addition to, an assessment made by the taxpayer; or
(c) an HMRC assessment in place of an assessment which ought to have been made by the taxpayer,

the start date is the date it would have been if the original assessment or self-assessment had been complete and accurate and made on the date (if any) by which it was required to be made, and the tax had been due and payable as a result of the original assessment or self-assessment.

Repayment interest runs from the start date until the date the payment or repayment is made. The start date in the case of an amount paid to HMRC is the later of—

(i) the date the amount was paid to HMRC; and
(ii) the date on which the amount became due and payable to HMRC (in a case where the amount has been paid in connection with a liability to make a payment to HMRC, and it is to be repaid by them).

The start date, in the case of an amount which has not been paid to HMRC and which is payable by virtue of a return or a claim having been submitted, is the later of—

(1) the date (if any) on which the return or claim was required to be submitted; and
(2) the date on which the return or claim was submitted.

The start date in the case of the carry back of losses or averaging claims is 31 January following the *later* tax year in relation to the claim.

# Interest on overdue tax

See p 4 regarding the **harmonised interest regime** and the taxes to which this currently applies. The provisions on interest on overdue tax continue to apply to taxes where the harmonised interest regime does not yet apply, and applied to other taxes before the transition to the harmonised regime.

## Income tax, capital gains tax, NICs Class 1, 1A, 1B, 4, stamp duty, stamp duty reserve tax and stamp duty land tax

For amounts outstanding in relation to income and capital gains tax self-assessment (including Class 4 NIC) immediately prior to 31 October 2011 the rules under TMA 1970 s 86 have effect up to and including 30 October 2011, and the rules under FA 2009 ss 101 and 103 on p 4 have effect thereafter.

These provisions apply to Class 1 NIC before 6 April 2014, and stamp duty reserve tax payable before 1 January 2015 only. The rules under FA 2009 ss 101 and 103 on p 4 have effect thereafter.

Interest runs from the due date (see p 2 for income tax and p 1 for capital gains tax) to the date of payment, on the amount outstanding. Interest is payable gross and is not tax deductible.

| *Period* | *Rate* |
|---|---|
| **from 23 August 2016** | **2.75%** |
| 29 September 2009–22 August 2016 | 3.00% |
| 24 March 2009–28 September 2009 | 2.50% |
| 27 January 2009–23 March 2009 | 3.50% |
| 6 January 2009–26 January 2009 | 4.50% |

## Corporation tax

Interest runs from the due date (see p 1) to the date of payment. For instalment payments by large companies for accounting periods ending after 30 June 1999, a special rate of interest runs from the due date to the earlier of the date of payment and nine months after the end of the accounting period (after which the normal rate applies).

**Corporation tax self-assessment** (accounting periods ending after 30 June 1999)

| *Period* | *Normal rate* |
|---|---|
| **from 23 August 2016** | **2.75%** |
| 29 September 2009–22 August 2016 | 3.00% |
| 24 March 2009–28 September 2009 | 2.50% |
| 27 January 2009–23 March 2009 | 3.50% |
| 6 January 2009–26 January 2009 | 4.50% |

| *Period* | *Special rate for instalment payments (except where still unpaid nine months after end of accounting period)* |
|---|---|
| **from 15 August 2016** | **1.25%** |
| 16 March 2009–14 August 2016 | 1.50% |
| 16 February 2009–15 March 2009 | 2.00% |
| 19 January 2009–15 February 2009 | 2.50% |

**Corporation tax pay and file** (accounting periods ending after 30 September 1993)

| *Period* | *Rate* |
|---|---|
| **from 23 August 2016** | **2.75%** |
| 29 September 2009–22 August 2016 | 3.00% |
| 24 March 2009– 28 September 2009 | 1.75% |
| 27 January 2009–23 March 2009 | 2.75% |
| 6 January 2009–26 January 2009 | 3.50% |

## Income tax on company payments (due on or after 14 October 1999)

| *Period* | *Rate* |
|---|---|
| **from 23 August 2016** | **2.75%** |
| 29 September 2009–22 August 2016 | 3.00% |
| 24 March 2009– 28 September 2009 | 2.50% |
| 27 January 2009–23 March 2009 | 3.50% |
| 6 January 2009–26 January 2009 | 4.50% |

## Inheritance tax[1]

Interest runs from the due date[2] (see p 2) to the date of payment.

| *Period* | *Rate* |
|---|---|
| **from 23 August 2016** | **2.75%** |
| 29 September 2009–22 August 2016 | 3.00% |
| 24 March 2009–28 September 2009 | 0.00% |
| 27 January 2009–23 March 2009 | 1.00% |
| 6 January 2009–26 January 2009 | 2.00% |

1 Appointed Day Orders will be made in due course to align the treatment of interest and penalties for inheritance tax purposes with other taxes.

2 Where higher IHT is payable as a result of IHTA 1984 Sch A1 or the F(No 2)A 2017 domicile changes, interest runs from the last day of the month following the month of Royal Assent to F(No 2)A 2017 if later than normal payment date.

# Interest on overpaid tax

See p 4 regarding the **harmonised interest regime** and the taxes to which this currently applies. The provisions on interest on overpaid tax continue to apply to taxes where the harmonised interest regime does not yet apply, and applied to other taxes before the transition to the harmonised regime.

## Income tax, capital gains tax, NICs Class 1, 1A, 1B, 4, stamp duty, stamp duty reserve tax and stamp duty land tax

For amounts in relation to income and capital gains tax self-assessment (including Class 4 NIC) outstanding immediately prior to 31 October 2011 the rules under TA 1988 s 824 and TCGA 1992 s 283 have effect up to and including 30 October 2011, and the rules under FA 2009 ss 102 and 103 on p 4 have effect thereafter.

These provisions apply to Class 1 NIC before 6 April 2014, and stamp duty reserve tax payable before 1 January 2015 only. The rules under FA 2009 ss 101 and 103 on p 4 have effect thereafter.

Calculated as simple interest on the amount of tax repaid. The supplement is tax free.

| *Period* | *Rate* |
|---|---|
| **from 29 September 2009** | **0.50%** |
| 27 January 2009–28 September 2009 | 0.00% |
| 6 January 2009–26 January 2009 | 0.75% |

### Income tax

(TA 1988 s 824; FA 1997 s 92; ITTOIA 2005 s 749; SI 2011/701)

From 1996–97 for amounts which become repayable up to and including 30 October 2011 (from 1997–98 for partnerships whose trade, profession or business commenced before 6 April 1994) repayment supplement applies to:

- (a) amounts paid on account of income tax
- (b) income tax paid by or on behalf of an individual
- (c) late payment penalties for income and capital gains tax self-assessment under FA 2009 Sch 56
- (d) penalties incurred by an individual under any provision of TMA 1970

but excluding amounts paid in excess of the maximum the taxpayer is required to pay.

Except for tax deducted at source, the repayment supplement runs *from* the date on which the tax or penalty was paid *to* the date on which the order for repayment is issued. For tax deducted at source, repayment supplement runs from 31 January after the end of the tax year for which the tax was deducted.

### Capital gains tax

(TCGA 1992 s 283; SI 2011/701)

From 1996–97 for amounts which become repayable up to and including 30 October 2011 repayment supplement runs *from* the date on which the tax was paid *to* the date on which the order for repayment is issued.

### Inheritance tax

(IHTA 1984 s 235)

Repayments of inheritance tax or interest paid carries interest *from* the date of payment *to* the date on which the order for repayment is issued. Before 29 September 2009, the prescribed rates for unpaid tax applied equally to repayment supplements. From 29 September 2009, the rate is 0.5%.

Appointed Day Orders will be made in due course to align the treatment of interest and penalties for inheritance tax purposes with other taxes.

## Companies

### Corporation tax self-assessment (accounting periods ending after 30 June 1999)

*Normal rates*

Rates on overpaid corporation tax in respect of periods after normal due date (SI 1989/1297 reg 3BB).

| *Period* | *Rate* |
|---|---|
| **from 29 September 2009** | **0.50%** |
| 27 January 2009–28 September 2009 | 0.00% |
| 6 January 2009–26 January 2009 | 1.00% |

*Special rates*

For instalment payments by large companies and early payments by other companies, a special rate of interest runs from the date the excess arises (but not earlier than the due date of the first instalment) to the earlier of the date the repayment order is issued and nine months and one day after the end of the accounting period, after which the normal rate of interest (as above) applies.

Rates on overpaid instalment payments and on corporation tax paid early (but not due by instalments).

| *Period* | *Rate* |
|---|---|
| **from 21 September 2009** | **0.50%** |
| 16 March 2009–20 September 2009 | 0.25% |
| 16 February 2009–15 March 2009 | 0.75% |
| 19 January 2009–15 February 2009 | 1.25% |

### Corporation tax pay and file (accounting periods ending before 1 July 1999)

| *Period* | *Rate* |
|---|---|
| **from 29 September 2009** | **0.50%** |
| 27 January 2009–28 September 2009 | 0.00% |
| 6 January 2009–26 January 2009 | 0.50% |

# Direct recovery of debt

(F(No 2)A 2015 Sch 8)

From 18 November 2015 HMRC are able to secure payment of tax and tax credit debts directly from debtors' bank and building society accounts (including funds held in cash in Individual Savings Accounts) that have a minimum aggregate credit of £5,000. HMRC will only take action against debtors who owe over £1,000 of debt, and will only put a hold on the funds in the affected account up to the value of the debt. Safeguards in place include a face-to-face visit with an HMRC officer, a specialist unit to deal with cases involving the vulnerable, and availability of appeal to the County Court.

# Remission of tax

(Concession A19)

By concession, arrears of tax may be waived if they result from HMRC's failure to make proper and timely use of information supplied by the taxpayer or, where it affects the taxpayer's coding, by his or her employer. The concession also applies to information supplied by the Department for Work and Pensions affecting the taxpayer's entitlement to a retirement, disability or widow's pension. The concession only applies where the taxpayer could reasonably have believed that his or her affairs were in order and (unless the circumstances are exceptional) where the taxpayer is notified of the arrears more than 12 months after the end of the tax year in which HMRC received the information indicating that more tax was due.

# Special relief

(TMA 1970 Sch 1AB para 3A; FA 1998 Sch 18 para 51BA)

From 1 April 2011 a statutory 'special relief' is available which allows HMRC to give effect to a claim for repayment or discharge of an amount of tax that a person is liable to pay, but which the person believes is not due or, if it has been paid, was not due, where the usual time limits for such relief have expired. Relief is only available to taxpayers in receipt of an income tax or corporation tax self-assessment determination made by HMRC in the absence of a self-assessment return being submitted, and where the following specific conditions are met: (a) it would be unconscionable for HMRC to seek to recover the amount or to refuse to repay it if it has already been paid; (b) that the person's tax affairs are otherwise up to date, or arrangements have been put in place to HMRC's satisfaction, to bring them up to date as far as possible; and (c) the person has not previously claimed special relief, or its concessionary predecessor equitable liability, whether or not such a claim was successful. This latter condition may be waived in exceptional circumstances. There is no time limit for claiming the relief.

# Certificates of tax deposit

Certificates are not available for purchase for use against corporation tax or PAYE liabilities. Certificates are available to individuals, partnerships, individual partners, trustees, personal representatives and companies for the payment of income tax, Class 4 NIC, capital gains tax (but not that payable by companies etc on disposals of high value UK residential property, see p 65), inheritance tax, or petroleum revenue tax. Minimum first deposit £500; subsequent deposits not less than £250 or amount required to bring total deposits up to £500 (ie where total deposits have fallen below that amount). Interest is paid gross and is chargeable to tax. It will only be paid for the first six years of a deposit. A deposit bears interest for the first year at the rate in force at the time of the deposit and for each subsequent year at the rate in force on the anniversary of the deposit.

HMRC provide an interest calculator tool on their website.

| *Date of deposit* | *Amount* | *Held for (mths in yr)* | *Pay't of tax %* | *Cashed %* |
|---|---|---|---|---|
| 9.1.09–5.2.09 | Under £100,000 | No limit | 0.00 | 0.00 |
| | £100,000 or over | under 1 | 0.00 | 0.00 |
| | | 1–under 3 | 1.50 | 0.75 |
| | | 3–under 6 | 1.25 | 0.50 |
| | | 6–under 9 | 1.25 | 0.50 |
| | | 9–12 | 1.25 | 0.50 |
| 6.2.09–5.3.09 | Under £100,000 | No limit | 0.00 | 0.00 |
| | £100,000 or over | under 1 | 0.00 | 0.00 |
| | | 1–under 3 | 1.00 | 0.50 |
| | | 3–under 6 | 1.00 | 0.50 |
| | | 6–under 9 | 1.00 | 0.50 |
| | | 9–12 | 0.75 | 0.25 |
| **6.3.09–** | Under £100,000 | No limit | 0.00 | 0.00 |
| | £100,000 or over | under 1 | 0.00 | 0.00 |
| | | 1–under 3 | 0.75 | 0.25 |
| | | 3–under 6 | 0.75 | 0.25 |
| | | 6–under 9 | 0.75 | 0.25 |
| | | 9–12 | 0.75 | 0.25 |

# Student loan deductions

## Plan 1

| | Percentage of income above the threshold | Threshold |
|---|---|---|
| **2017–18** | **9%** | **£17,775 per year<br>£1,481 per month<br>£341 per week** |
| 2016–17 | 9% | £17,495 per year<br>£1,457 per month<br>£336 per week |
| 2015–16 | 9% | £17,335 per year<br>£1,444 per month<br>£333 per week |
| 2014–15 | 9% | £16,910 per year<br>£1,409.16 per month<br>£325.19 per week |
| 2013–14 | 9% | £16,365 per year<br>£1,363.75 per month<br>£314.71 per week |
| 2012–13 | 9% | £15,795 per year<br>£1,316.25 per month<br>£303.75 per week |

## Plan 2

| | Percentage of income above the threshold | Threshold |
|---|---|---|
| **2017–18** | **9%** | **£21,000 per year<br>£1,750 per month<br>£403 per week** |
| 2016–17 | 9% | £21,000 per year<br>£1,750 per month<br>£403 per week |

# Filing dates

## Corporation tax

(FA 1998 Sch 18 paras 14, 15; SI 2003/282 reg 3(2A))

The return must be filed on the latest of the following dates—

(a) 12 months from the end of the period for which the return is made;

(b) where the company makes up its accounts for a period not exceeding 18 months, 12 months from the end of that period;

(c) where the company makes up its accounts for a period exceeding 18 months, 30 months from the start of that period;

(d) 3 months from the date of issue of the notice requiring the return.

From 1 April 2011 all company returns for accounting periods ending after 31 March 2010 must be filed online. Computations and, in most cases, accounts must be submitted in iXBRL format. From October 2014 micro-entities have the option to file simplified accounts.

## Income tax and capital gains tax

(TMA 1970 ss 8, 8A, 12AA; SI 2003/2682 reg 186)

| | |
|---|---|
| Basic position for paper returns. | On or before 31 October following end of tax year. |
| Basic position for electronic returns. | On or before 31 January following end of tax year. |
| Paper return and notice to file return issued after 31 July but on or before 31 October following end of tax year. | Within 3 months of date of notice. |
| Electronic return and notice to file return issued after 31 July but on or before 31 October following end of tax year. | On or before 31 January following end of tax year. |
| Paper or electronic return and notice to file return issued after 31 October following end of tax year. | Within 3 months of date of notice. |
| Paper return and taxpayer wishes tax underpayment of less than £3,000 to be coded out. | On or before 31 October following end of tax year. |
| Electronic return and taxpayer wishes tax underpayment of less than £3,000 to be coded out. | Before 31 December following end of tax year. |

## Non-resident capital gains tax

(TMA 1970 s 12ZB)

30 days after the date of completion of sale via online NRCGT return.

## Withdrawal of self-assessment notice

(TMA 1970 s 8B)

HMRC may withdraw a notice to file a self-assessment tax return in certain circumstances. The statutory power has effect for returns for 2012–13 onwards. Penalties for failure to make a return may be cancelled.

## Simple assessment

(TMA 1970 ss 28H–28J, 31AA)

From 2016–17 HMRC may make an assessment of an individual's or trustee's income tax or capital gains tax liability without that person first being required to complete a self-assessment return. HMRC will instead assess their tax liability on the basis of information already held. The assessment notice must include details of the information used and the amount of tax due. The assessment may be appealed or queried without formal appeal. HMRC may withdraw a simple assessment notice.

# Penalties

## Penalties — modernised penalty regime

A modernised penalty regime is being rolled out to all taxes and duties with the exception of tax credits. The penalty regime in force in respect of various defaults is set out below.

### Inaccuracy in return or other document

(FA 2007 Sch 24 para 1; SI 2017/355; SI 2017/259)

| *Applies to* | *Commencement date* | *Penalty details* |
|---|---|---|
| IT, CGT, CT, VAT, CIS, NIC Classes 1 and 4[1] | Return periods starting 1 April 2008 where the return is due to be filed on or after 1 April 2009 | Penalty based on potential lost revenue<br>Careless inaccuracy — 30%<br>Deliberate but not concealed — 70%<br>Deliberate and concealed — 100%<br>*Reductions for disclosure*<br>Unprompted disclosure minimum penalties nil, 20% and 30%<br>Prompted disclosure minimum penalties 15%, 35% and 50% |
| IHT, SDLT, SDRT, other taxes, levies and duties (except tax credits) | Return periods starting 1 April 2009 where the return is due to be filed on or after 1 April 2010, or where the liability arises on or after 1 April 2010; for IHT in respect of deaths from 1 April 2009 | |
| Class 1A NIC | 2010–11 returns | |
| Corporation tax credit, return by registered pension scheme | Return periods starting 1 April 2009 where the return is due to be filed on or after 1 April 2010 | |
| Annual tax on enveloped dwellings | 2013–14 returns | |
| Non-resident CGT | 6 April 2015 | |
| Class 2 NIC | 6 April 2015 | |
| Apprenticeship levy | 6 April 2017 | |
| IT, CGT but offshore matter Extended to IHT and offshore transfers (see note)[2] | 6 April 2011 (see note)[2] | Penalties above are increased by either 0%, 50% or 100% depending on the territory concerned (see table on pp 14–15 for a list of territories in each category)<br>Statutory limits for reductions for disclosure apply |

1 From 2013–14 for RTI purposes an inaccuracy in any full payment submission can attract a penalty. HMRC may issue one penalty notice for multiple inaccuracy penalties in a year.

2 From 1 April 2016 the offshore penalty regime is amended to include IHT. From 1 April 2017 for IHT transfers and from 6 April 2016 otherwise, the regime also applies to domestic offences where the proceeds are hidden offshore. From a date to be appointed the territory classification system will be updated to reflect the jurisdictions that adopt the new global standard of automatic tax information exchange and there will be four levels of penalty instead of three.

### Inaccuracy in return or other document as a result of third party providing incorrect (or withholding) information

(FA 2007 Sch 24 para 1A)

| *Applies to* | *Commencement date* | *Penalty details* |
|---|---|---|
| IT, CGT, CT, VAT, IHT, CIS, NIC Classes 1 and 4, SDLT, SDRT, other taxes, levies and duties (except tax credits) | 1 April 2009 where the return is due to be filed on or after 1 April 2010 | 100% of potential lost revenue<br>Subject to reduction for disclosure as for inaccuracies above |
| Class 1A NIC | 2010–11 returns | |
| Annual tax on enveloped dwellings | 2013–14 returns | |

## Failure to notify HMRC of an error in an assessment (within 30 days)

(FA 2007 Sch 24 para 2)

| *Applies to* | *Commencement date* | *Penalty details* |
|---|---|---|
| IT, CGT, CT, VAT, CIS, NIC Classes 1 and 4 | 1 April 2008 where the return is due to be filed on or after 1 April 2009 | 30% of potential lost revenue<br>*Reductions for disclosure*<br>Unprompted disclosure minimum penalty nil<br>Prompted disclosure minimum penalty 15% |
| IHT, SDLT, SDRT, other taxes, levies and duties (except tax credits) | 1 April 2009 where the return is due to be filed on or after 1 April 2010 | |
| Class 1A NIC | 2010–11 returns | |
| Annual tax on enveloped dwellings | 2013–14 returns | |

## Failure to notify chargeability (includes failure to register for VAT)

(FA 2008 Sch 41; SI 2017/259)

| *Applies to* | *Commencement date* | *Penalty details* |
|---|---|---|
| IT, CGT, NIC Class 4[2] | 2009–10 | Penalty based on potential lost revenue<br>Failure to notify — 30%<br>Deliberate but not concealed — 70%<br>Deliberate and concealed — 100%<br>*Reductions for disclosure*<br>Unprompted disclosure minimum penalties nil (within 12 months late), 10% (more than 12 months late), 20% and 30%<br>Prompted disclosure minimum penalties 15%, 35%, 50% |
| CT | Accounting periods ending on or after 31 March 2010 | |
| Other taxes, levies and duties (not IHT, SDLT, SDRT) | Obligations arising on or after 1 April 2010 | |
| Diverted profits tax | Accounting periods beginning on or after 1 April 2015 | |
| IT, CGT but offshore matter Extended to offshore transfers (see note)[1] | 6 April 2011 (see note)[1] | Penalties above are increased by either 0%, 50% or 100% depending on the territory concerned (see table on pp 14–15 for a list of territories in each category)<br>Statutory limits for reductions for disclosure apply |

1 From 6 April 2016 the offshore penalty regime is amended to apply to domestic offences where the proceeds are hidden offshore. From a date to be appointed the territory classification system will be updated to reflect the jurisdictions that adopt the new global standard of automatic tax information exchange and there will be four levels of penalty instead of three.

2 Before 6 April 2015, there were similar provisions for Class 2 NIC but in separate legislation.

## Failure to make returns on time

(FA 2009 Sch 55; FA 2010 Sch 1; SI 2003/2682; SI 2017/259)

<table>
<tr><th>Applies to</th><th>Commencement date</th><th>Penalty details</th></tr>
<tr><td>Bank Payroll Tax</td><td>31 August 2010</td><td rowspan="6">Initial penalty £100<br>Failure continues for more than three months — with notice — £10 per day for up to 90 days<br>Six months late — greater of 5% of the tax due and £300<br>12 months late — same penalty as for 6 months late unless deliberately withholding the return<br>Deliberate withholding of the return more than 12 months — 70% of tax due (minimum £300)<br>Deliberate and concealed withholding of the return more than 12 months — 100% of tax due (minimum £300)<br>Reductions for disclosure<br>Unprompted disclosure minimum penalty 20% and 30%<br>Prompted disclosure minimum penalties 35% and 50%</td></tr>
<tr><td>IT, CGT, NIC Class 4[5]</td><td>6 April 2011</td></tr>
<tr><td>Return by Registered Pension scheme</td><td>1 April 2011</td></tr>
<tr><td>Annual tax on enveloped dwellings</td><td>2013–14 returns due 1 October 2013</td></tr>
<tr><td>Stamp duty reserve tax</td><td>1 January 2015</td></tr>
<tr><td>Class 2 NIC</td><td>6 April 2015</td></tr>
<tr><td>Non-resident CGT[6]</td><td>26 March 2015</td><td>Penalties as above except the £10 daily penalty</td></tr>
<tr><td>CIS returns</td><td>6 October 2011</td><td>Initial penalty £100<br>After two months — £200<br>Six months late — greater of 5% of the tax due and £300<br>12 months late — same penalty as for 6 months late unless deliberately withholding the return<br>Deliberate withholding of the return more than 12 months — 70% of tax due (minimum £1,500)<br>Deliberate and concealed withholding of the return more than 12 months — 100% of tax due (minimum £3,000)<br>Reductions for disclosure<br>Unprompted disclosure minimum penalty 20% and 30%<br>Prompted disclosure minimum penalties 35% and 50%<br>Special rules apply to the first returns made on registration for CIS so that the maximum total penalty that can apply for the initial and second fixed penalties for all such returns is £3,000. Subsequent tax-geared penalties may still be incurred.<br>Where a CIS return only relates to persons registered for 'gross payment' a tax-geared penalty after 6 months or 12 months cannot apply. In these cases the person is liable to the fixed amount penalty.</td></tr>
<tr><td>PAYE Real Time Information. Failure during a tax month to make a return on or before the filing date (normally the date employee is paid)</td><td>6 October 2014 in relation to 2014–15 onwards for employers with 50 or more employees<br>6 March 2015 for employers with fewer than 50 employees[1]</td><td>First failure in a tax year — nil<br>Second and subsequent failure in tax year<br>1–9 employees — £100<br>10–49 employees — £200<br>50–249 employees — £300<br>250 or more employees — £400[2]<br>Failure continues for more than three months — with notice — 5% of tax due<br>New employers only: A failure in the 'initial period'[3] — nil</td></tr>
</table>

| Applies to | Commencement date | Penalty details |
|---|---|---|
| IT, CGT but offshore matter<br>Extended to offshore transfers (see note)[4] | 6 April 2011(see note)[4] | Penalties above for a return later than 12 months which has been withheld are increased by either 0%, 50% or 100% depending on the territory concerned (see table on pp 14–15 for a list of territories in each category)<br>Statutory limits for reductions for disclosure apply |

1 For 2013–14 the rules in the PAYE table on p 16 under 'failure to submit year-end PAYE returns' apply.

2 Before 6 April 2018 employers will not incur penalties for delays of up to 3 days in filing PAYE information. HMRC now take a more proportionate approach and concentrate on the more serious defaults on a risk-assessed basis.

3 A penalty will not be issued to a new employer if their first FPS is received within 30 days of making the first payment to their employee(s) (known as the 'initial period'). After that, normal penalties rules will apply if there is a failure to file on time.

4 From 6 April 2016 the offshore penalty regime is amended to apply to domestic offences where the proceeds are hidden offshore. From a date to be appointed the territory classification system will be updated to reflect the jurisdictions that adopt the new global standard of automatic tax information exchange and there will be four levels of penalty instead of three. Proposed to be extended to IHT failures.

5 HMRC will accept reasonable excuses from taxpayers who are generally compliant without further investigation.

6 Does not apply to an elective return made under TMA 1970 s 12ZBA. HMRC confirmed in June 2017 that they no longer issue the £10 daily penalty and such past penalties will be withdrawn.

## Failure to pay tax on time

(FA 2009 Sch 56; FA 2010 Sch 1)

| Applies to | Commencement date | Penalty details |
|---|---|---|
| PAYE[1], NIC Class 1, CIS[2], student loan deductions. | 2010–11 liabilities (on a risk assessed basis at present) | Penalty based on number of late payments in a year applied to the amounts paid late<br>1 late payment — nil<br>2, 3, 4 late payments — 1%<br>5, 6, 7 late payments — 2%<br>8, 9, 10 late payments — 3%<br>11, 12 late payments — 4%<br>Any amount paid 6 months late — 5%<br>Any amount paid 12 months late — 5% |
| NIC Class 1A and 1B (SI 2001/1004 reg 67B) | 2010–11 | 31 days late — 5%<br>6 months late — 5%<br>12 months late — 5% |
| Bank Payroll Tax | 31 August 2010 | 1 day late — 5%<br>5 months late — 5%<br>11 months late — 5% |
| Tax due by Registered Pension schemes | Payments due 30 September 2010 | 31 days late — 5%<br>6 months late — 5%<br>12 months late — 5% |
| IT, CGT payable under self-assessment | 6 April 2011 for self-assessment for 2010–11 onwards | 31 days late — 5%<br>6 months late — 5%<br>12 months late — 5% |
| Annual tax on enveloped dwellings | 2013–14 payments due 31 October 2013 | 31 days late — 5%<br>6 months late — 5%<br>12 months late — 5% |
| Stamp duty reserve tax | 1 January 2015 | 31 days late — 5%<br>6 months late — 5%<br>12 months late — 5% |
| Class 2 NIC | 6 April 2015 | 31 days late — 5%<br>6 months late — 5%<br>12 months late — 5% |

1 It had been intended to charge automatic in-year late payment penalties for RTI from 6 April 2015 but HMRC confirmed that late payment penalties will continue to be reviewed on a risk-assessed basis rather than be issued automatically. From 2014–15 a 'tolerance' of £100 has been introduced for PAYE in-year late payment penalties. Where the difference between the total of all the amounts that the employer is due to pay to HMRC for a tax period and the amount paid over for that period is no more than £100 the employer will not be liable to a late payment penalty.

2 From 2014–15 a 'tolerance' of £100 has been introduced for CIS in-year late payment penalties. Where the difference between the amount that the contractor is due to pay to HMRC for a tax period and the amount paid over for that period is no more than £100 the contractor will not be liable to a late payment penalty.

## Offshore penalties — territory categories[8]

*Category 1*

| | | | |
|---|---|---|---|
| Anguilla | Estonia | Japan | Poland |
| Aruba | Finland | Korea, South | Portugal[4] |
| Australia | France[2] | Latvia | Romania |
| Belgium | Germany | Liechtenstein (from 24 July 2013)[7] | Slovakia |
| Bulgaria | Greece | Lithuania | Slovenia |
| Canada | Guernsey[3] | Malta | Spain[5] |
| Cayman Islands | Hungary | Montserrat | Sweden |
| Cyprus | Ireland | Netherlands (not including Bonaire, Sint Eustatius and Saba) | Switzerland (from 24 July 2013)[7] |
| Czech Republic | Isle of Man | New Zealand (not including Tokelau) | USA (not including overseas territories and possessions)[6] |
| Denmark (not including Faroe Islands or Greenland)[1] | Italy | Norway | |

1 Faroe Islands and Greenland are in Category 2.
2 Includes overseas Departments of France; the overseas collectivities of France are in Category 2.
3 Includes Alderney and Sark.
4 Includes Madeira and the Azores.
5 Includes the Canary Islands and other overseas territories of Spain.
6 The overseas territories and possessions of the USA are in Category 2.
7 SI 2013/1618 changed the level of penalties which may be charged for 14 specified countries from 24 July 2013. This is to reflect the entry into force of tax information exchange and enhanced tax cooperation agreements with those countries. Liechtenstein and Switzerland were previously in Category 2.
8 From a date to be set by Treasury Order the territory classification system will be updated to reflect the jurisdictions that adopt the new global standard of automatic tax information exchange.

*Category 2*

Territories not listed in Categories 1 or 3 (other than the UK) will be in Category 2. Crown Dependencies and Overseas Territories of the UK are, unless listed, in Category 2.

*Category 3*

| | | | |
|---|---|---|---|
| Albania | Costa Rica | Kyrgyzstan | (Before 24 July 2013) *Saint Lucia*[2] |
| Algeria | Curaçao | Lebanon | (Before 24 July 2013) *Saint Vincent and the Grenadines*[2] |
| Andorra | Cuba | Macau[1] | (Before 24 July 2013) *San Marino*[2] |
| (Before 24 July 2013) *Antigua and Barbuda*[2] | Democratic People's Republic of Korea | Marshall Islands | Seychelles |
| (Before 24 July 2013) *Armenia*[2] | (Before 24 July 2013) *Dominica*[2] | (Before 24 July 2013) *Mauritius*[2] | Sint Maarten |
| (Before 24 July 2013) *Bahrain*[2] | Dominican Republic | Micronesia, Federated States of | Suriname |
| (Before 24 July 2013) *Barbados*[2] | Ecuador | Monaco | Syria |
| (Before 24 July 2013) *Belize*[2] | El Salvador | Nauru | Tokelau |
| Bonaire, Sint Eustatius and Saba | Gabon | Nicaragua | Tonga |
| Brazil | (Before 24 July 2013) *Grenada*[2] | Niue | Trinidad and Tobago |
| Cameroon | Guatemala | Palau | United Arab Emirates |
| Cape Verde | Honduras | Panama | Uruguay |
| Colombia | Iran | Paraguay | |
| Congo, Republic of | Iraq | Peru | |
| Cook Islands | Jamaica | (Before 24 July 2013) *Saint Kitts and Nevis*[2] | |

1 China and Hong Kong are in Category 2.

2 SI 2013/1618 changed the level of penalties which may be charged for 14 specified countries from 24.7.13. This is to reflect the entry into force of tax information exchange and enhanced tax cooperation agreements with those countries. 12 of the countries highlighted in this table are in Category 2 from 24.7.13.

## Offshore assets moves

(FA 2015 Sch 21; SI 2015/866; SI 2017/989)

| Applies to | Commencement date | Penalty details |
|---|---|---|
| Offshore assets move from a specified territory to a non-specified territory where IT, CGT or IHT penalty under FA 2007 Sch 24 para 1, FA 2008 Sch 41, or FA 2009 Sch 55 above already applies for a deliberate failure (see table below for a list of specified territories) | 27 March 2015 | 50% of amount of original penalty |

### Offshore assets move penalties — specified territories

| | | | |
|---|---|---|---|
| Andorra | Curaçao | Japan | Qatar |
| Anguilla | Cyprus | Jersey | Romania |
| Antigua and Barbuda | Czech Republic | Korea, South | Russia |
| Argentina | Denmark | Kuwait[1] | Saint Kitts and Nevis |
| Aruba | Dominica | Latvia | Saint Lucia |
| Australia | Estonia | Lebanon[1] | Saint Vincent and the Grenadines |
| Austria | Faroe Islands | Liechtenstein | Samoa |
| The Bahamas | Finland | Lithuania | San Marino |
| Bahrain[1] | France | Luxembourg | Saudi Arabia |
| Barbados | Germany | Macau | Seychelles |
| Belgium | Ghana[1] | Malaysia | Singapore |
| Belize | Gibraltar | Malta | Sint Maarten |
| Bermuda | Greece | Marshall Islands | Slovak Republic |
| Brazil | Greenland | Mauritius | Slovenia |
| British Virgin Islands | Grenada | Mexico | South Africa |
| Brunei Darussalam | Guernsey | Monaco | Spain |
| Bulgaria | Hong Kong | Montserrat | Sweden |
| Canada | Hungary | Nauru[1] | Switzerland |
| Cayman Islands | Iceland | Netherlands (including Bonaire, Sint Eustatius and Saba) | Trinidad and Tobago |
| Chile | India | New Zealand (not including Tokelau) | Turkey |
| China | Indonesia | Niue | Turks and Caicos Islands |
| Colombia | Ireland | Norway | United Arab Emirates |
| Cook Islands[1] | Isle of Man | Panama[1] | Uruguay |
| Costa Rica | Israel | Poland | Vanuatu[1] |
| Croatia | Italy | Portugal | |

1 Added from 3.11.17 when Albania and USA (excluding overseas territories and possessions) removed.

### Deliberate enablers of offshore evasion or non-compliance

| Applies to | Commencement date | Penalty details |
|---|---|---|
| A person who has enabled another person (Q) to commit a relevant offence in relation to IT, CGT or IHT, or to engage in conduct which makes Q liable to a penalty under FA 2007 Sch 24 para 1, FA 2008 Sch 41, FA 2009 Sch 55, or FA 2015 Sch 21 above, provided certain other conditions are met (FA 2016 Sch 20; SI 2016/1249). | 1 January 2017 | For penalties other than under FA 2015 Sch 21, the higher of—<br>(a) 100% of potential lost revenue; and<br>(b) £3,000<br>For penalties under FA 2015 Sch 21, the higher of—<br>(a) 50% of potential lost revenue in respect of the original tax non-compliance; and<br>(b) £3,000<br>Reductions available for disclosure |

## Asset-based penalty for offshore inaccuracies and failures

| Applies to | Commencement date | Penalty details |
|---|---|---|
| A person to whom a CGT, IHT or asset-based IT penalty under FA 2007 Sch 24 para 1, FA 2008 Sch 41, or FA 2009 Sch 55 above already applies for a deliberate failure in relation to an offshore matter or transfer for a tax year in which the potential lost revenue exceeds £25,000 (FA 2016 Sch 22; SI 2017/277). | 2016–17 onwards for CGT and IT<br>Transfers of value on or after 1 April 2017 for IHT | The lower of—<br>(a) 10% of the value of the asset; and<br>(b) 10 times the offshore potential lost revenue (as defined)<br>Reductions available for disclosure |

## Personal tax and corporation tax

| *Offence* | *Penalty* |
|---|---|
| **Failure to render return** for corporation tax (FA 1998 Sch 18 paras 17, 18). | (*a*) £100 if up to three months late (£500 if previous two returns also late);<br>(*b*) £200 if over three months late (£1,000 if previous two returns also late);<br>(*c*) if failure continues, on final day for delivery of return or, if later, 18 months after return period, 10% of tax unpaid 18 months after return period (20% of tax unpaid at that date if return not made within two years of return period). |
| **Failure to maintain records** supporting personal and trustees' returns of partnership returns (TMA 1970 s 12B). | Up to £3,000. |
| **Fraudulently or negligently** making an incorrect statement in connection with a claim to reduce payments on account (TMA 1970 s 59A(6)). | Up to the amount (or additional amount) payable on account if a correct statement had been made. |
| **Deliberately or recklessly failing to pay corporation tax due** in respect of total liability of company for accounting period, or fraudulently or negligently making claim for repayment (TMA 1970 s 59E(4); SI 1998/3175 reg 13). | Penalty not exceeding twice amount of interest charged under SI 1998/3175 reg 7. |

## PAYE

| *Offence* | *Penalty* |
|---|---|
| **Failure to submit return P9D or P11D** (benefits in kind) by due date (6 July following subsequent tax years) (TMA 1970 s 98(1)). | (*a*) Initial penalty up to £300; and<br>(*b*) continuing penalty up to £60 for each day on which the failure continues. |
| **Failure to submit information in connection with mandatory e-filing** from 2004–05 onwards (SI 2003/2682 as amended by 2009/2029 reg 14). | Penalty based on number of employees not exceeding £3,000 for 1,000 or more employees. |
| **Failure to submit returns P11D(b)** (Class 1A NIC returns) by due date (6 July following tax year, but by concession until 31 March 2013, 19 July applied) (SI 2001/1004 reg 81(2)). | (*a*) First 12 months: penalty of £100 for each 50 employees (or part thereof) for each month the failure continues (but total penalty not to exceed total Class 1A NIC due);<br>(*b*) failures exceeding 12 months: a penalty not exceeding the amount of Class 1A NIC due and unpaid after 19 July following tax year. |
| ***Repealed provisions*** | |
| **Failure to submit year-end PAYE returns** final FPS, or EPS, or EYU as applicable, formerly P14 (individual end of year summary), P35 (annual return), P38 or P38A (supplementary returns for employees not on P35) by due date (19 May following tax year) (TMA 1970 s 98A). | (*a*) *First 12 months: penalty of £100 for each 50 employees (or part thereof) for each month the failure continues;*<br>(*b*) *failures exceeding 12 months: penalty up to amount of PAYE or NIC due and unpaid after 19 April following tax year.*<br>***Replaced by penalty under FA 2009 Sch 55 from 6 October 2014 for 2014–15 onwards.*** |

## Inheritance tax returns and information[1]

| Offence | Penalty |
|---|---|
| **Failure to deliver an account** within 12 months of death (unless tax is less than £100 or there is a reasonable excuse) (IHTA 1984 s 245). | (*a*) Initial penalty of £100 (or the amount of tax payable if less);<br>(*b*) further penalty up to £60 (where penalty determined by court or tribunal) for each day on which the failure continues;<br>(*c*) if failure continues after six months after the date on which account is due, and proceedings not commenced, a further penalty of £100 (or amount of tax payable if less); and<br>(*d*) if failure continues one year after end of the period in which account is due, and IHT is payable, a penalty not exceeding £3,000. |
| **Failure to submit account or notify** HMRC under IHTA 1984 s 218A if a disposition on a death is varied within six months of the variation and additional tax is payable (IHTA 1984 s 245A(1A), (1B)). | (*a*) Initial penalty up to £100;<br>(*b*) further penalty up to £60 (if determined by court or tribunal) for each day on which the failure continues;<br>(*c*) up to £3,000 if failure continues after 12 months from date notification is due. |
| **Failure to provide information etc** under IHTA 1984 s 218 concerning a settlement by a UK-domiciled settlor with non-resident trustees (IHTA 1984 s 245A(1)). | (*a*) Initial penalty up to £300; and<br>(*b*) further penalty up to £60 (where penalty determined by court or tribunal) for each day on which the failure continues. |
| **Person other than the taxpayer fraudulently or negligently** delivering, furnishing or producing incorrect accounts, information or documents (IHTA 1984 s 247(3); FA 2004 s 295(4), (9)). | Up to £3,000. |
| ***Repealed provisions*** | |
| **Incorrect return etc:** Assisting in or inducing the delivery, furnishing or production of any account, information or document knowing it to be incorrect (IHTA 1984 s 247(4)). | *Up to £3,000.*<br>***Repealed with effect from 1 April 2013. See now tax agent dishonest conduct penalties under FA 2012 Sch 38 (see p 19).*** |

1 Appointed Day Orders will be made in due course to align the treatment of interest and penalties for inheritance tax purposes with other taxes.

## Special returns of information

| Offence | Penalty |
|---|---|
| **Failure to comply with a notice** to deliver a return or other document, furnish particulars or make anything available for inspection under any of the provisions listed in column 1 of the table in TMA 1970 s 98. | (*a*) Initial penalty up to £300;<br>(*b*) further penalty up to £60 for each day on which the failure continues. |
| **Failure to furnish information**, give certificates or produce documents or records under any of the provisions listed in column 2 of the table in TMA 1970 s 98. | (*a*) Initial penalty up to £300; and<br>(*b*) further penalty up to £60 for each day on which the failure continues. |
| **Failure to deduct income tax at source** from payments of interest or royalties under ITA 2007 Part 15 where the exemption does not apply and the company did not believe or could not reasonably have believed that it would apply (TMA 1970 s 98(4A)–(4E)). | (*a*) Initial penalty up to £3,000; and<br>(*b*) further penalty up to £600 for each day on which the failure continues. |
| **Failure of an employment intermediary** to furnish information or produce documents or records (TMA 1970 s 98(4F)). | (*a*) Initial penalty up to £3,000; and<br>(*b*) further penalty up to £600 for each day on which the failure continues. |
| **Advance pricing agreements:** Fraudulently or negligently making a false or misleading statement in the preparation of, or application to enter into, any advance pricing agreement (TIOPA 2010 s 227). | Penalty up to £10,000. |
| **Declaration of non-UK residence:** Fraudulently or negligently making a false or misleading declaration of non-UK residence to a deposit-taker or building society under ITA 2007 ss 858-861 (TMA 1970 s 99B). | Penalty up to £3,000. |
| ***Repealed provisions*** | |
| **Fraudulently or negligently** delivering any incorrect document, information etc required under the above provisions (TMA 1970 s 99; SI 2013/279). | *Penalty up to £3,000.*<br>***Repealed with effect from 1 April 2013. See now tax agent dishonest conduct penalties under FA 2012 Sch 38 (see p 19).*** |

## Other offences by taxpayers, agents etc

| *Offence* | *Penalty* |
|---|---|
| **GAAR.** Applies to arrangements entered into after 15 September 2016 if a taxpayer (or in some cases another person) submits a return, claim, or other document on the basis that a tax advantage arises from the tax arrangements and all or part of that tax advantage is later counteracted under the GAAR (FA 2013 s 212A). | 60% of the value of the counteracted advantage. |
| **Serial tax avoiders.** Use of any avoidance schemes in the warning period after the defeat of a relevant scheme. Applies to defeats incurred after 15 September 2016 (FA 2016 Sch 18). | (*a*) 20% of the tax understated or overclaimed for the first defeat of a scheme used during the warning period;<br>(*b*) 40% for the second such defeat; and<br>(*c*) 60% for any subsequent defeats. |
| **Falsification of documents.** Intentionally falsifying, concealing or destroying documents required under TMA 1970 ss 20A (repealed with effect from 1 April 2013) or 20BA (TMA 1970 s 20BB). | On summary conviction, a fine up to the statutory maximum (£5,000); on conviction on indictment, imprisonment for a term not exceeding two years or a fine or both. |
| **European Economic Interest Groupings**– Offences in connection with the supply of information: | |
| (i) failure to supply information | Initial penalty up to £300 per member of the Grouping at the time of failure and after direction by the tribunal: continuing penalty up to £60 per member of the Grouping at the end of the day for each day on which the failure continues. |
| (ii) fraudulent or negligent delivery of an incorrect return, accounts or statement<br>(TMA 1970 s 98B). | Up to £3,000 for each member of the Grouping at the time of delivery. |
| **Certificates of non-liability to income tax:** Fraudulently or negligently giving such a certificate for the purposes of receiving interest gross on a bank or building society account, or failing to comply with an undertaking given in such a certificate (TMA 1970 s 99A). | Penalty up to £3,000. |
| **Refusal to allow a deduction of income tax at source** (TMA 1970 s 106). | £50. |
| **Construction Industry Scheme:** (post 31 March 2007 scheme) Making false statements etc for the purpose of obtaining a gross payment certificate (FA 2004 s 72). | Up to £3,000. |
| **Fraudulent evasion of income tax** (TMA 1970 s 106A). | On summary conviction, imprisonment for up to six months or a fine up to the statutory maximum (£5,000) or both; on conviction on indictment, imprisonment for up to seven years or a fine or both. |
| **Enterprise investment scheme relief:** Issue by a company of a certificate of approval for such relief fraudulently or negligently or without the authority of HMRC (ITA 2007 s 207). | Not exceeding £3,000. |
| **Failure of a company to maintain records** (other than those only required for claims, etc, or dividend vouchers and certificates of income tax deducted where other evidence is available) (FA 1998 Sch 18 para 23). | Penalty not exceeding £3,000. |
| **Failure to notify notifiable proposals or notifiable arrangements**, or failure to notify the client of the relevant scheme reference number under the provisions of FA 2004 ss 306–319 (TMA 1970 s 98C; SI 2007/3104; SI 2008/1935; SI 2010/3019; FA 2013 s 223; FA 2014 s 284; FA 2015 Sch 17). | (*a*) Up to 31 December 2010 an initial penalty not exceeding £5,000;<br>(i) From 1 January 2011 in the case of provisions under FA 2004 ss 308(1) and (3), 309(1) and 310 up to £600 per day in 'initial period' (but a tribunal can determine a higher penalty up to £1 million);<br>(ii) From 1 January 2011 in the case of provisions in FA 2004 ss 312(2), 312A(2), 313ZA, 313A, 313B, 313C, from 17 July 2013 in the case of provisions in ss 312B and 313ZB, and from 26 March 2015 in the case of ss 310C, 312A(2A), 313ZC, and 316A, an initial penalty up to £5,000.<br>Where a disclosure order is made the amount in (i) above is increased up to £5,000 per day that failure continues from ten days after the order is made.<br>(*b*) a continuing penalty not exceeding £600 for each day on which the failure continues after imposition of initial penalty.<br>Where a disclosure order is made the amount is increased up to £5,000 per day that failure continues from ten days after the order is made. |

| *Offence* | *Penalty* |
|---|---|
| **Failure to notify scheme reference number etc** under FA 2004 s 313(1); | Penalty not exceeding £5,000[1] in respect of each scheme to which the failure relates; |
| for second failure, occurring within three years from the date on which the first failure began; | penalty not exceeding £7,500[1] in respect of each scheme to which the failure relates; |
| for subsequent failures, occurring within three years from the date on which the previous failure began. | penalty not exceeding £10,000[1] in respect of each scheme to which the failure relates. |
| (TMA 1970 s 98C; FA 2004 s 315(1)). | |
| **Failure to comply with HMRC investigatory powers** under FA 2008 Sch 36. | (*a*) an initial penalty of £300; |
| Failure to comply with an information notice within FA 2008 Sch 36 Pt 1 or deliberately obstructing an HMRC officer in the course of an inspection of business premises under FA 2008 Sch 36 Pt 2 which has been approved by the First-tier Tribunal. Applies to IT (including PAYE and CIS), CT, CGT, VAT and certain foreign taxes with effect from 1 April 2009. Extended to IHT, SDLT and other taxes from 1 April 2010, to Bank Payroll Tax (BPT) from 31 August 2010, to ATED from 17 July 2013; to pension scheme registration applications from 17 July 2014; and to Diverted Profits Tax from 1 April 2015. | (*b*) if failure/obstruction continues, a further penalty up to £60 per day;<br>(*c*) if failure/obstruction continues after penalty under (*a*) imposed, a tax-related amount determined by the Upper Tribunal. |
| Carelessly or deliberately providing inaccurate information or an inaccurate document in response to an information notice. | Up to £3,000 per inaccuracy. |
| **Failure of a senior accounting officer to ensure a company maintains appropriate tax accounting arrangements** (FA 2009 Sch 46). | £5,000. |
| **Failure of a senior accounting officer to provide a certificate** stating whether the company had appropriate tax accounting arrangements (FA 2009 Sch 46). | £5,000. |
| **Failure to notify Commissioners of name of senior accounting officer** (FA 2009 Sch 46). | £5,000. |
| **Failure of a third party to notify the contact details of a debtor** (FA 2009 Sch 49). | £300. |
| **Failure to comply with data-holder notice** (FA 2011 Sch 23). | (*a*) an initial penalty of £300.<br>(*b*) if failure continues, a further penalty up to £60 per day.<br>(*c*) increased daily penalty of up to £1,000 to be set by Tribunal if notice still not complied with within 30 days of a daily penalty being notified. |
| **Tax agent failure to comply with file access notice** (FA 2012 Sch 38). | (*a*) an initial penalty of £300.<br>(*b*) if failure continues, a further penalty up to £60 per day. |
| **Tax agent engaging in dishonest conduct** (FA 2012 Sch 38). | £5,000 minimum to £50,0000 maximum subject to the quality of disclosure and compliance with any access notice, with possible special reduction of £5,000 penalty to nil at HMRC's discretion. |
| **Failure to keep records** for the purposes of the annual tax on enveloped dwellings (FA 2013 Sch 33). | Up to £3,000 |
| **Corrective action not taken in response to follower notice** (FA 2014 s 208). | 50% of value of the denied advantage (20% for relevant partners).<br>May be reduced for co-operation. |
| **Failure to pay accelerated payment** (FA 2014 s 226). | (*a*) Initial penalty of 5% of any amount unpaid at end of payment period (or where the accelerated payment relates to an instalment of IHT, 5% of any amount unpaid by the later due date of that instalment if applicable).<br>(*b*) Further penalty of 5% of any amount unpaid after 5 months.<br>(*c*) Further penalty of 5% of any amount unpaid after 11 months. |
| **Failure of monitored promoter of a tax avoidance scheme**, or their intermediary, to comply with various duties to notify clients, provide information or produce documents (FA 2014 Sch 35 para 2). | (*a*) Initial maximum penalty of £5,000, £7,500, £10,000, or £1,000,000 depending on failure.<br>(*b*) Further daily penalty for each day on which failure continues of up to £10,000 where the maximum penalty could have been £1,000,000, or otherwise, £600. |
| **Provision of inaccurate information or document by a monitored promoter of a tax avoidance scheme** when complying with an information duty (FA 2014 Sch 35 para 4). | Maximum penalty of £5,000, £10,000, or £1,000,000 depending on duty being complied with. |
| **Concealing, destroying etc documents** required to be produced in connection with a monitored promoter of a tax avoidance scheme (FA 2014 s 280). | On summary conviction, a fine; on conviction on indictment, imprisonment for up to two years or a fine or both. |

| Offence | Penalty |
| --- | --- |
| **Failure of a company to provide a return** in respect of a SIP, SAYE option, CSOP, EMI or other employee share scheme (ITEPA 2003 Sch 2 para 81C; Sch 3 para 40C; Sch 4 para 28C; Sch 5 para 57B; s 421JC). | (*a*) Initial penalty of £100.<br>(*b*) Further penalty of £300 if failure continues for 3 months.<br>(*c*) Further penalty of £300 if failure continues for 6 months.<br>(*d*) Further penalty of £10 for each day that failure continues beyond 9 months (with notice). |
| **Inaccurate return provided by a company**, or return not filed electronically as required in respect of a SIP, SAYE option, CSOP, EMI or other employee share scheme (ITEPA 2003 Sch 2 para 81E; Sch 3 para 40E; Sch 4 para 28E; Sch 5 para 57C; s 421JD). | Up to £5,000. |
| **Failure of a company to comply with** the rules in respect of a SIP, SAYE option, or CSOP scheme (ITEPA 2003 Sch 2 para 81H–81I; Sch 3 para 40H–41I; Sch 4 para 28H–28I). | If scheme does not comply at all, penalty not exceeding twice the tax and NIC HMRC estimate has been 'saved'.<br>Otherwise, up to £5,000. |
| **Failure of a company to provide** to HMRC a declaration under ITEPA 2003 Sch 5 para 44(6) by individual to whom an EMI option is granted (ITEPA 2003 Sch 5 para 57A). | £500. |
| **A social enterprise fraudulently or negligently** issuing a compliance certificate or statement (ITA 2007 s 257PD). | Up to £3,000. |
| **Failure by a qualifying company or partnership, or by the head of a UK group of companies or by the head of a UK sub-group of a foreign group of companies** to publish the company's, partnership's, group's or sub-group's tax strategy or to make it freely available after publication. Applies to financial years beginning on or after 15 September 2016 (FA 2016 Sch 19). | (*a*) Initial penalty of up to £7,500.<br>(*b*) further penalty of £7,500 if failure continues for 6 months; and<br>(*c*) further penalty of £7,500 for every subsequent month that failure continues. |
| **Enablers of defeated tax avoidance**. Penalty applies to persons who enable the use of abusive tax avoidance arrangements which are later defeated (F(No 2)A 2017 Sch 16). | The amount of consideration received or receivable by enabler for enabling the tax avoidance arrangements. |
| **Failure to correct** on or by 30 September 2018 irregularities in relation to undeclared past UK IT, CGT and IHT liabilities involving offshore interests which exist at 5 April 2017 (F(No 2)A 2017 Sch 18). | 200% of the offshore potential lost revenue (PLR). Reductions apply for disclosure but minimum penalty will be 100% of PLR. |
| ***Repealed provisions*** | |
| **Assisting in the delivery of incorrect returns**, accounts or information (TMA 1970 s 99; SI 2013/279). | *Penalty up to £3,000.*<br>***Repealed with effect from 1 April 2013. See now tax agent dishonest conduct penalties under FA 2012 Sch 38 on p 19.*** |

1 Before 26 March 2015 the penalties were fixed amounts of £100, £500, and £1,000 respectively.

## Mitigation of penalties

HMRC have discretion to mitigate or entirely remit any penalty or to stay or compound any penalty proceedings (TMA 1970 s 102).

## Interest on penalties

Penalties under TMA 1970 Parts II (ss 7–12B), IV (ss 28A–43B), VA (ss 59A–59D) and X (ss 93–107), and FA 1998 Sch 18 carry interest at the prescribed rate (see p 5): TMA 1970 s 103A. This applies to penalties in relation to promoters of tax avoidance schemes from 17 July 2014. For interest which applies to penalties under the **harmonised interest regime** see p 4.

## Publishing details of deliberate tax defaulters

From 1 April 2010 HMRC have the power to publish the names and details of taxpayers who are penalised for deliberate defaults leading to a loss of tax of more than £25,000. From 1 April 2017 the power applies to certain individuals who control a body corporate or a partnership, or who are trustees of a settlement, which is penalised for such deliberate defaults relating to an offshore matter or transfer, but only where the individual would obtain a tax advantage from the default. From the same date, only taxpayers who make full unprompted disclosures are protected (FA 2009 s 94; SI 2017/261).

## Publishing details of deliberate enablers of offshore evasion or non-compliance

From 1 January 2017 HMRC have the power to publish the names and details of enablers of offshore tax evasion or non-compliance who are found liable for a penalty and the potential lost revenue involved exceeds £25,000. They may also publish information about a person who has been found to have incurred 5 or more penalties in any 5-year period (FA 2016 Sch 20; SI 2016/1249).

## Publishing details of serial tax avoiders

Broadly from 15 September 2016 HMRC have the power to publish the names and details of serial tax avoiders if they are given three warning notices in respect of schemes used while in a warning period and which are defeated (FA 2016 Sch 18).

## Publishing details of persistently uncooperative large businesses

HMRC have the power to publish the names and details of a large company, partnership, UK group of companies, or UK sub-group of a foreign group of companies which is subject to a confirmed special measures notice. The provisions apply in relation to the body or entity's first financial year and subsequent years following 15 September 2016 (FA 2016 Sch 19).

## Publishing details of enablers of defeated abusive tax avoidance arrangements

HMRC have the power to publish the names and details of persons who have been assessed to a penalty which has become final in relation to enabling defeated tax avoidance arrangements, provided they have incurred at least 50 other such penalties, or total penalties incurred including the current one will exceed £25,000 (F(No 2)A 2017 Sch 16).

## Criminal offence for offshore matters

From 7 October 2017 a criminal offence which does not require the need to prove intent will apply for failing to accurately declare taxable offshore income and gains. The specific offences are failure to notify, failure to deliver a return and making an inaccurate return. It will apply where the loss of tax exceeds £25,000 (TMA 1970 ss 106B–106H; SI 2017/970; SI 2017/988).

## Corporate offence of failure to prevent criminal facilitation of tax evasion

From 30 September 2017 an offence will be committed where a body corporate or partnership fails to prevent an associated person (broadly an employee, agent or other person who performs services for them) criminally facilitating the evasion of a tax in the UK or abroad (Criminal Finances Act 2017 ss 44–52; SI 2017/739).

## Tax agent dishonest conduct

From 1 April 2013, in addition to the penalties listed above, HMRC have the power to publish names and details of tax agents who incur penalties for dishonest conduct over £5,000 (FA 2012 Sch 38; SI 2013/279).

## Failure to provide security

A person who fails to comply with a requirement imposed under the PAYE regulations to give security or further security is liable on summary conviction to a fine not exceeding level 5 on the standard scale (£5,000) (ITEPA 2003 s 684(4A)).

# Time limits for claims and elections

Whenever possible, a claim or election must be made on the tax return or by an amendment to the return (TMA 1970 s 42 and FA 1998 Sch 18 paras 9, 10, 67 and 79). Exceptions to this general rule are dealt with in TMA 1970 Sch 1A. Except where another period is expressly prescribed, a claim for relief in respect of income tax and capital gains tax must be made within four years after the end of the tax year. (TMA 1970 s 43(1); FA 2008 Sch 39 para 12.) The time limit for claims by companies is four years from the end of the accounting period to which it relates (FA 1998 Sch 18 para 55; FA 2008 Sch 39 para 45). The tables below set out some of the main exceptions to the general limits.

## Income tax

| *Claim* | *Time limit* |
|---|---|
| **Trading losses:** Loss sustained in a trade, profession or vocation to be set against other income of the year or the last preceding year. Extended to certain pre-trading expenditure by ITTOIA 2005 s 57 (ITA 2007 s 64). | One year after 31 January next following tax year in which loss arose. |
| Unrelieved trading losses to be set against capital gains (TCGA 1992 ss 261B, 261C). | One year after 31 January next following tax year in which loss arose. |
| **Losses of new trade etc:** Loss sustained in the first four years of a new trade, profession or vocation to be offset against other income arising in the three years immediately preceding the year of loss. Extended to certain pre-trading expenditure by ITTOIA 2005 s 57 (ITA 2007 s 72). | One year after 31 January next following tax year in which loss arose. |
| **Property business losses:** Claim for relief against total income (ITA 2007 s 124). | One year after 31 January next following tax year specified in claim. |
| **Simplified cash basis for unincorporated property businesses:** Cash basis *not* to apply (ITTOIA 2005 s 271A; F(No 2)A 2017 s 16, Sch 2). | One year after 31 January next following tax year specified in claim. |
| **Loss on disposal of unlisted shares:** Loss on disposal of shares in an EIS company or a qualifying trading company to be offset against other income of the year of loss or the last preceding year (ITA 2007 s 132). | One year after 31 January next following tax year in which loss arose. |
| **Gift aid:** Election to treat donations to charity under gift aid made after 5 April 2003 as made in the previous tax year (ITA 2007 s 426). | On or before date on which donor delivers tax return for the previous tax year and not later than 31 January after that year. |
| **Enterprise investment scheme relief:** Income tax relief of 30% on amount invested within specified limits (ITA 2007 s 202). | 5 years after 31 January next following tax year in which shares are issued. |
| **Seed enterprise investment scheme relief:** Income tax relief of 50% on amount invested within specified limits (ITA 2007 s 357EA). | 5 years after 31 January next following tax year in which shares are issued. |
| **Social investment tax relief:** Income tax relief of 30% on amount invested within specified limits (ITA 2007 s 257P). | 5 years after 31 January next following tax year in which investment is made. |
| **Rent-a-room relief:** Relief not to apply; to apply to gross income in excess of limit; withdrawal of claim (ITTOIA 2005 ss 799, 800). | One year after 31 January next following tax year specified in claim. |
| **Trading or property allowance:** Full relief not to apply; partial relief to apply (ITTOIA 2005 ss 783AL, 783AM, 783BJ, 783BK; F(No 2)A 2017 s 17, Sch 3). | One year after 31 January next following tax year specified in claim. |

## Capital gains

| *Claim* | *Time limit* |
|---|---|
| **Assets of negligible value:** Loss to be allowed where the value of an asset has become negligible (TCGA 1992 s 24(2)). | Two years after end of chargeable period of deemed sale (and reacquisition). |
| **Assets held on 31 March 1982 for corporation tax purposes only:** Events occurring prior to 31 March 1982 to be ignored in computing gains arising after 5 April 1988 (TCGA 1992 s 35(5), (6) as amended). | Two years after end of accounting period in which first relevant disposal made after 31.3.88; or such further time as HMRC may allow. |
| **Main residence:** Determination of main residence for principal private residence exemption (TCGA 1992 s 222(5)(*a*)). | Two years after acquisition of second residence. |
| **Relief for loans to traders:** Losses on certain loans to traders to be allowed as capital losses at the time of claim or 'earlier time' (TCGA 1992 s 253(3A)). | Two years after the end of the tax year or accounting period of loss. |
| **Relief for loans to traders (payments by guarantor):** Losses arising from payments by guarantor of certain irrecoverable loans to traders to be allowed as capital losses at time of claim or 'earlier time' (TCGA 1992 s 253(4), (4A)). | Four years after the end of the tax year or accounting period in which payment made (for claims before 1 April 2010, five years after 31 January following tax year in which payment made (capital gains tax); six years after end of accounting period in which payment made (corporation tax)). |
| **Election for valuation at 6 April 1965 for corporation tax purposes only:** Gain on a disposal of an asset held at 6 April 1965 to be computed as if the asset had been acquired on that date. An election once made is irrevocable (TCGA 1992 Sch 2 para 17). | Two years after end of accounting period in which disposal made; or such further time as HMRC may allow. |
| **Entrepreneurs' relief:** Gain to be taxed at reduced rate of 10% (TCGA 1992 s 169M). | One year after 31 January next following tax year of qualifying business disposal. |

## Corporation tax

| *Claim* | *Time limit* |
|---|---|
| **Trading losses:** Loss sustained by a company in a trade in an accounting period to be offset against profits of that accounting period and profits of the preceding year. Extended to certain pre-trading expenditure by CTA 2009 s 61 (CTA 2010 s 37(7)). | Two years after end of loss-making period; or such further period as HMRC may allow. |
| **Trading losses:** Post-1 April 2017 loss to be offset against *total* profits of a later accounting period (CTA 2010 s 45A(7); F(No 2)A 2017 s 18, Sch 4). | Two years after end of loss-making period; or such further period as HMRC may allow. |
| **Trading losses:** Post-1 April 2017 loss *not* to be carried forward against *trade* profits of next accounting period (CTA 2010 s 45B(6); F(No 2)A 2017 s 18, Sch 4). | Two years after end of loss-making period; or such further period as HMRC may allow. |
| **Property losses:** Carry forward of post-1 April 2017 losses (CTA 2010 s 62(5C); F(No 2)A 2017 s 18, Sch 4). | Two years after end of loss-making period; or such further period as HMRC may allow. |
| **Group relief:** Group relief to be given for accounting periods ending after 30 June 1999. The surrendering company must consent to the claim (FA 1998 Sch 18 paras 66–77). | The last of:<br>(*a*) one year from filing date of claimant company's return for accounting period for which claim is made;<br>(*b*) 30 days after end of an enquiry into return;<br>(*c*) if HMRC amend return after an enquiry, 30 days after issue of notice of amendment;<br>(*d*) if an appeal is made against amendment, 30 days after determination of appeal;<br>(or such later time as HMRC may allow). |
| **Non-trading deficit on loan relationship:** Claim for non-trading deficits on loan relationships (including non-trading debits on derivative contracts) in an accounting period to be: | |
| (*a*) offset against profits of same period or carried back (CTA 2009 s 460); | Two years after end of accounting period in which deficit arose (or such later time as HMRC may allow). |
| (*b*) not treated as non-trading deficit of subsequent accounting period but to be carried forward to succeeding accounting periods (CTA 2009 ss 458, 463B; F(No 2)A 2017 s 18, Sch 4). | Two years after end of that subsequent accounting period. |
| (*c*) for post-1 April 2017 deficits only, carried forward against *total* profits of succeeding accounting periods (CTA 2009 s 463G; F(No 2)A 2017 s 18, Sch 4). | Two years after end of that subsequent accounting period. |
| **Intangible assets:** Election to replace accounts depreciation with fixed writing-down allowance of 4% (CTA 2009 s 730). | Two years after end of the accounting period in which asset was created or acquired. |
| **Research and development:** Claim for tax relief to be made, amended or withdrawn in company tax return (or amended return) (FA 1998 Sch 18 para 83E). | One year from the filing date for return or such later time as HMRC may allow. |

## Capital allowances

| *Claim* | *Time limit* |
|---|---|
| **Corporation tax claims:** Claims, amended claims and withdrawals of claims in respect of corporation tax capital allowances (CAA 2001 s 3(2), (3)(*b*); FA 1998 Sch 18 para 82). | The last of:<br>(*a*) one year after filing date of claimant company's return for accounting period for which claim is made;<br>(*b*) 30 days after end of enquiry into return;<br>(*c*) if HMRC amend the return after an enquiry, 30 days after issue of notice of amendment;<br>(*d*) if appeal is made against amendment, 30 days after determination of appeal;<br>(or such later time as HMRC may allow). |
| **Short life assets:** Plant or machinery to be treated as a short life asset (CAA 2001 s 85(2)). | One year after 31 January after tax year in which chargeable period ends (income tax); two years after end of chargeable period (corporation tax). |
| **Connected persons:** Succession to a trade between connected persons to be ignored in computing capital allowances (CAA 2001 s 266). | Two years after date of the succession. |
| **Sales between persons under common control** treated as made at the lower of open market value and tax written down value (CAA 2001 s 570(5)). | Two years after date of the disposal. |

# Exchanges

## Recognised stock exchanges

The following is a list of countries with exchanges which have been designated as recognised stock exchanges under ITA 2007 s 1005; CTA 2010 s 1137. Unless otherwise specified, any stock exchange (or options exchange) in a country listed below is a recognised stock exchange provided it is recognised under the law of the country concerned relating to stock exchanges.

HMRC may make an order designating a market in the UK as a recognised stock exchange.

| *Country* | *Date of recognition* |
|---|---|
| Australian Stock Exchange and its stock exchange subsidiaries | 22 September 1988 |
| National Stock Exchange of Australia | 19 June 2014 |
| Austria[3] | 22 October 1970 |
| Bahamas | |
| Bahamas International Securities Exchange | 19 April 2010 |
| Belgium[3] | 22 October 1970 |
| Bermuda | 4 December 2007 |
| Brazil | |
| Rio De Janeiro Stock Exchange | 17 August 1995 |
| São Paulo Stock Exchange | 11 December 1995 |
| Canada | |
| Any stock exchange prescribed for the purposes of the Canadian Income Tax Act | 22 October 1970 |
| Caribbean | |
| Dutch Caribbean Securities Exchange | 8 December 2014 |
| Cayman Islands Stock Exchange | 4 March 2004 |
| Channel Islands Securities Exchange Authority | 20 December 2013 |
| China | |
| Hong Kong – Any stock exchange recognised under Section 2A(1) of the Hong Kong Companies Ordinance | 26 February 1971 |
| Cyprus | |
| Cyprus Stock Exchange | 22 June 2009 |
| Denmark | |
| Copenhagen Stock Exchange | 22 October 1970 |
| Estonia | |
| NASDAQ OMX Tallinn | 5 May 2010 |
| European Wholesale Securities Market | 18 January 2013 |
| Finland | |
| Helsinki Stock Exchange | 22 October 1970 |
| France[3] | 22 October 1970 |
| Germany[3] | 5 August 1971 |
| Gibraltar | 16 August 2016 |
| Global Board of Trade | 30 July 2013 |
| Greece | |
| Athens Stock Exchange | 14 June 1993 |
| Guernsey[3] | 10 December 2002 |
| GXG Main Quote | 23 September 2013 |
| GXG Official List | 16 May 2013 |
| Iceland | 31 March 2006 |
| Irish Republic[3] | 22 October 1970 |
| Italy[3] | 3 May 1972 |
| Japan[3] | 22 October 1970 |
| Korea | 10 October 1994 |
| Lithuania | |
| NASDAQ OMX Vilnius | 12 March 2012 |
| Luxembourg[3] | 21 February 1972 |
| Malaysia | |
| Kuala Lumpur Stock Exchange | 10 October 1994 |
| Malta Stock Exchange | 29 December 2005 |
| Mauritius Stock Exchange | 31 January 2011 |
| Mexico | 10 October 1994 |
| Netherlands[3] | 22 October 1970 |
| New Zealand | 22 September 1988 |
| Norway[3] | 22 October 1970 |
| Poland | |
| Warsaw Stock Exchange | 25 February 2010 |
| Portugal[3] | 21 February 1972 |
| Russia | |
| MICEX Stock Exchange | 5 January 2011 |
| Singapore | 30 June 1977 |
| Singapore Exchange Securities Trading Limited (SGX-ST)[4] | 7 October 2014 |
| Singapore Exchange Derivatives Trading Limited (SGX-DT)[4] | 7 October 2014 |
| South Africa | |
| Bond Exchange of South Africa | 16 April 2008 |
| Johannesburg Stock Exchange | 22 October 1970 |

| *Country* | *Date of recognition* |
|---|---|
| Spain[3] | 5 August 1971 |
| Sri Lanka | |
| Colombo Stock Exchange | 21 February 1972 |
| Sweden | |
| Stockholm Stock Exchange | 16 July 1985 |
| Swiss Stock Exchange | 12 May 1997 |
| Thailand | 10 October 1994 |
| United Kingdom | |
| London Stock Exchange | 19 July 2007 |
| PLUS-listed Market | 19 July 2007 |
| ICAP Securities & Derivatives Exchange Ltd | 25 April 2013 |
| LIFFE Administration and Management | 26 September 2011 |
| Euronext London | 4 February 2015 |
| United States | |
| Any stock exchange registered with the SEC as a national securities exchange[1] | 22 October 1970 |
| Nasdaq Stock Market[2] | 10 March 1992 |

1 'National securities exchange' does not include any local exchanges registered with Securities and Exchange Commission.
2 As maintained through the facilities of the National Association of Securities Dealers Inc and its subsidiaries.
3 i.e., a stock exchange according to the law of the country concerned relating to stock exchanges.
4 The original Singapore Stock Exchange merged with two other exchanges and is now known as SGX. The SGX-ST market was identified as representing the originally designated exchange.

## Recognised futures exchanges

The following is a list of exchanges which have been designated as recognised futures exchanges under TCGA 1992 s 288(6). By concession, those exchanges were recognised futures exchanges for the tax year of recognition onwards.

| *Recognised futures exchanges* | *Date of recognition* |
|---|---|
| International Petroleum Exchange of London | 6 August 1985 |
| London Metal Exchange | 6 August 1985 |
| London Gold Market | 12 December 1985 |
| London Silver Market | 12 December 1985 |
| CME Group (formerly Chicago Mercantile Exchange and Chicago Board of Trade) | 19 December 1986 |
| New York Mercantile Exchange | 19 December 1986 |
| Philadelphia Board of Trade | 19 December 1986 |
| Mid America Commodity Exchange | 29 July 1987 |
| Montreal Exchange | 29 July 1987 |
| Hong Kong Futures Exchange | 15 December 1987 |
| Commodity Exchange (Comex) | 25 August 1988 |
| Sydney Futures Exchange | 13 October 1988 |
| Euronext (London International Financial Futures and Options Exchange) | 22 March 1992 |
| OM Stockholm | 18 March 1992 |
| OMLX (formerly OM London) | 18 March 1992 |
| New York Board of Trade | 10 June 2004 |
| Eurex Deutschland | 13 March 2015 |

## Recognised investment exchanges and clearing houses

The following is a list of investment exchanges and clearing houses recognised as investment exchanges under the Financial Services and Markets Act 2000 and able to carry out investment business in the UK.

| *Recognised investment exchanges* | *Date of recognition* |
|---|---|
| London Stock Exchange plc | 22 November 2001 |
| *LIFFE Administration and Management*[1] | 22 November 2001 |
| The London Metal Exchange Ltd | 22 November 2001 |
| ICE Futures Europe | 22 November 2001 |
| NEX Exchange Ltd (formerly ICAP Securities & Derivatives Exchange Ltd) | 19 July 2007 |
| BATS Trading Ltd | 20 May 2013 |
| CME Europe Ltd | 10 March 2014 |
| Euronext UK Markets Ltd | 2 June 2014 |

1 Taken over by ICE Futures Europe in December 2013.

| *Recognised clearing houses*[2] | *Date of recognition* |
|---|---|
| LCH.Clearnet Ltd[1] | 22 November 2001 |
| Euroclear UK & Ireland Ltd | 23 November 2001 |
| ICE Clear Europe Ltd[1] | 15 May 2008 |
| CME Clearing Europe Ltd[1] | 15 December 2010 |
| LME Clear Ltd[1] | 3 September 2014 |

1 These clearing houses are recognised central counterparties. LCH.Clearnet Ltd was recognised as such on 12 June 2014. CME Clearing Europe Ltd was recognised as such on 4 August 2014. LME Clear Ltd was recognised as such on 3 September 2014. ICE Clear Europe Ltd was recognised as such on 19 September 2016.

2 List as at 27 September 2017 on Bank of England website.

## Recognised overseas investment exchanges and clearing houses

The following is a list of overseas investment exchanges and clearing houses recognised under the Financial Services and Markets Act 2000 and able to conduct investment business in the UK.

| *Recognised overseas investment exchange* | *Date of recognition* |
|---|---|
| National Association of Securities Dealers Automated Quotations (NASDAQ) | 23 November 2001 |
| Australian Securities Exchange Ltd | 30 January 2002 |
| The Chicago Mercantile Exchange (CME) | 23 November 2001 |
| Chicago Board of Trade (CBOT) | 23 November 2001 |
| New York Mercantile Exchange Inc (NYMEX Inc) | 23 November 2001 |
| SIX Swiss Exchange AG | 23 November 2001 |
| EUREX (Zurich) | 23 November 2001 |
| ICE Futures US Inc | 17 May 2007 |

| *Recognised clearing house*[1] | *Date of recognition* |
|---|---|
| None | |

1 List as at 27 September 2017 on Bank of England website.

## Alternative finance investment bonds

List of recognised stock exchanges designated solely for the purposes of ITA 2007 s 564G, TCGA 1992 s 151N, CTA 2009 s 507.

| *Recognised stock exchanges* | *Date of recognition* |
|---|---|
| Abu Dhabi Securities Market | 1 April 2007 |
| Bahrain Stock Exchange | 1 April 2007 |
| Dubai Financial Market | 1 April 2007 |
| NASDAQ Dubai (formerly Dubai International Financial Exchange) | 1 April 2007 |
| Labuan International Financial Exchange | 1 April 2007 |
| Saudi Stock Exchange (Tadawul) | 1 April 2007 |
| Surabaya Stock Exchange | 1 April 2007 |

# Applications for clearances and approvals

| *Statutory clearance applications and approvals* | *Address* |
|---|---|
| Demergers (CTA 2010 s 1091); Company purchase of own shares (CTA 2010 s 1044); Transactions in securities (CTA 2010 s 748; ITA 2007 s 701); Enterprise Investment Scheme – acquisition of shares by new company (ITA 2007 s 247(1)(f)); Share exchanges (TCGA 1992 s 138); Reconstruction regarding transfer of a business (TCGA 1992 s 139); Transfer of a UK trade between EU member states (TCGA 1992 ss 140B, 140D); Intangible fixed assets (CTA 2009 s 831); Loan relationships transfers/mergers (CTA 2009 ss 426, 427, 438); Derivative contracts transfers/mergers (CTA 2009 ss 677, 686); Schemes converting income to capital (TCGA 1992 ss 184G–H); Assignment of lease granted at undervalue (CTA 2009 s 237; ITTOIA 2005 s 300); Transactions in land (CTA 2010 s 831; ITA 2007 s 770); Collective investment schemes (TCGA 1992 s 103K) | HM Revenue & Customs, CTIS Clearance S0483, Newcastle NE98 1ZZ (Applications should be marked "market sensitive" or "non-market sensitive" as appropriate.)[1] |
| Employee share schemes (ITEPA 2003 Schs 2, 3, 4) | Self-certification applies and can be made through HMRC Online services; see www.gov.uk/guidance/self-certify-your-tax-advantaged-employment-related-securities |
| Pensions | Registration of a pension scheme from 6 April 2006 must be done online, but HMRC can be contacted at Pension Schemes Services, Ferrers House, Castle Meadow Road, Nottingham, NG2 1BB |
| Qualifying life assurance policies (TA 1988 Sch 15) | HM Revenue & Customs, CTISA Corporation Tax and Business Income Tax, Financial Services Team, 3rd Floor, 100 Parliament Street, London SW1A 2BQ |
| Transactions in shares or debentures (TA 1988 ss 765 and 765A) | The recommendation is that businesses should address the reports directly to the customer relationship manager dealing with their affairs |

| *Non-statutory clearance applications* | *Address* |
|---|---|
| Controlled foreign companies (TIOPA 2010 Part 9A; TA 1988 ss 747–756, Schs 24–26) | HM Revenue & Customs, Business, Assets and International, Foreign Profits Team Registry (CFC clearances), Room 3C/21, 100 Parliament Street, London SW1A 2BQ |
| Company migration (TMA 1970 s 109B–F, formerly FA 1988 s 130) | HM Revenue & Customs, Business, Assets and International, Foreign Profits Team, Room 3C/21, 100 Parliament Street, London SW1A 2BQ |
| Inward investment (in Statement of Practice 02/07) | Inward Investment Support, HM Revenue & Customs, CTIAA Business International, 100 Parliament Street, London SW1A 2BQ |
| Creative industries (CTA 2009 Pts 15, 15A, 15B) | Creative Industries Unit (Film, Television/Animation and Video Games Tax Reliefs), Local Compliance S0717, PO Box 3900, Glasgow G70 6AA |
| Enterprise Investment Scheme (EIS), Seed Enterprise Investment Scheme (SEIS) and Venture Capital Trust (VCT) scheme (ITA 2007 Pts 5, 5A, 6) | Local Compliance, Small Company Enterprise Centre Admin Team, HM Revenue & Customs, SO777, PO Box 3900, Glasgow G70 6AA |
| Business investment relief (ITA 2007 s 809VC) | Wealthy and Mid-sized Business Compliance, HM Revenue & Customs, BX9 1BN |
| IHT business property relief (IHTA 1984 Pt 5 Ch 1) | HM Revenue & Customs, Trusts & Estates Technical Team (Clearances), Ferrers House, Castle Meadow Road, Nottingham NG2 1BB |
| Social investment tax relief (ITA 2007 Pt 5B) | Small Company Enterprise Centre (Admin team), Mid-size Business S0777, PO Box 3900, Glasgow G70 6AA |
| Other non-statutory clearances including VAT | Large businesses should contact their client relationship manager. All other businesses and their agents should send applications to HM Revenue & Customs Non-statutory Clearances Team, 5th Floor Alexander House, 21 Victoria Avenue, Southend-on-Sea, Essex SS99 1AA[2] or email hmrc.southendteam@hmrc.gsi.gov.uk. Regarding emails see[1] |

| *Confirmation or pre-transaction or general advice* | *Address* |
|---|---|
| General enquiries on IR35 | HM Revenue & Customs, IR35 Customer Service Unit, S0733, Newcastle Upon Tyne, NE98 1ZZ Telephone 0300 123 2326 |

| *Confirmation or pre-transaction or general advice* | *Address* |
|---|---|
| Advance thin capitalisation agreements (Statement of Practice 1/12) | The first contact for information about advance thin capitalisation agreements under the Statement of Practice should be the Customer Relationship Manager (CRM) or Customer Contact (CC) of the business concerned, and they will engage the assistance of a transfer pricing specialist. If there is no known CRM or CC, the application may be sent to the local Transfer Pricing team leader |
| CGT post-transaction value checks | Completed form CG34 which must be received by HMRC at least two months before the relevant filing deadline |
| Professional bodies (relief for subscriptions) (ITEPA 2003 s 343) | A list of approved professional bodies and learned societies is available on the HMRC website (at www.gov.uk/government/publications/professional-bodies-approved-for-tax-relief-list-3) |
| General advice on specialist technical issues | See www.gov.uk/contact-hmrc |
| SDLT transactions | See www.gov.uk/stamp-duty-land-tax |
| Post-transaction clearances connected to an offshore disclosure | HM Revenue & Customs, WDF Clearance Team, Individual & Small Business Compliance, Compliance Centres, Digital Disclosure Service Room BP3002, Benton Park View, S1250 Newcastle upon Tyne, NE98 1YX<br>Email isbc.disclosureposttransactionclearance@hmrc.gsi.gov.uk |

1 Where clearance is sought under any one or more of the sections handled by the Clearance and Counteraction Team, clearance applications may be sent in a single letter to the above Newcastle address for clearances under those sections. The letter should make clear what clearance(s) is required. HMRC acknowledge only those applications that request acknowledgement. An email acknowledgement may be requested. E-mail applications can be sent to reconstructions@hmrc.gsi.gov.uk. Attachments to emails should be no larger than 2MB. Self-extracting zip files should not be sent as HMRC software will block them. Security of emails is not guaranteed. Information about market or price sensitive matters, or well known individuals, should not be sent by email.

2 Non-statutory clearances: Taxpayers may apply for a non-statutory clearance where they require clarification on guidance or legislation for other circumstances after having checked that the transaction is not covered by a more appropriate clearance or approval route. Taxpayers must provide all the necessary information requested in the relevant checklist. HMRC will not give clearances or advice in respect of the application of the 'settlements legislation' in ITTOIA 2005 Pt 5 Ch 5 or the tax consequences of executing non-charitable trust deeds or settlements. See www.gov.uk/non-statutory-clearance-service-guidance.

# Capital allowances

## Rates

### Agricultural buildings *for periods before April 2011*

| | Expenditure incurred after | % Rate |
|---|---|---|
| *Initial allowance* | 31 October 1992[1] | 20 |
| | 31 October 1993 | Nil |
| *Writing-down allowance* | 31 March 1986 and before 6 April 2011 (1 April 2011 for companies) | 4[2, 3] |

1 Initial allowances were temporarily reintroduced for 1 year in respect of capital expenditure on agricultural buildings or works. The allowances applied to buildings or works constructed under a contract entered into between 1 November 1992 and 31 October 1993, and brought into use for the purposes of the farming trade by 31 December 1994. See CAA 1990 s 124A.

2 Agricultural buildings allowances are abolished for income tax purposes for 2011–12 onwards and for corporation tax purposes for the financial year beginning 1 April 2011 onwards. (FA 2008, s 84.)

3 As a transitional measure, writing-down allowances were stepped down over the three financial or tax years prior to abolition. For 2008–09 (for corporation tax, the financial year beginning 1 April 2008) only 75% of the allowance was given. For 2009–10 (or financial year beginning 1 April 2009) only 50% was given and for 2010–11 (or financial year beginning 1 April 2010) only 25%. Where a chargeable period fell in more than one tax or financial year, time apportionment applied to determine the amount of the allowance. (FA 2008, s 85.)

**Note:** For balancing events on or after 21 March 2007, no election for a balancing adjustment could be made so that the new holder of the relevant interest, in all cases, calculated writing-down allowances based on the previous owner's balance of qualifying expenditure (cost less allowances claimed).

### Dredging

| | Expenditure incurred after | % Rate |
|---|---|---|
| *Writing-down allowance* | **5 November 1962** | **4** |

### Enterprise zones

***Before 1 April 2011 (corporation tax) or 6 April 2011 (income tax)*** — See below for allowances for expenditure by businesses on industrial or commercial buildings within enterprise zones. There was no phasing out of the allowance between 2008 and 2011.

For 100% first-year allowances available for companies investing in plant or machinery for use primarily in designated assisted areas within certain enterprise zones see under **plant and machinery**.

### Industrial buildings and structures *for periods before April 2011*

| | Expenditure[1] incurred after | % Rate |
|---|---|---|
| *Initial allowance* | | |
| Generally: | 31 October 1992 | 20 |
| | 31 October 1993 | Nil |
| Exception: Enterprise zones | within 10 years of site being included in zone[2] | 100 |
| *Writing-down allowance* | | |
| Generally: | 5 April 1946 | 2 |
| | 5 November 1962[3] and before 6 April 2011 (1 April 2011 for companies)[4, 5] | 4 |
| Exception: Enterprise zones | within 10 years of site being included in zone[2, 4] | 25 |

1 The amount qualifying for allowance is the price paid for the relevant interest *minus* (i) the value of the land element and (ii) any value attributable to elements over and above those which would feature in a normal commercial lease negotiated in the open market: FA 1995 s 100 confirming previous practice.

2 CAA 2001 s 306, 310. Includes expenditure on qualifying hotels.

3 Includes expenditure on qualifying hotels (other than in an enterprise zone).
Also includes expenditure on the construction of toll roads incurred for accounting periods or basis periods ending after 5 April 1991.

4 Industrial buildings allowances and allowances for buildings in enterprise zones are abolished for income tax purposes for 2011–12 onwards and for corporation tax purposes for the financial year beginning 1 April 2011 onwards. (FA 2008, ss 84, 86.)

5 As a transitional measure, writing-down allowances (other than those on enterprise zones) were stepped down over the three financial or tax years prior to abolition. For 2008–09 (for corporation tax, the financial year beginning 1 April 2008) only 75% of the allowance was given. For 2009–10 (or financial year beginning 1 April 2009) only 50% was given and for 2010–11 (or financial year beginning 1 April 2010) only 25%. Where a chargeable period fell in more than one tax or financial year, time apportionment applied to determine the amount of the allowance. (FA 2008, ss 85, 87.)

**Note:** For balancing events on or after 21 March 2007, no balancing adjustment arose and the new holder of the relevant interest calculated writing-down allowances based on the previous owner's balance of qualifying expenditure (cost less allowances claimed).

## Flat conversions *for periods before April 2013*

| *Initial allowance* | *Expenditure incurred* | *% Rate* |
|---|---|---|
| | 10 May 2001 to 1 or 6 April 2013 | 100 |

Applies to expenditure incurred on renovating or converting vacant or storage space above commercial properties to provide low value flats for rent. A writing-down allowance is given at 25% (on a straight-line basis) on unrelieved expenditure. (CAA 2001 ss 393A–393W; FA 2001 s 67, Sch 19.)
This relief is withdrawn for expenditure incurred on or after 1 April 2013 (corporation tax) and on or after 6 April 2013 (income tax). The entitlement to claim writing down allowance on any outstanding residue of qualifying expenditure also ceased with effect from the same dates (FA 2012 Sch 39).

## Know-how

Expenditure incurred after 31 March 1986: **annual 25% writing-down allowance** (reducing balance basis).

## Mineral extraction

*First-year allowance:* **100% FYA** is available for certain expenditure incurred after 16 April 2002 wholly for the purposes of a North Sea Oil ring-fence trade or on plant and machinery used in such a trade.
*Writing-down allowance:* for expenditure incurred after 31 March 1986, **10%** for expenditure on the acquisition of a mineral asset and certain pre-trading expenditure, otherwise **25%** (on reducing balance basis). (CAA 2001 s 418.)

## Motor cars

**Expenditure *on or after* 1 April 2009 (corporation tax) or 6 April 2009 (income tax)** on cars is allocated to the special rate (**currently 8%**) plant and machinery pool if the car's $CO_2$ emissions exceed 130g/km (160g/km for expenditure incurred before 1 April 2013 (corporation tax) or 6 April 2013 (income tax)) and otherwise to the (**currently 18%**) main pool. Cars that have an element of non-business use are still dealt with in a single asset pool, but the rate of WDA depends on the emissions. (CAA 2001 ss 104AA, 104F, 208A, 268A–268D; SI 2016/984.) **From April 2018 the $CO_2$ threshold will be reduced to 110g/km.**

**The position for expenditure *before* 1 April 2009 (corporation tax) or 6 April 2009 (income tax)** is as follows. Transitional rules applied — see note 2.

| | | % Rate[1, 2] |
|---|---|---|
| *Writing-down allowance (WDA)* | Chargeable period ending before 1 April 2008 for corporation tax and 5 April 2008 for income tax | 25% |
| | Chargeable period straddling 1 April 2008 for corporation tax and 6 April 2008 for income tax | hybrid rate |
| | Chargeable period ending before 1 April 2012 for corporation tax or 6 April 2012 income tax | 20% |
| | Chargeable period straddling 1 April 2012 for corporation tax and 6 April 2012 for income tax | hybrid rate |
| | Chargeable period beginning on or after 1 April 2012 for corporation tax or 6 April 2012 for income tax | 18% |

1 Restricted to £3,000 for cars costing more than £12,000 and bought outright, on hire purchase or by way of a lease with an option to purchase (CAA 2001 ss 74, 75).
2 Expenditure still in a single asset pool for cars costing more than £12,000 on the last day of the first chargeable period ending on or after 31 March 2014 (corporation tax) or 5 April 2014 (income tax) was carried forward to the main pool (FA 2009 Sch 11 para 31).
3 See also note 5, p 32 and Car hire, p 82.

## Patent rights

*Writing-down allowance*
Expenditure incurred after 31 March 1986: **annual 25% writing-down allowance** (reducing balance basis). (CAA 2001 s 472.)

## Plant and machinery

| | Expenditure incurred after | Expenditure incurred before | Up to pa |
|---|---|---|---|
| ***Annual investment allowance***[1] | | | |
| for income tax purposes | **31 December 2015** | | **£200,000** |
| | 5 April 2014 | 1 January 2016 | £500,000 |
| | 31 December 2012 | 6 April 2014 | £250,000 |
| | 5 April 2012 | 1 January 2013 | £25,000 |
| | 5 April 2010 | 6 April 2012 | £100,000 |
| | 5 April 2008 | 6 April 2010 | £50,000 |
| for corporation tax purposes | **31 December 2015** | | **£200,000** |
| | 31 March 2014 | 1 January 2016 | £500,000 |
| | 31 December 2012 | 1 April 2014 | £250,000 |
| | 31 March 2012 | 1 January 2013 | £25,000 |
| | 31 March 2010 | 1 April 2012 | £100,000 |
| | 31 March 2008 | 1 April 2010 | £50,000 |
| ***First-year allowance (FYA)***[13] | | | |
| General[12] | | | ***% Rate*** |
| for income tax purposes | 5 April 2009 | 6 April 2010 | 40 |
| for corporation tax purposes | 31 March 2009 | 1 April 2010 | 40 |
| Small and medium-sized businesses[2] | | | |
| for income tax purposes | 1 July 1998 | 6 April 2008 | 40 |
| for corporation tax purposes | 1 July 1998 | 1 April 2008 | 40 |
| | 1 July 1997 | 2 July 1998 | 50 |
| in Northern Ireland *only* | 11 May 1998 | 12 May 2002 | 100 |
| Small businesses[3] | | | |
| for income tax purposes | 5 April 2006 | 6 April 2008 | 50 |
| | 5 April 2004 | 6 April 2005 | 50 |
| for corporation tax purposes | 31 March 2006 | 1 April 2008 | 50 |
| | 31 March 2004 | 1 April 2005 | 50 |
| ICT | 31 March 2000 | 1 April 2004 | 100 |
| Energy-saving plant or machinery[4] | **31 March 2001** | | 100 |
| New low-emission cars[5] | **16 April 2002** | **1 April 2021**[5] | 100 |
| Certain refuelling equipment[5] | **16 April 2002** | **1 April 2018**[5] | 100 |
| Environmentally beneficial plant or machinery[6] | **31 March 2003** | | 100 |
| Zero-emission goods vehicles[7] | | | |
| for income tax purposes | **5 April 2010** | **6 April 2018**[7] | **100** |
| for corporation tax purposes | **31 March 2010** | **1 April 2018**[7] | **100** |
| Enterprise zones[18] | **31 March 2012** | | **100** |
| Electric charge-point equipment[19] | | | |
| for income tax purposes | **22 November 2016** | **6 April 2019** | **100** |
| for corporation tax purposes | **22 November 2016** | **1 April 2019** | **100** |
| ***Writing-down allowance (WDA)***[8] | | | |
| Foreign leased assets[11] | 9 March 1982 | 1 April 2006 | 10 |
| | **Chargeable period beginning on or after** | | |
| Long-life assets[8, 9] | | | |
| for income tax purposes | **6 April 2012** | | **8** |
| for corporation tax purposes | **1 April 2012** | | **8** |
| | Chargeable period ending before | | |
| for income tax purposes | 6 April 2012 | | 10 |
| for corporation tax purposes | 1 April 2012 | | 10 |
| for income tax purposes | 6 April 2008 | | 6 |
| for corporation tax purposes | 1 April 2008 | | 6 |
| Integral features[8, 10] | **Chargeable period beginning on or after** | | |
| for income tax purposes | **6 April 2012** | | **8** |
| for corporation tax purposes | **1 April 2012** | | **8** |
| | Chargeable period ending before | | |
| for income tax purposes | 6 April 2012 | | 10 |
| for corporation tax purposes | 1 April 2012 | | 10 |
| Thermal insulation[8, 15] | **Chargeable period beginning on or after** | | |
| for income tax purposes | **6 April 2012** | | **8** |
| for corporation tax purposes | **1 April 2012** | | **8** |

| | | |
|---|---|---|
| | Chargeable period ending before | |
| for income tax purposes | 6 April 2012 | 10 |
| for corporation tax purposes | 1 April 2012 | 10 |
| Certain cars[8, 14] | **Chargeable period beginning on or after** | |
| for income tax purposes | **6 April 2012** | **8** |
| for corporation tax purposes | **1 April 2012** | **8** |
| | Chargeable period ending before | |
| for income tax purposes | 6 April 2012 | 10 |
| for corporation tax purposes | 1 April 2012 | 10 |
| Solar panels[8, 17] | **Chargeable period beginning on or after** | |
| for income tax purposes | **6 April 2012** | **8** |
| for corporation tax purposes | **1 April 2012** | **8** |
| Cushion gas[8, 16] | **Chargeable period beginning on or after** | |
| for income tax purposes | **6 April 2012** | **8** |
| for corporation tax purposes | **1 April 2012** | **8** |
| | Chargeable period ending before | |
| for income tax purposes | 6 April 2012 | 10 |
| for corporation tax purposes | 1 April 2012 | 10 |
| Generally | **Chargeable periods beginning on or after** | |
| for income tax purposes | **6 April 2012** | **18** |
| for corporation tax purposes | **1 April 2012** | **18** |
| | Chargeable period ending before | |
| for income tax purposes | 6 April 2012 | 20 |
| for corporation tax purposes | 1 April 2012 | 20 |
| for income tax purposes | 6 April 2008 | 25 |
| for corporation tax purposes | 1 April 2008 | 25 |
| | Chargeable periods straddling | |
| for income tax purposes | **6 April 2012** | **Hybrid rate**[8, 9] |
| for corporation tax purposes | **1 April 2012** | **Hybrid rate**[8, 9] |
| for income tax purposes | 6 April 2008 | Hybrid rate[8, 9] |
| for corporation tax purposes | 1 April 2008 | Hybrid rate[8, 9] |

1 **Annual investment allowance:** The first £200,000 (for expenditure on or after 1 January 2016; see table for earlier amounts) of qualifying expenditure incurred in a chargeable period qualifies for the annual investment allowance at 100%. Where a chargeable period spans the date of an increase or decrease, transitional rules apply. The limit is proportionately increased or decreased where the chargeable period is longer or shorter than a year. A group of companies (defined as for company law purposes) can only receive a single allowance. This restriction also applies to certain related businesses or companies. Expenditure on cars does not qualify (CAA 2001 ss 38A, 38B, 51A–51N; FA 2011 s 11; FA 2013 Sch 1; FA 2014 s 10, Sch 2, F(No 2)A 2015 s 8).

2 **Small and medium-sized businesses:** The allowance did not apply to certain expenditure including that on plant and machinery for leasing, motor cars, ships, railway assets or long-life assets. After the first year, allowances revert to the normal WDA. The rate of 50% applied only for expenditure incurred during the year ended 1 July 1998 when a 12% FYA applied to long-life assets. (See note 9 below.) Small and medium-sized businesses are, broadly, those satisfying any two of the following conditions: (*a*) turnover £22,800,000 or less (*b*) assets £11,400,000 or less (*c*) not more than 250 employees (CAA 1990 ss 22(3C), (6B), 22A, 44, 46–49). For accounting periods ending before 30 January 2004, the thresholds were: (*a*) turnover £11,200,000 or less (*b*) assets £5,600,000 or less.

3 **Small businesses:** See note 2 above for conditions for relief. Small businesses are, broadly, those satisfying any two of the following conditions: (*a*) turnover £5,600,000 or less (*b*) assets £2,800,000 or less (*c*) not more than 50 employees. For accounting periods ending before 30 January 2004, the thresholds were: (*a*) turnover £2,800,000 or less (*b*) assets £1,400,000 or less (FA 2004 s 142).

4 **Energy-saving plant or machinery:** The allowances are available for investment by *any* business in designated energy-saving plant and machinery in accordance with the Government's Energy Technology Product List. 100% first-year allowances are not available for expenditure incurred on or after 1 April 2012 (corporation tax) or 6 April 2012 (income tax) on plant or machinery to generate renewable electricity or heat where tariff payments are received under either of the renewable energy schemes introduced by the Department of Energy and Climate Change. The restriction applies from April 2014 for combined heat and power equipment (CAA 2001 ss 45A–45C, 46; FA 2001 s 65, Sch 17; SI 2001/2541; SI 2005/1114). The product lists are available at www.gov.uk/energy-technology-list.

5 **Low-emission cars:** The allowance is given on (*a*) new cars which are either electrically propelled or emit not more than 75g/km of $CO_2$ (95g/km for expenditure incurred before 1 April 2015, 110g/km for expenditure incurred before 1 April 2013, 120g/km for expenditure incurred before 1 April 2008), registered after 16 April 2002 and (*b*) new plant and machinery to refuel vehicles in a gas refuelling station with natural gas, hydrogen fuels, or (for expenditure on or after 1 April 2008) biogas. For expenditure incurred after 31 March 2013 cars provided for leasing no longer qualify for the FYA (CAA 2001 ss 45D, 45E, 46; SI 2016/984).**The qualifying threshold will be reduced to 50g/km from 1 April 2018**.

6 **Environmentally beneficial plant or machinery:** Allowances are available for expenditure by *any* business on new and unused designated technologies and products which satisfy the relevant environmental criteria in accordance with the Government's technologies or products lists (CAA 2001 ss 45H–45J, 46; FA 2003 s 167, Sch 30; SI 2003/2076). The product lists are available at www.gov.uk/government/publications/water-efficient-enhanced-capital-allowances.

7 **Zero-emission goods vehicles:** The allowance is given on new (and not second hand) vehicles which cannot under any circumstances produce $CO_2$ emissions when driven and which are of a design primarily suited to the conveyance of goods or burden. The expenditure must be incurred before 1 April 2018 (corporation tax) or 6 April 2018 (income tax) and is limited to expenditure of € 85 million per undertaking (as defined) over the period for which the provisions apply. The allowance is not available where another State aid has been or will be received towards the qualifying expenditure. Other exclusions apply (CAA 2001 ss 45DA–45DB, 212T; FA 2015 s 45).

8 **WDAs** are calculated on a reducing balance basis. For chargeable periods beginning before 6 April 2012 and ending on or after that date (income tax) or, beginning before 1 April 2012 and ending on or after that date (corporation tax) a hybrid rate of WDAs applies, calculated by time apportionment of the 20% and 18% rates, or, for the special rate expenditure, the 10% and 8% rates. For chargeable periods beginning on or after 6 April 2008 (income tax) or 1 April 2008 (corporation tax), a WDA of up to £1,000 can be claimed in respect of the main pool and/or the special rate pool where the unrelieved expenditure in the pool concerned is £1,000 or less.

9 **Long-life assets:** Applies to plant or machinery with an expected working life, when new, of 25 years or more. Applies where expenditure on long-life assets in a year is £100,000 or more (in the case of companies the de minimis limit is £100,000 divided by one plus the number of associated companies). Transitional provisions apply to maintain a 25% allowance for expenditure incurred before 1 January 2001 under a contract entered into before 26 November 1996 and to expenditure on second-hand plant or machinery if old rules applied to vendor. It does not apply to plant or machinery in a building used wholly or mainly as, or for purposes ancillary to, a dwelling-house, retail shop, showroom, hotel or office; cars; or sea-going ships and railway assets acquired before 1 January 2011. Expenditure on or after 1 April 2008 (corporation tax) or 6 April 2008 (income tax) qualifies, as special rate expenditure, for a writing down allowance of 8% (10% for periods before 1 or 6 April 2012, see note 8 above) reducing balance. The balance of the long-life asset pool at 1 or 6 April 2008 was also transferred into the special rate pool. The rate applying for chargeable periods beginning before 1 or 6 April 2008 was 6% and a hybrid rate applied for chargeable periods spanning those dates calculated by a time apportionment of the 6% and 10% rates (CAA 2001 ss 90–104, Sch 3 para 20).

10 **Integral features** of a building are electrical systems (including lighting systems); cold water systems; space or water heating systems, powered ventilation systems, air cooling or purification and any floor or ceiling comprised in such systems; lifts, escalators and moving walkways and external solar shading. Applies to expenditure incurred on or after 1 April 2008 (corporation tax) and 6 April 2008 (income tax). They all fall into the special rate pool and qualify for a 8% (10% for periods before 1 or 6 April 2012, see note 8 above) writing down allowance (CAA 2001 ss 33A, 104A).

11 **Foreign leased assets:** The relief applies only to leases finalised before 1 April 2006 (CAA 2001 s 109; FA 2006 Sch 9 para 13).

12 **First-year tax credits:** For expenditure incurred on or after 1 April 2008, a company can surrender a tax loss attributable to first-year allowances for energy-saving or environmentally beneficial equipment in exchange for a cash payment from the Government. The cash payment is equal to 19% of the loss surrendered, subject to an upper limit of the greater of £250,000 and the company's PAYE and NIC liability for the period concerned. (CAA 2001 Sch A1). Relief extended to 31 March 2018 by SI 2013/464.

13 **First year allowances**, where applicable, are available on expenditure over the annual investment allowance level or on which annual investment allowance has not been claimed, which would otherwise qualify for writing down allowance at 18% in the general plant and machinery pool.

14 **Cars:** For expenditure on and after 1 April 2009 (corporation tax), 6 April 2009 (income tax), cars with $CO_2$ emissions exceeding 130g/km (160g/km for expenditure incurred before 1 April 2013 (corporation tax) or 6 April 2013 (income tax)) will be allocated to the special rate pool. All other cars will go into the general pool (CAA 2001 ss 104A, 104AA; SI 2016/984). **From April 2018 the $CO_2$ threshold will be reduced to 110g/km**.

15 **Thermal insulation**: Expenditure on thermal insulation incurred on or after 1 April 2008 (corporation tax) and 6 April 2008 (income tax) falls into the special rate pool and qualifies for a 8% (10% for periods before 1 or 6 April 2012, see note 8 above) writing down allowance (CAA 2001 ss 28, 104A).

16 **Cushion gas:** Expenditure on cushion gas incurred on or after 1 April 2010 falls into the special rate pool and qualifies for a 8% (10% for periods before 1 or 6 April 2012, see note 8 above) writing down allowance (CAA 2001 ss 70J, 104A).

17 **Solar panels**: Expenditure on solar panels incurred on or after 1 April 2012 (corporation tax) and 6 April 2012 (income tax) falls into the special rate pool and qualifies for a 8% writing down allowance (CAA 2001 s 104A).

18 **Enterprise zones:** For expenditure incurred for the purpose of a qualifying activity in the eight-year period from the date the area is (or is treated as) designated, 100% first-year allowances are available for companies chargeable to corporation tax which invest in unused (not second hand) plant or machinery for use primarily in designated assisted areas within certain enterprise zones. Expenditure must be incurred for the purposes of broadly a new or expanding business carried on by the company, must not be replacement expenditure and is limited to €125 million per single investment project (as defined) over the eight years. Exclusions apply. See SI 2014/3183, SI 2015/2047 and SI 2016/751 for details of the current enterprise zones. The Northern Ireland Executive proposes to establish a pilot enterprise zone in Northern Ireland which, if implemented, will benefit from the enhanced capital allowances (CAA 2001 ss 45K–N, 212U).

19 **Electric charge-point equipment**. 100% first-year allowance is available for expenditure incurred in the period from 23 November 2016 to 31 March 2019 (corporation tax) and 23 November 2016 to 5 April

2019 (income tax) on new (not second hand), unused electric vehicle charging point equipment installed solely for the purpose of charging electric vehicles (CAA 2001 s 45EA; F(No 2)A 2017 s 38).

**Cars:** Car hire p 82.

## Renovation of business premises

| | Expenditure incurred between | % Rate |
|---|---|---|
| *First-year allowance* | **11 April 2007 and 1 or 6 April 2017** | **100** |

The expenditure must be incurred on renovating or converting vacant business properties in Northern Ireland or the designated disadvantaged areas in the UK that have been vacant for at least a year, to bring the property back into business use. From April 2014 the type of qualifying expenditure has been specifically clarified. Premises refurbished by or used by businesses in the following trades are excluded from the scheme: fisheries and aquaculture, shipbuilding, the coal or steel industries, synthetic fibres, primary production of certain agricultural products and the manufacture of products which imitate or substitute for milk or milk products. For qualifying expenditure incurred on or after 1 April 2014 (corporation tax) and on or after 6 April 2014 (income tax), allowances are not available if another form of State aid has been, or will be, received. A writing-down allowance is given at 25% (on a straight-line basis) on unrelieved expenditure. (FA 2005 s 92, Sch 6; SI 2012/868)

The relief is withdrawn for expenditure incurred on or after 1 April 2017 (corporation tax) and 6 April 2017 (income tax). (SI 2012/868)

## Research and development (formerly scientific research)

| | Expenditure incurred after | % Rate |
|---|---|---|
| *Allowance in year 1* | **5 November 1962** | **100** |

*Note:* Land and houses are excluded from 1 April 1985.

# Capital gains

## Annual exemption

(TCGA 1992 s 3; SI 2017/377)

### Individuals[a], personal representatives[b] and certain trusts[c]

a For 2008–09 onwards, an individual who claims to use the remittance basis for a tax year is not entitled to the capital gains tax annual exemption for that year. This does not apply if the individual's unremitted foreign income and gains for the year are less than £2,000 (TCGA 1992 s 3(1A); ITA 2007 s 809D).

b Year of death and following two years (maximum) (TCGA 1992 s 3(7)).

c Trusts for disabled persons as defined. Exemption divided by number of qualifying settlements created (after 9 March 1981) by one settlor, subject to a minimum of one-tenth (TCGA 1992 Sch para 1(1); FA 2005 Sch 1A).

| *Exempt amount of net gains* | ***2012–13*** | ***2013–14*** | ***2014–15*** | ***2015–16*** | ***2016–17*** | ***2017–18*** |
|---|---|---|---|---|---|---|
| | £10,600 | £10,900 | £11,000 | £11,100 | £11,100 | **£11,300** |

### Trusts[a] generally

| *Exempt amount of net gains* | ***2012–13*** | ***2013–14*** | ***2014–15*** | ***2015–16*** | ***2016–17*** | ***2017–18*** |
|---|---|---|---|---|---|---|
| | £5,300 | £5,450 | £5,500 | £5,550 | £5,550 | **£5,650** |

a Exemption divided by number of qualifying settlements created (after 6 June 1978) by one settlor, subject to a minimum of one-fifth (TCGA 1992 Sch 1 para 1(4)).

## Chattel exemption

(TCGA 1992 s 262)

| | *Disposals exemption* | *Marginal relief: Maximum chargeable gain* |
|---|---|---|
| **From 1989–90 onwards** | £6,000 | 5/3 excess over £6,000 |

## Rates of tax

(TCGA 1992 s 4)

| | | | | |
|---|---|---|---|---|
| **2017–18*** | **Gains accruing on the disposal of interests in residential properties (where not exempt), and gains arising in respect of carried interest** | | | |
| | *Individuals* | • | to income tax basic rate limit £33,500 (see note) | **18%** |
| | | • | above income tax basic rate limit £33,500 | **28%** |
| | *Trusts and personal representatives* | | | **28%** |
| | **Other gains** | | | |
| | *Individuals* | • | to income tax basic rate limit £33,500 | **10%** |
| | | • | above income tax basic rate limit £33,500 | **20%** |
| | *Trusts and personal representatives* | | | **20%** |
| **2016–17*** | **Gains accruing on the disposal of interests in residential properties (where not exempt), and gains arising in respect of carried interest** | | | |
| | *Individuals* | • | to income tax basic rate limit £32,000 | 18% |
| | | • | above income tax basic rate limit £32,000 | 28% |
| | *Trusts and personal representatives* | | | 28% |
| | **Other gains** | | | |
| | *Individuals* | • | to income tax basic rate limit £32,000 | 10% |
| | | • | above income tax basic rate limit £32,000 | 20% |
| | *Trusts and personal representatives* | | | 20% |
| **2015–16*** | *Individuals* | • | to income tax basic rate limit £31,785 | 18% |
| | | • | above income tax basic rate limit £31,785 | 28% |
| | *Trusts and personal representatives* | | | 28% |
| **2014–15*** | *Individuals* | • | to income tax basic rate limit £31,865 | 18% |
| | | • | above income tax basic rate limit £31,865 | 28% |
| | *Trusts and personal representatives* | | | 28% |
| **2013–14*** | *Individuals* | • | to income tax basic rate limit £32,010 | 18% |
| | | • | above income tax basic rate limit £32,010 | 28% |
| | *Trusts and personal representatives* | | | 28% |
| **2012–13*** | *Individuals* | • | to income tax basic rate limit £34,370 | 18% |
| | | • | above income tax basic rate limit £34,370 | 28% |
| | *Trusts and personal representatives* | | | 28% |

* A rate of **10% applies where entrepreneurs' relief is claimed** — see p 37.
For gains arising on or after 23 June 2010, the rate of tax for an individual is determined by treating gains as the top slice of income.
**Scottish taxpayers**: In 2017–18, the lower Scottish basic rate limit (see p 75) does not apply to determine the rate of capital gains tax payable.
**Disposals of high value UK residential property by certain non-natural persons**: A rate of 28% applies to gains arising on disposals on or after 6 April 2013 of high value UK residential property by certain non-natural persons — see p 65.
**Non-resident CGT gains on disposal of UK residential property by certain companies**: A rate of 20% applies to NRCGT gains arising on disposals on or after 6 April 2015 of UK residential property interests at a time when the company is not resident in the UK. The normal rates above apply to individuals subject to the charge.

**Trusts for vulnerable persons:** From 2004–05 onwards, gains taxed at beneficiary's rates (on beneficiary if UK resident or on trustees if beneficiary not UK-resident) (FA 2005 ss 30–32).

# Share identification rules

(TCGA 1992 ss 104–106A)

**For disposals on or after 6 April 2008 by individuals, trustees or personal representatives**, shares and securities of the same class in the same company are identified with acquisitions in the following order[2]:

- acquisitions on the same day as the disposal;
- acquisitions within 30 days after the day of disposal on a first in/first out basis[1];
- shares comprised in a single pool incorporating all other shares of the same class, whenever acquired.

**For the purposes of corporation tax on chargeable gains**, disposals of shares etc are identified with acquisitions in the following order:

- same day acquisitions;
- acquisitions within the previous nine days on a first in/first out basis;
- the pool of shares acquired after 31 March 1982;
- any shares held at 31 March 1982;
- any shares acquired on or before 6 April 1965 on a last in/first out basis;
- (if shares disposed of still not fully matched) subsequent acquisitions.

[1] The 30-day matching rule does not apply in relation to acquisitions after 21 March 2006 where the individual making the disposal is not (or is not treated as) resident (or before 6 April 2013, ordinarily resident) in the UK at the time of the acquisition.

[2] Different rules apply for SIP shares, exempt employee shareholder shares, BES shares, community investment tax relief shares, relevant EMI shares, EIS shares, VCT shares, SEIS shares, EOT exempt shares and social investment tax relief shares.

# Entrepreneurs' relief

(TCGA 1992 ss 169H–169V)

Entrepreneurs' relief applies to disposals by an individual on or after 6 April 2008 of:

- all or part of a trade carried on alone or in partnership;
- assets of such a trade following cessation; or
- shares or securities in the individual's 'personal trading company' (as defined).

Where a disposal of shares or of an interest in the assets of a partnership qualifies for relief, an associated disposal of assets owned by the individual and used by the company or partnership also qualifies for relief. However, for disposals on or after 18 March 2015, in order to qualify for this relief the claimant must generally reduce his participation in the business by also disposing of a minimum 5% of the shares of the company carrying on the business, or (where the business is carried on in partnership) of a minimum 5% share in the assets of the partnership carrying on the business. However, the disposal may be of less than a 5% share in the assets of the partnership providing the claimant disposes of the whole of his interest and owned 5% or more of the assets for a continuous period of three years in the eight years preceding the disposal. In addition, for assets acquired on or after 13 June 2016, the asset must have been held for three years before disposal.

Where a qualifying disposal is not of shares or securities in the individual's 'personal trading company', entrepreneurs' relief is given only in respect of the disposal of 'relevant business assets' comprised in the qualifying business disposal (assets used for purpose of the business but excluding shares and securities and assets, other than shares or securities, which are held as investments). Relief is not available for disposals of goodwill on or after 3 December 2014 to a close company to which the seller is related (this type of goodwill is excluded from the definition of relevant business assets) unless the business is transferred to a company controlled by 5 or fewer persons or by its directors and the claimant holds less than 5% of the shares, and less than 5% of the voting power, in the acquiring company. Relief will still also be due where the claimant does hold 5% or more of the shares or voting power provided the transfer of the business to the company is part of arrangements for the company to be sold to a new, independent owner.

Trustees can claim relief where a qualifying beneficiary has an interest in the business concerned.

Relief is extended to a disposal by an employee or officer of a trading company (or one or more companies in same trading group) of relevant EMI shares (as defined). Relief applies from 6 April 2013 where the shares were acquired on or after 6 April 2012.

The relief is available where the relevant conditions are met throughout a period of one year. The relief operates by charging qualifying net gains to CGT at 10% and is subject to a lifetime limit of gains of £10 million (£5 million for disposals before 6 April 2011; £2 million for disposals before 23 June 2010; £1 million for disposals before 6 April 2010), but disposals before 6 April 2008 do not count towards the limit. Relief given to trustees counts towards the limit of the qualifying beneficiary.

Transitional rules apply to allow relief to be claimed in certain circumstances where a gain made before 6 April 2008 is deferred and becomes chargeable on or after that date. In addition, gains which would have originally accrued on or after 3 December 2014 but which are deferred into the Enterprise Investment Scheme (see p 38) or Social Investment Tax Relief (see p 39) remain eligible for relief when the deferred gain becomes chargeable.

# Investors' relief

(TCGA 1992 ss 169VA–169VY, Sch 7ZB)

Relief is available for gains accruing on the disposal of ordinary shares in an unlisted trading company, held for a period of at least three years starting on or after 6 April 2016, which are newly issued to the claimant and acquired for new consideration on or after 17 March 2016. Generally neither the investor nor a person connected to them can be an employee or officer of the company or a connected company, though some exceptions apply. The relief operates by charging relevant gains to CGT at 10% and is subject to a lifetime limit of £10 million. Relief can be claimed by trustees where an eligible beneficiary has an interest in settled property which includes the qualifying shares.

# Other reliefs

The following is a summary of the other main capital gains tax reliefs and exemptions.

## Charities

Gains accruing to charities which are both applicable and applied for charitable purposes are exempt. The exemption also applies from 1 April 2002 to Community Amateur Sports Clubs (CASCs).

## Individuals

| | |
|---|---|
| Companies owned by employee-ownership trusts | From 6 April 2014 relief from capital gains tax is available for disposals by a person other than a company of shares in either a trading company which is not a member of a group, or a parent company of a trading group, where the disposal is to a trust with specified characteristics. The disposal is treated as being made at no gain/no loss if the settlement is for the benefit of all eligible employees of the company or group and the settlement acquires a controlling interest in the company during the tax year in which the disposal is made. Further conditions apply. |
| Compensation (injury to person, profession or vocation) | Exempt. |
| Decorations for valour (acquired otherwise than for money or money's worth) | Gain exempt. |
| Employee shareholder shares (see p 98) | Gains on or after 1 September 2013 on disposals of shares which were worth up to £50,000 on acquisition are exempt, provided the Employee Shareholder Agreement was entered into before 1 December 2016 (or 2 December 2016 where professional advice was given in relation to the share offer on 23 November 2016 before 1.30pm). A lifetime limit of £100,000 applies to exempt gains on disposal of shares acquired under Employee Shareholder Agreements entered into after 16 March 2016. |
| Enterprise Investment Scheme (see p 96) | Gain on disposal after relevant three-year period exempt to extent full relief given on shares. Deferral relief is available on gains on assets where the disposal proceeds are reinvested in EIS shares within one year before and three years after the disposal. |
| Entrepreneurs' relief (see p 37) | Gains on specified assets chargeable at 10% rate up to lifetime limit. |
| Foreign currency acquired for personal expenditure | Gain exempt. |
| Gifts for public benefit, works of art, historic buildings etc | No chargeable gain/allowable loss. |
| Gifts of pre-eminent objects | Donors who gift pre-eminent objects to the nation will receive a reduction in their UK tax liability of 30% of the value of the object they are donating. The tax reduction can be against income or capital gains tax and can be spread forward across a period of up to five years starting with the tax year in which the object is offered. The legislation has effect in relation to liabilities for tax years and accounting periods beginning on or after 1 April 2012. The gift must be accepted as pre-eminent by the Arts Council under the Cultural Gifts Scheme. See p 64 for relief applying to companies. |
| Gilt-edged stock | No chargeable gain/allowable loss. |
| Hold-over relief for gifts | Restricted to:<br>(1) gifts of business assets (including unquoted shares in trading companies and holding companies of trading groups). Relief is not available on the transfer of shares or securities to a company made after 8 November 1999 (other than transfers between 6 April 2003 and 20 October 2003);<br>(2) gifts of heritage property;<br>(3) gifts to heritage maintenance funds;<br>(4) gifts to political parties; and<br>(5) gifts which are chargeable transfers for inheritance tax.<br>Where available, transferee's acquisition cost treated as reduced by held-over gain. |
| Investors' relief (see p 37) | Gains on qualifying ordinary shares in an unlisted trading company chargeable at 10% rate up to lifetime limit. |
| Married persons or civil partners living together | No chargeable gain/allowable loss on transfers between spouses or civil partners. |
| Motor vehicles | Gain exempt. |

| | |
|---|---|
| Principal private residence | Gain exempt if property is main residence throughout period of ownership, or throughout the period of ownership except for all or any part of the last 18 months of that period (36 months for disposals before 6 April 2014). The 36-month period continues to apply where property is disposed of by an individual who is, or whose spouse or civil partner is, a disabled person or long-term resident of a care home, provided that neither holds an interest in any other dwelling on which private residence relief can be claimed. For disposals after 5 April 2015 property is treated as not being occupied as a residence for tax years when neither the taxpayer nor their spouse or civil partner is tax-resident in the territory in which the property is situated, and they do not stay overnight at the property at least 90 times during the year (pro-rated for part tax years). Period of ownership does not include any period before 31 March 1982. Certain other periods of absence qualify for exemption. |
| If residence is partly let, exemption for the let part is limited to the smaller of– | (1) exemption on owner-occupied part; and<br>(2) £40,000. |
| Qualifying corporate bonds | No chargeable gain (for loans made before 17 March 1998, allowable loss in certain cases if all or part of loss is irrecoverable). |
| Seed enterprise investment scheme (see p 96) | From 2012–13 reinvestment relief may be claimed where an individual realises capital gains on disposals of assets in a tax year and in the same year makes investments that qualify for, and he claims, the main seed enterprise investment scheme (SEIS) relief from income tax. For disposals of assets in 2012–13 the relief applies to the full qualifying re-invested amount. From 2013–14 the relief applies to half the qualifying re-invested amount. SEIS shares can be treated as issued in the previous tax year as a result of a SEIS income tax relief carry-back claim. SEIS re-investment relief then also has effect as if those shares had been issued on a day in the previous tax year. The maximum exemption is £100,000 of gains for 2012–13 and £50,000 thereafter. A disposal of shares on which SEIS income tax relief has been given and not withdrawn is exempt. |
| Social investment tax relief (see p 97) | Deferral relief is available for gains arising on assets in the period 6 April 2014 to 5 April 2019 where the disposal proceeds are reinvested in shares or debt investments which qualify for the social investment tax relief (SITR) income tax relief and investor is UK-resident. The qualifying investment must be made in the period from one year before to three years after the disposal. Limit of £1 million of gains which can be relieved in a tax year. A gain on a disposal of shares on which SITR income tax relief has been given and not withdrawn is exempt from capital gains tax where shares held for at least 3 years. |
| Venture capital trusts (see p 97) | Gain on disposal of shares by original investor exempt if company still a venture capital trust. Exemption applies only to shares acquired up to the permitted maximum of £200,000 per year of assessment. Deferral relief was available on gains on assets where the disposal proceeds were reinvested in VCT shares issued before 6 April 2004 and within one year before or after the disposal. This relief is withdrawn for shares issued after that date. |

## Businesses

*Roll-over relief for replacement of business assets*

(TCGA 1992 s 155)

| Qualifying assets: |
|---|
| Buildings and land both occupied and used for the purposes of the trade.<br>Fixed plant and machinery.<br>Ships, aircraft and hovercraft.<br>Satellites, space stations and spacecraft.<br>Goodwill[1].<br>Milk and potato quotas[1].<br>Ewe and suckler cow premium quotas[1].<br>Fish quotas[1].<br>Payment entitlement under farmers' single payment scheme.<br>Payment entitlement under farmers' basic payment scheme (from 20 December 2013).<br>Lloyd's syndicate rights. |

1 From 1 April 2002 onwards, subject to transitional rules, these items are removed from the list for companies only (as they fall within the intangible assets regime from that date (FA 2002 Sch 29 para 132(5)).

2 The 'replacement' assets must be acquired within 12 months before or three years after the disposal of the old asset. Both assets must be within any of the above classes. Holdover relief is available where the new asset is a depreciating asset (having a predictable useful life not exceeding 60 years).

*Roll-over relief on the transfer of a business ('incorporation relief')*
(TCGA 1992 s 162)

| |
|---|
| On incorporation of a business, the assets of the business are transferred to a company which then carries on the business in succession to the former proprietor. Gains realised on the transfer can be rolled over where the transfer is wholly or partly in consideration for the issue of shares. Relief is automatic (no claim is required). |

See p 64 for disincorporation relief for companies. See p 39 for gifts of business assets.

## Personal representatives

*Allowable expenses*
(SP 2/04)

Expenses allowable for the costs of establishing title in computing chargeable gains on disposal of assets in a deceased person's estate: deaths occurring after 5 April 2004. (HMRC accepts computations based either on the scale or on the actual allowable expenditure incurred.)

| *Gross value of estate* | *Allowable expenditure* |
|---|---|
| Up to £50,000 | 1.8% of the probate value of the assets sold by the personal representatives. |
| Between £50,001 and £90,000 | £900, to be divided between all the assets of the estate in proportion to the probate values and allowed in those proportions on assets sold by the personal representatives. |
| Between £90,001 and £400,000 | 1% of the probate value of the assets sold. |
| Between £400,001 and £500,000 | £4,000, to be divided between all the assets of the estate in proportion to the probate values and allowed in those proportions on assets sold by the personal representatives. |
| Between £500,001 and £1,000,000 | 0.8% of the probate value of the assets sold. |
| Between £1,000,001 and £5,000,000 | £8,000 to be divided between all the assets of the estate in proportion to the probate values and allowed in those proportions on assets sold by the personal representatives. |
| Exceeding £5,000,000 | 0.16% of the probate value of the assets sold subject to a maximum of £10,000. |

## Trustees

*Allowable expenses*
(SP 2/04)

Expenses allowable in computing chargeable gains of corporate trustees in the administration of trusts and estates: acquisition, disposals and deemed disposals after 5 April 2004. (HMRC accepts computations based either on the scale or on the actual allowable expenditure incurred.)

| | |
|---|---|
| *Transfers of assets to beneficiaries etc* | |
| (*a*) Quoted stocks and shares | |
| (i) One beneficiary | £25 per holding. |
| (ii) More than one beneficiary | £25 per holding, divided equally between the beneficiaries. |
| (*b*) Unquoted shares | As (*a*) above, plus any exceptional expenditure. |
| (*c*) Other assets | As (*a*) above, plus any exceptional expenditure. |
| *Actual disposals and acquisitions* | |
| (*a*) Quoted stocks and shares | Investment fee as charged by the trustees (where a comprehensive annual management fee is charged, the investment fee is taken to be £0.25 per £100 of the sale or purchase moneys). |
| (*b*) Unquoted shares | As (*a*) above, plus actual valuation costs. |
| (*c*) Other assets | Investment fee (as (*a*) above), subject to a maximum of £75, plus actual valuation costs. |
| *Deemed disposals by trustees* | |
| (*a*) Quoted stocks and shares | £8 per holding. |
| (*b*) Unquoted shares | Actual valuation costs. |
| (*c*) Other assets | Actual valuation costs. |

## Indexation allowance – corporation tax on chargeable gains

(TCGA 1992 ss 53–57, 109)

For corporation tax purposes, an indexation allowance is given as a deduction in calculating gains on disposals from the amount realised (or deemed to be realised) on disposal. The indexation allowance is calculated by multiplying each item of allowable expenditure by:

$$\frac{RD - RI}{RI}$$

Where:

RD is the retail prices index figure for month of disposal;

RI is the retail prices index for month of expenditure (or March 1982 if later).

Indexation allowance can only be used to reduce or extinguish a gain. It cannot be used to create or increase a capital loss. It is not available to individuals, trustees and personal representatives. See p 60 for RPI values. The factors below can be used to calculate the indexation allowance for corporation tax purposes.

MONTH OF DISPOSAL

| | ***2015*** | | | | | | | | | | ***2016*** | | | | |
|---|---|---|---|---|---|---|---|---|---|---|---|---|---|---|---|
| **1982** | Mar | Apr | May | June | July | Aug | Sep | Oct | Nov | Dec | Jan | Feb | Mar | Apr | May |
| Mar | 2.236 | 2.248 | 2.254 | 2.259 | 2.255 | 2.270 | 2.268 | 2.267 | 2.270 | 2.280 | 2.258 | 2.273 | 2.287 | 2.290 | 2.299 |
| Apr | 2.173 | 2.184 | 2.190 | 2.195 | 2.191 | 2.206 | 2.203 | 2.202 | 2.206 | 2.216 | 2.194 | 2.208 | 2.222 | 2.226 | 2.234 |
| May | 2.150 | 2.161 | 2.167 | 2.172 | 2.168 | 2.183 | 2.181 | 2.179 | 2.183 | 2.193 | 2.171 | 2.185 | 2.199 | 2.203 | 2.211 |
| June | 2.141 | 2.152 | 2.158 | 2.163 | 2.159 | 2.174 | 2.172 | 2.170 | 2.174 | 2.184 | 2.162 | 2.177 | 2.190 | 2.194 | 2.202 |
| July | 2.140 | 2.151 | 2.157 | 2.162 | 2.158 | 2.173 | 2.171 | 2.169 | 2.173 | 2.183 | 2.161 | 2.176 | 2.189 | 2.193 | 2.201 |
| Aug | 2.139 | 2.150 | 2.156 | 2.161 | 2.157 | 2.172 | 2.170 | 2.168 | 2.172 | 2.182 | 2.160 | 2.175 | 2.188 | 2.192 | 2.200 |
| Sept | 2.141 | 2.152 | 2.158 | 2.163 | 2.159 | 2.174 | 2.172 | 2.170 | 2.174 | 2.184 | 2.162 | 2.177 | 2.190 | 2.194 | 2.202 |
| Oct | 2.126 | 2.137 | 2.143 | 2.147 | 2.144 | 2.158 | 2.156 | 2.155 | 2.158 | 2.168 | 2.146 | 2.161 | 2.174 | 2.178 | 2.186 |
| Nov | 2.110 | 2.121 | 2.127 | 2.132 | 2.128 | 2.143 | 2.141 | 2.139 | 2.143 | 2.153 | 2.131 | 2.145 | 2.159 | 2.162 | 2.171 |
| Dec | 2.116 | 2.127 | 2.133 | 2.138 | 2.134 | 2.149 | 2.146 | 2.145 | 2.149 | 2.158 | 2.137 | 2.151 | 2.164 | 2.168 | 2.177 |
| **1983** | Mar | Apr | May | June | July | Aug | Sep | Oct | Nov | Dec | Jan | Feb | Mar | Apr | May |
| Jan | 2.112 | 2.123 | 2.129 | 2.134 | 2.130 | 2.145 | 2.142 | 2.141 | 2.145 | 2.155 | 2.133 | 2.147 | 2.161 | 2.164 | 2.173 |
| Feb | 2.099 | 2.110 | 2.116 | 2.121 | 2.117 | 2.131 | 2.129 | 2.128 | 2.131 | 2.141 | 2.119 | 2.134 | 2.147 | 2.151 | 2.159 |
| Mar | 2.093 | 2.104 | 2.110 | 2.115 | 2.111 | 2.126 | 2.123 | 2.122 | 2.126 | 2.135 | 2.114 | 2.128 | 2.141 | 2.145 | 2.153 |
| Apr | 2.050 | 2.061 | 2.067 | 2.072 | 2.068 | 2.082 | 2.080 | 2.079 | 2.082 | 2.092 | 2.071 | 2.085 | 2.098 | 2.101 | 2.110 |
| May | 2.038 | 2.048 | 2.054 | 2.059 | 2.055 | 2.070 | 2.067 | 2.066 | 2.070 | 2.079 | 2.058 | 2.072 | 2.085 | 2.088 | 2.097 |
| June | 2.030 | 2.041 | 2.047 | 2.052 | 2.048 | 2.062 | 2.060 | 2.059 | 2.062 | 2.072 | 2.050 | 2.065 | 2.078 | 2.081 | 2.089 |
| July | 2.014 | 2.025 | 2.031 | 2.035 | 2.032 | 2.046 | 2.043 | 2.042 | 2.046 | 2.055 | 2.034 | 2.048 | 2.061 | 2.065 | 2.073 |
| Aug | 2.001 | 2.011 | 2.017 | 2.022 | 2.018 | 2.032 | 2.030 | 2.029 | 2.032 | 2.042 | 2.021 | 2.035 | 2.047 | 2.051 | 2.059 |
| Sept | 1.988 | 1.998 | 2.004 | 2.008 | 2.005 | 2.019 | 2.017 | 2.015 | 2.019 | 2.028 | 2.007 | 2.021 | 2.034 | 2.037 | 2.046 |
| Oct | 1.977 | 1.987 | 1.993 | 1.998 | 1.994 | 2.008 | 2.006 | 2.005 | 2.008 | 2.018 | 1.997 | 2.011 | 2.023 | 2.027 | 2.035 |
| Nov | 1.967 | 1.977 | 1.983 | 1.987 | 1.984 | 1.998 | 1.995 | 1.994 | 1.998 | 2.007 | 1.986 | 2.000 | 2.013 | 2.016 | 2.024 |
| Dec | 1.959 | 1.969 | 1.975 | 1.979 | 1.976 | 1.990 | 1.988 | 1.986 | 1.990 | 1.999 | 1.978 | 1.992 | 2.005 | 2.008 | 2.016 |
| **1984** | Mar | Apr | May | June | July | Aug | Sep | Oct | Nov | Dec | Jan | Feb | Mar | Apr | May |
| Jan | 1.960 | 1.971 | 1.977 | 1.981 | 1.978 | 1.992 | 1.989 | 1.988 | 1.992 | 2.001 | 1.980 | 1.994 | 2.007 | 2.010 | 2.018 |
| Feb | 1.948 | 1.959 | 1.964 | 1.969 | 1.968 | 1.979 | 1.977 | 1.976 | 1.979 | 1.989 | 1.968 | 1.982 | 1.994 | 1.998 | 2.006 |
| Mar | 1.939 | 1.949 | 1.955 | 1.960 | 1.956 | 1.970 | 1.968 | 1.966 | 1.970 | 1.979 | 1.958 | 1.972 | 1.985 | 1.988 | 1.996 |
| Apr | 1.900 | 1.911 | 1.916 | 1.921 | 1.917 | 1.931 | 1.929 | 1.927 | 1.931 | 1.940 | 1.920 | 1.933 | 1.945 | 1.949 | 1.957 |
| May | 1.890 | 1.900 | 1.905 | 1.910 | 1.906 | 1.920 | 1.918 | 1.917 | 1.920 | 1.929 | 1.909 | 1.922 | 1.935 | 1.938 | 1.946 |
| June | 1.882 | 1.892 | 1.898 | 1.902 | 1.899 | 1.913 | 1.910 | 1.909 | 1.913 | 1.921 | 1.901 | 1.915 | 1.927 | 1.930 | 1.938 |
| July | 1.886 | 1.896 | 1.901 | 1.906 | 1.902 | 1.916 | 1.914 | 1.912 | 1.916 | 1.925 | 1.905 | 1.918 | 1.930 | 1.934 | 1.942 |
| Aug | 1.859 | 1.869 | 1.874 | 1.879 | 1.875 | 1.889 | 1.886 | 1.885 | 1.889 | 1.898 | 1.878 | 1.891 | 1.903 | 1.906 | 1.914 |
| Sept | 1.853 | 1.863 | 1.869 | 1.873 | 1.870 | 1.883 | 1.881 | 1.880 | 1.883 | 1.892 | 1.872 | 1.885 | 1.897 | 1.901 | 1.909 |
| Oct | 1.836 | 1.845 | 1.851 | 1.855 | 1.852 | 1.865 | 1.863 | 1.862 | 1.865 | 1.874 | 1.854 | 1.867 | 1.880 | 1.883 | 1.891 |
| Nov | 1.827 | 1.837 | 1.842 | 1.847 | 1.843 | 1.856 | 1.854 | 1.853 | 1.856 | 1.865 | 1.846 | 1.859 | 1.871 | 1.874 | 1.882 |
| Dec | 1.829 | 1.839 | 1.845 | 1.849 | 1.846 | 1.859 | 1.857 | 1.856 | 1.859 | 1.868 | 1.848 | 1.861 | 1.873 | 1.876 | 1.884 |
| **1985** | Mar | Apr | May | June | July | Aug | Sep | Oct | Nov | Dec | Jan | Feb | Mar | Apr | May |
| Jan | 1.819 | 1.829 | 1.834 | 1.839 | 1.835 | 1.849 | 1.846 | 1.845 | 1.849 | 1.857 | 1.838 | 1.851 | 1.863 | 1.866 | 1.874 |
| Feb | 1.796 | 1.806 | 1.812 | 1.816 | 1.813 | 1.826 | 1.824 | 1.823 | 1.826 | 1.834 | 1.815 | 1.828 | 1.840 | 1.843 | 1.851 |
| Mar | 1.770 | 1.780 | 1.786 | 1.790 | 1.787 | 1.800 | 1.797 | 1.796 | 1.800 | 1.808 | 1.789 | 1.802 | 1.814 | 1.817 | 1.824 |
| Apr | 1.713 | 1.722 | 1.727 | 1.732 | 1.728 | 1.741 | 1.739 | 1.738 | 1.741 | 1.750 | 1.731 | 1.743 | 1.755 | 1.758 | 1.765 |
| May | 1.700 | 1.710 | 1.715 | 1.719 | 1.716 | 1.729 | 1.727 | 1.726 | 1.729 | 1.737 | 1.718 | 1.731 | 1.742 | 1.746 | 1.753 |
| June | 1.695 | 1.704 | 1.709 | 1.713 | 1.710 | 1.723 | 1.721 | 1.720 | 1.723 | 1.731 | 1.712 | 1.725 | 1.737 | 1.740 | 1.747 |
| July | 1.700 | 1.709 | 1.714 | 1.719 | 1.715 | 1.728 | 1.726 | 1.725 | 1.728 | 1.736 | 1.718 | 1.730 | 1.742 | 1.745 | 1.752 |
| Aug | 1.692 | 1.702 | 1.707 | 1.711 | 1.708 | 1.721 | 1.719 | 1.718 | 1.721 | 1.729 | 1.710 | 1.723 | 1.734 | 1.738 | 1.745 |
| Sept | 1.694 | 1.703 | 1.709 | 1.713 | 1.710 | 1.722 | 1.720 | 1.719 | 1.722 | 1.731 | 1.712 | 1.724 | 1.736 | 1.739 | 1.746 |
| Oct | 1.690 | 1.699 | 1.704 | 1.708 | 1.705 | 1.718 | 1.716 | 1.715 | 1.718 | 1.726 | 1.707 | 1.720 | 1.731 | 1.735 | 1.742 |
| Nov | 1.680 | 1.690 | 1.695 | 1.699 | 1.696 | 1.709 | 1.706 | 1.705 | 1.709 | 1.717 | 1.698 | 1.711 | 1.722 | 1.725 | 1.733 |
| Dec | 1.677 | 1.686 | 1.691 | 1.696 | 1.692 | 1.705 | 1.703 | 1.702 | 1.705 | 1.713 | 1.695 | 1.707 | 1.718 | 1.722 | 1.729 |

MONTH OF DISPOSAL

| | ***2016*** | | | | | | | ***2017*** | | | | | | | |
|---|---|---|---|---|---|---|---|---|---|---|---|---|---|---|---|
| **1982** | June | July | Aug | Sep | Oct | Nov | Dec | Jan | Feb | Mar | Apr | May | June | July | Aug |
| Mar | 2.312 | 2.316 | 2.328 | 2.334 | 2.333 | 2.342 | 2.362 | 2.342 | 2.379 | 2.390 | 2.406 | 2.420 | 2.428 | 2.435 | 2.433 |
| Apr | 2.247 | 2.250 | 2.263 | 2.269 | 2.268 | 2.276 | 2.296 | 2.276 | 2.312 | 2.323 | 2.339 | 2.353 | 2.360 | 2.368 | 2.365 |
| May | 2.223 | 2.227 | 2.239 | 2.245 | 2.244 | 2.253 | 2.272 | 2.253 | 2.288 | 2.299 | 2.315 | 2.329 | 2.336 | 2.343 | 2.341 |
| June | 2.214 | 2.218 | 2.230 | 2.236 | 2.235 | 2.244 | 2.263 | 2.244 | 2.279 | 2.290 | 2.306 | 2.319 | 2.327 | 2.334 | 2.332 |
| July | 2.213 | 2.217 | 2.229 | 2.235 | 2.234 | 2.243 | 2.262 | 2.243 | 2.278 | 2.289 | 2.305 | 2.318 | 2.326 | 2.333 | 2.331 |
| Aug | 2.212 | 2.216 | 2.228 | 2.234 | 2.233 | 2.242 | 2.261 | 2.242 | 2.277 | 2.288 | 2.304 | 2.317 | 2.325 | 2.332 | 2.330 |
| Sept | 2.214 | 2.218 | 2.230 | 2.236 | 2.235 | 2.244 | 2.263 | 2.244 | 2.279 | 2.290 | 2.306 | 2.319 | 2.327 | 2.334 | 2.332 |
| Oct | 2.199 | 2.202 | 2.214 | 2.220 | 2.219 | 2.228 | 2.247 | 2.228 | 2.263 | 2.274 | 2.290 | 2.303 | 2.310 | 2.318 | 2.315 |
| Nov | 2.183 | 2.186 | 2.199 | 2.205 | 2.203 | 2.212 | 2.231 | 2.212 | 2.247 | 2.258 | 2.274 | 2.287 | 2.294 | 2.301 | 2.299 |
| Dec | 2.189 | 2.192 | 2.204 | 2.211 | 2.209 | 2.218 | 2.237 | 2.218 | 2.253 | 2.264 | 2.280 | 2.293 | 2.300 | 2.307 | 2.305 |
| **1983** | June | July | Aug | Sep | Oct | Nov | Dec | Jan | Feb | Mar | Apr | May | June | July | Aug |
| Jan | 2.185 | 2.188 | 2.201 | 2.207 | 2.205 | 2.214 | 2.233 | 2.214 | 2.249 | 2.260 | 2.276 | 2.289 | 2.296 | 2.303 | 2.301 |
| Feb | 2.171 | 2.175 | 2.187 | 2.193 | 2.192 | 2.200 | 2.219 | 2.200 | 2.235 | 2.246 | 2.262 | 2.275 | 2.282 | 2.289 | 2.287 |
| Mar | 2.165 | 2.169 | 2.181 | 2.187 | 2.186 | 2.194 | 2.214 | 2.194 | 2.229 | 2.240 | 2.256 | 2.269 | 2.276 | 2.283 | 2.281 |
| Apr | 2.122 | 2.125 | 2.137 | 2.143 | 2.142 | 2.150 | 2.169 | 2.150 | 2.184 | 2.195 | 2.211 | 2.224 | 2.231 | 2.238 | 2.235 |
| May | 2.109 | 2.112 | 2.124 | 2.130 | 2.129 | 2.137 | 2.156 | 2.137 | 2.171 | 2.182 | 2.197 | 2.210 | 2.217 | 2.224 | 2.222 |
| June | 2.101 | 2.105 | 2.116 | 2.122 | 2.121 | 2.129 | 2.148 | 2.129 | 2.164 | 2.174 | 2.189 | 2.202 | 2.210 | 2.217 | 2.214 |
| July | 2.084 | 2.088 | 2.100 | 2.106 | 2.104 | 2.113 | 2.131 | 2.113 | 2.147 | 2.157 | 2.172 | 2.185 | 2.192 | 2.199 | 2.197 |
| Aug | 2.071 | 2.074 | 2.086 | 2.092 | 2.091 | 2.099 | 2.117 | 2.099 | 2.133 | 2.143 | 2.158 | 2.171 | 2.178 | 2.185 | 2.183 |
| Sept | 2.057 | 2.061 | 2.072 | 2.078 | 2.077 | 2.085 | 2.104 | 2.085 | 2.119 | 2.129 | 2.144 | 2.157 | 2.164 | 2.171 | 2.169 |
| Oct | 2.046 | 2.050 | 2.062 | 2.067 | 2.066 | 2.074 | 2.093 | 2.074 | 2.108 | 2.118 | 2.133 | 2.146 | 2.153 | 2.160 | 2.158 |
| Nov | 2.036 | 2.039 | 2.051 | 2.057 | 2.055 | 2.063 | 2.082 | 2.063 | 2.097 | 2.107 | 2.122 | 2.135 | 2.142 | 2.149 | 2.147 |
| Dec | 2.028 | 2.031 | 2.043 | 2.049 | 2.047 | 2.055 | 2.074 | 2.055 | 2.089 | 2.099 | 2.114 | 2.127 | 2.134 | 2.141 | 2.138 |
| **1984** | June | July | Aug | Sep | Oct | Nov | Dec | Jan | Feb | Mar | Apr | May | June | July | Aug |
| Jan | 2.030 | 2.033 | 2.045 | 2.050 | 2.049 | 2.057 | 2.076 | 2.057 | 2.091 | 2.101 | 2.116 | 2.129 | 2.136 | 2.142 | 2.140 |
| Feb | 2.017 | 2.021 | 2.032 | 2.038 | 2.037 | 2.045 | 2.063 | 2.045 | 2.078 | 2.088 | 2.103 | 2.116 | 2.123 | 2.130 | 2.127 |
| Mar | 2.008 | 2.011 | 2.022 | 2.028 | 2.027 | 2.035 | 2.053 | 2.035 | 2.068 | 2.078 | 2.093 | 2.106 | 2.113 | 2.120 | 2.117 |
| Apr | 1.968 | 1.971 | 1.983 | 1.988 | 1.987 | 1.995 | 2.013 | 1.995 | 2.028 | 2.038 | 2.053 | 2.065 | 2.072 | 2.079 | 2.076 |
| May | 1.957 | 1.960 | 1.972 | 1.977 | 1.976 | 1.984 | 2.002 | 1.984 | 2.017 | 2.027 | 2.041 | 2.054 | 2.060 | 2.067 | 2.065 |
| June | 1.950 | 1.953 | 1.964 | 1.970 | 1.969 | 1.976 | 1.994 | 1.976 | 2.009 | 2.019 | 2.034 | 2.046 | 2.053 | 2.059 | 2.057 |
| July | 1.953 | 1.956 | 1.967 | 1.973 | 1.972 | 1.980 | 1.998 | 1.980 | 2.012 | 2.022 | 2.037 | 2.049 | 2.056 | 2.063 | 2.061 |
| Aug | 1.925 | 1.929 | 1.940 | 1.945 | 1.944 | 1.952 | 1.970 | 1.952 | 1.984 | 1.994 | 2.009 | 2.021 | 2.028 | 2.034 | 2.032 |
| Sept | 1.920 | 1.923 | 1.934 | 1.940 | 1.938 | 1.946 | 1.964 | 1.946 | 1.978 | 1.988 | 2.003 | 2.015 | 2.022 | 2.028 | 2.026 |
| Oct | 1.902 | 1.905 | 1.916 | 1.922 | 1.920 | 1.928 | 1.946 | 1.928 | 1.960 | 1.970 | 1.984 | 1.997 | 2.003 | 2.010 | 2.008 |
| Nov | 1.893 | 1.896 | 1.907 | 1.913 | 1.911 | 1.919 | 1.937 | 1.919 | 1.951 | 1.961 | 1.975 | 1.987 | 1.994 | 2.001 | 1.998 |
| Dec | 1.895 | 1.899 | 1.910 | 1.915 | 1.914 | 1.922 | 1.939 | 1.922 | 1.954 | 1.963 | 1.978 | 1.990 | 1.996 | 2.003 | 2.001 |
| **1985** | June | July | Aug | Sep | Oct | Nov | Dec | Jan | Feb | Mar | Apr | May | June | July | Aug |
| Jan | 1.885 | 1.888 | 1.899 | 1.904 | 1.903 | 1.911 | 1.929 | 1.911 | 1.943 | 1.953 | 1.967 | 1.979 | 1.986 | 1.992 | 1.990 |
| Feb | 1.862 | 1.865 | 1.876 | 1.881 | 1.880 | 1.888 | 1.905 | 1.888 | 1.919 | 1.929 | 1.943 | 1.955 | 1.962 | 1.968 | 1.966 |
| Mar | 1.835 | 1.838 | 1.849 | 1.854 | 1.853 | 1.861 | 1.878 | 1.861 | 1.892 | 1.902 | 1.916 | 1.928 | 1.934 | 1.941 | 1.939 |
| Apr | 1.776 | 1.779 | 1.790 | 1.795 | 1.794 | 1.801 | 1.818 | 1.801 | 1.832 | 1.841 | 1.855 | 1.867 | 1.873 | 1.879 | 1.877 |
| May | 1.763 | 1.767 | 1.777 | 1.782 | 1.781 | 1.789 | 1.805 | 1.789 | 1.819 | 1.829 | 1.842 | 1.854 | 1.860 | 1.866 | 1.864 |
| June | 1.758 | 1.761 | 1.771 | 1.776 | 1.775 | 1.783 | 1.799 | 1.783 | 1.813 | 1.822 | 1.836 | 1.848 | 1.854 | 1.860 | 1.858 |
| July | 1.763 | 1.766 | 1.776 | 1.782 | 1.781 | 1.788 | 1.805 | 1.788 | 1.818 | 1.828 | 1.841 | 1.853 | 1.859 | 1.866 | 1.863 |
| Aug | 1.755 | 1.758 | 1.769 | 1.774 | 1.773 | 1.780 | 1.797 | 1.780 | 1.811 | 1.820 | 1.834 | 1.845 | 1.852 | 1.858 | 1.856 |
| Sept | 1.757 | 1.760 | 1.770 | 1.776 | 1.775 | 1.782 | 1.799 | 1.782 | 1.812 | 1.822 | 1.835 | 1.847 | 1.853 | 1.859 | 1.857 |
| Oct | 1.752 | 1.756 | 1.766 | 1.771 | 1.770 | 1.778 | 1.794 | 1.778 | 1.808 | 1.817 | 1.831 | 1.842 | 1.849 | 1.855 | 1.853 |
| Nov | 1.743 | 1.746 | 1.756 | 1.762 | 1.761 | 1.768 | 1.785 | 1.768 | 1.798 | 1.808 | 1.821 | 1.833 | 1.839 | 1.845 | 1.843 |
| Dec | 1.739 | 1.742 | 1.753 | 1.758 | 1.757 | 1.764 | 1.781 | 1.764 | 1.795 | 1.804 | 1.817 | 1.829 | 1.835 | 1.841 | 1.839 |

## MONTH OF DISPOSAL

| | **2015** | | | | | | | | | | **2016** | | | | |
|---|---|---|---|---|---|---|---|---|---|---|---|---|---|---|---|
| **1986** | Mar | Apr | May | June | July | Aug | Sep | Oct | Nov | Dec | Jan | Feb | Mar | Apr | May |
| Jan | 1.671 | 1.681 | 1.686 | 1.690 | 1.687 | 1.699 | 1.697 | 1.696 | 1.699 | 1.708 | 1.689 | 1.701 | 1.713 | 1.716 | 1.723 |
| Feb | 1.661 | 1.671 | 1.676 | 1.680 | 1.677 | 1.689 | 1.687 | 1.686 | 1.689 | 1.698 | 1.679 | 1.691 | 1.703 | 1.706 | 1.713 |
| Mar | 1.658 | 1.667 | 1.672 | 1.677 | 1.673 | 1.686 | 1.684 | 1.683 | 1.686 | 1.694 | 1.675 | 1.688 | 1.699 | 1.702 | 1.710 |
| Apr | 1.632 | 1.642 | 1.647 | 1.651 | 1.648 | 1.660 | 1.658 | 1.657 | 1.660 | 1.668 | 1.650 | 1.662 | 1.673 | 1.676 | 1.684 |
| May | 1.628 | 1.637 | 1.642 | 1.646 | 1.643 | 1.655 | 1.653 | 1.652 | 1.655 | 1.663 | 1.645 | 1.657 | 1.668 | 1.672 | 1.679 |
| June | 1.629 | 1.638 | 1.643 | 1.647 | 1.644 | 1.657 | 1.655 | 1.654 | 1.657 | 1.665 | 1.646 | 1.659 | 1.670 | 1.673 | 1.680 |
| July | 1.636 | 1.646 | 1.651 | 1.655 | 1.652 | 1.664 | 1.662 | 1.661 | 1.664 | 1.672 | 1.654 | 1.666 | 1.678 | 1.681 | 1.688 |
| Aug | 1.628 | 1.637 | 1.643 | 1.647 | 1.644 | 1.656 | 1.654 | 1.653 | 1.656 | 1.664 | 1.646 | 1.658 | 1.669 | 1.672 | 1.679 |
| Sept | 1.615 | 1.625 | 1.630 | 1.634 | 1.631 | 1.643 | 1.641 | 1.640 | 1.643 | 1.651 | 1.633 | 1.645 | 1.656 | 1.659 | 1.666 |
| Oct | 1.611 | 1.621 | 1.626 | 1.630 | 1.627 | 1.639 | 1.637 | 1.636 | 1.639 | 1.647 | 1.629 | 1.641 | 1.652 | 1.655 | 1.662 |
| Nov | 1.589 | 1.598 | 1.603 | 1.608 | 1.604 | 1.617 | 1.615 | 1.614 | 1.617 | 1.625 | 1.606 | 1.619 | 1.630 | 1.633 | 1.640 |
| Dec | 1.581 | 1.590 | 1.595 | 1.599 | 1.596 | 1.608 | 1.606 | 1.605 | 1.608 | 1.616 | 1.598 | 1.610 | 1.621 | 1.624 | 1.631 |
| **1987** | Mar | Apr | May | June | July | Aug | Sep | Oct | Nov | Dec | Jan | Feb | Mar | Apr | May |
| Jan | 1.571 | 1.580 | 1.585 | 1.589 | 1.586 | 1.598 | 1.596 | 1.595 | 1.598 | 1.606 | 1.588 | 1.600 | 1.611 | 1.614 | 1.621 |
| Feb | 1.561 | 1.570 | 1.575 | 1.579 | 1.576 | 1.588 | 1.586 | 1.585 | 1.588 | 1.596 | 1.578 | 1.590 | 1.601 | 1.604 | 1.611 |
| Mar | 1.556 | 1.565 | 1.570 | 1.574 | 1.571 | 1.583 | 1.581 | 1.580 | 1.583 | 1.590 | 1.573 | 1.584 | 1.595 | 1.598 | 1.605 |
| Apr | 1.526 | 1.534 | 1.539 | 1.543 | 1.540 | 1.552 | 1.550 | 1.549 | 1.552 | 1.560 | 1.542 | 1.554 | 1.565 | 1.568 | 1.575 |
| May | 1.523 | 1.532 | 1.537 | 1.541 | 1.538 | 1.550 | 1.548 | 1.547 | 1.550 | 1.557 | 1.540 | 1.552 | 1.562 | 1.565 | 1.572 |
| June | 1.523 | 1.532 | 1.537 | 1.541 | 1.538 | 1.550 | 1.548 | 1.547 | 1.550 | 1.557 | 1.540 | 1.552 | 1.562 | 1.565 | 1.572 |
| July | 1.526 | 1.534 | 1.539 | 1.543 | 1.540 | 1.552 | 1.550 | 1.549 | 1.552 | 1.560 | 1.542 | 1.554 | 1.565 | 1.568 | 1.575 |
| Aug | 1.518 | 1.527 | 1.532 | 1.536 | 1.533 | 1.545 | 1.543 | 1.542 | 1.545 | 1.552 | 1.535 | 1.547 | 1.557 | 1.560 | 1.567 |
| Sept | 1.511 | 1.520 | 1.524 | 1.528 | 1.525 | 1.537 | 1.535 | 1.534 | 1.537 | 1.545 | 1.527 | 1.539 | 1.550 | 1.553 | 1.560 |
| Oct | 1.499 | 1.507 | 1.512 | 1.516 | 1.513 | 1.525 | 1.523 | 1.522 | 1.525 | 1.533 | 1.515 | 1.527 | 1.537 | 1.540 | 1.547 |
| Nov | 1.486 | 1.495 | 1.500 | 1.504 | 1.501 | 1.513 | 1.511 | 1.510 | 1.513 | 1.520 | 1.503 | 1.515 | 1.525 | 1.528 | 1.535 |
| Dec | 1.489 | 1.498 | 1.502 | 1.506 | 1.503 | 1.515 | 1.513 | 1.512 | 1.515 | 1.523 | 1.505 | 1.517 | 1.528 | 1.530 | 1.537 |
| **1988** | Mar | Apr | May | June | July | Aug | Sep | Oct | Nov | Dec | Jan | Feb | Mar | Apr | May |
| Jan | 1.489 | 1.498 | 1.502 | 1.506 | 1.503 | 1.515 | 1.513 | 1.512 | 1.515 | 1.523 | 1.505 | 1.517 | 1.528 | 1.530 | 1.537 |
| Feb | 1.479 | 1.488 | 1.493 | 1.497 | 1.494 | 1.505 | 1.503 | 1.502 | 1.505 | 1.513 | 1.496 | 1.507 | 1.518 | 1.521 | 1.527 |
| Mar | 1.470 | 1.478 | 1.483 | 1.487 | 1.484 | 1.496 | 1.494 | 1.493 | 1.496 | 1.503 | 1.486 | 1.498 | 1.508 | 1.511 | 1.518 |
| Apr | 1.430 | 1.439 | 1.443 | 1.447 | 1.444 | 1.456 | 1.454 | 1.453 | 1.456 | 1.463 | 1.446 | 1.457 | 1.468 | 1.471 | 1.477 |
| May | 1.421 | 1.429 | 1.434 | 1.438 | 1.435 | 1.446 | 1.444 | 1.444 | 1.446 | 1.454 | 1.437 | 1.448 | 1.459 | 1.461 | 1.468 |
| June | 1.412 | 1.420 | 1.425 | 1.429 | 1.426 | 1.437 | 1.435 | 1.434 | 1.437 | 1.445 | 1.428 | 1.439 | 1.449 | 1.452 | 1.459 |
| July | 1.410 | 1.418 | 1.423 | 1.426 | 1.424 | 1.435 | 1.433 | 1.432 | 1.435 | 1.442 | 1.425 | 1.437 | 1.447 | 1.450 | 1.456 |
| Aug | 1.383 | 1.391 | 1.396 | 1.399 | 1.397 | 1.408 | 1.406 | 1.405 | 1.408 | 1.415 | 1.399 | 1.410 | 1.420 | 1.423 | 1.429 |
| Sept | 1.372 | 1.380 | 1.385 | 1.388 | 1.386 | 1.397 | 1.395 | 1.394 | 1.397 | 1.404 | 1.387 | 1.399 | 1.409 | 1.411 | 1.418 |
| Oct | 1.348 | 1.356 | 1.361 | 1.364 | 1.362 | 1.373 | 1.371 | 1.370 | 1.373 | 1.380 | 1.363 | 1.374 | 1.384 | 1.387 | 1.394 |
| Nov | 1.337 | 1.345 | 1.350 | 1.354 | 1.351 | 1.362 | 1.360 | 1.359 | 1.362 | 1.369 | 1.353 | 1.364 | 1.374 | 1.376 | 1.383 |
| Dec | 1.331 | 1.339 | 1.344 | 1.347 | 1.345 | 1.355 | 1.354 | 1.353 | 1.355 | 1.363 | 1.346 | 1.357 | 1.367 | 1.370 | 1.376 |
| **1989** | Mar | Apr | May | June | July | Aug | Sep | Oct | Nov | Dec | Jan | Feb | Mar | Apr | May |
| Jan | 1.316 | 1.324 | 1.329 | 1.332 | 1.330 | 1.341 | 1.339 | 1.338 | 1.341 | 1.348 | 1.332 | 1.342 | 1.352 | 1.355 | 1.361 |
| Feb | 1.300 | 1.308 | 1.312 | 1.316 | 1.313 | 1.324 | 1.322 | 1.321 | 1.324 | 1.331 | 1.315 | 1.326 | 1.335 | 1.338 | 1.344 |
| Mar | 1.289 | 1.297 | 1.302 | 1.305 | 1.303 | 1.313 | 1.312 | 1.311 | 1.313 | 1.321 | 1.305 | 1.315 | 1.325 | 1.328 | 1.334 |
| Apr | 1.249 | 1.257 | 1.262 | 1.265 | 1.262 | 1.273 | 1.271 | 1.270 | 1.273 | 1.280 | 1.264 | 1.275 | 1.284 | 1.287 | 1.293 |
| May | 1.236 | 1.243 | 1.248 | 1.251 | 1.249 | 1.259 | 1.257 | 1.257 | 1.259 | 1.266 | 1.250 | 1.261 | 1.270 | 1.273 | 1.279 |
| June | 1.228 | 1.236 | 1.240 | 1.244 | 1.241 | 1.251 | 1.250 | 1.249 | 1.251 | 1.258 | 1.243 | 1.253 | 1.263 | 1.265 | 1.271 |
| July | 1.226 | 1.234 | 1.238 | 1.242 | 1.239 | 1.249 | 1.248 | 1.247 | 1.249 | 1.256 | 1.241 | 1.251 | 1.261 | 1.263 | 1.269 |
| Aug | 1.220 | 1.228 | 1.232 | 1.236 | 1.233 | 1.244 | 1.242 | 1.241 | 1.244 | 1.250 | 1.235 | 1.245 | 1.255 | 1.257 | 1.263 |
| Sept | 1.205 | 1.213 | 1.217 | 1.220 | 1.218 | 1.228 | 1.226 | 1.226 | 1.228 | 1.235 | 1.220 | 1.230 | 1.239 | 1.242 | 1.248 |
| Oct | 1.188 | 1.196 | 1.200 | 1.203 | 1.201 | 1.211 | 1.209 | 1.209 | 1.211 | 1.218 | 1.203 | 1.213 | 1.222 | 1.225 | 1.231 |
| Nov | 1.170 | 1.177 | 1.181 | 1.185 | 1.182 | 1.192 | 1.191 | 1.190 | 1.192 | 1.199 | 1.184 | 1.194 | 1.203 | 1.206 | 1.212 |
| Dec | 1.164 | 1.172 | 1.176 | 1.179 | 1.177 | 1.187 | 1.185 | 1.184 | 1.187 | 1.194 | 1.178 | 1.189 | 1.198 | 1.200 | 1.206 |

MONTH OF DISPOSAL

| | 2016 | | | | | | | 2017 | | | | | | | |
|---|---|---|---|---|---|---|---|---|---|---|---|---|---|---|---|
| **1986** | June | July | Aug | Sep | Oct | Nov | Dec | Jan | Feb | Mar | Apr | May | June | July | Aug |
| Jan | 1.734 | 1.737 | 1.747 | 1.752 | 1.751 | 1.758 | 1.775 | 1.758 | 1.789 | 1.798 | 1.811 | 1.823 | 1.829 | 1.835 | 1.833 |
| Feb | 1.724 | 1.727 | 1.737 | 1.742 | 1.741 | 1.748 | 1.765 | 1.748 | 1.778 | 1.788 | 1.801 | 1.813 | 1.819 | 1.825 | 1.823 |
| Mar | 1.720 | 1.723 | 1.733 | 1.739 | 1.738 | 1.745 | 1.761 | 1.745 | 1.775 | 1.784 | 1.797 | 1.809 | 1.815 | 1.821 | 1.819 |
| Apr | 1.694 | 1.697 | 1.707 | 1.712 | 1.711 | 1.718 | 1.735 | 1.718 | 1.748 | 1.757 | 1.771 | 1.782 | 1.788 | 1.794 | 1.792 |
| May | 1.689 | 1.692 | 1.702 | 1.707 | 1.706 | 1.713 | 1.730 | 1.713 | 1.743 | 1.752 | 1.766 | 1.777 | 1.783 | 1.789 | 1.787 |
| June | 1.690 | 1.693 | 1.704 | 1.709 | 1.708 | 1.715 | 1.731 | 1.715 | 1.745 | 1.754 | 1.767 | 1.778 | 1.784 | 1.791 | 1.788 |
| July | 1.698 | 1.701 | 1.711 | 1.716 | 1.715 | 1.723 | 1.739 | 1.723 | 1.752 | 1.762 | 1.775 | 1.786 | 1.792 | 1.799 | 1.796 |
| Aug | 1.690 | 1.693 | 1.703 | 1.708 | 1.707 | 1.714 | 1.731 | 1.714 | 1.744 | 1.753 | 1.766 | 1.778 | 1.784 | 1.790 | 1.788 |
| Sept | 1.676 | 1.680 | 1.690 | 1.695 | 1.694 | 1.701 | 1.717 | 1.701 | 1.730 | 1.740 | 1.753 | 1.764 | 1.770 | 1.776 | 1.774 |
| Oct | 1.672 | 1.675 | 1.686 | 1.691 | 1.690 | 1.697 | 1.713 | 1.697 | 1.726 | 1.735 | 1.748 | 1.760 | 1.766 | 1.772 | 1.770 |
| Nov | 1.650 | 1.653 | 1.663 | 1.668 | 1.667 | 1.674 | 1.690 | 1.674 | 1.703 | 1.712 | 1.725 | 1.736 | 1.742 | 1.749 | 1.746 |
| Dec | 1.641 | 1.644 | 1.654 | 1.659 | 1.658 | 1.665 | 1.681 | 1.665 | 1.694 | 1.703 | 1.716 | 1.727 | 1.733 | 1.739 | 1.737 |
| **1987** | June | July | Aug | Sep | Oct | Nov | Dec | Jan | Feb | Mar | Apr | May | June | July | Aug |
| Jan | 1.631 | 1.634 | 1.644 | 1.649 | 1.648 | 1.655 | 1.671 | 1.655 | 1.684 | 1.693 | 1.706 | 1.717 | 1.723 | 1.729 | 1.727 |
| Feb | 1.621 | 1.624 | 1.633 | 1.638 | 1.637 | 1.644 | 1.660 | 1.644 | 1.673 | 1.682 | 1.695 | 1.706 | 1.712 | 1.718 | 1.716 |
| Mar | 1.615 | 1.618 | 1.628 | 1.633 | 1.632 | 1.639 | 1.655 | 1.639 | 1.668 | 1.677 | 1.690 | 1.701 | 1.707 | 1.713 | 1.711 |
| Apr | 1.584 | 1.587 | 1.597 | 1.602 | 1.601 | 1.608 | 1.624 | 1.608 | 1.637 | 1.645 | 1.658 | 1.669 | 1.675 | 1.681 | 1.679 |
| May | 1.582 | 1.585 | 1.595 | 1.600 | 1.599 | 1.605 | 1.621 | 1.605 | 1.634 | 1.643 | 1.656 | 1.666 | 1.672 | 1.678 | 1.676 |
| June | 1.582 | 1.585 | 1.595 | 1.600 | 1.599 | 1.605 | 1.621 | 1.605 | 1.634 | 1.643 | 1.656 | 1.666 | 1.672 | 1.678 | 1.676 |
| July | 1.584 | 1.587 | 1.597 | 1.602 | 1.601 | 1.608 | 1.624 | 1.608 | 1.637 | 1.645 | 1.658 | 1.669 | 1.675 | 1.681 | 1.679 |
| Aug | 1.577 | 1.580 | 1.590 | 1.595 | 1.594 | 1.600 | 1.616 | 1.600 | 1.629 | 1.638 | 1.650 | 1.661 | 1.667 | 1.673 | 1.671 |
| Sept | 1.569 | 1.572 | 1.582 | 1.587 | 1.586 | 1.593 | 1.608 | 1.593 | 1.621 | 1.630 | 1.643 | 1.653 | 1.659 | 1.665 | 1.663 |
| Oct | 1.557 | 1.560 | 1.569 | 1.574 | 1.573 | 1.580 | 1.596 | 1.580 | 1.608 | 1.617 | 1.630 | 1.640 | 1.646 | 1.652 | 1.650 |
| Nov | 1.544 | 1.547 | 1.557 | 1.562 | 1.561 | 1.568 | 1.583 | 1.568 | 1.596 | 1.604 | 1.617 | 1.628 | 1.633 | 1.639 | 1.637 |
| Dec | 1.547 | 1.550 | 1.560 | 1.564 | 1.563 | 1.570 | 1.586 | 1.570 | 1.598 | 1.607 | 1.620 | 1.630 | 1.636 | 1.642 | 1.640 |
| **1988** | June | July | Aug | Sep | Oct | Nov | Dec | Jan | Feb | Mar | Apr | May | June | July | Aug |
| Jan | 1.547 | 1.550 | 1.560 | 1.564 | 1.563 | 1.570 | 1.586 | 1.570 | 1.598 | 1.607 | 1.620 | 1.630 | 1.636 | 1.642 | 1.640 |
| Feb | 1.537 | 1.540 | 1.550 | 1.554 | 1.554 | 1.560 | 1.576 | 1.560 | 1.588 | 1.597 | 1.609 | 1.620 | 1.626 | 1.632 | 1.630 |
| Mar | 1.527 | 1.530 | 1.540 | 1.545 | 1.544 | 1.550 | 1.566 | 1.550 | 1.578 | 1.587 | 1.599 | 1.610 | 1.616 | 1.622 | 1.620 |
| Apr | 1.487 | 1.490 | 1.499 | 1.504 | 1.503 | 1.509 | 1.525 | 1.509 | 1.537 | 1.545 | 1.558 | 1.568 | 1.574 | 1.579 | 1.578 |
| May | 1.477 | 1.480 | 1.490 | 1.494 | 1.493 | 1.500 | 1.515 | 1.500 | 1.527 | 1.536 | 1.548 | 1.558 | 1.564 | 1.570 | 1.568 |
| June | 1.468 | 1.471 | 1.480 | 1.485 | 1.484 | 1.491 | 1.506 | 1.491 | 1.518 | 1.526 | 1.538 | 1.549 | 1.554 | 1.560 | 1.558 |
| July | 1.466 | 1.469 | 1.478 | 1.483 | 1.482 | 1.488 | 1.503 | 1.488 | 1.515 | 1.524 | 1.536 | 1.546 | 1.552 | 1.558 | 1.556 |
| Aug | 1.438 | 1.441 | 1.450 | 1.455 | 1.454 | 1.461 | 1.475 | 1.461 | 1.487 | 1.496 | 1.508 | 1.518 | 1.524 | 1.529 | 1.527 |
| Sept | 1.427 | 1.430 | 1.439 | 1.444 | 1.443 | 1.449 | 1.464 | 1.449 | 1.476 | 1.484 | 1.496 | 1.506 | 1.512 | 1.518 | 1.516 |
| Oct | 1.403 | 1.405 | 1.415 | 1.419 | 1.418 | 1.425 | 1.439 | 1.425 | 1.451 | 1.459 | 1.471 | 1.481 | 1.487 | 1.492 | 1.490 |
| Nov | 1.392 | 1.395 | 1.404 | 1.408 | 1.407 | 1.414 | 1.428 | 1.414 | 1.440 | 1.448 | 1.460 | 1.470 | 1.475 | 1.481 | 1.479 |
| Dec | 1.385 | 1.388 | 1.397 | 1.402 | 1.401 | 1.407 | 1.422 | 1.407 | 1.433 | 1.442 | 1.453 | 1.463 | 1.469 | 1.474 | 1.472 |
| **1989** | June | July | Aug | Sep | Oct | Nov | Dec | Jan | Feb | Mar | Apr | May | June | July | Aug |
| Jan | 1.370 | 1.373 | 1.382 | 1.386 | 1.386 | 1.392 | 1.406 | 1.392 | 1.418 | 1.426 | 1.438 | 1.448 | 1.453 | 1.459 | 1.457 |
| Feb | 1.353 | 1.356 | 1.365 | 1.369 | 1.369 | 1.375 | 1.389 | 1.375 | 1.401 | 1.409 | 1.420 | 1.430 | 1.436 | 1.441 | 1.439 |
| Mar | 1.343 | 1.346 | 1.354 | 1.359 | 1.358 | 1.364 | 1.378 | 1.364 | 1.390 | 1.398 | 1.410 | 1.419 | 1.425 | 1.430 | 1.428 |
| Apr | 1.302 | 1.304 | 1.313 | 1.318 | 1.317 | 1.323 | 1.337 | 1.323 | 1.348 | 1.356 | 1.367 | 1.377 | 1.382 | 1.388 | 1.386 |
| May | 1.288 | 1.290 | 1.299 | 1.303 | 1.303 | 1.309 | 1.323 | 1.309 | 1.334 | 1.342 | 1.353 | 1.363 | 1.368 | 1.373 | 1.371 |
| June | 1.280 | 1.282 | 1.291 | 1.295 | 1.295 | 1.301 | 1.315 | 1.301 | 1.326 | 1.334 | 1.345 | 1.354 | 1.360 | 1.365 | 1.363 |
| July | 1.278 | 1.281 | 1.289 | 1.294 | 1.293 | 1.299 | 1.313 | 1.299 | 1.324 | 1.332 | 1.343 | 1.352 | 1.358 | 1.363 | 1.361 |
| Aug | 1.272 | 1.275 | 1.283 | 1.288 | 1.287 | 1.293 | 1.307 | 1.293 | 1.318 | 1.326 | 1.337 | 1.346 | 1.351 | 1.357 | 1.355 |
| Sept | 1.256 | 1.259 | 1.268 | 1.272 | 1.271 | 1.277 | 1.291 | 1.277 | 1.302 | 1.310 | 1.321 | 1.330 | 1.335 | 1.340 | 1.339 |
| Oct | 1.239 | 1.242 | 1.250 | 1.254 | 1.254 | 1.260 | 1.273 | 1.260 | 1.284 | 1.292 | 1.303 | 1.312 | 1.317 | 1.323 | 1.321 |
| Nov | 1.220 | 1.223 | 1.231 | 1.235 | 1.235 | 1.241 | 1.254 | 1.241 | 1.265 | 1.273 | 1.284 | 1.293 | 1.298 | 1.303 | 1.301 |
| Dec | 1.215 | 1.217 | 1.226 | 1.230 | 1.229 | 1.235 | 1.248 | 1.235 | 1.259 | 1.267 | 1.278 | 1.287 | 1.292 | 1.297 | 1.295 |

MONTH OF DISPOSAL

| | ***2015*** | | | | | | | | | | ***2016*** | | | | |
|---|---|---|---|---|---|---|---|---|---|---|---|---|---|---|---|
| **1990** | Mar | Apr | May | June | July | Aug | Sep | Oct | Nov | Dec | Jan | Feb | Mar | Apr | May |
| Jan | 1.151 | 1.159 | 1.163 | 1.167 | 1.164 | 1.174 | 1.172 | 1.172 | 1.174 | 1.181 | 1.166 | 1.176 | 1.185 | 1.187 | 1.193 |
| Feb | 1.139 | 1.146 | 1.151 | 1.154 | 1.151 | 1.161 | 1.160 | 1.159 | 1.161 | 1.168 | 1.153 | 1.163 | 1.172 | 1.175 | 1.181 |
| Mar | 1.118 | 1.125 | 1.129 | 1.133 | 1.130 | 1.140 | 1.138 | 1.138 | 1.140 | 1.147 | 1.132 | 1.142 | 1.151 | 1.153 | 1.159 |
| Apr | 1.055 | 1.062 | 1.066 | 1.070 | 1.067 | 1.077 | 1.075 | 1.074 | 1.077 | 1.083 | 1.069 | 1.078 | 1.087 | 1.090 | 1.095 |
| May | 1.037 | 1.044 | 1.048 | 1.052 | 1.049 | 1.059 | 1.057 | 1.056 | 1.059 | 1.065 | 1.051 | 1.060 | 1.069 | 1.071 | 1.077 |
| June | 1.029 | 1.036 | 1.040 | 1.043 | 1.041 | 1.051 | 1.049 | 1.048 | 1.051 | 1.057 | 1.043 | 1.052 | 1.061 | 1.063 | 1.069 |
| July | 1.028 | 1.035 | 1.039 | 1.042 | 1.039 | 1.049 | 1.047 | 1.047 | 1.049 | 1.055 | 1.041 | 1.050 | 1.059 | 1.062 | 1.067 |
| Aug | 1.007 | 1.014 | 1.018 | 1.021 | 1.019 | 1.028 | 1.027 | 1.026 | 1.028 | 1.034 | 1.020 | 1.030 | 1.038 | 1.041 | 1.046 |
| Sept | .988 | .995 | .999 | 1.002 | 1.000 | 1.009 | 1.008 | 1.007 | 1.009 | 1.015 | 1.002 | 1.011 | 1.019 | 1.022 | 1.027 |
| Oct | .973 | .980 | .984 | .987 | .985 | .994 | .992 | .992 | .994 | 1.000 | .986 | .995 | 1.004 | 1.006 | 1.012 |
| Nov | .978 | .985 | .988 | .992 | .989 | .998 | .997 | .996 | .998 | 1.005 | .991 | 1.000 | 1.008 | 1.011 | 1.016 |
| Dec | .979 | .986 | .990 | .993 | .991 | 1.000 | .998 | .998 | 1.000 | 1.006 | .992 | 1.002 | 1.010 | 1.012 | 1.018 |
| **1991** | Mar | Apr | May | June | July | Aug | Sep | Oct | Nov | Dec | Jan | Feb | Mar | Apr | May |
| Jan | .975 | .982 | .985 | .988 | .986 | .995 | .994 | .993 | .995 | 1.002 | .988 | .997 | 1.005 | 1.008 | 1.013 |
| Feb | .964 | .971 | .975 | .978 | .976 | .985 | .983 | .982 | .985 | .991 | .977 | .986 | .995 | .997 | 1.002 |
| Mar | .957 | .963 | .967 | .970 | .968 | .977 | .976 | .975 | .977 | .983 | .970 | .979 | .987 | .989 | .995 |
| Apr | .932 | .938 | .942 | .945 | .943 | .952 | .950 | .950 | .952 | .958 | .944 | .953 | .962 | .964 | .969 |
| May | .926 | .933 | .936 | .939 | .937 | .946 | .945 | .944 | .946 | .952 | .939 | .948 | .956 | .958 | .963 |
| June | .917 | .924 | .928 | .931 | .928 | .937 | .936 | .935 | .937 | .943 | .930 | .939 | .947 | .949 | .955 |
| July | .922 | .928 | .932 | .935 | .933 | .942 | .940 | .939 | .942 | .948 | .934 | .943 | .951 | .954 | .959 |
| Aug | .917 | .924 | .928 | .931 | .928 | .937 | .936 | .935 | .937 | .943 | .930 | .939 | .947 | .949 | .955 |
| Sept | .910 | .917 | .921 | .923 | .921 | .930 | .929 | .928 | .930 | .936 | .923 | .932 | .940 | .942 | .947 |
| Oct | .903 | .910 | .913 | .916 | .914 | .923 | .922 | .921 | .923 | .929 | .916 | .925 | .933 | .935 | .940 |
| Nov | .896 | .903 | .906 | .909 | .907 | .916 | .914 | .914 | .916 | .922 | .909 | .917 | .926 | .928 | .933 |
| Dec | .895 | .901 | .905 | .908 | .906 | .915 | .913 | .912 | .915 | .920 | .907 | .916 | .924 | .926 | .931 |
| **1992** | Mar | Apr | May | June | July | Aug | Sep | Oct | Nov | Dec | Jan | Feb | Mar | Apr | May |
| Jan | .896 | .903 | .906 | .909 | .907 | .916 | .914 | .914 | .916 | .922 | .909 | .917 | .926 | .928 | .933 |
| Feb | .886 | .893 | .897 | .899 | .897 | .906 | .905 | .904 | .906 | .912 | .899 | .908 | .916 | .918 | .923 |
| Mar | .881 | .887 | .891 | .894 | .892 | .901 | .899 | .898 | .901 | .906 | .893 | .902 | .910 | .912 | .917 |
| Apr | .852 | .859 | .862 | .865 | .863 | .872 | .870 | .870 | .872 | .878 | .865 | .873 | .881 | .883 | .888 |
| May | .846 | .852 | .856 | .859 | .856 | .865 | .864 | .863 | .865 | .871 | .858 | .866 | .874 | .877 | .882 |
| June | .846 | .852 | .856 | .859 | .856 | .865 | .864 | .863 | .865 | .871 | .858 | .866 | .874 | .877 | .882 |
| July | .852 | .859 | .862 | .865 | .863 | .872 | .870 | .870 | .872 | .878 | .865 | .873 | .881 | .883 | .888 |
| Aug | .851 | .857 | .861 | .864 | .862 | .870 | .869 | .868 | .870 | .876 | .863 | .872 | .880 | .882 | .887 |
| Sept | .844 | .851 | .854 | .857 | .855 | .864 | .862 | .862 | .864 | .869 | .857 | .865 | .873 | .875 | .880 |
| Oct | .838 | .844 | .848 | .851 | .848 | .857 | .856 | .855 | .857 | .863 | .850 | .858 | .866 | .868 | .873 |
| Nov | .840 | .847 | .850 | .853 | .851 | .860 | .858 | .858 | .860 | .865 | .853 | .861 | .869 | .871 | .876 |
| Dec | .847 | .853 | .857 | .860 | .858 | .866 | .865 | .864 | .866 | .872 | .859 | .868 | .876 | .878 | .883 |
| **1993** | Mar | Apr | May | June | July | Aug | Sep | Oct | Nov | Dec | Jan | Feb | Mar | Apr | May |
| Jan | .864 | .871 | .875 | .877 | .875 | .884 | .883 | .882 | .884 | .890 | .877 | .885 | .893 | .896 | .901 |
| Feb | .852 | .859 | .862 | .865 | .863 | .872 | .870 | .870 | .872 | .878 | .865 | .873 | .881 | .883 | .888 |
| Mar | .846 | .852 | .856 | .859 | .856 | .865 | .864 | .863 | .865 | .871 | .858 | .866 | .874 | .877 | .882 |
| Apr | .829 | .835 | .839 | .841 | .839 | .848 | .846 | .846 | .848 | .853 | .841 | .849 | .857 | .859 | .864 |
| May | .822 | .828 | .832 | .835 | .833 | .841 | .840 | .839 | .841 | .847 | .834 | .843 | .850 | .853 | .858 |
| June | .823 | .830 | .833 | .836 | .834 | .843 | .841 | .840 | .843 | .848 | .835 | .844 | .852 | .854 | .859 |
| July | .827 | .834 | .837 | .840 | .838 | .846 | .845 | .844 | .846 | .852 | .839 | .848 | .856 | .858 | .863 |
| Aug | .820 | .826 | .829 | .832 | .830 | .839 | .837 | .837 | .839 | .844 | .832 | .840 | .848 | .850 | .855 |
| Sept | .812 | .818 | .822 | .825 | .822 | .831 | .829 | .829 | .831 | .837 | .824 | .832 | .840 | .842 | .847 |
| Oct | .813 | .819 | .823 | .826 | .824 | .832 | .831 | .830 | .832 | .838 | .825 | .834 | .841 | .843 | .848 |
| Nov | .816 | .822 | .826 | .828 | .826 | .835 | .833 | .833 | .835 | .840 | .828 | .836 | .844 | .846 | .851 |
| Dec | .812 | .818 | .822 | .825 | .822 | .831 | .829 | .829 | .831 | .837 | .824 | .832 | .840 | .842 | .847 |

MONTH OF DISPOSAL

| | 2016 | | | | | | | 2017 | | | | | | | |
|---|---|---|---|---|---|---|---|---|---|---|---|---|---|---|---|
| **1990** | June | July | Aug | Sep | Oct | Nov | Dec | Jan | Feb | Mar | Apr | May | June | July | Aug |
| Jan | 1.202 | 1.204 | 1.213 | 1.217 | 1.216 | 1.222 | 1.235 | 1.222 | 1.246 | 1.254 | 1.264 | 1.274 | 1.279 | 1.284 | 1.282 |
| Feb | 1.189 | 1.191 | 1.200 | 1.204 | 1.203 | 1.209 | 1.222 | 1.209 | 1.233 | 1.240 | 1.251 | 1.260 | 1.265 | 1.270 | 1.269 |
| Mar | 1.167 | 1.170 | 1.178 | 1.182 | 1.181 | 1.187 | 1.200 | 1.187 | 1.211 | 1.218 | 1.229 | 1.238 | 1.243 | 1.248 | 1.246 |
| Apr | 1.103 | 1.106 | 1.114 | 1.118 | 1.117 | 1.122 | 1.135 | 1.122 | 1.145 | 1.153 | 1.163 | 1.172 | 1.177 | 1.181 | 1.180 |
| May | 1.085 | 1.087 | 1.095 | 1.099 | 1.098 | 1.104 | 1.116 | 1.104 | 1.127 | 1.134 | 1.144 | 1.153 | 1.158 | 1.162 | 1.161 |
| June | 1.077 | 1.079 | 1.087 | 1.091 | 1.090 | 1.096 | 1.108 | 1.096 | 1.118 | 1.125 | 1.136 | 1.144 | 1.149 | 1.154 | 1.152 |
| July | 1.075 | 1.077 | 1.085 | 1.089 | 1.088 | 1.094 | 1.106 | 1.094 | 1.117 | 1.124 | 1.134 | 1.143 | 1.147 | 1.152 | 1.151 |
| Aug | 1.054 | 1.056 | 1.064 | 1.068 | 1.067 | 1.073 | 1.085 | 1.073 | 1.095 | 1.102 | 1.112 | 1.121 | 1.126 | 1.130 | 1.129 |
| Sept | 1.035 | 1.037 | 1.045 | 1.049 | 1.048 | 1.053 | 1.066 | 1.053 | 1.076 | 1.083 | 1.093 | 1.101 | 1.106 | 1.111 | 1.109 |
| Oct | 1.019 | 1.021 | 1.029 | 1.033 | 1.032 | 1.038 | 1.050 | 1.038 | 1.060 | 1.067 | 1.077 | 1.085 | 1.090 | 1.094 | 1.093 |
| Nov | 1.024 | 1.026 | 1.034 | 1.038 | 1.037 | 1.042 | 1.055 | 1.042 | 1.065 | 1.072 | 1.082 | 1.090 | 1.095 | 1.099 | 1.098 |
| Dec | 1.025 | 1.028 | 1.035 | 1.039 | 1.038 | 1.044 | 1.056 | 1.044 | 1.066 | 1.073 | 1.083 | 1.092 | 1.096 | 1.101 | 1.099 |
| **1991** | June | July | Aug | Sep | Oct | Nov | Dec | Jan | Feb | Mar | Apr | May | June | July | Aug |
| Jan | 1.021 | 1.023 | 1.031 | 1.035 | 1.034 | 1.039 | 1.051 | 1.039 | 1.061 | 1.068 | 1.078 | 1.087 | 1.091 | 1.096 | 1.094 |
| Feb | 1.010 | 1.012 | 1.020 | 1.024 | 1.023 | 1.028 | 1.040 | 1.028 | 1.050 | 1.057 | 1.067 | 1.076 | 1.080 | 1.085 | 1.083 |
| Mar | 1.002 | 1.005 | 1.012 | 1.016 | 1.015 | 1.021 | 1.033 | 1.021 | 1.043 | 1.049 | 1.059 | 1.068 | 1.072 | 1.077 | 1.075 |
| Apr | .977 | .979 | .986 | .990 | .989 | .995 | 1.007 | .995 | 1.017 | 1.023 | 1.033 | 1.041 | 1.046 | 1.050 | 1.049 |
| May | .971 | .973 | .981 | .984 | .984 | .989 | 1.001 | .989 | 1.010 | 1.017 | 1.027 | 1.035 | 1.040 | 1.044 | 1.043 |
| June | .962 | .964 | .972 | .975 | .975 | .980 | .992 | .980 | 1.001 | 1.008 | 1.018 | 1.026 | 1.031 | 1.035 | 1.034 |
| July | .966 | .969 | .976 | .980 | .979 | .984 | .996 | .984 | 1.006 | 1.013 | 1.022 | 1.031 | 1.035 | 1.040 | 1.038 |
| Aug | .962 | .964 | .972 | .975 | .975 | .980 | .992 | .980 | 1.001 | 1.008 | 1.018 | 1.026 | 1.031 | 1.035 | 1.034 |
| Sept | .955 | .957 | .964 | .968 | .967 | .973 | .984 | .973 | .994 | 1.001 | 1.010 | 1.019 | 1.023 | 1.027 | 1.026 |
| Oct | .947 | .950 | .957 | .961 | .960 | .965 | .977 | .965 | .987 | .993 | 1.003 | 1.011 | 1.016 | 1.020 | 1.019 |
| Nov | .940 | .942 | .950 | .954 | .953 | .958 | .970 | .958 | .979 | .986 | .996 | 1.004 | 1.008 | 1.013 | 1.011 |
| Dec | .939 | .941 | .948 | .952 | .951 | .957 | .968 | .957 | .978 | .985 | .994 | 1.002 | 1.007 | 1.011 | 1.010 |
| **1992** | June | July | Aug | Sep | Oct | Nov | Dec | Jan | Feb | Mar | Apr | May | June | July | Aug |
| Jan | .940 | .942 | .950 | .954 | .953 | .958 | .970 | .958 | .979 | .986 | .996 | 1.004 | 1.008 | 1.013 | 1.011 |
| Feb | .930 | .933 | .940 | .944 | .943 | .948 | .960 | .948 | .969 | .976 | .985 | .993 | .998 | 1.002 | 1.001 |
| Mar | .925 | .927 | .934 | .938 | .937 | .942 | .954 | .942 | .963 | .970 | .980 | .988 | .992 | .996 | .995 |
| Apr | .896 | .898 | .905 | .909 | .908 | .913 | .924 | .913 | .934 | .940 | .950 | .957 | .962 | .966 | .965 |
| May | .889 | .891 | .898 | .902 | .901 | .906 | .917 | .906 | .927 | .933 | .943 | .950 | .955 | .959 | .958 |
| June | .889 | .891 | .898 | .902 | .901 | .906 | .917 | .906 | .927 | .933 | .943 | .950 | .955 | .959 | .958 |
| July | .896 | .898 | .905 | .909 | .908 | .913 | .924 | .913 | .934 | .940 | .950 | .957 | .962 | .966 | .965 |
| Aug | .894 | .896 | .904 | .907 | .906 | .911 | .923 | .911 | .932 | .939 | .948 | .956 | .960 | .965 | .963 |
| Sept | .887 | .890 | .897 | .900 | .900 | .905 | .916 | .905 | .925 | .932 | .941 | .949 | .953 | .958 | .956 |
| Oct | .881 | .883 | .890 | .893 | .893 | .898 | .909 | .898 | .919 | .925 | .934 | .942 | .946 | .951 | .949 |
| Nov | .883 | .885 | .893 | .896 | .895 | .901 | .912 | .901 | .921 | .928 | .937 | .945 | .949 | .953 | .952 |
| Dec | .890 | .892 | .899 | .903 | .902 | .907 | .919 | .907 | .928 | .935 | .944 | .952 | .956 | .960 | .959 |
| **1993** | June | July | Aug | Sep | Oct | Nov | Dec | Jan | Feb | Mar | Apr | May | June | July | Aug |
| Jan | .908 | .910 | .917 | .921 | .920 | .925 | .937 | .925 | .946 | .953 | .962 | .970 | .975 | .979 | .978 |
| Feb | .896 | .898 | .905 | .909 | .908 | .913 | .924 | .913 | .934 | .940 | .950 | .957 | .962 | .966 | .965 |
| Mar | .889 | .891 | .898 | .902 | .901 | .906 | .917 | .906 | .927 | .933 | .943 | .950 | .955 | .959 | .958 |
| Apr | .871 | .873 | .881 | .884 | .883 | .888 | .900 | .888 | .909 | .915 | .925 | .932 | .937 | .941 | .940 |
| May | .865 | .867 | .874 | .877 | .877 | .882 | .893 | .882 | .902 | .909 | .918 | .926 | .930 | .934 | .933 |
| June | .866 | .868 | .875 | .879 | .878 | .883 | .894 | .883 | .904 | .910 | .919 | .927 | .931 | .935 | .934 |
| July | .870 | .872 | .879 | .883 | .882 | .887 | .898 | .887 | .908 | .914 | .923 | .931 | .935 | .940 | .938 |
| Aug | .862 | .864 | .871 | .875 | .874 | .879 | .890 | .879 | .900 | .906 | .915 | .923 | .927 | .931 | .930 |
| Sept | .854 | .856 | .863 | .867 | .866 | .871 | .882 | .871 | .891 | .898 | .907 | .915 | .919 | .923 | .922 |
| Oct | .855 | .858 | .865 | .868 | .867 | .872 | .884 | .872 | .893 | .899 | .908 | .916 | .920 | .925 | .923 |
| Nov | .858 | .860 | .867 | .871 | .870 | .875 | .886 | .875 | .895 | .902 | .911 | .919 | .923 | .927 | .926 |
| Dec | .854 | .856 | .863 | .867 | .866 | .871 | .882 | .871 | .891 | .898 | .907 | .915 | .919 | .923 | .922 |

MONTH OF DISPOSAL

| | ***2015*** | | | | | | | | | | ***2016*** | | | | |
|---|---|---|---|---|---|---|---|---|---|---|---|---|---|---|---|
| **1994** | Mar | Apr | May | June | July | Aug | Sep | Oct | Nov | Dec | Jan | Feb | Mar | Apr | May |
| Jan | .820 | .826 | .829 | .832 | .830 | .839 | .837 | .837 | .839 | .844 | .832 | .840 | .848 | .850 | .855 |
| Feb | .809 | .816 | .819 | .822 | .820 | .828 | .827 | .826 | .828 | .834 | .821 | .830 | .837 | .840 | .844 |
| Mar | .804 | .811 | .814 | .817 | .815 | .823 | .822 | .821 | .823 | .829 | .816 | .825 | .832 | .834 | .839 |
| Apr | .783 | .789 | .793 | .795 | .793 | .802 | .800 | .800 | .802 | .807 | .795 | .803 | .811 | .813 | .818 |
| May | .777 | .783 | .786 | .789 | .787 | .795 | .794 | .793 | .795 | .801 | .789 | .797 | .804 | .806 | .811 |
| June | .777 | .783 | .786 | .789 | .787 | .795 | .794 | .793 | .795 | .801 | .789 | .797 | .804 | .806 | .811 |
| July | .785 | .792 | .795 | .798 | .796 | .804 | .803 | .802 | .804 | .810 | .797 | .806 | .813 | .815 | .820 |
| Aug | .777 | .783 | .786 | .789 | .787 | .795 | .794 | .793 | .795 | .801 | .789 | .797 | .804 | .806 | .811 |
| Sept | .773 | .779 | .783 | .786 | .783 | .792 | .790 | .790 | .792 | .797 | .785 | .793 | .801 | .803 | .808 |
| Oct | .771 | .777 | .780 | .783 | .781 | .789 | .788 | .787 | .789 | .795 | .782 | .791 | .798 | .800 | .805 |
| Nov | .769 | .776 | .779 | .782 | .780 | .788 | .787 | .786 | .788 | .794 | .781 | .789 | .797 | .799 | .804 |
| Dec | .761 | .767 | .771 | .773 | .771 | .779 | .778 | .777 | .779 | .785 | .773 | .781 | .788 | .790 | .795 |
| **1995** | Mar | Apr | May | June | July | Aug | Sep | Oct | Nov | Dec | Jan | Feb | Mar | Apr | May |
| Jan | .761 | .767 | .771 | .773 | .771 | .779 | .778 | .777 | .779 | .785 | .773 | .781 | .788 | .790 | .795 |
| Feb | .750 | .756 | .760 | .762 | .760 | .769 | .767 | .767 | .769 | .774 | .762 | .770 | .777 | .779 | .784 |
| Mar | .743 | .749 | .753 | .755 | .753 | .761 | .760 | .759 | .761 | .767 | .755 | .763 | .770 | .772 | .777 |
| Apr | .726 | .732 | .735 | .738 | .736 | .744 | .742 | .742 | .744 | .749 | .737 | .745 | .752 | .754 | .759 |
| May | .719 | .725 | .728 | .731 | .729 | .737 | .735 | .735 | .737 | .742 | .730 | .738 | .745 | .747 | .752 |
| June | .716 | .722 | .726 | .728 | .726 | .734 | .733 | .732 | .734 | .740 | .728 | .736 | .743 | .745 | .750 |
| July | .724 | .730 | .734 | .736 | .734 | .742 | .741 | .740 | .742 | .748 | .736 | .744 | .751 | .753 | .758 |
| Aug | .715 | .721 | .724 | .727 | .725 | .733 | .732 | .731 | .733 | .738 | .726 | .734 | .742 | .744 | .748 |
| Sept | .707 | .713 | .716 | .719 | .717 | .725 | .724 | .723 | .725 | .730 | .718 | .726 | .734 | .736 | .740 |
| Oct | .716 | .722 | .726 | .728 | .726 | .734 | .733 | .732 | .734 | .740 | .728 | .736 | .743 | .745 | .750 |
| Nov | .716 | .722 | .726 | .728 | .726 | .734 | .733 | .732 | .734 | .740 | .728 | .736 | .743 | .745 | .750 |
| Dec | .706 | .712 | .715 | .718 | .716 | .724 | .723 | .722 | .724 | .729 | .717 | .725 | .733 | .735 | .739 |
| **1996** | Mar | Apr | May | June | July | Aug | Sep | Oct | Nov | Dec | Jan | Feb | Mar | Apr | May |
| Jan | .712 | .718 | .721 | .724 | .722 | .730 | .728 | .728 | .730 | .735 | .723 | .731 | .738 | .740 | .745 |
| Feb | .704 | .710 | .713 | .716 | .714 | .722 | .720 | .720 | .722 | .727 | .715 | .723 | .730 | .732 | .737 |
| Mar | .697 | .703 | .706 | .709 | .707 | .715 | .714 | .713 | .715 | .720 | .708 | .716 | .723 | .725 | .730 |
| Apr | .685 | .691 | .694 | .697 | .695 | .702 | .701 | .701 | .702 | .708 | .696 | .704 | .711 | .713 | .718 |
| May | .681 | .687 | .691 | .693 | .691 | .699 | .698 | .697 | .699 | .704 | .693 | .700 | .708 | .710 | .714 |
| June | .680 | .686 | .690 | .692 | .690 | .698 | .697 | .696 | .698 | .703 | .692 | .699 | .707 | .708 | .713 |
| July | .687 | .693 | .696 | .699 | .697 | .705 | .703 | .703 | .705 | .710 | .698 | .706 | .713 | .715 | .720 |
| Aug | .679 | .685 | .688 | .691 | .689 | .697 | .696 | .695 | .697 | .702 | .690 | .698 | .705 | .707 | .712 |
| Sept | .672 | .678 | .681 | .683 | .681 | .689 | .688 | .687 | .689 | .694 | .683 | .691 | .698 | .700 | .704 |
| Oct | .672 | .678 | .681 | .683 | .681 | .689 | .688 | .687 | .689 | .694 | .683 | .691 | .698 | .700 | .704 |
| Nov | .671 | .676 | .680 | .682 | .680 | .688 | .687 | .686 | .688 | .693 | .682 | .689 | .697 | .699 | .703 |
| Dec | .665 | .671 | .674 | .677 | .675 | .683 | .681 | .681 | .683 | .688 | .676 | .684 | .691 | .693 | .698 |
| **1997** | Mar | Apr | May | June | July | Aug | Sep | Oct | Nov | Dec | Jan | Feb | Mar | Apr | May |
| Jan | .665 | .671 | .674 | .677 | .675 | .683 | .681 | .681 | .683 | .688 | .676 | .684 | .691 | .693 | .698 |
| Feb | .659 | .665 | .668 | .670 | .668 | .676 | .675 | .674 | .676 | .681 | .670 | .677 | .685 | .686 | .691 |
| Mar | .654 | .660 | .663 | .666 | .664 | .672 | .671 | .670 | .672 | .677 | .665 | .673 | .680 | .682 | .687 |
| Apr | .645 | .651 | .654 | .656 | .655 | .662 | .661 | .660 | .662 | .667 | .656 | .663 | .671 | .672 | .677 |
| May | .639 | .644 | .648 | .650 | .648 | .656 | .655 | .654 | .656 | .661 | .649 | .657 | .664 | .666 | .670 |
| June | .632 | .638 | .641 | .644 | .642 | .650 | .648 | .648 | .650 | .655 | .643 | .651 | .658 | .660 | .664 |
| July | .632 | .638 | .641 | .644 | .642 | .650 | .648 | .648 | .650 | .655 | .643 | .651 | .658 | .660 | .664 |
| Aug | .622 | .628 | .631 | .633 | .632 | .639 | .638 | .637 | .639 | .644 | .633 | .640 | .647 | .649 | .654 |
| Sept | .614 | .620 | .623 | .625 | .623 | .631 | .630 | .629 | .631 | .636 | .625 | .632 | .639 | .641 | .645 |
| Oct | .612 | .618 | .621 | .623 | .621 | .629 | .628 | .627 | .629 | .634 | .623 | .630 | .637 | .639 | .643 |
| Nov | .611 | .617 | .620 | .622 | .620 | .628 | .627 | .626 | .628 | .633 | .622 | .629 | .636 | .638 | .642 |
| Dec | .607 | .613 | .616 | .618 | .616 | .624 | .623 | .622 | .624 | .629 | .618 | .625 | .632 | .634 | .638 |

MONTH OF DISPOSAL

| | **2016** | | | | | | | **2017** | | | | | | | |
|---|---|---|---|---|---|---|---|---|---|---|---|---|---|---|---|
| **1994** | June | July | Aug | Sep | Oct | Nov | Dec | Jan | Feb | Mar | Apr | May | June | July | Aug |
| Jan | .862 | .864 | .871 | .875 | .874 | .879 | .890 | .879 | .900 | .906 | .915 | .923 | .927 | .931 | .930 |
| Feb | .852 | .854 | .861 | .864 | .863 | .868 | .880 | .868 | .889 | .895 | .904 | .912 | .916 | .920 | .919 |
| Mar | .846 | .848 | .855 | .859 | .858 | .863 | .874 | .863 | .884 | .890 | .899 | .907 | .911 | .915 | .914 |
| Apr | .825 | .827 | .834 | .837 | .836 | .841 | .852 | .841 | .861 | .868 | .877 | .884 | .888 | .893 | .891 |
| May | .818 | .820 | .827 | .831 | .830 | .835 | .846 | .835 | .855 | .861 | .870 | .878 | .882 | .886 | .885 |
| June | .818 | .820 | .827 | .831 | .830 | .835 | .846 | .835 | .855 | .861 | .870 | .878 | .882 | .886 | .885 |
| July | .827 | .829 | .836 | .840 | .839 | .844 | .855 | .844 | .864 | .870 | .879 | .887 | .891 | .895 | .894 |
| Aug | .818 | .820 | .827 | .831 | .830 | .835 | .846 | .835 | .855 | .861 | .870 | .878 | .882 | .886 | .885 |
| Sept | .814 | .817 | .823 | .827 | .826 | .831 | .842 | .831 | .851 | .857 | .866 | .874 | .878 | .882 | .881 |
| Oct | .812 | .814 | .821 | .824 | .824 | .829 | .840 | .829 | .848 | .855 | .864 | .871 | .875 | .879 | .878 |
| Nov | .811 | .813 | .820 | .823 | .822 | .827 | .838 | .827 | .847 | .853 | .862 | .870 | .874 | .878 | .877 |
| Dec | .802 | .804 | .811 | .814 | .814 | .818 | .829 | .818 | .838 | .845 | .853 | .861 | .865 | .869 | .868 |
| **1995** | June | July | Aug | Sep | Oct | Nov | Dec | Jan | Feb | Mar | Apr | May | June | July | Aug |
| Jan | .802 | .804 | .811 | .814 | .814 | .818 | .829 | .818 | .838 | .845 | .853 | .861 | .865 | .869 | .868 |
| Feb | .791 | .793 | .800 | .803 | .803 | .807 | .818 | .807 | .827 | .833 | .842 | .850 | .854 | .858 | .856 |
| Mar | .784 | .786 | .793 | .796 | .795 | .800 | .811 | .800 | .820 | .826 | .835 | .842 | .846 | .850 | .849 |
| Apr | .766 | .768 | .774 | .778 | .777 | .782 | .793 | .782 | .801 | .807 | .816 | .823 | .828 | .832 | .830 |
| May | .759 | .761 | .767 | .771 | .770 | .775 | .785 | .775 | .794 | .800 | .809 | .816 | .820 | .824 | .823 |
| June | .756 | .758 | .765 | .768 | .768 | .772 | .783 | .772 | .792 | .798 | .806 | .814 | .818 | .822 | .820 |
| July | .765 | .767 | .773 | .777 | .776 | .781 | .791 | .781 | .800 | .806 | .815 | .822 | .826 | .830 | .829 |
| Aug | .755 | .757 | .764 | .767 | .767 | .771 | .782 | .771 | .791 | .797 | .805 | .813 | .817 | .821 | .819 |
| Sept | .747 | .749 | .756 | .759 | .758 | .763 | .774 | .763 | .782 | .788 | .797 | .804 | .808 | .812 | .811 |
| Oct | .756 | .758 | .765 | .768 | .768 | .772 | .783 | .772 | .792 | .798 | .806 | .814 | .818 | .822 | .820 |
| Nov | .756 | .758 | .765 | .768 | .768 | .772 | .783 | .772 | .792 | .798 | .806 | .814 | .818 | .822 | .820 |
| Dec | .746 | .748 | .754 | .758 | .757 | .762 | .772 | .762 | .781 | .787 | .796 | .803 | .807 | .811 | .810 |
| **1996** | June | July | Aug | Sep | Oct | Nov | Dec | Jan | Feb | Mar | Apr | May | June | July | Aug |
| Jan | .752 | .754 | .760 | .764 | .763 | .768 | .778 | .768 | .787 | .793 | .802 | .809 | .813 | .817 | .816 |
| Feb | .744 | .746 | .752 | .755 | .755 | .759 | .770 | .759 | .779 | .785 | .793 | .801 | .805 | .808 | .807 |
| Mar | .737 | .739 | .745 | .749 | .748 | .752 | .763 | .752 | .772 | .778 | .786 | .793 | .797 | .801 | .800 |
| Apr | .724 | .726 | .733 | .736 | .735 | .740 | .750 | .740 | .759 | .765 | .773 | .780 | .784 | .788 | .787 |
| May | .721 | .723 | .729 | .733 | .732 | .736 | .747 | .736 | .755 | .761 | .770 | .777 | .781 | .785 | .784 |
| June | .720 | .722 | .728 | .731 | .731 | .735 | .746 | .735 | .754 | .760 | .769 | .776 | .780 | .784 | .782 |
| July | .726 | .728 | .735 | .738 | .738 | .742 | .753 | .742 | .761 | .767 | .776 | .783 | .787 | .791 | .789 |
| Aug | .718 | .720 | .727 | .730 | .730 | .734 | .745 | .734 | .753 | .759 | .767 | .775 | .779 | .782 | .781 |
| Sept | .711 | .713 | .719 | .722 | .722 | .726 | .737 | .726 | .745 | .751 | .759 | .767 | .770 | .774 | .773 |
| Oct | .711 | .713 | .719 | .722 | .722 | .726 | .737 | .726 | .745 | .751 | .759 | .767 | .770 | .774 | .773 |
| Nov | .710 | .712 | .718 | .721 | .721 | .725 | .736 | .725 | .744 | .750 | .758 | .765 | .769 | .773 | .772 |
| Dec | .704 | .706 | .712 | .716 | .715 | .720 | .730 | .720 | .738 | .744 | .753 | .760 | .764 | .767 | .766 |
| **1997** | June | July | Aug | Sep | Oct | Nov | Dec | Jan | Feb | Mar | Apr | May | June | July | Aug |
| Jan | .704 | .706 | .712 | .716 | .715 | .720 | .730 | .720 | .738 | .744 | .753 | .760 | .764 | .767 | .766 |
| Feb | .697 | .699 | .706 | .709 | .708 | .713 | .723 | .713 | .732 | .737 | .746 | .753 | .757 | .761 | .759 |
| Mar | .693 | .695 | .701 | .705 | .704 | .708 | .719 | .708 | .727 | .733 | .741 | .748 | .752 | .756 | .755 |
| Apr | .683 | .685 | .692 | .695 | .694 | .699 | .709 | .699 | .717 | .723 | .731 | .738 | .742 | .746 | .745 |
| May | .677 | .679 | .685 | .688 | .688 | .692 | .702 | .692 | .711 | .716 | .725 | .732 | .736 | .739 | .738 |
| June | .670 | .672 | .679 | .682 | .681 | .686 | .696 | .686 | .704 | .710 | .718 | .725 | .729 | .733 | .731 |
| July | .670 | .672 | .679 | .682 | .681 | .686 | .696 | .686 | .704 | .710 | .718 | .725 | .729 | .733 | .731 |
| Aug | .660 | .662 | .668 | .671 | .671 | .675 | .685 | .675 | .693 | .699 | .707 | .714 | .718 | .722 | .721 |
| Sept | .652 | .653 | .660 | .663 | .662 | .667 | .677 | .667 | .685 | .691 | .699 | .706 | .709 | .713 | .712 |
| Oct | .650 | .651 | .658 | .661 | .660 | .665 | .675 | .665 | .683 | .688 | .697 | .703 | .707 | .711 | .710 |
| Nov | .648 | .650 | .657 | .660 | .659 | .664 | .674 | .664 | .682 | .687 | .695 | .702 | .706 | .710 | .709 |
| Dec | .644 | .646 | .653 | .656 | .655 | .659 | .669 | .659 | .678 | .683 | .691 | .698 | .702 | .706 | .704 |

MONTH OF DISPOSAL

| | ***2015*** | | | | | | | | | | ***2016*** | | | | |
|---|---|---|---|---|---|---|---|---|---|---|---|---|---|---|---|
| **1998** | Mar | Apr | May | June | July | Aug | Sep | Oct | Nov | Dec | Jan | Feb | Mar | Apr | May |
| Jan | .612 | .618 | .621 | .623 | .621 | .629 | .628 | .627 | .629 | .634 | .623 | .630 | .637 | .639 | .643 |
| Feb | .604 | .609 | .613 | .615 | .613 | .621 | .619 | .619 | .621 | .626 | .614 | .622 | .629 | .631 | .635 |
| Mar | .599 | .604 | .608 | .610 | .608 | .616 | .614 | .614 | .616 | .621 | .609 | .617 | .624 | .626 | .630 |
| Apr | .581 | .587 | .590 | .592 | .590 | .598 | .597 | .596 | .598 | .603 | .592 | .599 | .606 | .608 | .612 |
| May | .572 | .578 | .581 | .583 | .582 | .589 | .588 | .587 | .589 | .594 | .583 | .590 | .597 | .599 | .603 |
| June | .573 | .579 | .582 | .584 | .583 | .590 | .589 | .588 | .590 | .595 | .584 | .591 | .598 | .600 | .604 |
| July | .577 | .583 | .586 | .588 | .587 | .594 | .593 | .592 | .594 | .599 | .588 | .595 | .602 | .604 | .608 |
| Aug | .571 | .576 | .579 | .582 | .580 | .587 | .586 | .585 | .587 | .592 | .581 | .588 | .595 | .597 | .601 |
| Sept | .564 | .569 | .572 | .575 | .573 | .580 | .579 | .578 | .580 | .585 | .574 | .582 | .588 | .590 | .594 |
| Oct | .563 | .568 | .571 | .574 | .572 | .579 | .578 | .578 | .579 | .584 | .573 | .581 | .587 | .589 | .593 |
| Nov | .564 | .569 | .572 | .575 | .573 | .580 | .579 | .578 | .580 | .585 | .574 | .582 | .588 | .590 | .594 |
| Dec | .564 | .569 | .572 | .575 | .573 | .580 | .579 | .578 | .580 | .585 | .574 | .582 | .588 | .590 | .594 |
| **1999** | Mar | Apr | May | June | July | Aug | Sep | Oct | Nov | Dec | Jan | Feb | Mar | Apr | May |
| Jan | .573 | .579 | .582 | .584 | .583 | .590 | .589 | .588 | .590 | .595 | .584 | .591 | .598 | .600 | .604 |
| Feb | .571 | .576 | .579 | .582 | .580 | .587 | .586 | .585 | .587 | .592 | .581 | .588 | .595 | .597 | .601 |
| Mar | .567 | .572 | .575 | .578 | .576 | .583 | .582 | .581 | .583 | .588 | .577 | .584 | .591 | .593 | .597 |
| Apr | .556 | .562 | .565 | .567 | .565 | .573 | .571 | .571 | .573 | .577 | .567 | .574 | .581 | .582 | .587 |
| May | .553 | .558 | .561 | .563 | .562 | .569 | .568 | .567 | .569 | .574 | .563 | .570 | .577 | .579 | .583 |
| June | .553 | .558 | .561 | .563 | .562 | .569 | .568 | .567 | .569 | .574 | .563 | .570 | .577 | .579 | .583 |
| July | .557 | .563 | .566 | .568 | .566 | .574 | .572 | .572 | .574 | .578 | .568 | .575 | .581 | .583 | .588 |
| Aug | .553 | .559 | .562 | .564 | .563 | .570 | .569 | .568 | .570 | .575 | .564 | .571 | .578 | .579 | .584 |
| Sept | .547 | .552 | .555 | .558 | .556 | .563 | .562 | .561 | .563 | .568 | .557 | .564 | .571 | .573 | .577 |
| Oct | .544 | .550 | .553 | .555 | .553 | .560 | .559 | .559 | .560 | .565 | .554 | .562 | .568 | .570 | .574 |
| Nov | .542 | .548 | .551 | .553 | .551 | .558 | .557 | .557 | .558 | .563 | .552 | .560 | .566 | .568 | .572 |
| Dec | .537 | .542 | .545 | .548 | .546 | .553 | .552 | .551 | .553 | .558 | .547 | .554 | .561 | .562 | .567 |
| **2000** | Mar | Apr | May | June | July | Aug | Sep | Oct | Nov | Dec | Jan | Feb | Mar | Apr | May |
| Jan | .543 | .549 | .552 | .554 | .552 | .559 | .558 | .558 | .559 | .564 | .553 | .561 | .567 | .569 | .573 |
| Feb | .535 | .540 | .543 | .546 | .544 | .551 | .550 | .549 | .551 | .556 | .545 | .552 | .559 | .561 | .565 |
| Mar | .527 | .532 | .535 | .537 | .536 | .543 | .542 | .541 | .543 | .548 | .537 | .544 | .550 | .552 | .556 |
| Apr | .511 | .517 | .520 | .522 | .520 | .527 | .526 | .526 | .527 | .532 | .521 | .529 | .535 | .537 | .541 |
| May | .506 | .511 | .514 | .517 | .515 | .522 | .521 | .520 | .522 | .527 | .516 | .523 | .530 | .531 | .535 |
| June | .503 | .508 | .511 | .513 | .511 | .518 | .517 | .517 | .518 | .523 | .513 | .520 | .526 | .528 | .532 |
| July | .508 | .513 | .516 | .518 | .517 | .524 | .523 | .522 | .524 | .528 | .518 | .525 | .531 | .533 | .537 |
| Aug | .508 | .513 | .516 | .518 | .517 | .524 | .523 | .522 | .524 | .528 | .518 | .525 | .531 | .533 | .537 |
| Sept | .497 | .503 | .506 | .508 | .506 | .513 | .512 | .511 | .513 | .518 | .507 | .514 | .521 | .522 | .526 |
| Oct | .498 | .503 | .506 | .509 | .507 | .514 | .513 | .512 | .514 | .519 | .508 | .515 | .522 | .523 | .527 |
| Nov | .494 | .499 | .502 | .504 | .503 | .510 | .508 | .508 | .510 | .514 | .504 | .511 | .517 | .519 | .523 |
| Dec | .493 | .498 | .501 | .503 | .502 | .509 | .508 | .507 | .509 | .513 | .503 | .510 | .516 | .518 | .522 |
| **2001** | Mar | Apr | May | June | July | Aug | Sep | Oct | Nov | Dec | Jan | Feb | Mar | Apr | May |
| Jan | .503 | .508 | .511 | .513 | .511 | .518 | .517 | .517 | .518 | .523 | .513 | .520 | .526 | .528 | .532 |
| Feb | .495 | .500 | .503 | .505 | .503 | .510 | .509 | .509 | .510 | .515 | .505 | .512 | .518 | .520 | .524 |
| Mar | .493 | .498 | .501 | .503 | .502 | .509 | .508 | .507 | .509 | .513 | .503 | .510 | .516 | .518 | .522 |
| Apr | .485 | .490 | .493 | .496 | .494 | .501 | .500 | .499 | .501 | .505 | .495 | .502 | .508 | .510 | .514 |
| May | .476 | .481 | .484 | .486 | .485 | .491 | .490 | .490 | .491 | .496 | .486 | .493 | .499 | .501 | .505 |
| June | .474 | .479 | .482 | .485 | .483 | .490 | .489 | .488 | .490 | .494 | .484 | .491 | .497 | .499 | .503 |
| July | .484 | .489 | .492 | .494 | .492 | .499 | .498 | .497 | .499 | .504 | .493 | .500 | .507 | .508 | .512 |
| Aug | .478 | .483 | .486 | .488 | .486 | .493 | .492 | .491 | .493 | .498 | .487 | .494 | .501 | .502 | .506 |
| Sept | .473 | .478 | .481 | .483 | .481 | .488 | .487 | .486 | .488 | .493 | .482 | .489 | .495 | .497 | .501 |
| Oct | .475 | .480 | .483 | .485 | .484 | .491 | .489 | .489 | .491 | .495 | .485 | .492 | .498 | .500 | .504 |
| Nov | .481 | .486 | .489 | .491 | .490 | .497 | .495 | .495 | .497 | .501 | .491 | .498 | .504 | .506 | .510 |
| Dec | .483 | .488 | .491 | .493 | .491 | .498 | .497 | .497 | .498 | .503 | .493 | .499 | .506 | .507 | .512 |

MONTH OF DISPOSAL

| | ***2016*** | | | | | | | ***2017*** | | | | | | | |
|---|---|---|---|---|---|---|---|---|---|---|---|---|---|---|---|
| **1998** | June | July | Aug | Sep | Oct | Nov | Dec | Jan | Feb | Mar | Apr | May | June | July | Aug |
| Jan | .650 | .651 | .658 | .661 | .660 | .665 | .675 | .665 | .683 | .688 | .697 | .703 | .707 | .711 | .710 |
| Feb | .641 | .643 | .649 | .653 | .652 | .656 | .666 | .656 | .674 | .680 | .688 | .695 | .699 | .702 | .701 |
| Mar | .636 | .638 | .644 | .647 | .647 | .651 | .661 | .651 | .669 | .675 | .683 | .690 | .693 | .697 | .696 |
| Apr | .618 | .620 | .626 | .629 | .629 | .633 | .643 | .633 | .651 | .656 | .664 | .671 | .675 | .678 | .677 |
| May | .609 | .611 | .617 | .620 | .620 | .624 | .634 | .624 | .642 | .647 | .655 | .662 | .665 | .669 | .668 |
| June | .610 | .612 | .618 | .621 | .621 | .625 | .635 | .625 | .643 | .648 | .656 | .663 | .666 | .670 | .669 |
| July | .614 | .616 | .622 | .625 | .625 | .629 | .639 | .629 | .647 | .652 | .660 | .667 | .671 | .674 | .673 |
| Aug | .607 | .609 | .615 | .618 | .618 | .622 | .632 | .622 | .640 | .645 | .653 | .660 | .663 | .667 | .666 |
| Sept | .600 | .602 | .608 | .611 | .611 | .615 | .625 | .615 | .633 | .638 | .646 | .653 | .656 | .660 | .659 |
| Oct | .599 | .601 | .607 | .610 | .610 | .614 | .624 | .614 | .632 | .637 | .645 | .652 | .655 | .659 | .658 |
| Nov | .600 | .602 | .608 | .611 | .611 | .615 | .625 | .615 | .633 | .638 | .646 | .653 | .656 | .660 | .659 |
| Dec | .600 | .602 | .608 | .611 | .611 | .615 | .625 | .615 | .633 | .638 | .646 | .653 | .656 | .660 | .659 |
| **1999** | June | July | Aug | Sep | Oct | Nov | Dec | Jan | Feb | Mar | Apr | May | June | July | Aug |
| Jan | .610 | .612 | .618 | .621 | .621 | .625 | .635 | .625 | .643 | .648 | .656 | .663 | .666 | .670 | .669 |
| Feb | .607 | .609 | .615 | .618 | .618 | .622 | .632 | .622 | .640 | .645 | .653 | .660 | .663 | .667 | .666 |
| Mar | .603 | .605 | .611 | .614 | .614 | .618 | .628 | .618 | .636 | .641 | .649 | .656 | .659 | .663 | .662 |
| Apr | .593 | .594 | .600 | .604 | .603 | .607 | .617 | .607 | .625 | .630 | .638 | .645 | .648 | .652 | .651 |
| May | .589 | .591 | .597 | .600 | .599 | .603 | .613 | .603 | .621 | .626 | .634 | .641 | .644 | .648 | .647 |
| June | .589 | .591 | .597 | .600 | .599 | .603 | .613 | .603 | .621 | .626 | .634 | .641 | .644 | .648 | .647 |
| July | .594 | .595 | .601 | .604 | .604 | .608 | .618 | .608 | .626 | .631 | .639 | .646 | .649 | .653 | .652 |
| Aug | .590 | .592 | .598 | .601 | .600 | .604 | .614 | .604 | .622 | .627 | .635 | .642 | .645 | .649 | .648 |
| Sept | .583 | .585 | .591 | .594 | .593 | .597 | .607 | .597 | .615 | .620 | .628 | .635 | .638 | .642 | .641 |
| Oct | .580 | .582 | .588 | .591 | .590 | .595 | .604 | .595 | .612 | .617 | .625 | .632 | .635 | .639 | .638 |
| Nov | .578 | .580 | .586 | .589 | .588 | .593 | .602 | .593 | .610 | .615 | .623 | .630 | .633 | .637 | .636 |
| Dec | .573 | .574 | .580 | .583 | .583 | .587 | .597 | .587 | .604 | .610 | .617 | .624 | .628 | .631 | .630 |
| **2000** | June | July | Aug | Sep | Oct | Nov | Dec | Jan | Feb | Mar | Apr | May | June | July | Aug |
| Jan | .579 | .581 | .587 | .590 | .589 | .594 | .603 | .594 | .611 | .616 | .624 | .631 | .634 | .638 | .637 |
| Feb | .571 | .573 | .579 | .581 | .581 | .585 | .595 | .585 | .602 | .608 | .616 | .622 | .626 | .629 | .628 |
| Mar | .562 | .564 | .570 | .573 | .572 | .577 | .586 | .577 | .594 | .599 | .607 | .613 | .617 | .621 | .619 |
| Apr | .547 | .549 | .554 | .557 | .557 | .561 | .570 | .561 | .578 | .583 | .591 | .597 | .601 | .604 | .603 |
| May | .541 | .543 | .549 | .552 | .551 | .555 | .565 | .555 | .572 | .578 | .585 | .592 | .595 | .599 | .598 |
| June | .538 | .539 | .545 | .548 | .548 | .552 | .561 | .552 | .569 | .574 | .582 | .588 | .591 | .595 | .594 |
| July | .543 | .545 | .551 | .554 | .553 | .557 | .567 | .557 | .574 | .579 | .587 | .594 | .597 | .601 | .599 |
| Aug | .543 | .545 | .551 | .554 | .553 | .557 | .567 | .557 | .574 | .579 | .587 | .594 | .597 | .601 | .599 |
| Sept | .532 | .534 | .540 | .543 | .542 | .546 | .556 | .546 | .563 | .568 | .576 | .582 | .586 | .589 | .588 |
| Oct | .533 | .535 | .541 | .544 | .543 | .547 | .557 | .547 | .564 | .569 | .577 | .583 | .587 | .590 | .589 |
| Nov | .529 | .531 | .536 | .539 | .539 | .543 | .552 | .543 | .560 | .565 | .572 | .579 | .582 | .586 | .585 |
| Dec | .528 | .530 | .535 | .538 | .538 | .542 | .551 | .542 | .559 | .564 | .571 | .578 | .581 | .585 | .584 |
| **2001** | June | July | Aug | Sep | Oct | Nov | Dec | Jan | Feb | Mar | Apr | May | June | July | Aug |
| Jan | .538 | .539 | .545 | .548 | .548 | .552 | .561 | .552 | .569 | .574 | .582 | .588 | .591 | .595 | .594 |
| Feb | .530 | .531 | .537 | .540 | .540 | .544 | .553 | .544 | .560 | .566 | .573 | .580 | .583 | .587 | .585 |
| Mar | .528 | .530 | .535 | .538 | .538 | .542 | .551 | .542 | .559 | .564 | .571 | .578 | .581 | .585 | .584 |
| Apr | .520 | .522 | .527 | .530 | .530 | .534 | .543 | .534 | .551 | .556 | .563 | .570 | .573 | .577 | .575 |
| May | .510 | .512 | .518 | .521 | .520 | .524 | .533 | .524 | .541 | .546 | .553 | .560 | .563 | .567 | .565 |
| June | .509 | .510 | .516 | .519 | .518 | .522 | .532 | .522 | .539 | .544 | .552 | .558 | .561 | .565 | .564 |
| July | .518 | .520 | .526 | .529 | .528 | .532 | .541 | .532 | .549 | .554 | .561 | .568 | .571 | .575 | .574 |
| Aug | .512 | .514 | .520 | .522 | .522 | .526 | .535 | .526 | .543 | .548 | .555 | .561 | .565 | .568 | .567 |
| Sept | .507 | .509 | .514 | .517 | .517 | .521 | .530 | .521 | .537 | .542 | .550 | .556 | .560 | .563 | .562 |
| Oct | .509 | .511 | .517 | .520 | .519 | .523 | .532 | .523 | .540 | .545 | .552 | .559 | .562 | .566 | .565 |
| Nov | .516 | .517 | .523 | .526 | .525 | .529 | .539 | .529 | .546 | .551 | .559 | .565 | .569 | .572 | .571 |
| Dec | .517 | .519 | .525 | .528 | .527 | .531 | .540 | .531 | .548 | .553 | .561 | .567 | .570 | .574 | .573 |

MONTH OF DISPOSAL

| | ***2015*** | | | | | | | | | | ***2016*** | | | | |
|---|---|---|---|---|---|---|---|---|---|---|---|---|---|---|---|
| **2002** | Mar | Apr | May | June | July | Aug | Sep | Oct | Nov | Dec | Jan | Feb | Mar | Apr | May |
| Jan | .484 | .489 | .492 | .494 | .492 | .499 | .498 | .497 | .499 | .504 | .493 | .500 | .507 | .508 | .512 |
| Feb | .479 | .484 | .487 | .490 | .488 | .495 | .494 | .493 | .495 | .499 | .489 | .496 | .502 | .504 | .508 |
| Mar | .473 | .479 | .481 | .484 | .482 | .489 | .488 | .487 | .489 | .493 | .483 | .490 | .496 | .498 | .502 |
| Apr | .463 | .468 | .471 | .474 | .472 | .479 | .478 | .477 | .479 | .483 | .473 | .480 | .486 | .488 | .492 |
| May | .459 | .464 | .467 | .469 | .468 | .474 | .473 | .473 | .474 | .479 | .469 | .476 | .482 | .484 | .488 |
| June | .459 | .464 | .467 | .469 | .468 | .474 | .473 | .473 | .474 | .479 | .469 | .476 | .482 | .484 | .488 |
| July | .462 | .467 | .470 | .472 | .470 | .477 | .476 | .475 | .477 | .482 | .471 | .478 | .484 | .486 | .490 |
| Aug | .457 | .463 | .465 | .468 | .466 | .473 | .472 | .471 | .473 | .477 | .467 | .474 | .480 | .482 | .486 |
| Sept | .448 | .453 | .456 | .458 | .456 | .463 | .462 | .461 | .463 | .467 | .457 | .464 | .470 | .472 | .476 |
| Oct | .445 | .450 | .453 | .455 | .454 | .460 | .459 | .459 | .460 | .465 | .455 | .461 | .468 | .469 | .473 |
| Nov | .443 | .448 | .451 | .453 | .451 | .458 | .457 | .456 | .458 | .462 | .452 | .459 | .465 | .467 | .471 |
| Dec | .440 | .445 | .448 | .450 | .449 | .455 | .454 | .454 | .455 | .460 | .450 | .457 | .463 | .464 | .468 |
| **2003** | Mar | Apr | May | June | July | Aug | Sep | Oct | Nov | Dec | Jan | Feb | Mar | Apr | May |
| Jan | .441 | .446 | .449 | .451 | .450 | .456 | .455 | .455 | .456 | .461 | .451 | .457 | .464 | .465 | .469 |
| Feb | .434 | .439 | .442 | .444 | .442 | .449 | .448 | .447 | .449 | .453 | .443 | .450 | .456 | .458 | .462 |
| Mar | .429 | .434 | .437 | .439 | .437 | .444 | .443 | .442 | .444 | .449 | .439 | .445 | .451 | .453 | .457 |
| Apr | .419 | .424 | .427 | .429 | .427 | .434 | .433 | .432 | .434 | .438 | .428 | .435 | .441 | .443 | .446 |
| May | .417 | .421 | .424 | .426 | .425 | .431 | .430 | .430 | .431 | .436 | .426 | .433 | .439 | .440 | .444 |
| June | .418 | .423 | .426 | .428 | .426 | .433 | .432 | .431 | .433 | .437 | .427 | .434 | .440 | .442 | .446 |
| July | .418 | .423 | .426 | .428 | .426 | .433 | .432 | .431 | .433 | .437 | .427 | .434 | .440 | .442 | .446 |
| Aug | .416 | .421 | .423 | .426 | .424 | .431 | .430 | .429 | .431 | .435 | .425 | .432 | .438 | .439 | .443 |
| Sept | .409 | .414 | .416 | .419 | .416 | .424 | .422 | .422 | .424 | .428 | .418 | .425 | .431 | .432 | .436 |
| Oct | .408 | .413 | .416 | .418 | .416 | .423 | .422 | .421 | .423 | .427 | .417 | .424 | .430 | .432 | .435 |
| Nov | .407 | .412 | .415 | .417 | .415 | .422 | .421 | .420 | .422 | .426 | .417 | .423 | .429 | .431 | .435 |
| Dec | .401 | .406 | .409 | .411 | .409 | .416 | .415 | .414 | .416 | .420 | .410 | .417 | .423 | .425 | .428 |
| **2004** | Mar | Apr | May | June | July | Aug | Sep | Oct | Nov | Dec | Jan | Feb | Mar | Apr | May |
| Jan | .404 | .409 | .412 | .414 | .412 | .419 | .418 | .417 | .419 | .423 | .413 | .420 | .426 | .428 | .431 |
| Feb | .399 | .404 | .406 | .409 | .407 | .413 | .412 | .412 | .413 | .418 | .408 | .415 | .421 | .422 | .426 |
| Mar | .393 | .398 | .400 | .402 | .401 | .407 | .406 | .406 | .407 | .412 | .402 | .408 | .414 | .416 | .420 |
| Apr | .384 | .389 | .392 | .394 | .393 | .399 | .398 | .397 | .399 | .403 | .394 | .400 | .406 | .408 | .411 |
| May | .379 | .383 | .386 | .388 | .387 | .393 | .392 | .391 | .393 | .397 | .388 | .394 | .400 | .402 | .405 |
| June | .376 | .381 | .384 | .386 | .384 | .391 | .390 | .389 | .391 | .395 | .385 | .392 | .398 | .399 | .403 |
| July | .376 | .381 | .384 | .386 | .384 | .391 | .390 | .389 | .391 | .395 | .385 | .392 | .398 | .399 | .403 |
| Aug | .372 | .377 | .379 | .382 | .380 | .386 | .385 | .385 | .386 | .391 | .381 | .387 | .393 | .395 | .399 |
| Sept | .367 | .372 | .374 | .376 | .375 | .381 | .380 | .380 | .381 | .385 | .376 | .382 | .388 | .390 | .393 |
| Oct | .363 | .368 | .371 | .373 | .371 | .378 | .376 | .376 | .378 | .382 | .372 | .379 | .384 | .386 | .390 |
| Nov | .360 | .365 | .368 | .370 | .368 | .375 | .374 | .373 | .375 | .379 | .369 | .376 | .381 | .383 | .387 |
| Dec | .354 | .359 | .361 | .363 | .362 | .368 | .367 | .367 | .368 | .372 | .363 | .369 | .375 | .377 | .380 |
| **2005** | Mar | Apr | May | June | July | Aug | Sep | Oct | Nov | Dec | Jan | Feb | Mar | Apr | May |
| Jan | .361 | .366 | .368 | .371 | .369 | .375 | .374 | .374 | .375 | .380 | .370 | .376 | .382 | .384 | .388 |
| Feb | .356 | .361 | .363 | .366 | .364 | .370 | .369 | .369 | .370 | .374 | .365 | .371 | .377 | .379 | .382 |
| Mar | .350 | .354 | .357 | .359 | .357 | .364 | .363 | .362 | .364 | .368 | .359 | .365 | .371 | .372 | .376 |
| Apr | .342 | .347 | .349 | .351 | .350 | .356 | .355 | .354 | .356 | .360 | .351 | .357 | .363 | .364 | .368 |
| May | .339 | .344 | .346 | .348 | .347 | .353 | .352 | .352 | .353 | .357 | .348 | .354 | .360 | .361 | .365 |
| June | .338 | .342 | .345 | .347 | .345 | .352 | .351 | .350 | .352 | .356 | .347 | .353 | .358 | .360 | .364 |
| July | .338 | .342 | .345 | .347 | .345 | .352 | .351 | .350 | .352 | .356 | .347 | .353 | .358 | .360 | .364 |
| Aug | .335 | .340 | .342 | .344 | .343 | .349 | .348 | .347 | .349 | .353 | .344 | .350 | .356 | .357 | .361 |
| Sept | .331 | .336 | .339 | .341 | .339 | .345 | .344 | .344 | .345 | .350 | .340 | .346 | .352 | .354 | .357 |
| Oct | .330 | .335 | .337 | .339 | .338 | .344 | .343 | .342 | .344 | .348 | .339 | .345 | .351 | .352 | .356 |
| Nov | .328 | .333 | .335 | .337 | .336 | .342 | .341 | .340 | .342 | .346 | .337 | .343 | .349 | .350 | .354 |
| Dec | .325 | .329 | .332 | .334 | .332 | .338 | .337 | .337 | .338 | .343 | .333 | .340 | .345 | .347 | .350 |

MONTH OF DISPOSAL

| | 2016 | | | | | | | 2017 | | | | | | | |
|---|---|---|---|---|---|---|---|---|---|---|---|---|---|---|---|
| **2002** | June | July | Aug | Sep | Oct | Nov | Dec | Jan | Feb | Mar | Apr | May | June | July | Aug |
| Jan | .518 | .520 | .526 | .529 | .528 | .532 | .541 | .532 | .549 | .554 | .561 | .568 | .571 | .575 | .574 |
| Feb | .514 | .516 | .521 | .524 | .524 | .528 | .537 | .528 | .544 | .549 | .557 | .563 | .567 | .570 | .569 |
| Mar | .508 | .509 | .515 | .518 | .517 | .521 | .531 | .521 | .538 | .543 | .551 | .557 | .560 | .564 | .563 |
| Apr | .497 | .499 | .505 | .508 | .507 | .511 | .520 | .511 | .528 | .533 | .540 | .546 | .550 | .553 | .552 |
| May | .493 | .495 | .501 | .503 | .503 | .507 | .516 | .507 | .523 | .528 | .536 | .542 | .545 | .549 | .548 |
| June | .493 | .495 | .501 | .503 | .503 | .507 | .516 | .507 | .523 | .528 | .536 | .542 | .545 | .549 | .548 |
| July | .496 | .497 | .503 | .506 | .505 | .509 | .518 | .509 | .526 | .531 | .538 | .545 | .548 | .551 | .550 |
| Aug | .491 | .493 | .499 | .502 | .501 | .505 | .514 | .505 | .522 | .527 | .534 | .540 | .544 | .547 | .546 |
| Sept | .481 | .483 | .489 | .492 | .491 | .495 | .504 | .495 | .511 | .516 | .524 | .530 | .533 | .537 | .535 |
| Oct | .479 | .481 | .486 | .489 | .488 | .492 | .501 | .492 | .509 | .514 | .521 | .527 | .531 | .534 | .533 |
| Nov | .476 | .478 | .484 | .487 | .486 | .490 | .499 | .490 | .506 | .511 | .519 | .525 | .528 | .531 | .530 |
| Dec | .474 | .476 | .481 | .484 | .483 | .487 | .496 | .487 | .504 | .509 | .516 | .522 | .525 | .529 | .528 |
| **2003** | June | July | Aug | Sep | Oct | Nov | Dec | Jan | Feb | Mar | Apr | May | June | July | Aug |
| Jan | .475 | .476 | .482 | .485 | .484 | .488 | .497 | .488 | .504 | .510 | .517 | .523 | .526 | .530 | .529 |
| Feb | .467 | .469 | .475 | .477 | .477 | .481 | .490 | .481 | .497 | .502 | .509 | .515 | .519 | .522 | .521 |
| Mar | .462 | .464 | .470 | .472 | .472 | .476 | .485 | .476 | .492 | .497 | .504 | .510 | .514 | .517 | .516 |
| Apr | .452 | .454 | .459 | .462 | .461 | .465 | .474 | .465 | .481 | .486 | .493 | .499 | .503 | .506 | .505 |
| May | .450 | .451 | .457 | .460 | .459 | .463 | .472 | .463 | .479 | .484 | .491 | .497 | .500 | .504 | .502 |
| June | .451 | .453 | .458 | .461 | .461 | .464 | .473 | .464 | .480 | .485 | .493 | .499 | .502 | .505 | .504 |
| July | .451 | .453 | .458 | .461 | .461 | .464 | .473 | .464 | .480 | .485 | .493 | .499 | .502 | .505 | .504 |
| Aug | .449 | .450 | .456 | .459 | .458 | .462 | .471 | .462 | .478 | .483 | .490 | .496 | .499 | .503 | .502 |
| Sept | .442 | .443 | .449 | .452 | .451 | .455 | .464 | .455 | .471 | .476 | .483 | .489 | .492 | .495 | .494 |
| Oct | .441 | .442 | .448 | .451 | .450 | .454 | .463 | .454 | .470 | .475 | .482 | .488 | .491 | .495 | .493 |
| Nov | .440 | .442 | .447 | .450 | .449 | .453 | .462 | .453 | .469 | .474 | .481 | .487 | .490 | .494 | .493 |
| Dec | .434 | .435 | .441 | .444 | .443 | .447 | .456 | .447 | .463 | .468 | .475 | .481 | .484 | .487 | .486 |
| **2004** | June | July | Aug | Sep | Oct | Nov | Dec | Jan | Feb | Mar | Apr | May | June | July | Aug |
| Jan | .437 | .439 | .444 | .447 | .446 | .450 | .459 | .450 | .466 | .471 | .478 | .484 | .487 | .490 | .489 |
| Feb | .431 | .433 | .439 | .441 | .441 | .445 | .453 | .445 | .460 | .465 | .472 | .478 | .482 | .485 | .484 |
| Mar | .425 | .427 | .432 | .435 | .434 | .438 | .447 | .438 | .454 | .459 | .466 | .472 | .475 | .478 | .477 |
| Apr | .417 | .418 | .424 | .426 | .426 | .430 | .438 | .430 | .445 | .450 | .457 | .463 | .466 | .470 | .468 |
| May | .411 | .412 | .418 | .420 | .420 | .424 | .432 | .424 | .439 | .444 | .451 | .457 | .460 | .463 | .462 |
| June | .408 | .410 | .415 | .418 | .418 | .421 | .430 | .421 | .437 | .442 | .449 | .454 | .458 | .461 | .460 |
| July | .408 | .410 | .415 | .418 | .418 | .421 | .430 | .421 | .437 | .442 | .449 | .454 | .458 | .461 | .460 |
| Aug | .404 | .406 | .411 | .414 | .413 | .417 | .425 | .417 | .432 | .437 | .444 | .450 | .453 | .456 | .455 |
| Sept | .399 | .400 | .406 | .408 | .408 | .411 | .420 | .411 | .427 | .432 | .439 | .444 | .448 | .451 | .450 |
| Oct | .395 | .397 | .402 | .405 | .404 | .408 | .416 | .408 | .423 | .428 | .435 | .441 | .444 | .447 | .446 |
| Nov | .392 | .394 | .399 | .402 | .401 | .405 | .413 | .405 | .420 | .425 | .432 | .438 | .441 | .444 | .443 |
| Dec | .385 | .387 | .392 | .395 | .394 | .398 | .407 | .398 | .413 | . 418 | .425 | .431 | .434 | .437 | .436 |
| **2005** | June | July | Aug | Sep | Oct | Nov | Dec | Jan | Feb | Mar | Apr | May | June | July | Aug |
| Jan | .393 | .394 | .400 | .402 | .402 | .406 | .414 | .406 | .421 | .426 | .433 | .438 | .442 | .445 | .444 |
| Feb | .388 | .389 | .395 | .397 | .397 | .400 | .409 | .400 | .416 | .420 | .427 | .433 | .436 | .439 | .438 |
| Mar | .381 | .383 | .388 | .391 | .390 | .394 | .402 | .394 | .409 | .414 | .420 | .426 | .429 | .433 | .431 |
| Apr | .373 | .375 | .380 | .383 | .382 | .386 | .394 | .386 | .401 | .406 | .412 | .418 | .421 | .424 | .423 |
| May | .370 | .372 | .377 | .380 | .379 | .383 | .391 | .383 | .398 | .403 | .409 | .415 | .418 | .421 | .420 |
| June | .369 | .370 | .376 | .378 | .378 | .381 | .390 | .381 | .396 | .401 | .408 | .414 | .417 | .420 | .419 |
| July | .369 | .370 | .376 | .378 | .378 | .381 | .390 | .381 | .396 | .401 | .408 | .414 | .417 | .420 | .419 |
| Aug | .366 | .368 | .373 | .375 | .375 | .379 | .387 | .379 | .394 | .398 | .405 | .411 | .414 | .417 | .416 |
| Sept | .363 | .364 | .369 | .372 | .371 | .375 | .383 | .375 | .390 | .395 | .401 | .407 | .410 | .413 | .412 |
| Oct | .361 | .363 | .368 | .370 | .370 | .374 | .382 | .374 | .389 | .393 | .400 | .406 | .409 | .412 | .411 |
| Nov | .359 | .361 | .366 | .368 | .368 | .371 | .380 | .371 | .386 | .391 | .398 | .403 | .407 | .410 | .409 |
| Dec | .355 | .357 | .362 | .365 | .364 | .368 | .376 | .368 | .383 | .387 | .394 | .400 | .403 | .406 | .405 |

MONTH OF DISPOSAL

| | ***2015*** | | | | | | | | | | ***2016*** | | | | |
|---|---|---|---|---|---|---|---|---|---|---|---|---|---|---|---|
| **2006** | Mar | Apr | May | June | July | Aug | Sep | Oct | Nov | Dec | Jan | Feb | Mar | Apr | May |
| Jan | .329 | .334 | .337 | .339 | .337 | .343 | .342 | .342 | .343 | .347 | .338 | .344 | .350 | .352 | .355 |
| Feb | .324 | .329 | .331 | .333 | .332 | .338 | .337 | .336 | .338 | .342 | .333 | .339 | .344 | .346 | .350 |
| Mar | .318 | .323 | .326 | .328 | .326 | .332 | .331 | .331 | .332 | .336 | .327 | .333 | .339 | .341 | .344 |
| Apr | .308 | .313 | .316 | .318 | .316 | .322 | .321 | .321 | .322 | .326 | .317 | .323 | .329 | .330 | .334 |
| May | .300 | .305 | .308 | .310 | .308 | .314 | .313 | .313 | .314 | .318 | .309 | .315 | .321 | .322 | .326 |
| June | .295 | .300 | .302 | .304 | .303 | .309 | .308 | .307 | .309 | .313 | .304 | .310 | .315 | .317 | .320 |
| July | .295 | .300 | .302 | .304 | .303 | .309 | .308 | .307 | .309 | .313 | .304 | .310 | .315 | .317 | .320 |
| Aug | .291 | .295 | .298 | .300 | .298 | .304 | .303 | .303 | .304 | .308 | .299 | .305 | .311 | .312 | .316 |
| Sept | .285 | .289 | .292 | .294 | .292 | .298 | .297 | .297 | .298 | .302 | .293 | .299 | .305 | .306 | .310 |
| Oct | .283 | .287 | .290 | .292 | .290 | .296 | .295 | .295 | .296 | .300 | .291 | .297 | .303 | .304 | .308 |
| Nov | .278 | .283 | .285 | .287 | .286 | .292 | .291 | .290 | .292 | .296 | .287 | .293 | .298 | .300 | .303 |
| Dec | .268 | .273 | .275 | .277 | .276 | .282 | .281 | .280 | .282 | .286 | .277 | .283 | .288 | .290 | .293 |
| **2007** | Mar | Apr | May | June | July | Aug | Sep | Oct | Nov | Dec | Jan | Feb | Mar | Apr | May |
| Jan | .275 | .280 | .282 | .284 | .283 | .289 | .288 | .287 | .289 | .293 | .284 | .290 | .295 | .297 | .300 |
| Feb | .266 | .270 | .273 | .275 | .273 | .279 | .278 | .278 | .279 | .283 | .274 | .280 | .286 | .287 | .290 |
| Mar | .258 | .262 | .265 | .267 | .265 | .271 | .270 | .270 | .271 | .275 | .266 | .272 | .277 | .279 | .282 |
| Apr | .252 | .256 | .259 | .260 | .259 | .265 | .264 | .263 | .265 | .269 | .260 | .266 | .271 | .273 | .276 |
| May | .247 | .251 | .254 | .256 | .254 | .260 | .259 | .258 | .260 | .264 | .255 | .261 | .266 | .268 | .271 |
| June | .240 | .245 | .247 | .249 | .247 | .253 | .252 | .252 | .253 | .257 | .248 | .254 | .260 | .261 | .264 |
| July | .247 | .252 | .254 | .256 | .255 | .261 | .260 | .259 | .261 | .264 | .256 | .262 | .267 | .268 | .272 |
| Aug | .240 | .245 | .247 | .249 | .247 | .253 | .252 | .252 | .253 | .257 | .248 | .254 | .260 | .261 | .264 |
| Sept | .236 | .240 | .243 | .245 | .243 | .249 | .248 | .248 | .249 | .253 | .244 | .250 | .255 | .257 | .260 |
| Oct | .231 | .235 | .237 | .239 | .238 | .244 | .243 | .242 | .244 | .247 | .239 | .245 | .250 | .251 | .255 |
| Nov | .226 | .230 | .233 | .235 | .233 | .239 | .238 | .237 | .239 | .243 | .234 | .240 | .245 | .247 | .250 |
| Dec | .219 | .223 | .226 | .228 | .226 | .232 | .231 | .230 | .232 | .236 | .227 | .233 | .238 | .239 | .243 |
| **2008** | Mar | Apr | May | June | July | Aug | Sep | Oct | Nov | Dec | Jan | Feb | Mar | Apr | May |
| Jan | .225 | .230 | .232 | .234 | .233 | .238 | .237 | .237 | .238 | .242 | .234 | .239 | .245 | .246 | .249 |
| Feb | .216 | .220 | .223 | .225 | .223 | .229 | .228 | .228 | .229 | .233 | .224 | .230 | .235 | .237 | .240 |
| Mar | .212 | .216 | .219 | .221 | .219 | .225 | .224 | .223 | .225 | .229 | .220 | .226 | .231 | .232 | .236 |
| Apr | .201 | .206 | .208 | .210 | .208 | .214 | .213 | .213 | .214 | .218 | .209 | .215 | .220 | .221 | .225 |
| May | .195 | .199 | .202 | .204 | .202 | .208 | .207 | .206 | .208 | .212 | .203 | .209 | .214 | .215 | .219 |
| June | .186 | .190 | .192 | .194 | .193 | .198 | .197 | .197 | .198 | .202 | .194 | .199 | .204 | .206 | .209 |
| July | .188 | .192 | .194 | .196 | .194 | .200 | .199 | .199 | .200 | .204 | .195 | .201 | .206 | .207 | .211 |
| Aug | .184 | .188 | .190 | .192 | .191 | .196 | .195 | .195 | .196 | .200 | .192 | .197 | .202 | .203 | .207 |
| Sept | .177 | .181 | .184 | .185 | .184 | .190 | .189 | .188 | .190 | .193 | .185 | .190 | .196 | .197 | .200 |
| Oct | .181 | .185 | .187 | .189 | .188 | .193 | .192 | .192 | .193 | .197 | .189 | .194 | .199 | .201 | .204 |
| Nov | .190 | .194 | .197 | .199 | .197 | .203 | .202 | .201 | .203 | .206 | .198 | .204 | .209 | .210 | .213 |
| Dec | .208 | .212 | .214 | .216 | .215 | .220 | .219 | .219 | .220 | .224 | .216 | .221 | .226 | .228 | .231 |
| **2009** | Mar | Apr | May | June | July | Aug | Sep | Oct | Nov | Dec | Jan | Feb | Mar | Apr | May |
| Jan | .224 | .228 | .230 | .232 | .231 | .237 | .236 | .235 | .237 | .240 | .232 | .238 | .243 | .244 | .248 |
| Feb | .216 | .220 | .223 | .225 | .223 | .229 | .228 | .228 | .229 | .233 | .224 | .230 | .235 | .237 | .240 |
| Mar | .217 | .221 | .223 | .225 | .224 | .230 | .229 | .228 | .230 | .233 | .225 | .230 | .236 | .237 | .240 |
| Apr | .216 | .220 | .222 | .224 | .223 | .228 | .227 | .227 | .228 | .232 | .224 | .229 | .235 | .236 | .239 |
| May | .208 | .212 | .215 | .217 | .215 | .221 | .220 | .219 | .221 | .225 | .216 | .222 | .227 | .228 | .232 |
| June | .205 | .209 | .211 | .213 | .212 | .217 | .216 | .216 | .217 | .221 | .213 | .218 | .224 | .225 | .228 |
| July | .205 | .209 | .211 | .213 | .212 | .217 | .216 | .216 | .217 | .221 | .213 | .218 | .224 | .225 | .228 |
| Aug | .199 | .203 | .206 | .208 | .206 | .212 | .211 | .210 | .212 | .215 | .207 | .213 | .218 | .219 | .222 |
| Sept | .194 | .198 | .201 | .203 | .201 | .207 | .206 | .205 | .207 | .210 | .202 | .208 | .213 | .214 | .217 |
| Oct | .190 | .194 | .197 | .199 | .197 | .203 | .202 | .201 | .203 | .206 | .198 | .204 | .209 | .210 | .213 |
| Nov | .187 | .191 | .193 | .195 | .194 | .199 | .199 | .198 | .199 | .203 | .195 | .200 | .205 | .207 | .210 |
| Dec | .179 | .183 | .186 | .188 | .186 | .192 | .191 | .190 | .192 | .195 | .187 | .193 | .198 | .199 | .202 |

MONTH OF DISPOSAL

| | 2016 | | | | | | | 2017 | | | | | | | |
|---|---|---|---|---|---|---|---|---|---|---|---|---|---|---|---|
| **2006** | June | July | Aug | Sep | Oct | Nov | Dec | Jan | Feb | Mar | Apr | May | June | July | Aug |
| Jan | .360 | .362 | .367 | .370 | .369 | .373 | .381 | .373 | .388 | .392 | .399 | .405 | .408 | .411 | .410 |
| Feb | .355 | .356 | .361 | .364 | .364 | .367 | .375 | .367 | .382 | .387 | .393 | .399 | .402 | .405 | .404 |
| Mar | .349 | .351 | .356 | .358 | .358 | .362 | .370 | .362 | .376 | .381 | .388 | .393 | .396 | .399 | .398 |
| Apr | .339 | .340 | .346 | .348 | .348 | .351 | .359 | .351 | .366 | .370 | .377 | .383 | .386 | .389 | .388 |
| May | .331 | .332 | .337 | .340 | .339 | .343 | .351 | .343 | .358 | .362 | .369 | .374 | .377 | .380 | .379 |
| June | .325 | .327 | .332 | .335 | .334 | .338 | .346 | .338 | .352 | .357 | .363 | .369 | .372 | .375 | .374 |
| July | .325 | .327 | .332 | .335 | .334 | .338 | .346 | .338 | .352 | .357 | .363 | .369 | .372 | .375 | .374 |
| Aug | .321 | .322 | .327 | .330 | .329 | .333 | .341 | .333 | .347 | .352 | .358 | .364 | .367 | .370 | .369 |
| Sept | .315 | .316 | .321 | .324 | .323 | .327 | .335 | .327 | .341 | .346 | .352 | .358 | .361 | .364 | .363 |
| Oct | .313 | .314 | .319 | .322 | .321 | .325 | .333 | .325 | .339 | .344 | .350 | .356 | .359 | .362 | .361 |
| Nov | .308 | .310 | .315 | .317 | .317 | .320 | .328 | .320 | .335 | .339 | .346 | .351 | .354 | .357 | .356 |
| Dec | .298 | .299 | .304 | .307 | .306 | .310 | .318 | .310 | .324 | .329 | .335 | .340 | .343 | .346 | .345 |
| **2007** | June | July | Aug | Sep | Oct | Nov | Dec | Jan | Feb | Mar | Apr | May | June | July | Aug |
| Jan | .305 | .307 | .312 | .314 | .313 | .317 | .325 | .317 | .331 | .336 | .342 | .348 | .351 | .354 | .353 |
| Feb | .295 | .297 | .302 | .304 | .304 | .307 | .315 | .307 | .322 | .326 | .332 | .338 | .341 | .344 | .343 |
| Mar | .287 | .289 | .294 | .296 | .295 | .299 | .307 | .299 | .313 | .318 | .324 | .329 | .332 | .335 | .334 |
| Apr | .281 | .282 | .287 | .290 | .289 | .293 | .300 | .293 | .307 | .311 | .317 | .323 | .326 | .329 | .328 |
| May | .276 | .277 | .282 | .285 | .284 | .288 | .295 | .288 | .302 | .306 | .312 | .318 | .321 | .323 | .323 |
| June | .269 | .271 | .275 | .278 | .277 | .281 | .288 | .281 | .295 | .299 | .305 | .311 | .314 | .316 | .315 |
| July | .277 | .278 | .283 | .285 | .285 | .288 | .296 | .288 | .302 | .307 | .313 | .318 | .321 | .324 | .323 |
| Aug | .269 | .271 | .275 | .278 | .277 | .281 | .288 | .281 | .295 | .299 | .305 | .311 | .314 | .316 | .315 |
| Sept | .265 | .266 | .271 | .274 | .273 | .276 | .284 | .276 | .290 | .295 | .301 | .306 | .309 | .312 | .311 |
| Oct | .259 | .261 | .266 | .268 | .268 | .271 | .279 | .271 | .285 | .289 | .295 | .301 | .303 | .306 | .305 |
| Nov | .255 | .256 | .261 | .263 | .263 | .266 | .274 | .266 | .280 | .284 | .290 | .296 | .299 | .301 | .300 |
| Dec | .248 | .249 | .254 | .256 | .256 | .259 | .266 | .259 | .273 | .277 | .283 | .288 | .291 | .294 | .293 |
| **2008** | June | July | Aug | Sep | Oct | Nov | Dec | Jan | Feb | Mar | Apr | May | June | July | Aug |
| Jan | .254 | .255 | .260 | .263 | .262 | .265 | .273 | .265 | .279 | .284 | .290 | .295 | .298 | .301 | .300 |
| Feb | .245 | .246 | .251 | .253 | .253 | .256 | .263 | .256 | .270 | .274 | .280 | .285 | .288 | .291 | .290 |
| Mar | .240 | .242 | .247 | .249 | .248 | .252 | .259 | .252 | .265 | .270 | .276 | .281 | .284 | .287 | .286 |
| Apr | .229 | .231 | .236 | .238 | .237 | .241 | .248 | .241 | .254 | .258 | .264 | .270 | .272 | .275 | .274 |
| May | .223 | .225 | .229 | .232 | .231 | .234 | .242 | .234 | .248 | .252 | .258 | .263 | .266 | .269 | .268 |
| June | .214 | .215 | .220 | .222 | .221 | .225 | .232 | .225 | .238 | .242 | .248 | .253 | .256 | .259 | .258 |
| July | .215 | .217 | .221 | .224 | .223 | .226 | .234 | .226 | .240 | .244 | .250 | .255 | .258 | .261 | .260 |
| Aug | .211 | .213 | .217 | .220 | .219 | .222 | .230 | .222 | .236 | .240 | .246 | .251 | .254 | .256 | .256 |
| Sept | .205 | .206 | .211 | .213 | .212 | .216 | .223 | .216 | .229 | .233 | .239 | .244 | .247 | .250 | .249 |
| Oct | .209 | .210 | .215 | .217 | .216 | .220 | .227 | .220 | .233 | .237 | .243 | .248 | .251 | .254 | .253 |
| Nov | .218 | .219 | .224 | .226 | .226 | .229 | .237 | .229 | .243 | .247 | .253 | .258 | .261 | .263 | .263 |
| Dec | .236 | .237 | .242 | .244 | .244 | .247 | .255 | .247 | .261 | .265 | .271 | .276 | .279 | .282 | .281 |
| **2009** | June | July | Aug | Sep | Oct | Nov | Dec | Jan | Feb | Mar | Apr | May | June | July | Aug |
| Jan | .252 | .254 | .258 | .261 | .260 | .264 | .271 | .264 | .277 | .282 | .288 | .293 | .296 | .299 | .298 |
| Feb | .245 | .246 | .251 | .253 | .253 | .256 | .263 | .256 | .270 | .274 | .280 | .285 | .288 | .291 | .290 |
| Mar | .245 | .247 | .251 | .252 | .253 | .257 | .264 | .257 | .270 | .274 | .281 | .286 | .289 | .292 | .291 |
| Apr | .244 | .245 | .250 | .252 | .252 | .255 | .263 | .255 | .269 | .273 | .279 | .285 | .287 | .290 | .289 |
| May | .236 | .238 | .242 | .245 | .244 | .248 | .255 | .248 | .261 | .266 | .272 | .277 | .280 | .282 | .281 |
| June | .233 | .234 | .239 | .241 | .241 | .244 | .252 | .244 | .258 | .262 | .268 | .273 | .276 | .279 | .278 |
| July | .233 | .234 | .239 | .241 | .241 | .244 | .252 | .244 | .258 | .262 | .268 | .273 | .276 | .279 | .278 |
| Aug | .227 | .229 | .233 | .236 | .235 | .238 | .246 | .238 | .252 | .256 | .262 | .267 | .270 | .273 | .272 |
| Sept | .222 | .223 | .228 | .230 | .230 | .233 | .241 | .233 | .247 | .251 | 257 | .262 | .265 | .268 | .267 |
| Oct | .218 | .219 | .224 | .226 | .226 | .229 | .237 | .229 | .243 | .247 | .253 | .258 | .261 | .263 | .263 |
| Nov | .215 | .216 | .221 | .223 | .223 | .226 | .233 | .226 | .239 | .243 | .249 | .254 | .257 | .260 | .259 |
| Dec | .207 | .208 | .213 | .215 | .215 | .218 | .225 | .218 | .231 | .235 | .241 | .246 | .249 | .252 | .251 |

MONTH OF DISPOSAL

| | *2015* | | | | | | | | | | *2016* | | | | |
|---|---|---|---|---|---|---|---|---|---|---|---|---|---|---|---|
| **2010** | Mar | Apr | May | June | July | Aug | Sep | Oct | Nov | Dec | Jan | Feb | Mar | Apr | May |
| Jan | .180 | .184 | .186 | .188 | .187 | .192 | .191 | .191 | .192 | .196 | .188 | .193 | .198 | .200 | .203 |
| Feb | .173 | .177 | .179 | .181 | .180 | .185 | .184 | .184 | .185 | .189 | .181 | .186 | .191 | .193 | .196 |
| Mar | .165 | .169 | .171 | .173 | .172 | .177 | .176 | .176 | .177 | .181 | .173 | .178 | .183 | .184 | .188 |
| Apr | .154 | .158 | .160 | .162 | .161 | .166 | .165 | .165 | .166 | .170 | .162 | .167 | .172 | .173 | .176 |
| May | .150 | .154 | .156 | .158 | .157 | .162 | .161 | .161 | .162 | .165 | .157 | .163 | .168 | .169 | .172 |
| June | .147 | .151 | .154 | .155 | .154 | .159 | .158 | .158 | .159 | .163 | .155 | .160 | .165 | .166 | .170 |
| July | .150 | .154 | .156 | .158 | .157 | .162 | .161 | .161 | .162 | .165 | .157 | .163 | .168 | .169 | .172 |
| Aug | .145 | .149 | .151 | .153 | .152 | .157 | .156 | .156 | .157 | .161 | .153 | .158 | .163 | .164 | .167 |
| Sept | .141 | .145 | .147 | .149 | .148 | .153 | .152 | .152 | .153 | .157 | .149 | .154 | .159 | .160 | .163 |
| Oct | .139 | .143 | .145 | .147 | .145 | .151 | .150 | .149 | .151 | .154 | .146 | .151 | .156 | .158 | .161 |
| Nov | .134 | .138 | .140 | .142 | .140 | .146 | .145 | .144 | .146 | .149 | .141 | .146 | .151 | .153 | .156 |
| Dec | .126 | .130 | .132 | .134 | .132 | .137 | .137 | .136 | .137 | .141 | .133 | .138 | .143 | .144 | .148 |
| **2011** | Mar | Apr | May | June | July | Aug | Sep | Oct | Nov | Dec | Jan | Feb | Mar | Apr | May |
| Jan | .123 | .127 | .129 | .131 | .129 | .134 | .134 | .133 | .134 | .138 | .130 | .135 | .140 | .141 | .145 |
| Feb | .112 | .115 | .118 | .119 | .118 | .123 | .122 | .122 | .123 | .127 | .119 | .124 | .129 | .130 | .133 |
| Mar | .106 | .110 | .112 | .114 | .112 | .117 | .117 | .116 | .117 | .121 | .113 | .118 | .123 | .124 | .127 |
| Apr | .097 | .101 | .103 | .105 | .103 | .108 | .108 | .107 | .108 | .112 | .104 | .109 | .114 | .115 | .118 |
| May | .093 | .097 | .099 | .101 | .099 | .105 | .104 | .103 | .105 | .108 | .100 | .105 | .110 | .111 | .114 |
| Jun | .093 | .097 | .099 | .101 | .099 | .105 | .104 | .103 | .105 | .108 | .100 | .105 | .110 | .111 | .114 |
| July | .095 | .099 | .101 | .103 | .102 | .107 | .106 | .106 | .107 | .110 | .103 | .108 | .112 | .114 | .117 |
| Aug | .089 | .093 | .095 | .097 | .095 | .100 | .100 | .099 | .100 | .104 | .096 | .101 | .106 | .107 | .110 |
| Sept | .081 | .084 | .087 | .088 | .087 | .092 | .091 | .091 | .092 | .095 | .088 | .093 | .098 | .099 | .102 |
| Oct | .080 | .084 | .086 | .088 | .087 | .092 | .091 | .090 | .092 | .095 | .087 | .092 | .097 | .098 | .101 |
| Nov | .078 | .082 | .084 | .086 | .084 | .089 | .088 | .088 | .089 | .093 | .085 | .090 | .095 | .096 | .099 |
| Dec | .074 | .078 | .080 | .081 | .080 | .085 | .084 | .084 | .085 | .089 | .081 | .086 | .091 | .092 | .095 |
| **2012** | Mar | Apr | May | June | July | Aug | Sep | Oct | Nov | Dec | Jan | Feb | Mar | Apr | May |
| Jan | .080 | .084 | .086 | .088 | .087 | .092 | .091 | .090 | .092 | .095 | .087 | .092 | .097 | .098 | .101 |
| Feb | .072 | .075 | .078 | .079 | .078 | .083 | .082 | .082 | .083 | .086 | .079 | .084 | .088 | .090 | .093 |
| Mar | .068 | .071 | .074 | .075 | .074 | .079 | .078 | .078 | .079 | .082 | .075 | .080 | .084 | .086 | .088 |
| Apr | .060 | .064 | .066 | .068 | .066 | .071 | .071 | .070 | .071 | .075 | .067 | .072 | .077 | .078 | .081 |
| May | .061 | .064 | .066 | .068 | .067 | .072 | .071 | .071 | .072 | .075 | .068 | .073 | .077 | .078 | .081 |
| June | .063 | .067 | .069 | .071 | .069 | .074 | .074 | .073 | .074 | .078 | .070 | .075 | .080 | .081 | .084 |
| July | .062 | .066 | .068 | .069 | .068 | .073 | .072 | .072 | .073 | .076 | .069 | .074 | .078 | .080 | .083 |
| Aug | .058 | .062 | .064 | .065 | .064 | .069 | .068 | .068 | .069 | .072 | .065 | .070 | .074 | .076 | .079 |
| Sept | .053 | .057 | .059 | .060 | .059 | .064 | .063 | .063 | .064 | .067 | .060 | .065 | .069 | .070 | .073 |
| Oct | .047 | .050 | .053 | .054 | .053 | .058 | .057 | .057 | .058 | .061 | .054 | .059 | .063 | .064 | .067 |
| Nov | .047 | .050 | .053 | .054 | .053 | .058 | .057 | .057 | .058 | .061 | .054 | .059 | .063 | .064 | .067 |
| Dec | .042 | .045 | .047 | .049 | .048 | .053 | .052 | .051 | .053 | .056 | .049 | .053 | .058 | .059 | .062 |
| **2013** | Mar | Apr | May | June | July | Aug | Sep | Oct | Nov | Dec | Jan | Feb | Mar | Apr | May |
| Jan | .046 | .050 | .052 | .053 | .052 | .057 | .056 | .056 | .057 | .060 | .053 | .058 | .062 | .063 | .066 |
| Feb | .038 | .042 | .044 | .046 | .044 | .049 | .048 | .048 | .049 | .053 | .045 | .050 | .055 | .056 | .059 |
| Mar | .034 | .037 | .039 | .041 | .040 | .045 | .044 | .043 | .045 | .048 | .041 | .045 | .050 | .051 | .054 |
| Apr | .030 | .034 | .036 | .038 | .036 | .041 | .040 | .040 | .041 | .044 | .037 | .042 | .046 | .048 | .051 |
| May | .028 | .032 | .034 | .036 | .034 | .039 | .038 | .038 | .039 | .042 | .035 | .040 | .044 | .046 | .048 |
| June | .030 | .033 | .035 | .037 | .036 | .040 | .040 | .039 | .040 | .044 | .036 | .041 | .046 | .047 | .050 |
| July | .030 | .033 | .035 | .037 | .036 | .040 | .040 | .039 | .040 | .044 | .036 | .041 | .046 | .047 | .050 |
| Aug | .024 | .028 | .030 | .031 | .030 | .035 | .034 | .034 | .035 | .038 | .031 | .036 | .040 | .041 | .044 |
| Sept | .021 | .024 | .026 | .028 | .027 | .031 | .031 | .030 | .031 | .035 | .027 | .032 | .037 | .038 | .040 |
| Oct | .021 | .024 | .026 | .028 | .027 | .031 | .031 | .030 | .031 | .035 | .027 | .032 | .037 | .038 | .040 |
| Nov | .020 | .023 | .025 | .027 | .026 | .031 | .030 | .029 | .031 | .034 | .027 | .031 | .036 | .037 | .040 |
| Dec | .018 | .021 | .023 | .025 | .024 | .029 | .028 | .027 | .029 | .032 | .025 | .029 | .034 | .035 | .038 |

MONTH OF DISPOSAL

| | ***2016*** | | | | | | | ***2017*** | | | | | | | |
|---|---|---|---|---|---|---|---|---|---|---|---|---|---|---|---|
| **2010** | June | July | Aug | Sep | Oct | Nov | Dec | Jan | Feb | Mar | Apr | May | June | July | Aug |
| Jan | .207 | .209 | .213 | .216 | .215 | .218 | .226 | .218 | .232 | .236 | .242 | .247 | .250 | .252 | .251 |
| Feb | .200 | .202 | .206 | .208 | .208 | .211 | .219 | .211 | .224 | .229 | .234 | .240 | .242 | .245 | .244 |
| Mar | .192 | .193 | .198 | .200 | .200 | .203 | .210 | .203 | .216 | .220 | .226 | .231 | .234 | .237 | .236 |
| Apr | .181 | .182 | .187 | .189 | .189 | .192 | .199 | .192 | .205 | .209 | .215 | .219 | .222 | .225 | .224 |
| May | .177 | .178 | .182 | .185 | .184 | .187 | .195 | .187 | .200 | .204 | .210 | .215 | .218 | .220 | .220 |
| June | .174 | .175 | .180 | .182 | .182 | .185 | .192 | .185 | .198 | .202 | .207 | .212 | .215 | .218 | .217 |
| July | .177 | .178 | .182 | .185 | .184 | .187 | .195 | .187 | .200 | .204 | .210 | .215 | .218 | .220 | .220 |
| Aug | .172 | .173 | .178 | .180 | .180 | .183 | .190 | .183 | .196 | .200 | .205 | .210 | .213 | .216 | .215 |
| Sept | .168 | .169 | .174 | .176 | .175 | .178 | .186 | .178 | .191 | .195 | .201 | .206 | .209 | .211 | .210 |
| Oct | .165 | .167 | .171 | .173 | .173 | .176 | .183 | .176 | .189 | .193 | .198 | .203 | .206 | .209 | .208 |
| Nov | .160 | .161 | .166 | .168 | .168 | .171 | .178 | .171 | .183 | .187 | .193 | .198 | .201 | .203 | .202 |
| Dec | .152 | .153 | .158 | .160 | .159 | .162 | .169 | .162 | .175 | .179 | .185 | .190 | .192 | .195 | .194 |
| **2011** | June | July | Aug | Sep | Oct | Nov | Dec | Jan | Feb | Mar | Apr | May | June | July | Aug |
| Jan | .149 | .150 | .155 | .157 | .156 | .159 | .166 | .159 | .172 | .176 | .182 | .186 | .189 | .192 | .191 |
| Feb | .137 | .139 | .143 | .145 | .145 | .148 | .155 | .148 | .160 | .164 | .170 | .175 | .177 | .180 | .179 |
| Mar | .132 | .133 | .137 | .139 | .139 | .142 | .149 | .142 | .154 | .158 | .164 | .169 | .171 | .174 | .173 |
| Apr | .122 | .124 | .128 | .130 | .130 | .133 | .140 | .133 | .145 | .149 | .154 | .159 | .162 | .164 | .163 |
| May | .119 | .120 | .124 | .126 | .126 | .129 | .136 | .129 | .141 | .145 | .151 | .155 | .158 | .160 | .159 |
| June | .119 | .120 | .124 | .126 | .126 | .129 | .136 | .129 | .141 | .145 | .151 | .155 | .158 | .160 | .159 |
| July | .121 | .122 | .127 | .129 | .128 | .131 | .138 | .131 | .144 | .147 | .153 | .158 | .160 | .163 | .162 |
| Aug | .114 | .116 | .120 | .122 | .122 | .125 | .131 | .125 | .137 | .141 | .146 | .151 | .153 | .156 | .155 |
| Sept | .106 | .107 | .111 | .113 | .113 | .116 | .123 | .116 | .128 | .132 | .137 | .142 | .145 | .147 | .146 |
| Oct | .105 | .107 | .111 | .113 | .113 | .116 | .122 | .116 | .128 | .132 | .137 | .142 | .144 | .147 | .146 |
| Nov | .103 | .104 | .109 | .111 | .110 | .113 | .120 | .113 | .125 | .129 | .135 | .139 | .142 | .144 | .143 |
| Dec | .099 | .100 | .104 | .107 | .106 | .109 | .116 | .109 | .121 | .125 | .130 | .135 | .137 | .140 | .139 |
| **2012** | June | July | Aug | Sep | Oct | Nov | Dec | Jan | Feb | Mar | Apr | May | June | July | Aug |
| Jan | .105 | .107 | .111 | .113 | .113 | .116 | .122 | .116 | .128 | .132 | .137 | .142 | .144 | .147 | .146 |
| Feb | .097 | .098 | .102 | .104 | .104 | .107 | .113 | .107 | .119 | .123 | .128 | .133 | .135 | .138 | .137 |
| Mar | .093 | .094 | .098 | .100 | .100 | .103 | .109 | .103 | .115 | .118 | .124 | .128 | .131 | .133 | .132 |
| Apr | .085 | .086 | .090 | .092 | .092 | .095 | .101 | .095 | .107 | .111 | .116 | .120 | .123 | .125 | .125 |
| May | .085 | .087 | .091 | .093 | .092 | .095 | .102 | .095 | .107 | .111 | .116 | .121 | .123 | .126 | .125 |
| June | .088 | .089 | .093 | .096 | .095 | .098 | .105 | .098 | .110 | .114 | .119 | .124 | .126 | .129 | .128 |
| July | .087 | .088 | .092 | .094 | .094 | .097 | .103 | .097 | .109 | .112 | .118 | .122 | .125 | .127 | .126 |
| Aug | .083 | .084 | .088 | .090 | .090 | .093 | .099 | .093 | .105 | .108 | .114 | .118 | .121 | .123 | .122 |
| Sept | .077 | .079 | .083 | .085 | .084 | .087 | .094 | .087 | .099 | .103 | .108 | .113 | .115 | .118 | .117 |
| Oct | .071 | .072 | .077 | .079 | .078 | .081 | .088 | .081 | .093 | .096 | .102 | .106 | .109 | .111 | .110 |
| Nov | .071 | .072 | .077 | .079 | .078 | .081 | .088 | .081 | .093 | .096 | .102 | .106 | .109 | .111 | .110 |
| Dec | .066 | .067 | .071 | .073 | .073 | .076 | .082 | .076 | .088 | .091 | .096 | .101 | .103 | .106 | .105 |
| **2013** | June | July | Aug | Sep | Oct | Nov | Dec | Jan | Feb | Mar | Apr | May | June | July | Aug |
| Jan | .070 | .072 | .076 | .078 | .077 | .080 | .087 | .080 | .092 | .096 | .101 | .105 | .108 | .110 | .109 |
| Feb | .063 | .064 | .068 | .070 | .069 | .072 | .079 | .072 | .084 | .088 | .093 | .097 | .100 | .102 | .101 |
| Mar | .058 | .059 | .063 | .065 | .065 | .068 | .074 | .068 | .079 | .083 | .088 | .092 | .095 | .097 | .097 |
| Apr | .055 | .056 | .060 | .062 | .061 | .064 | .071 | .064 | .076 | .079 | .085 | .089 | .091 | .094 | .093 |
| May | .052 | .054 | .058 | .060 | .059 | .062 | .068 | .062 | .074 | .077 | .082 | .087 | .089 | .092 | .091 |
| June | .054 | .055 | .059 | .061 | .060 | .063 | .070 | .063 | .075 | .078 | .084 | .088 | .091 | .093 | .092 |
| July | .054 | .055 | .059 | .061 | .060 | .063 | .070 | .063 | .075 | .078 | .084 | .088 | .091 | .093 | .092 |
| Aug | .048 | .049 | .053 | .055 | .055 | .058 | .064 | .058 | .069 | .073 | .078 | .082 | .085 | .087 | .086 |
| Sept | .044 | .046 | .050 | .052 | .051 | .054 | .060 | .054 | .066 | .069 | .074 | .079 | .081 | .083 | .083 |
| Oct | .044 | .046 | .050 | .052 | .051 | .054 | .060 | .054 | .066 | .069 | .074 | .079 | .081 | .083 | .083 |
| Nov | .044 | .045 | .049 | .051 | .050 | .053 | .060 | .053 | .065 | .068 | .073 | .078 | .080 | .083 | .082 |
| Dec | .042 | .043 | .047 | .049 | .048 | .051 | .057 | .051 | .063 | .066 | .071 | .076 | .078 | .080 | .080 |

MONTH OF DISPOSAL

| | 2015 | | | | | | | | | | 2016 | | | | |
|---|---|---|---|---|---|---|---|---|---|---|---|---|---|---|---|
| **2014** | Mar | Apr | May | June | July | Aug | Sep | Oct | Nov | Dec | Jan | Feb | Mar | Apr | May |
| Jan | .018 | .021 | .023 | .025 | .024 | .029 | .028 | .027 | .029 | .032 | .025 | .029 | .034 | .035 | .038 |
| Feb | .011 | .015 | .017 | .018 | .017 | .022 | .021 | .021 | .022 | .025 | .018 | .023 | .027 | .028 | .031 |
| Mar | .009 | .013 | .015 | .016 | .015 | .020 | .019 | .018 | .020 | .023 | .016 | .020 | .025 | .026 | .029 |
| Apr | .005 | .009 | .011 | .013 | .011 | .016 | .015 | .015 | .016 | .019 | .012 | .017 | .021 | .022 | .025 |
| May | .005 | .008 | .010 | .012 | .011 | .015 | .014 | .014 | .015 | .018 | .011 | .016 | .020 | .021 | .024 |
| June | .003 | .007 | .009 | .010 | .010 | .014 | .013 | .012 | .014 | .017 | .010 | .014 | .019 | .020 | .023 |
| July | .004 | .008 | .010 | .011 | .010 | .015 | .014 | .014 | .015 | .018 | .011 | .016 | .020 | .021 | .024 |
| Aug | .000 | .004 | .006 | .007 | .006 | .011 | .010 | .010 | .011 | .014 | .007 | .012 | .016 | .017 | .020 |
| Sep | .000 | .002 | .003 | .005 | .004 | .009 | .008 | .007 | .009 | .012 | .005 | .009 | .014 | .015 | .017 |
| Oct | .000 | .001 | .003 | .005 | .003 | .008 | .007 | .007 | .008 | .011 | .004 | .009 | .013 | .014 | .017 |
| Nov | .000 | .004 | .005 | .007 | .006 | .011 | .010 | .009 | .011 | .014 | .007 | .011 | .016 | .017 | .019 |
| Dec | .000 | .002 | .004 | .005 | .004 | .009 | .008 | .008 | .009 | .012 | .005 | .010 | .014 | .015 | .018 |
| **2015** | Mar | Apr | May | June | July | Aug | Sep | Oct | Nov | Dec | Jan | Feb | Mar | Apr | May |
| Jan | .007 | .010 | .012 | .014 | .013 | .017 | .016 | .016 | .017 | .020 | .013 | .018 | .022 | .023 | .026 |
| Feb | .002 | .005 | .007 | .009 | .007 | .012 | .011 | .011 | .012 | .015 | .008 | .013 | .017 | .018 | .021 |
| Mar | — | .004 | .005 | .007 | .006 | .011 | .010 | .009 | .011 | .014 | .007 | .011 | .016 | .017 | .019 |
| Apr | — | — | .002 | .003 | .002 | .007 | .006 | .006 | .007 | .010 | .003 | .008 | .012 | .013 | .016 |
| May | — | — | — | .002 | .000 | .005 | .004 | .004 | .005 | .008 | .001 | .006 | .010 | .011 | .014 |
| June | — | — | — | — | .000 | .003 | .003 | .002 | .003 | .007 | .000 | .004 | .008 | .010 | .012 |
| July | — | — | — | — | — | .005 | .004 | .003 | .005 | .008 | .001 | .005 | .010 | .011 | .014 |
| Aug | — | — | — | — | — | — | .000 | .000 | .000 | .003 | .000 | .001 | .005 | .006 | .009 |
| Sep | — | — | — | — | — | — | — | .000 | .001 | .004 | .000 | .002 | .006 | .007 | .010 |
| Oct | — | — | — | — | — | — | — | — | .001 | .004 | .000 | .002 | .006 | .007 | .010 |
| Nov | — | — | — | — | — | — | — | — | — | .003 | .000 | .001 | .005 | .006 | .009 |
| Dec | — | — | — | — | — | — | — | — | — | — | .000 | .000 | .002 | .003 | .006 |
| **2016** | Mar | Apr | May | June | July | Aug | Sep | Oct | Nov | Dec | Jan | Feb | Mar | Apr | May |
| Jan | — | — | — | — | — | — | — | — | — | — | — | .005 | .009 | .010 | .013 |
| Feb | — | — | — | — | — | — | — | — | — | — | — | — | .004 | .005 | .008 |
| Mar | — | — | — | — | — | — | — | — | — | — | — | — | — | .001 | .004 |
| Apr | — | — | — | — | — | — | — | — | — | — | — | — | — | — | .003 |
| May | — | — | — | — | — | — | — | — | — | — | — | — | — | — | — |
| June | — | — | — | — | — | — | — | — | — | — | — | — | — | — | — |
| July | — | — | — | — | — | — | — | — | — | — | — | — | — | — | — |
| Aug | — | — | — | — | — | — | — | — | — | — | — | — | — | — | — |
| Sep | — | — | — | — | — | — | — | — | — | — | — | — | — | — | — |
| Oct | — | — | — | — | — | — | — | — | — | — | — | — | — | — | — |
| Nov | — | — | — | — | — | — | — | — | — | — | — | — | — | — | — |
| Dec | — | — | — | — | — | — | — | — | — | — | — | — | — | — | — |
| **2017** | Mar | Apr | May | June | July | Aug | Sep | Oct | Nov | Dec | Jan | Feb | Mar | Apr | May |
| Jan | — | — | — | — | — | — | — | — | — | — | — | — | — | — | — |
| Feb | — | — | — | — | — | — | — | — | — | — | — | — | — | — | — |
| Mar | — | — | — | — | — | — | — | — | — | — | — | — | — | — | — |
| Apr | — | — | — | — | — | — | — | — | — | — | — | — | — | — | — |
| May | — | — | — | — | — | — | — | — | — | — | — | — | — | — | — |
| June | — | — | — | — | — | — | — | — | — | — | — | — | — | — | — |
| July | — | — | — | — | — | — | — | — | — | — | — | — | — | — | — |
| Aug | — | — | — | — | — | — | — | — | — | — | — | — | — | — | — |

MONTH OF DISPOSAL

| | **2016** | | | | | | | **2017** | | | | | | | |
|---|---|---|---|---|---|---|---|---|---|---|---|---|---|---|---|
| **2014** | June | July | Aug | Sep | Oct | Nov | Dec | Jan | Feb | Mar | Apr | May | June | July | Aug |
| Jan | .042 | .043 | .047 | .049 | .048 | .051 | .057 | .051 | .063 | .066 | .071 | .076 | .078 | .080 | .080 |
| Feb | .035 | .036 | .040 | .042 | .042 | .044 | .051 | .044 | .056 | .059 | .065 | .069 | .071 | .074 | .073 |
| Mar | .033 | .034 | .038 | .040 | .039 | .042 | .048 | .042 | .053 | .057 | .062 | .066 | .069 | .071 | .070 |
| Apr | .029 | .030 | .034 | .036 | .036 | .038 | .045 | .038 | .050 | .053 | .058 | .063 | .065 | .067 | .066 |
| May | .028 | .029 | .033 | .035 | .035 | .038 | .044 | .038 | .049 | .052 | .057 | .062 | .064 | .066 | .066 |
| June | .027 | .028 | .032 | .034 | .033 | .036 | .042 | .036 | .047 | .051 | .056 | .060 | .062 | .065 | .064 |
| July | .028 | .029 | .033 | .035 | .034 | .037 | .043 | .037 | .048 | .052 | .057 | .061 | .064 | .066 | .065 |
| Aug | .024 | .025 | .029 | .031 | .030 | .033 | .039 | .033 | .044 | .048 | .053 | .057 | .060 | .062 | .061 |
| Sep | .021 | .023 | .026 | .028 | .028 | .031 | .037 | .031 | .042 | .045 | .050 | .055 | .057 | .059 | .059 |
| Oct | .021 | .022 | .026 | .028 | .028 | .030 | .036 | .030 | .042 | .045 | .050 | .054 | .057 | .059 | .058 |
| Nov | .023 | .025 | .028 | .030 | .030 | .033 | .039 | .033 | .044 | .047 | .053 | .057 | .059 | .061 | .061 |
| Dec | .022 | .023 | .027 | .029 | .028 | .031 | .037 | .031 | .042 | .046 | .051 | .055 | .057 | .060 | .059 |
| **2015** | June | July | Aug | Sep | Oct | Nov | Dec | Jan | Feb | Mar | Apr | May | June | July | Aug |
| Jan | .030 | .031 | .035 | .037 | .037 | .040 | .046 | .040 | .051 | .054 | .060 | .064 | .066 | .069 | .068 |
| Feb | .025 | .026 | .030 | .032 | .032 | .034 | .041 | .034 | .046 | .049 | .054 | .058 | .061 | .063 | .062 |
| Mar | .023 | .025 | .028 | .030 | .030 | .033 | .039 | .033 | .044 | .047 | .053 | .057 | .059 | .061 | .061 |
| Apr | .020 | .021 | .025 | .027 | .026 | .029 | .035 | .029 | .040 | .044 | .049 | .053 | .055 | .058 | .057 |
| May | .018 | .019 | .023 | .025 | .024 | .027 | .033 | .027 | .038 | .042 | .047 | .051 | .053 | .056 | .055 |
| June | .016 | .017 | .021 | .023 | .023 | .025 | .032 | .025 | .037 | .040 | .045 | .049 | .052 | .054 | .053 |
| July | .017 | .019 | .022 | .024 | .024 | .027 | .033 | .027 | .038 | .041 | .046 | .051 | .053 | .055 | .055 |
| Aug | .013 | .014 | .018 | .020 | .019 | .022 | .028 | .022 | .033 | .037 | .042 | .046 | .048 | .050 | .050 |
| Sep | .013 | .015 | .018 | .020 | .020 | .023 | .029 | .023 | .034 | .037 | .042 | .047 | .049 | .051 | .050 |
| Oct | .014 | .015 | .019 | .021 | .020 | .023 | .029 | .023 | .034 | .038 | .043 | .047 | .049 | .052 | .051 |
| Nov | .013 | .014 | .018 | .020 | .019 | .022 | .028 | .022 | .033 | .037 | .042 | .046 | .048 | .050 | .050 |
| Dec | .010 | .011 | .015 | .017 | .016 | .019 | .025 | .019 | .030 | .033 | .038 | .043 | .045 | .047 | .046 |
| **2016** | June | July | Aug | Sep | Oct | Nov | Dec | Jan | Feb | Mar | Apr | May | June | July | Aug |
| Jan | .017 | .018 | .022 | .024 | .023 | .026 | .032 | .026 | .037 | .041 | .046 | .050 | .052 | .054 | .054 |
| Feb | .012 | .013 | .017 | .019 | .018 | .021 | .027 | .021 | .032 | .036 | .041 | .045 | .047 | .050 | .049 |
| Mar | .008 | .009 | .013 | .015 | .014 | .017 | .023 | .017 | .028 | .031 | .036 | .041 | .043 | .045 | .044 |
| Apr | .007 | .008 | .011 | .013 | .013 | .016 | .022 | .016 | .027 | .030 | .035 | .039 | .042 | .044 | .043 |
| May | .004 | .005 | .009 | .011 | .010 | .013 | .019 | .013 | .024 | .027 | .032 | .037 | .039 | .041 | .040 |
| June | — | .001 | .005 | .007 | .006 | .009 | .015 | .009 | .020 | .024 | .029 | .033 | .035 | .037 | .036 |
| July | — | — | .004 | .006 | .005 | .008 | .014 | .008 | .019 | .022 | .027 | .032 | .034 | .036 | .035 |
| Aug | — | — | — | .002 | .002 | .004 | .010 | .004 | .015 | .019 | .023 | .028 | .030 | .032 | .031 |
| Sep | — | — | — | — | .000 | .002 | .008 | .002 | .013 | .017 | .022 | .026 | .028 | .030 | .029 |
| Oct | — | — | — | — | — | .003 | .009 | .003 | .014 | .017 | .022 | .026 | .028 | .031 | .030 |
| Nov | — | — | — | — | — | — | .006 | .000 | .011 | .014 | .019 | .023 | .026 | .028 | .027 |
| Dec | — | — | — | — | — | — | — | .000 | .005 | .008 | .013 | .017 | .019 | .022 | .021 |
| **2017** | June | July | Aug | Sep | Oct | Nov | Dec | Jan | Feb | Mar | Apr | May | June | July | Aug |
| Jan | — | — | — | — | — | — | — | — | .011 | .014 | .019 | .023 | .026 | .028 | .027 |
| Feb | — | — | — | — | — | — | — | — | — | .003 | .008 | .012 | .015 | .017 | .016 |
| Mar | — | — | — | — | — | — | — | — | — | — | .005 | .009 | .011 | .013 | .013 |
| Apr | — | — | — | — | — | — | — | — | — | — | — | .004 | .006 | .008 | .008 |
| May | — | — | — | — | — | — | — | — | — | — | — | — | .002 | .004 | .004 |
| June | — | — | — | — | — | — | — | — | — | — | — | — | — | .002 | .001 |
| July | — | — | — | — | — | — | — | — | — | — | — | — | — | — | .000 |
| Aug | — | — | — | — | — | — | — | — | — | — | — | — | — | — | — |

# Retail prices index

| | Jan | Feb | Mar | Apr | May | Jun |
|---|---|---|---|---|---|---|
| **1982** | 78.73 | 78.76 | 79.44 | 81.04 | 81.62 | 81.85 |
| **1983** | 82.61 | 82.97 | 83.12 | 84.28 | 84.64 | 84.84 |
| **1984** | 86.84 | 87.20 | 87.48 | 88.64 | 88.97 | 89.20 |
| **1985** | 91.20 | 91.94 | 92.80 | 94.78 | 95.21 | 95.41 |
| **1986** | 96.25 | 96.60 | 96.73 | 97.67 | 97.85 | 97.79 |
| **1987** | 100.00 | 100.40 | 100.60 | 101.80 | 101.90 | 101.90 |
| **1988** | 103.30 | 103.70 | 104.10 | 105.80 | 106.20 | 106.60 |
| **1989** | 111.00 | 111.80 | 112.30 | 114.30 | 115.00 | 115.40 |
| **1990** | 119.50 | 120.20 | 121.40 | 125.10 | 126.20 | 126.70 |
| **1991** | 130.20 | 130.90 | 131.40 | 133.10 | 133.50 | 134.10 |
| **1992** | 135.60 | 136.30 | 136.70 | 138.80 | 139.30 | 139.30 |
| **1993** | 137.90 | 138.80 | 139.30 | 140.60 | 141.10 | 141.00 |
| **1994** | 141.30 | 142.10 | 142.50 | 144.20 | 144.70 | 144.70 |
| **1995** | 146.00 | 146.90 | 147.50 | 149.00 | 149.60 | 149.80 |
| **1996** | 150.20 | 150.90 | 151.50 | 152.60 | 152.90 | 153.00 |
| **1997** | 154.40 | 155.00 | 155.40 | 156.30 | 156.90 | 157.50 |
| **1998** | 159.50 | 160.30 | 160.80 | 162.60 | 163.50 | 163.40 |
| **1999** | 163.40 | 163.70 | 164.10 | 165.20 | 165.60 | 165.60 |
| **2000** | 166.60 | 167.50 | 168.40 | 170.10 | 170.70 | 171.10 |
| **2001** | 171.10 | 172.00 | 172.20 | 173.10 | 174.20 | 174.40 |
| **2002** | 173.30 | 173.80 | 174.50 | 175.70 | 176.20 | 176.20 |
| **2003** | 178.40 | 179.30 | 179.90 | 181.20 | 181.50 | 181.30 |
| **2004** | 183.10 | 183.80 | 184.60 | 185.70 | 186.50 | 186.80 |
| **2005** | 188.90 | 189.60 | 190.50 | 191.60 | 192.00 | 192.20 |
| **2006** | 193.40 | 194.20 | 195.00 | 196.50 | 197.70 | 198.50 |
| **2007** | 201.60 | 203.10 | 204.40 | 205.40 | 206.20 | 207.30 |
| **2008** | 209.80 | 211.40 | 212.10 | 214.00 | 215.10 | 216.80 |
| **2009** | 210.10 | 211.40 | 211.30 | 211.50 | 212.80 | 213.40 |
| **2010** | 218.00 | 219.20 | 220.70 | 222.80 | 223.60 | 224.10 |
| **2011** | 229.00 | 231.30 | 232.50 | 234.40 | 235.20 | 235.20 |
| **2012** | 238.00 | 239.90 | 240.80 | 242.50 | 242.40 | 241.80 |
| **2013** | 245.80 | 247.60 | 248.70 | 249.50 | 250.00 | 249.70 |
| **2014** | 252.60 | 254.20 | 254.80 | 255.70 | 255.90 | 256.30 |
| **2015** | 255.40 | 256.70 | 257.10 | 258.00 | 258.50 | 258.90 |
| **2016** | 258.80 | 260.00 | 261.10 | 261.40 | 262.10 | 263.10 |
| **2017** | 265.50 | 268.40 | 269.30 | 270.60 | 271.70 | 272.30 |

## Retail prices index, cont.

| | Jul | Aug | Sep | Oct | Nov | Dec |
|---|---|---|---|---|---|---|
| **1982** | 81.88 | 81.90 | 81.85 | 82.26 | 82.66 | 82.51 |
| **1983** | 85.30 | 85.68 | 86.06 | 86.36 | 86.67 | 86.89 |
| **1984** | 89.10 | 89.94 | 90.11 | 90.67 | 90.95 | 90.87 |
| **1985** | 95.23 | 95.49 | 95.44 | 95.59 | 95.92 | 96.05 |
| **1986** | 97.52 | 97.82 | 98.30 | 98.45 | 99.29 | 99.62 |
| **1987** | 101.80 | 102.10 | 102.40 | 102.90 | 103.40 | 103.30 |
| **1988** | 106.70 | 107.90 | 108.40 | 109.50 | 110.00 | 110.30 |
| **1989** | 115.50 | 115.80 | 116.60 | 117.50 | 118.50 | 118.80 |
| **1990** | 126.80 | 128.10 | 129.30 | 130.30 | 130.00 | 129.90 |
| **1991** | 133.80 | 134.10 | 134.60 | 135.10 | 135.60 | 135.70 |
| **1992** | 138.80 | 138.90 | 139.40 | 139.90 | 139.70 | 139.20 |
| **1993** | 140.70 | 141.30 | 141.90 | 141.80 | 141.60 | 141.90 |
| **1994** | 144.00 | 144.70 | 145.00 | 145.20 | 145.30 | 146.00 |
| **1995** | 149.10 | 149.90 | 150.60 | 149.80 | 149.80 | 150.70 |
| **1996** | 152.40 | 153.10 | 153.80 | 153.80 | 153.90 | 154.40 |
| **1997** | 157.50 | 158.50 | 159.30 | 159.50 | 159.60 | 160.00 |
| **1998** | 163.00 | 163.70 | 164.40 | 164.50 | 164.40 | 164.40 |
| **1999** | 165.10 | 165.50 | 166.20 | 166.50 | 166.70 | 167.30 |
| **2000** | 170.50 | 170.50 | 171.70 | 171.60 | 172.10 | 172.20 |
| **2001** | 173.30 | 174.00 | 174.60 | 174.30 | 173.60 | 173.40 |
| **2002** | 175.90 | 176.40 | 177.60 | 177.90 | 178.20 | 178.50 |
| **2003** | 181.30 | 181.60 | 182.50 | 182.60 | 182.70 | 183.50 |
| **2004** | 186.80 | 187.40 | 188.10 | 188.60 | 189.00 | 189.90 |
| **2005** | 192.20 | 192.60 | 193.10 | 193.30 | 193.60 | 194.10 |
| **2006** | 198.50 | 199.20 | 200.10 | 200.40 | 201.10 | 202.70 |
| **2007** | 206.10 | 207.30 | 208.00 | 208.90 | 209.70 | 210.90 |
| **2008** | 216.50 | 217.20 | 218.40 | 217.70 | 216.00 | 212.90 |
| **2009** | 213.40 | 214.40 | 215.30 | 216.00 | 216.60 | 218.00 |
| **2010** | 223.60 | 224.50 | 225.30 | 225.80 | 226.80 | 228.40 |
| **2011** | 234.70 | 236.10 | 237.90 | 238.00 | 238.50 | 239.40 |
| **2012** | 242.10 | 243.00 | 244.20 | 245.60 | 245.60 | 246.80 |
| **2013** | 249.70 | 251.00 | 251.90 | 251.90 | 252.10 | 253.40 |
| **2014** | 256.00 | 257.00 | 257.60 | 257.70 | 257.10 | 257.50 |
| **2015** | 258.60 | 259.80 | 259.60 | 259.50 | 259.80 | 260.60 |
| **2016** | 263.40 | 264.40 | 264.90 | 264.80 | 265.50 | 267.10 |
| **2017** | 272.90 | 274.70 | | | | |

# Leases

**Depreciation table** (TCGA 1992 Sch 8 para 1)

| *Yrs* | *%* | *Yrs* | *%* | *Yrs* | *%* | *Yrs* | *%* |
|---|---|---|---|---|---|---|---|
| 50 (or more) | 100 | 37 | 93.497 | 24 | 79.622 | 11 | 50.038 |
| 49 | 99.657 | 36 | 92.761 | 23 | 78.055 | 10 | 46.695 |
| 48 | 99.289 | 35 | 91.981 | 22 | 76.399 | 9 | 43.154 |
| 47 | 98.902 | 34 | 91.156 | 21 | 74.635 | 8 | 39.399 |
| 46 | 98.490 | 33 | 90.280 | 20 | 72.770 | 7 | 35.414 |
| 45 | 98.059 | 32 | 89.354 | 19 | 70.791 | 6 | 31.195 |
| 44 | 97.595 | 31 | 88.371 | 18 | 68.697 | 5 | 26.722 |
| 43 | 97.107 | 30 | 87.330 | 17 | 66.470 | 4 | 21.983 |
| 42 | 96.593 | 29 | 86.226 | 16 | 64.116 | 3 | 16.959 |
| 41 | 96.041 | 28 | 85.053 | 15 | 61.617 | 2 | 11.629 |
| 40 | 95.457 | 27 | 83.816 | 14 | 58.971 | 1 | 5.983 |
| 39 | 94.842 | 26 | 82.496 | 13 | 56.167 | 0 | 0 |
| 38 | 94.189 | 25 | 81.100 | 12 | 53.191 | | |

**Formula:** Fraction of expenditure disallowed—

$$\frac{AE - D}{AE}$$

Where:

AE is the percentage for duration of lease at acquisition or expenditure; and
D is the percentage for duration of lease at disposal.

**Fractions of years:** Add one-twelfth of the difference between the percentage for the whole year and the next higher percentage for each additional month. Odd days under 14 are not counted; 14 odd days or more count as a month.

**Short leases: premiums treated as rent** (TCGA 1992 Sch 8 para 5; ITTOIA 2005 ss 277–281A; CTA 2009 s 217–221A) Part of premium for grant of a short lease which is chargeable to income tax as property income:

$$P - (2\% \times (n - 1) \times P)$$

Where:

P is the amount of premium;
n is the number of complete years which lease has to run when granted.

| *Length of lease (complete years)* | *Amount chargeable to CGT %* | *Income tax charge %* | *Length of lease (complete years)* | *Amount chargeable to CGT %* | *Income tax charge %* | *Length of lease (complete years)* | *Amount chargeable to CGT %* | *Income tax charge %* |
|---|---|---|---|---|---|---|---|---|
| Over 50 | 100 | 0 | 34 | 66 | 34 | 17 | 32 | 68 |
| 50 | 98 | 2 | 33 | 64 | 36 | 16 | 30 | 70 |
| 49 | 96 | 4 | 32 | 62 | 38 | 15 | 28 | 72 |
| 48 | 94 | 6 | 31 | 60 | 40 | 14 | 26 | 74 |
| 47 | 92 | 8 | 30 | 58 | 42 | 13 | 24 | 76 |
| 46 | 90 | 10 | 29 | 56 | 44 | 12 | 22 | 78 |
| 45 | 88 | 12 | 28 | 54 | 46 | 11 | 20 | 80 |
| 44 | 86 | 14 | 27 | 52 | 48 | 10 | 18 | 82 |
| 43 | 84 | 16 | 26 | 50 | 50 | 9 | 16 | 84 |
| 42 | 82 | 18 | 25 | 48 | 52 | 8 | 14 | 86 |
| 41 | 80 | 20 | 24 | 46 | 54 | 7 | 12 | 88 |
| 40 | 78 | 22 | 23 | 44 | 56 | 6 | 10 | 90 |
| 39 | 76 | 24 | 22 | 42 | 58 | 5 | 8 | 92 |
| 38 | 74 | 26 | 21 | 40 | 60 | 4 | 6 | 94 |
| 37 | 72 | 28 | 20 | 38 | 62 | 3 | 4 | 96 |
| 36 | 70 | 30 | 19 | 36 | 64 | 2 | 2 | 98 |
| 35 | 68 | 32 | 18 | 34 | 66 | 1 or less | 0 | 100 |

# Corporation tax

## Rates for non-ring fence profits

(CTA 2010 ss 3, 18–34; FA 2015 s 6; F(No 2)A 2015 s 7)

| *Financial year* | **2012** | **2013** | **2014** | **2015** | **2016** | **2017** |
|---|---|---|---|---|---|---|
| Main rate | 24% | 23% | 21% | 20%[2] | 20%[2] | **19%**[2] |
| Small profits rate | 20% | 20% | 20% | N/A | N/A | **N/A** |
| lower limit[1] | £300,000 | £300,000 | £300,000 | N/A | N/A | **N/A** |
| upper limit[1] | £1.5m | £1.5m | £1.5m | N/A | N/A | **N/A** |
| marginal relief fraction | 1/100 | 3/400 | 1/400 | N/A | N/A | **N/A** |
| effective marginal rate | 25% | 23.75% | 21.25% | N/A | N/A | **N/A** |
| Tax credit: from 6 April | 10% | 10% | 10% | 10% | N/A[5] | **N/A**[5] |

1 Reduced proportionally for accounting periods of less than 12 months. For financial years before 2015 the limits are divided by the number of associated companies (including the company in question).

2 For financial year 2015 onwards there is one main rate and no small profits rate.

3 For financial years 2018 to 2019 the main rate will be 19%. For financial year 2020 it will be 17%.

4 The power to set the rate of corporation tax in Northern Ireland has been devolved to the Northern Ireland Assembly in relation to such financial year as HM Treasury may appoint. The Northern Ireland Executive has committed to setting a rate of 12.5% in April 2018.

5 Tax credits are abolished from 6 April 2016.

### Marginal relief before 1 April 2015

The small profits rate applies to taxable total profits where augmented profits (see below) do not exceed the lower limit. Where a company's profits exceed the lower limit but do not exceed the upper limit, the charge to corporation tax on the company's taxable total profits is reduced by an amount calculated in accordance with a statutory formula—

$$F \times (U - A) \times \frac{N}{A}$$

where—

F is the marginal relief fraction;
U is the upper limit;
N is the amount of the taxable total profits;
A is the amount of the augmented profits—its adjusted taxable total profits plus franked investment income (other than from UK companies in the same group or owned by a consortium of which the recipient is a member). A company's adjusted taxable total profits are its profits chargeable to corporation tax as if no part of its chargeable gains and allowable losses for the period were liable to capital gains tax (ie on disposals of certain high value UK property, see p 65) instead of to corporation tax.

**Bank levy** see p 66. **Patent box** see p 64. **Diverted profits tax** see p 66. **Bank corporation tax surcharge** see p 66. **Tax charge on restitution interest** see p 66.

## Rates for ring fence profits

(CTA 2010 ss 279A–279H)

| *Financial year* | **2012** | **2013** | **2014** | **2015** | **2016** | **2017** |
|---|---|---|---|---|---|---|
| Main rate | 30% | 30% | 30% | 30% | 30% | **30%** |
| Small profits rate | 19% | 19% | 19% | 19% | 19% | **19%** |
| lower limit[1] | £300,000 | £300,000 | £300,000 | £300,000 | £300,000 | **£300,000** |
| upper limit[1] | £1.5m | £1.5m | £1.5m | £1.5m | £1.5m | **£1.5m** |
| marginal relief fraction | 11/400 | 11/400 | 11/400 | 11/400 | 11/400 | **11/400** |

1 Reduced proportionally for accounting periods of less than 12 months. The limits are divided by the number of related 51% group companies (before 1 April 2015, number of associated companies), including the company in question.

### Marginal relief

**From 1 April 2015** Applies to ring fence profits only. The small ring fence profits rate applies to taxable total profits where augmented profits (see below) do not exceed the lower limit. Where a company's ring fence profits exceed the lower limit but do not exceed the upper limit, the charge to corporation tax on the company's taxable total profits is reduced by an amount calculated in accordance with a statutory formula—

$$R \times (U - A) \times \frac{N}{A}$$

where—

R is the marginal relief fraction;

U is the upper limit;

N is the amount of the taxable total profits;

A is the amount of the augmented profits—its adjusted taxable total profits plus exempt ABGH distributions (before 6 April 2016, franked investment income) (other than from UK companies in the same group or owned by a consortium of which the recipient is a member). A company's adjusted taxable total profits are its profits chargeable to corporation tax as if no part of its chargeable gains and allowable losses for the period were liable to capital gains tax (ie on disposals of certain high value UK property, see p 65) instead of to corporation tax.

# Reliefs

## Disincorporation relief

(FA 2013 ss 58–61)

With effect for disincorporations between 1 April 2013 and 31 March 2018 inclusive, joint claims may be made by a company and its shareholders to allow goodwill or interests in land not held as trading stock to be transferred at a reduced value so that no corporation tax will be payable by the company on the transfer. Relief is restricted to cases where the market value of the assets allowed for disincorporation relief does not exceed £100,000. Joint claims must be made to HMRC within two years of the date of the transfer and other eligibility criteria also apply. Shareholders to whom the assets are transferred will inherit the transfer value for the purpose of capital gains tax.

## Gifts of pre-eminent objects

(FA 2012 Sch 14)

Companies which gift pre-eminent objects to the nation will receive a reduction in their UK tax liability of 20% of the value of the object they are donating. The legislation has effect in relation to liabilities for tax years and accounting periods beginning on or after 1 April 2012. The gift must be accepted as pre-eminent by the Arts Council under the Cultural Gifts Scheme.

## Patent box

(CTA 2010 Pt 8A)

The patent box allows companies to elect to apply a 10% corporation tax rate to a proportion of profits attributable to qualifying patents, whether paid separately as royalties or embedded in the sales price of products, and to certain other qualifying intellectual property rights such as regulatory data protection (also called 'data exclusivity'), supplementary protection certificates and plant variety rights from 1 April 2013. In the first year the proportion of profits qualifying for the 10% rate was 60% and this was increased annually to 100% from April 2017. Thus, for financial year 2014 the proportion was 70%, for 2015 it was 80%, and for 2016 it was 90%.

## Real Estate Investment Trusts (REITs)

(CTA 2010 ss 518–609)

From 1 January 2007, qualifying rental income from and gains on disposals of investment properties by UK companies within the REIT scheme are exempt from corporation tax.

## Research and development

(CTA 2009 ss 1039–1142; F(No 2)A 2015 s 31)

### *Deduction scheme*

An '**SME**' incurring R&D expenditure (of at least £10,000 for accounting periods ending before 1 April 2012, though this minimum expenditure requirement is now removed) in a 12-month accounting period can obtain relief for 230% (applying from 1 April 2015) of that expenditure (225% for expenditure incurred between 1 April 2012 and 31 March 2015; 200% for expenditure incurred between 1 April 2011 and 1 April 2012; 175% for expenditure incurred between 1 August 2008 and 1 April 2011). **SMEs** not yet in profit or which have not yet started to trade can claim relief upfront as a cash payment (R&D tax credit).

An '**SME**' can also claim relief where it incurs expenditure on work contracted to it by a large company or by any person otherwise than in the course of carrying on a chargeable trade; or expenditure which is subsidised; or expenditure subject to the project limit (€7.5m for expenditure incurred after 31 July 2008). The relief is 130% of the expenditure. The minimum expenditure rules above applied for accounting periods ending before 1 April 2012.

An '**SME**' is a company with less than 500 employees and either annual turnover of €100m or less or annual balance sheet total of €86m or less.

**Large companies** can claim a similar relief to that for SMEs above, including tax credits, for expenditure incurred before 1 April 2017 on certain vaccines research. The relief was previously also available to SMEs but was withdrawn for them from April 2012.

Before 1 April 2016 **large companies** incurring R&D expenditure (of at least £10,000 for accounting periods ending before 1 April 2012) could obtain relief for 130% of that expenditure. From that date they must use the 'Above the line' credit scheme outlined below.

### *'Above the line' credit scheme for large companies*

This scheme applies from 1 April 2013. Large companies (and certain SMEs with sub-contracted or subsidised R&D, or R&D subject to the project limit) can claim R&D relief as a taxable above the line (ATL) credit to the value of 11% (10% before 1 April 2015) of their qualifying R&D expenditure (49% for ring fence trades). The credit is fully payable, net of tax, to companies with no corporation tax liability. The scheme was initially optional. Companies that did not elect to claim the ATL credit could continue claiming R&D relief under the large company deduction scheme (see above) until 31 March 2016. The ATL credit became mandatory for such companies on 1 April 2016. Universities and charities are unable to claim the credit for expenditure incurred on or after 1 August 2015.

## Annual tax on enveloped dwellings

(FA 2013 ss 94–174, Schs 33–35)

From 1 April 2013 a charge is imposed on certain non-natural persons (NNPs), ie companies, partnerships with at least one company member, and collective investment schemes which hold UK residential dwellings valued above a certain limit on specified valuation dates. The limit was set at £2 million from 1 April 2013, but lowered to £1 million from 1 April 2015, and £500,000 from 1 April 2016. Returns and payment are generally due by 30 April[2] each year. If the payer is not chargeable for the full year, a later repayment claim can be made. Various reliefs from the charge apply and from 1 April 2015 companies may be able to submit relief declaration returns. **A charge to capital gains tax** at 28% also applies to the disposal of such properties, whether by UK resident or non-resident NNPs. See also p 137 regarding the 15% **stamp duty land tax** which can apply to acquisitions of such properties.

Annual tax charge

| **Property value**[1] | **Annual tax 2013–14** | **Annual tax 2014–15** | **Annual tax 2015–16** | **Annual tax 2016–17** | **Annual tax 2017–18** |
|---|---|---|---|---|---|
| More than £500,000 to £1 million | N/A | N/A | N/A | £3,500 | **£3,500** |
| More than £1 million to £2 million | N/A | N/A | £7,000 | £7,000 | **£7,050** |
| More than £2 million to £5 million | £15,000 | £15,400 | £23,350 | £23,350 | **£23,550** |
| More than £5 million to £10 million | £35,000 | £35,900 | £54,450 | £54,450 | **£54,950** |
| More than £10 million to £20 million | £70,000 | £71,850 | £109,050 | £109,050 | **£110,100** |
| More than £20 million | £140,000 | £143,750 | £218,200 | £218,200 | **£220,350** |

1 The valuation is the market value on the last previous valuation date. The first valuation date is 1 April 2012 and then every five years thereafter. Other valuation dates can apply in certain circumstances, for example when a new property is purchased. The valuation is applied on the first day of the chargeable period if the chargeable person is within the charge on that day, otherwise the first day in the chargeable period on which they are first within the charge.

2 Returns applicable to the band applying from 1 April 2015 to residential properties worth more than £1 million and not more than £2 million were not required until 1 October 2015 with payment required by 31 October 2015.

Relief codes for relief declaration returns

| | *Code for type of relief* |
|---|---|
| Property rental business | 1 |
| Dwellings open to the public | 2 |
| Property developers | 3 |
| Property traders | 4 |
| Financial institutions acquiring dwellings | 5 |
| Regulated home reversion plans | 5A |
| Occupation by certain employees etc | 6 |
| Farmhouses | 7 |
| Providers of social housing | 8 |

# Bank corporation tax surcharge

(CTA 2010 ss 269D–269DO)

From 1 January 2016 a surcharge of 8% is levied on profits of banking companies and building societies.

# Bank levy

(FA 2011 Sch 19 para 6)

From 1 January 2011 a bank levy is charged based on the total chargeable equity and liabilities reported in the relevant balance sheets of affected banks, banking and building society groups at the end of the chargeable period. It is payable through the existing corporation tax self-assessment system. It is not charged on the first £20 billion of chargeable liabilities.

| | 1.1.13 – 31.12.13 | 1.1.14– 31.3.15 | 1.4.15– 31.12.15 | 1.1.16– 31.12.16 | **1.1.17– 31.12.17** | **1.1.18– 31.12.18** |
|---|---|---|---|---|---|---|
| Short-term chargeable liabilities | 0.130% | 0.156% | 0.21% | 0.18% | **0.17%** | **0.16%** |
| Long-term chargeable equity and liabilities | 0.065% | 0.078% | 0.105% | 0.09% | **0.085%** | **0.08%** |

# Diverted profits tax

(FA 2015 ss 77–116)

From 1 April 2015 a diverted profits tax of 25% applies to counter the use of aggressive tax planning techniques by multinational enterprises to divert profits from the UK. There are two basic rules which apply. The first rule counteracts arrangements by which foreign companies exploit the permanent establishment rules, and comes into effect if a person is carrying on activity in the UK in connection with supplies of goods and services by a non-UK resident company to customers in the UK, provided that the detailed conditions are met. The second rule applies to certain arrangements which lack economic substance involving entities with an existing UK taxable presence.

# Loans to participators

(CTA 2010 s 455)

A charge of 32.5% of the loan made or benefit conferred applies (25% for loans made and benefits conferred before 6 April 2016).

# Tax charge on restitution interest

(CTA 2010 ss 357YA–357YW)

Where tax has been overpaid by a company as a result of a mistake in law or following unlawful collection of tax by HMRC a restitution award may be made. Where the award is made as a result of a judgment or an agreement between the parties which became final on or after 21 October 2015, the interest element of the award, whether arising before, on or after 21 October 2015, is chargeable to corporation tax at a special rate of 45%.

# Environmental taxes and other levies

## Aggregates levy

(FA 2001 ss 16–49, Schs 4–10; SI 2004/1959; SI 2010/2598)

Levy on commercial exploitation of aggregates including rock, gravel or sand together with any other substance incorporated or naturally occurring with it. Applies to all aggregate (not recycled) extracted in the UK or territorial waters unless exempt. Before 1 April 2014 exemptions applied to quarried or mined products such as clay, shale, slate, metal and metal ores, gemstones, semi-precious gemstones and industrial minerals. From 1 April 2014, the Government had to suspend these exemptions, exclusions and reliefs as they were the subject of a State aid investigation by the European Commission. Following conclusion of the investigation, all the exemptions except that for shale were reinstated on 1 August 2015 with retrospective effect from 1 April 2014. There is an exempt process for shale which is not used as aggregate for construction purposes which applies from 1 April 2014. This enables a person who has commercially exploited and accounted for the levy chargeable on such shale to claim a tax credit for it, when it is used in this new exempt process (HMRC Brief 6/2015).

The aggregates levy has been devolved to the Scottish Parliament. From a date to be appointed a replacement tax will apply in Scotland.

| | |
|---|---|
| **From 1 April 2009** | **£2.00 per tonne** |

## Air passenger duty

(FA 1994 s 30, Sch 5A; FA 2017 s 19)

APD was extended to smaller aircraft and business jets (reducing the de minimis weight limit from 10 tonnes to 5.7 tonnes) from 1 April 2013 and passengers on 'luxury' business jets (20 tonnes or more and fewer than 19 seats) pay APD at twice the standard rate. From 1 November 2011 to 31 December 2012 the band A rates applied to all *direct* long haul flights departing from Northern Ireland. The rates for all *direct* long haul flights (ie in bands B to D) departing from Northern Ireland from 1 January 2013 are devolved to the Northern Ireland Assembly and set at £0.

Children under the age of 2 years on the date of the flight without their own seat are exempt from charge in all classes of travel. From 1 May 2015, children under the age of 12 years on the date of the flight are exempt from charge in standard class. From 1 March 2016 this exemption applies to children under age 16.

**From 1 April 2015 destinations from bands B, C and D are merged into a single band B.**

Air passenger duty has been devolved to the Scottish Parliament. From April 2018 a replacement tax (air departure tax) will apply in Scotland.

**Reduced rate (lowest class of travel)**

| Band and distance of capital city of destination country from UK in miles | | | | Band and distance of capital city of destination country from UK in miles | | | | |
|---|---|---|---|---|---|---|---|---|
| | 1.4.12–31.3.13 | 1.4.13–31.3.14 | 1.4.14–31.3.15 | | 1.4.15–31.3.16 | 1.4.16–31.3.17 | **1.4.17–31.3.18** | From 1.4.18 |
| **Band A** (0–2,000) | £13 | £13 | £13 | **Band A** (0–2,000) | £13 | £13 | **£13** | £13 |
| **Band B** (2,001–4,000) | £65 | £67 | £69 | **Band B** (over 2,000) | £71 | £73 | **£75** | £78 |
| **Band C** (4,001–6,000) | £81 | £83 | £85 | | | | | |
| **Band D** (over 6,000) | £92 | £94 | £97 | | | | | |

**Standard rate (all classes other than lowest class)**[1]

| Band and distance of capital city of destination country from UK in miles | | | | Band and distance of capital city of destination country from UK in miles | | | | |
|---|---|---|---|---|---|---|---|---|
| | 1.4.12–31.3.13 | 1.4.13–31.3.14 | 1.4.14–31.3.15 | | 1.4.15–31.3.16 | 1.4.16–31.3.17 | **1.4.17–31.3.18** | From 1.4.18 |
| **Band A** (0–2,000) | £26 | £26 | £26 | **Band A** (0–2,000) | £26 | £26 | **£26** | £26 |
| **Band B** (2,001–4,000) | £130 | £134 | £138 | **Band B** (over 2,000) | £142 | £146 | **£150** | £156 |
| **Band C** (4,001–6,000) | £162 | £166 | £170 | | | | | |
| **Band D** (over 6,000) | £184 | £188 | £194 | | | | | |

**Higher rate (flights aboard aircraft of 20 tonnes and above with fewer than 19 seats)**

| Band and distance of capital city of destination country from UK in miles | | | | Band and distance of capital city of destination country from UK in miles | | | | |
|---|---|---|---|---|---|---|---|---|
| | 1.4.12–31.3.13 | 1.4.13–31.3.14 | 1.4.14–31.3.15 | | 1.4.15–31.3.16 | 1.4.16–31.3.17 | **1.4.17–31.3.18** | From 1.4.18 |
| **Band A** (0–2,000) | N/A | £52 | £52 | **Band A** (0–2,000) | £78 | £78 | **£78** | £78 |
| **Band B** (2,001–4,000) | N/A | £268 | £276 | **Band B** (over 2,000) | £426 | £438 | **£450** | £468 |
| **Band C** (4,001–6,000) | N/A | £332 | £340 | | | | | |
| **Band D** (over 6,000) | N/A | £376 | £388 | | | | | |

1 From 1 November 2008, if a class of travel provides a seat pitch in excess of 1.016 metres (40 inches) the standard rate is the minimum rate that applies, even if it is the lowest or only class of travel.

The following specifies which countries come into which bands.

**Band A territories** — 0–2,000 miles from London

| | | |
|---|---|---|
| Albania | Greenland | Morocco |
| Algeria | Guernsey[3] | Netherlands |
| Andorra | Hungary | Norway (including Svalbard) |
| Austria | Iceland | Poland |
| Azores | Republic of Ireland | Portugal (including Madeira) |
| Belarus | Isle of Man | Romania |
| Belgium | Italy (including Sicily and Sardinia)[2] | Russian Federation (west of the Urals) |
| Bosnia and Herzegovina | Jersey[3] | San Marino |
| Bulgaria | Republic of Kosovo | Serbia |
| Croatia | Latvia | Slovak Republic |
| Cyprus | Libya | Slovenia |
| Czech Republic | Liechtenstein | Spain (including the Balearic Islands and the Canary Islands) |
| Denmark (including the Faroe Islands) | Lithuania | Sweden |
| Estonia | Luxembourg | Switzerland |
| Finland | former Yugoslav Republic of Macedonia | Tunisia |
| France (including Corsica) | Malta | Turkey |
| Germany | Moldova | Ukraine |
| Gibraltar | Monaco | Western Sahara[1] |
| Greece | Montenegro | |

1 HMRC Notice 550 Appendix 1 (updated March 2017) does not include Western Sahara.
2 HMRC Notice 550 Appendix 1 (updated March 2017) does include Vatican City even though this is not in the tables in FA 1994 Sch 5A.
3 HMRC Notice 550 Appendix 1 (updated March 2017) refers to the Channel Islands, rather than Guernsey and Jersey.

**Note: From 1 April 2015 destinations from bands B, C and D are merged into a single band B.**

**Band B territories** — 2,001–4,000 miles from London

| | | |
|---|---|---|
| Afghanistan | Gambia | Pakistan |
| Armenia | Georgia | Qatar |
| Azerbaijan | Ghana | Russian Federation (east of the Urals) |
| Bahrain | Guinea | Saint Pierre and Miquelon |
| Benin | Guinea-Bissau | Sao Tome and Principe |
| Bermuda | Iran | Saudi Arabia |
| Burkina Faso | Iraq | Senegal |
| Cameroon | Israel & Occupied Palestinian Territories | Sierra Leone |
| Canada | Ivory Coast | South Sudan |
| Cape Verde | Jordan | Sudan |
| Central African Republic | Kazakhstan | Syria |
| Chad | Kuwait | Tajikistan |
| Democratic Republic of Congo | Kyrgyzstan | Togo |
| Republic of Congo | Lebanon | Turkmenistan |
| Djibouti | Liberia | Uganda |
| Egypt | Mali | United Arab Emirates |
| Equatorial Guinea | Mauritania | United States of America |
| Eritrea | Niger | Uzbekistan |
| Ethiopia | Nigeria | Yemen |
| Gabon | Oman | |

**Note: From 1 April 2015 destinations from bands B, C and D are merged into a single band B.**

**Band C territories** — 4,001–6,000 miles from London

| | | |
|---|---|---|
| Angola | Guadeloupe | Puerto Rico |
| Anguilla | Guatemala | Reunion |
| Antigua and Barbuda | Guyana | Rwanda |
| Aruba | Haiti | Saba |
| Bahamas | Honduras | Saint Barthelemy |
| Bangladesh | Hong Kong SAR | Saint Christopher and Nevis (St Kitts and Nevis) |
| Barbados | India | Saint Helena, Ascension and Tristan da Cuhna |
| Belize | Jamaica | Saint Lucia |
| Bhutan | Japan | Saint Martin |
| Bonaire | Kenya | Saint Vincent and the Grenadines |
| Botswana | North Korea | Seychelles |
| Brazil | South Korea | Sint Eustatius |
| British Indian Ocean Territory | Laos | Sint Maarten |
| British Virgin Islands | Lesotho | Somalia |
| Burma | Macao SAR | South Africa |
| Burundi | Madagascar | Sri Lanka |
| Cayman Islands | Malawi | Suriname |
| China | Maldives | Swaziland |
| Colombia | Martinique | Tanzania |
| Comoros | Mauritius | Thailand |
| Costa Rica | Mayotte | Trinidad and Tobago |
| Cuba | Mexico | Turks and Caicos Islands |
| Curaçao | Mongolia | Venezuela |
| Dominica | Montserrat | Vietnam |
| Dominican Republic | Mozambique | Virgin Islands |
| Ecuador | Namibia | Zambia |
| El Salvador | Nepal | Zimbabwe |
| French Guiana | Nicaragua | |
| Grenada | Panama | |

**Band D** — journey ends in any other place.

**Note: From 1 April 2015 destinations from bands B, C and D are merged into a single band B.**

# Climate change levy

(FA 2000 s 30, Sch 6)

Levy on supply for industrial or commercial purposes of energy, from 1 April 2001, in the form of electricity, gas, petroleum and hydrocarbon gas supplied in a liquid state, coal and lignite, coke and semi-coke of coal or lignite and petroleum coke.

| *Taxable commodity supplied* | *Rate*[1] | | | | | | |
|---|---|---|---|---|---|---|---|
| | 1.4.12–31.3.13 | 1.4.13–31.3.14 | 1.4.14–31.3.15 | 1.4.15–31.3.16 | 1.4.16–31.3.17 | **1.4.17–31.3.18** | 1.4.18–31.3.19 |
| Electricity | 0.509p per kWh | 0.524p per kWh | 0.541p per kWh | 0.554p per kWh | 0.559p per kWh | **0.568p per kWh** | 0.583p per kWh |
| Gas supplied by a gas utility or any gas supplied in a gaseous state that is of a kind supplied by a gas utility | 0.177p per kWh | 0.182p per kWh | 0.188p per kWh | 0.193p per kWh | 0.195p per kWh | **0.198p per kWh** | 0.203p per kWh |
| Gas supplied as above in Northern Ireland | 0.062p per kWh | 0.064p per kWh until 31.10.13 then main rate applies | 0.188p per kWh | 0.193p per kWh | 0.195p per kWh | **0.198p per kWh** | 0.203p per kWh |
| Any petroleum gas, or other gaseous hydrocarbon supplied in a liquid state | 1.137p per kg | 1.172p per kg | 1.210p per kg | 1.240p per kg | 1.251p per kg | **1.272p per kg** | 1.304p per kg |
| Any other taxable commodity | 1.387p per kg | 1.429p per kg | 1.476p per kg | 1.512p per kg | 1.526p per kg | **1.551p per kg** | 1.591p per kg |

1 Rate at which payable if supply is not a reduced-rate supply. The levy is charged at a reduced rate for facilities covered by a climate change agreement, generally 35% of the full rate, but 20% from 1 April 2012 to 31 March 2014 for supplies of taxable commodities used in recycling of steel and aluminium (previously and subsequently exempt) and 10% from 1 April 2013 for electricity supplies. From 1 April 2014 supplies of taxable commodities used in metallurgical and mineralogical processes are exempt. From 1 August 2015 electricity generated from renewable sources is no longer eligible for exemption when supplied under a renewable source contract, though the exemption may still apply until 31 March 2018 to renewable source electricity generated before 1 August 2015.

## Carbon price support rates for climate change levy and fuel duty

The carbon price floor was introduced from 1 April 2013. Supplies of solid fossil fuels, gas and liquefied petroleum gas used in most forms of electricity generation are liable to the CPS rates of CCL, which differs from the main CCL rates (see above) levied on consumers' use of these commodities (and electricity). Oils and bioblends are not taxable commodities for CCL purposes, and are taxed under the fuel duty regime. There are, however, CPS rates of fuel duty for oils and bioblends used in the generation of electricity. Subject to state aid approval, the carbon price floor does not apply to Northern Ireland. The CPS rate is reduced by the carbon capture percentage where there is a supply of fossil fuels to an electricity generator which uses carbon capture and storage (CCS) technology. Small scale Combined Heat and Power (CHP) stations are not subject to the CPS rate. From 1 April 2015 fossil fuels used in a CHP station to generate good quality electricity consumed on-site are also excluded.

| *Supplies of commodity* | | | | |
|---|---|---|---|---|
| | 1.4.13–31.3.14 | 1.4.14–31.3.15 | 1.4.15–31.3.16 | **1.4.16–31.3.20** |
| Gas supplied by a gas utility or any gas supplied in a gaseous state that is of a kind supplied by a gas utility | 0.091p per kWh | 0.175p per kWh | 0.334p per kWh | **0.331p per kWh** |
| Any petroleum gas, or other gaseous hydrocarbon supplied in a liquid state | 1.460p per kg | 2.822p per kg | 5.307p per kg | **5.28p per kg** |
| Coal and other taxable solid fossil fuels | 44.264p per gross gigajoule | 81.906p per gross gigajoule | 156.86p per gross gigajoule | **154.79p per gross gigajoule** |
| Gas oil; rebated bioblend; kerosene[1] | 1.365p per litre | 2.642p per litre | 4.99p per litre | **4.916p per litre** |
| Fuel oil; other heavy oil; rebated light oil | 1.568p per litre | 3.011p per litre | 5.73p per litre | **5.711p per litre** |

1 The CPS rates of fuel duty apply to duty paid kerosene used in electricity generation from 1 May 2014.

# Fuel duty

(HODA 1979 s 6; SI 2011/2935; SI 2015/550)

A Rural Fuel Duty relief scheme for retailers of road fuel on the Inner and Outer Hebrides, the Northern Isles, the Islands of the Clyde and the Isles of Scilly applies from 1 January 2012 to 31 December 2017, though the government is seeking EU permission to extend the scheme. Retailers of road fuel within these areas are eligible to register with HMRC to claim back five pence per litre relief on unleaded petrol and diesel for retail sale within the eligible areas. The retailers have 60 days following registration for the scheme to reduce the cost of every litre of road fuel sold by the equivalent amount of the relief claimed (HMRC Brief 40/2011). The scheme is extended from 1 April 2015 to 31 March 2020 to the postal town of Hawes in North Yorkshire, and the following postcode districts: EX35, LA17, NE48, IV14, IV21, IV22, IV26, IV27, IV54, KW12, PA38, PA80, PH19, PH23, PH36, PH41 (HMRC Brief 3/2015).

| | Petrol/diesel | Biodiesel or bioethanol | LPG used as road fuel | Natural gas used as road fuel | Red diesel | Fuel oil | Aqua-methanol |
|---|---|---|---|---|---|---|---|
| **From 14 November 2016** | **57.95p per litre** | **57.95p per litre** | **31.61p per kg** | **24.70p per kg** | **11.14p per litre** | **10.70p per litre** | **7.90p per litre** |
| From 6pm 23 March 2011 to 13 November 2016 | 57.95p per litre | 57.95p per litre | 31.61p per kg | 24.70p per kg | 11.14p per litre | 10.70p per litre | 57.95p per litre |
| From 1 January 2011 to 6pm 23 March 2011 | 58.95p per litre | 58.95p per litre | 33.04p per kg | 26.15p per kg | 11.33p per litre | 10.88p per litre | N/A |
| From 1 October 2010 to 31 December 2010 | 58.19p per litre | 58.19p per litre | 31.95p per kg | 25.05p per kg | 11.18p per litre | 10.74p per litre | N/A |
| From 1 April 2010 to 30 September 2010 | 57.19p per litre | 57.19p per litre | 30.53p per kg | 23.60p per kg | 10.99p per litre | 10.55p per litre | N/A |

# Insurance premium tax

(FA 1994 ss 48–74, Schs 6A, 7, 7A; FA 2017 s 17)

IPT is a tax on premiums received under insurance contracts other than those which are specifically exempt.

| | *Standard rate* | *Higher rate*[1] |
|---|---|---|
| **From 1.6.17** | **12.0%** | **20.0%** |
| 1.10.16–31.5.17[3] | 10.0% | 20.0% |
| 1.11.15–30.9.16[2] | 9.5% | 20.0% |
| 4.1.11–31.10.15 | 6.0% | 20.0% |

1 The higher rate applies to sales of motor cars, light vans and motorcycles, electrical or mechanical domestic appliances, and travel insurance.

2 9.5% rate applies from 1 March 2016 for insurers who use a special accounting scheme rather than the cash receipt method, and where the premium relates to risks covered by the terms of a contract entered into before 1 November 2015.

3 10% rate applies from 1 February 2017 for insurers who use a special accounting scheme rather than the cash receipt method, and where the premium relates to risks covered by the terms of a contract entered into before 1 October 2016.

# Landfill tax

(FA 1996 ss 39–71, 197, Sch 5; SI 1996/1527; SI 1996/1528; SI 2016/376; Notice LFT 1 para 4.5; SI 2017/332)

Tax on disposal of waste imposed on operators of landfill sites calculated by reference to the weight and type of waste deposited. Exemption applies to mining and quarrying waste, dredging waste, pet cemeteries, disposals of NATO waste, and inert waste used to fill working and old quarries. An exemption for waste from reclamation of contaminated land was abolished with effect from 30 November 2008 although some exemption certificates remained valid until 31 March 2012. Legislation introduced in Finance Act 2012 brought landfill tax legislation in Scotland into line with the rest of the UK and had retrospective effect back to 21 March 2000. The power to raise landfill tax devolved to the Scottish Parliament from 1 April 2015 (see table below). That power has also been devolved to the Welsh Government from April 2018 (see table below).

| *Period* | *Active waste per tonne* | *Inert waste per tonne*[2] | *Maximum credit*[1] |
|---|---|---|---|
| From 1.4.18 | £88.95 | £2.80 | TBA |
| **1.4.17–31.3.18** | **£86.10** | **£2.70** | **5.3%** |
| 1.4.16–31.3.17 | £84.40 | £2.65 | 4.2% |
| 1.4.15–31.3.16 | £82.60 | £2.60 | 5.7% |
| 1.4.14–31.3.15 | £80 | £2.50 | 5.1% |
| 1.4.13–31.3.14 | £72 | £2.50 | 6.8% |
| 1.4.12–31.3.13 | £64 | £2.50 | 5.6% |
| 1.4.11–31.3.12 | £56 | £2.50 | 6.2% |

1 Tax credits are available to operators who make donations to environmental trusts of 90% of the donation to the maximum percentage above of the tax payable in a 12-month period (Landfill Communities Fund).

2 For details of waste materials liable at the lower rate see SI 2011/1017 as amended by SI 2012/940 and HMRC Briefs 15/2012 and 18/2012.

# Scottish landfill tax

(Landfill Tax (Scotland) Act 2014; SSI 2017/23)

Tax replaces landfill tax in Scotland from 1 April 2015.

| *Period* | *Active waste per tonne* | *Inert waste per tonne*[2] | *Maximum credit*[1] |
|---|---|---|---|
| **From 1.4.17** | **£86.10** | **£2.70** | **5.6%** |
| 1.4.16–31.3.17 | £84.40 | £2.65 | 5.6% |
| 1.4.15–31.3.16 | £82.60 | £2.60 | 5.6% |

1 Tax credits are available to operators who make donations to environmental trusts of 90% of the donation to the maximum percentage above of the tax payable in a 12-month period (Scottish Landfill Communities Fund).

2 For details of waste materials liable at the lower rate see SSIs 2015/45 and 2016/93.

# Landfill disposals tax (Wales)

(Landfill Disposals Tax (Wales) Act 2017; WSI 2017/955)

Tax replaces landfill tax in Wales from 1 April 2018.

| *Period* | *Active waste per tonne* | *Inert waste per tonne* | *Unauthorised disposals rate* | *Maximum credit* |
|---|---|---|---|---|
| From 1.4.18 | £88.95 | £2.80 | £133.45 | TBA |

# Vehicle excise duty

(VERA 1994 Sch 1; FA 2017 s 20)
Vehicle tax, or 'road tax' is charged according to $CO_2$ emissions, as follows:

## Standard and first-year rates for cars registered before 1 April 2017

| Band | $CO_2$ (g/km) | 2015–16 Standard rate | 2015–16 first-year rate | 2016–17 Standard rate | 2016–17 first-year rate | 2017–18 Standard rate |
|---|---|---|---|---|---|---|
| A | Up to 100 | £0 | £0 | £0 | £0 | **£0** |
| B | 101–110 | £20 | £0 | £20 | £0 | **£20** |
| C | 111–120 | £30 | £0 | £30 | £0 | **£30** |
| D | 121–130 | £110 | £0 | £110 | £0 | **£115** |
| E | 131–140 | £130 | £130 | £130 | £130 | **£135** |
| F | 141–150 | £145 | £145 | £145 | £145 | **£150** |
| G | 151–165 | £180 | £180 | £185 | £185 | **£190** |
| H | 166–175 | £205 | £295 | £210 | £300 | **£220** |
| I | 176–185 | £225 | £350 | £230 | £355 | **£240** |
| J | 186–200 | £265 | £490 | £270 | £500 | **£280** |
| K | 201–225 | £290 | £640 | £295 | £650 | **£305** |
| L | 226–255 | £490 | £870 | £500 | £885 | **£520** |
| M | Over 255 | £505 | £1,100 | £515 | £1,120 | **£535** |

There is an alternative fuel discount of £10 for all cars from 2010–11 onwards. From 1 April 2010, a different rate of tax applies in the year of purchase of a new vehicle. In later years, the standard rate applies.

**A revised banding system is introduced for cars registered on or after 1 April 2017**. There are no 2017–18 first-year rates for cars registered before 1 April 2017. First-year rates for cars registered on or after 1 April 2017 continue to be based on $CO_2$ emissions but a standard flat rate of £140 applies to all cars except those with zero emissions. Cars with a list price above £40,000 when new, pay an additional rate of £310 per year for the first 5 years in which the standard rate is paid.

## Standard and first-year rates for cars registered on or after 1 April 2017

| $CO_2$ (g/km) | 2017–18 Standard rates | 2017–18 first-year rates |
|---|---|---|
| 0 | **£0** | **£0** |
| 1–50 | **£140** | **£10** |
| 51–75 | **£140** | **£25** |
| 76–90 | **£140** | **£100** |
| 91–100 | **£140** | **£120** |
| 101–110 | **£140** | **£140** |
| 111–130 | **£140** | **£160** |
| 131–150 | **£140** | **£200** |
| 151–170 | **£140** | **£500** |
| 171–190 | **£140** | **£800** |
| 191–225 | **£140** | **£1,200** |
| 226–255 | **£140** | **£1,700** |
| Over 255 | **£140** | **£2,000** |

### Light goods vehicle rates

| Tax class | 2015–16 | 2016–17 | 2017–18 |
|---|---|---|---|
| Light goods vehicle[1] | £225 | £230 | **£240** |
| Euro 4 & 5 LGV | £140 | £140 | **£140** |

[1] Registered on or after 1 March 2001.

### Motorcycle rates

| VED band | 2015–16 | 2016–17 | 2017–18 |
|---|---|---|---|
| Up to 150 cc | £17 | £17 | **£18** |
| 151–400 cc | £38 | £39 | **£41** |
| 401–600 cc | £59 | £60 | **£62** |
| Over 600 cc | £81 | £82 | **£85** |

# Income tax

## Starting, basic, higher and additional rates

(ITA 2007 ss 6–21)

| Band of taxable income £ | Band £ | Rate[1] % | Tax £ | Cumulative tax £ |
|---|---|---|---|---|
| **2017–18** | | | | |
| **0–33,500** | **33,500** | **20** | **6,700** | **6,700** |
| **33,501–150,000** | **116,500** | **40** | **46,600** | **53,300** |
| **Over 150,000** | **–** | **45** | **–** | **–** |
| **2016–17** | | | | |
| 0–32,000 | 32,000 | 20 | 6,400 | 6,400 |
| 32,001–150,000 | 118,000 | 40 | 47,200 | 53,600 |
| Over 150,000 | – | 45 | – | – |
| **2015–16** | | | | |
| 0–31,785 | 31,785 | 20 | 6,357 | 6,357 |
| 31,786–150,000 | 118,215 | 40 | 47,286 | 53,643 |
| Over 150,000 | – | 45 | – | – |
| **2014–15** | | | | |
| 0–31,865 | 31,865 | 20 | 6,373 | 6,373 |
| 31,866–150,000 | 118,135 | 40 | 47,254 | 53,627 |
| Over 150,000 | – | 45 | – | – |
| **2013–14** | | | | |
| 0–32,010 | 32,010 | 20 | 6,402 | 6,402 |
| 32,011–150,000 | 117,990 | 40 | 47,196 | 53,598 |
| Over 150,000 | – | 45 | – | – |
| **2012–13** | | | | |
| 0–34,370 | 34,370 | 20 | 6,874 | 6,874 |
| 34,371–150,000 | 115,630 | 40 | 46,252 | 53,126 |
| Over 150,000 | – | 50 | – | – |

[1] A Scottish rate of income tax applies from 6 April 2016 — see below.

## Scottish rate of income tax

(Scotland Act 1998 s 80C; Scotland Act 2016 s 13)

| Band of taxable income £ | Band £ | Rate % | Tax £ | Cumulative tax £ |
|---|---|---|---|---|
| **2017–18** | | | | |
| **0–31,500** | **31,500** | **20** | **6,300** | **6,300** |
| **31,501–150,000** | **118,500** | **40** | **47,400** | **53,700** |
| **Over 150,000** | **–** | **45** | **–** | **–** |
| **2016–17** | | | | |
| 0–32,000 | 32,000 | 20 | 6,400 | 6,400 |
| 32,001–150,000 | 118,000 | 40 | 47,200 | 53,600 |
| Over 150,000 | – | 45 | – | – |

**From 6 April 2016 a Scottish rate of income tax applies to Scottish taxpayers'** non-dividend, non-savings income. From 2017–18 the Scottish Parliament can set its own Scottish income tax rates and bands. In 2017–18 the tax rates remain the same as the rest of the UK but the basic rate band applying to non-dividend, non-savings income is £31,500 rather than £33,500. The UK basic rate band of £33,500 still applies to Scottish taxpayers' dividend and savings income. In 2016–17 the Scottish basic, higher and additional rates were calculated by reducing each of the UK basic, higher and additional rates by ten percentage points and then adding a Scottish rate of 10%. This means for 2016–17 the rates of income tax paid by Scottish taxpayers stayed the same as for the rest of the UK. The definition of a Scottish taxpayer is based on the location of an individual's main place of residence.

## Taxation of savings

(ITA 2007 ss 6–21)

A starting rate for savings band for individuals applies. For **2015–16, 2016–17 and 2017–18 it is £5,000**. Previous rate bands were £2,880 for 2014–15, £2,790 for 2013–14, and £2,710 for 2012–13. Where an individual's taxable non-savings income is less than this limit, there is a **0% starting rate for 2015–16, 2016–17 and 2017–18** (10% for earlier years) for savings up to the limit. Where taxable non-savings income exceeds the limit, the starting rate for savings does not apply. Savings income includes interest from banks and building societies, interest distributions from authorised unit trusts, interest on gilts and other securities including corporate bonds, purchased life annuities and discounts.

**From 6 April 2016** a personal savings allowance (PSA) is available to basic and higher rate taxpayers but not to additional rate taxpayers. The allowance is **£1,000 per year for basic rate taxpayers and £500 per year for higher rate taxpayers**. Savings income above the allowance is taxable at the basic or higher rate as appropriate, with savings income generally being treated as the second top slice of income behind dividends. The PSA is not a deduction in arriving at total income or taxable income. **A 0% rate of income tax applies** to savings income covered by the PSA. It operates in conjunction with the 0% starting rate for savings and income taxable at this rate does not fall within the PSA. Also from 6 April 2016, banks, building societies and National Savings are no longer required to deduct 20% tax at source from interest payable. From 6 April 2017 there is no requirement to deduct income tax at source from interest distributions from open-ended investment companies, authorised unit trusts and investment trust companies and from interest on peer-to-peer loans. Savings income within an ISA continues to be tax-free, and does not need to be covered by the PSA.

**For tax years before 2016–17**, where income did not exceed the basic rate limit, there was no further tax to pay on savings income from which 20% tax had been deducted. Any tax over-deducted was repayable. Higher rate taxpayers liable to pay tax at 40% and additional rate taxpayers liable to pay tax at 45% (50% for 2012–13) on that part of their savings income falling above the basic rate limit or higher rate limit (as applicable) were entitled to a credit for any tax deducted at source. Non-taxpayers and those whose total savings income is eligible for the 0% starting rate could apply to have interest paid without deduction of tax.

# Taxation of dividends

(ITA 2007 ss 6–21; F(No 2)A 2017 s 8)

**From 6 April 2016** a **dividend allowance of £5,000** per year is available to all taxpayers, though this is reduced to **£2,000 from 2018–19**. The rates of tax on dividend income above the allowance are 7.5% for dividend income falling within the basic rate band, 32.5% for dividend income falling within the higher rate band, and 38.1% for dividend income falling within the additional rate band. The dividend allowance is not a deduction in arriving at total income or taxable income. A **0% rate of income tax applies** to dividends covered by the allowance. UK and foreign dividends (except those foreign dividends taxed under the remittance basis) form the top slice of taxable income.

**For tax years before 2016–17**, where income did not exceed the basic rate limit the tax rate was 10% (applied to the dividend grossed-up by a tax credit of 1/9) so that the liability was met by the tax credit. Higher rate taxpayers were liable to pay tax at 32.5% on that part of their dividend income falling above the basic rate limit. From 2013–14 additional rate taxpayers were liable to pay tax at 37.5% on that part of their dividend income falling above the higher rate limit (42.5% in 2012–13). Tax credits are abolished from 6 April 2016.

# Taxation of trusts

| | *Trust rate* | *Dividend trust rate* |
|---|---|---|
| **2016–17 onwards** | **45%** | **38.1%** |
| 2013–14 to 2015–16 | 45% | 37.5% |
| 2011–12 to 2012–13 | 50% | 42.5% |

**First slice of income:** For 2006–07 onwards the first £1,000 of income arising to a trust chargeable at the trust rate or the dividend trust rate is instead chargeable at the basic, savings or dividend rate.
**Vulnerable beneficiaries:** From 2004–05 onwards, trustees can be taxed (on election) on trust income as if it were income of the vulnerable beneficiary taking into account the beneficiary's personal allowances, starting and basic rate bands (FA 2005 ss 23–45).

# Construction industry sub-contractors

(SI 2007/46)

| | Rate of tax deduction at source |
|---|---|
| Registered sub-contractors | **20%** |
| Unregistered sub-contractors | **30%** |

# Child benefit income tax charge

(ITEPA 2003 ss 681B–H; Social Security Administration Act 1992, s 13A)

Where an individual or their partner is in receipt of child benefit a high income child benefit charge can arise from 7 January 2013. The charge is applied to the higher earner. Taxpayers with adjusted net income between £50,000 and £60,000 are subject to an income tax charge of 1% of the amount of child benefit for every £100 of income that exceeds £50,000. For taxpayers with income above £60,000, the amount of the charge will equal the amount of child benefit received. Alternatively, a taxpayer with expected income over £60,000 can elect not to receive any child benefit. The election has effect for weeks beginning after it is made. It can be revoked at any time to restore payment of child benefit, and, where the election was made in the erroneous belief that the charge would arise, it may be revoked up to two years after the end of the tax year to which it relates in order for child benefit to be paid for the period.

# Charities and Community Amateur Sports Clubs (CASCs)

## Gift Aid and Gift Aid Small Donations schemes

Under the **Gift Aid scheme** an individual donor can claim higher rate relief and, if applicable, additional rate relief on the grossed up amount of a monetary donation against income tax and capital gains tax. The charity or CASC claims basic rate relief on the grossed up amount of the donation. Donors must make a declaration that they are UK taxpayers to allow the charity to reclaim the repayment. One declaration can cover a series of donations to the same charity and the declaration can be made in writing, including fax, email and text, or orally, although an oral declaration is not effective until a written confirmation is sent to the donor. Template declarations are provided on Gov.uk. A declaration can be backdated for up to four years prior to the declaration. The basic rate tax deemed to have been deducted by the donor at source is clawed back if the donor's tax liability is insufficient to match it. Donors may elect in their self-assessment tax returns for donations to be treated as made in the preceding tax year for higher rate (and if applicable, additional rate) relief purposes.

Relief for payments under charitable covenants is given under the Gift Aid scheme.

From April 2013 the **Gift Aid Small Donations scheme** allows charities and CASCs to claim a gift aid style payment on broadly £8,000 (£5,000 before 6 April 2016) of small cash donations (or from 6 April 2017, contactless payments) of up to £20 each in circumstances where it is often difficult to obtain a gift aid declaration, such as street collections. The donations must not have been the subject of a gift aid declaration and must not be deductible in calculating the individual's income.

(ITA 2007 ss 413–430; FA 2012 s 50; Small Charitable Donations Act 2012; SI 2015/2027)

## Gifts in kind

Relief is available for gifts by traders to charities, community amateur sports clubs or educational establishments of goods produced or sold or of plant or machinery used for the purposes of the trade (CAA 2001 s 63(2)–(4); ITTOIA 2005 ss 107–109; CTA 2009 ss 105–107; CTA 2010 ss 658–671).

## Gifts of land, shares and securities etc

Relief is available where a person disposes of listed shares and securities, unit trust units, AIM shares, etc or of freehold or leasehold interests in land to a charity by way of a gift or sale at an undervalue. The amount deductible from total income is the market value of the shares etc on the date of disposal plus incidental disposal costs less any consideration or value of benefits received by the donor or a connected person. This is in addition to any capital gains tax relief (ITA 2007 ss 431–446).

## Payroll giving

Under the payroll giving scheme, employees authorise their employer to deduct charitable donations from their pay and receive tax relief on their donation at their top rate of tax (FA 2000 s 38; ITEPA 2003 ss 713–715; SI 1986/2211 as amended).

**Inheritance tax relief** see p 108. **Capital gains tax** see p 38. **Gifts of pre-eminent objects** see p 99.

# Table of income tax reliefs

| | 2017–18 | 2016–17 |
|---|---|---|
| | £ | £ |
| **Basic personal allowance**[6] | **11,500** | 11,000 |
| Total income limit[5] | **100,000** | 100,000 |
| Not beneficial if individual's | | |
| total income exceeds | **123,000** | 122,000 |
| Transferable marriage allowance[7] | **1,150** | 1,100 |
| *Age allowance* | | |
| Total income limit[1] | **N/A** | N/A |
| Personal allowance born after 5.4.1938 but before 6.4.1948 / age 65–74[6] | **N/A** | N/A |
| Not beneficial if individual's | | |
| total income exceeds | **N/A** | N/A |
| Personal allowance born before 6.4.1938 / age 75 and over | **N/A** | N/A |
| Not beneficial if individual's | | |
| total income exceeds | **N/A** | N/A |
| **Married couple's allowance**[2] | | |
| Either partner aged 75 and over and born before 6 April 1935 | | |
| Minimum amount | **3,260** | 3,220 |
| Total income limit[3] | **28,000** | 27,700 |
| Maximum amount | **8,445** | 8,355 |
| Reduced to minimum if income exceeds[3] | | |
| born after 5.4.1948 / under 65 and his total income exceeds | **38,370** | 37,970 |
| born after 5.4.1938 but before 6.4.1948 / 65–74 and his total income exceeds | **38,370** | 37,970 |
| born before 6.4.1938 / 75 or over and his total income exceeds | **38,370** | 37,970 |
| **Blind person's allowance**[4] | **2,320** | 2,290 |
| **Dividend allowance**[8] | **5,000** | 5,000 |
| **Personal savings allowance**[8] | | |
| Basic rate taxpayer | **1,000** | 1,000 |
| Higher rate taxpayer | **500** | 500 |
| **Trading allowance**[9] | **1,000** | N/A |
| **Property allowance**[9] | **1,000** | N/A |

1 The higher personal allowances for years before 2016–17 were available if the claimant's adjusted net income did not exceed the statutory income limit. If the limit was exceeded the maximum allowance was reduced by one-half of the excess until it was reduced to the basic personal allowance, but subject to a further reduction as outlined in note 5 if the adjusted net income exceeded £100,000.

2 The universal married couple's allowance was withdrawn for 2000–01 onwards but continues to be available to any married couple or, from 2005–06, civil partnership where at least one spouse or partner was born before 6 April 1935. The relief is given as a reduction in income tax liability restricted to the lower of 10% of the amount of the allowance or the claimant's total income tax liability.

For marriages before 5 December 2005, married couple's allowance is given to the husband (subject to right of transfer to the wife), the amount being determined by the level of the husband's income. For marriages and civil partnerships entered into on or after that date, the allowance is given to whichever of the two partners has the higher total income for the tax year in question, the amount being determined by the level of that partner's income (subject to the right to transfer half or all of the basic allowance or excess allowances to the partner). Couples married before 5 December 2005 could make a joint election to be brought within the rules for couples marrying on or after that date.

# National insurance contributions – self-employed

| | | 2017–18 | 2016–17 |
|---|---|---|---|
| **Class 2** | Flat rate per week | **£2.85** | £2.80 |
| | Small profits threshold/ small earnings exception | **6,025** | 5,965 |
| **Class 4** | Band | **8,164–45,000** | 8,060–43,000 |
| | Rate | **36,836@9%** | 34,940@9% |
| | Amount payable to upper limit | **3,315.24** | 3144.60 |
| | Charge on profits above the limit | **2%** | 2% |

# Table of income tax reliefs (cont.)

| *2015–16* | *2014–15* | *2013–14* | *2012–13* | *2011–12* |
|---|---|---|---|---|
| **£** | **£** | **£** | **£** | **£** |
| 10,600 | 10,000 | 9,440 | 8,105 | 7,475 |
| 100,000 | 100,000 | 100,000 | 100,000 | 100,000 |
| 121,200 | 120,000 | 118,880 | 116,210 | 114,950 |
| 1,060 | N/A | N/A | N/A | N/A |
| 27,700 | 27,000 | 26,100 | 25,400 | 24,000 |
| N/A | 10,500 | 10,500 | 10,500 | 9,940 |
| N/A | 28,000 | 28,220 | 30,190 | 28,930 |
| 10,660 | 10,660 | 10,660 | 10,660 | 10,090 |
| 27,820 | 28,320 | 28,540 | 30,510 | 29,230 |
| 3,220 | 3,140 | 3,040 | 2,960 | 2,800 |
| 27,700 | 27,000 | 26,100 | 25,400 | 24,000 |
| 8,355 | 8,165 | 7,915 | 7,705 | 7,295 |
| 37,970 | 37,050 | 35,850 | 34,890 | 32,990 |
| 37,970 | 38,050 | 37,970 | 39,680 | 37,920 |
| 38,090 | 38,370 | 38,290 | 40,000 | 38,220 |
| 2,290 | 2,230 | 2,160 | 2,100 | 1,980 |
| N/A | N/A | N/A | N/A | N/A |
| N/A | N/A | N/A | N/A | N/A |
| N/A | N/A | N/A | N/A | N/A |
| N/A | N/A | N/A | N/A | N/A |
| N/A | N/A | N/A | N/A | N/A |

3 The higher married couple's allowance is available if the claimant's adjusted net income does not exceed the statutory income limit (subject to relief given as a reduction in tax liability as in note 2 above). If the limit is exceeded the maximum allowance is reduced by one-half of the excess (less any reduction made in the personal age allowance as in note 1 above for years before 2016–17) but it cannot be reduced to less than the basic couple's allowance.

4 The allowance is available for persons registered blind but not for persons registered partially-sighted.

5 From 2010–11, the basic personal allowance for income tax is gradually reduced to nil for individuals with adjusted net incomes in excess of £100,000. The reduction is £1 for every £2 of income over the limit.

6 For 2012–13 and earlier years differing levels of personal allowances applied based on age. From 2013–14 the differing levels applied based on specified dates of birth. For 2015–16 there was one level of basic personal allowance for individuals born after 5 April 1938, and an age allowance for those born before 6 April 1938. From 2016–17 onwards there is one personal allowance regardless of age.

7 From 2015–16 a spouse or civil partner who is not liable to income tax above the basic rate is able to transfer an amount of their personal allowance to their spouse or civil partner, provided the transferee is also not liable to income tax above the basic rate. Married couples or civil partnerships entitled to claim the married couple's allowance will not be entitled to make a transfer. For 2017–18 they can transfer £1,150 (£1,100 for 2016–17, £1,060 for 2015–16).

8 See p 75 for the tax rates applying where allowance is exceeded.

9 See p 98 for details.

# National insurance contributions – self-employed (cont.)

| *2015–16* | *2014–15* | *2013–14* | *2012–13* | *2011–12* |
|---|---|---|---|---|
| £2.80 | £2.75 | £2.70 | £2.65 | £2.50 |
| 5,965 | 5,885 | £5,725 | 5,595 | 5,315 |
| 8,060–42,385 | 7,956–41,865 | 7,755–41,450 | 7,605–42,475 | 7,225–42,475 |
| 34,325@9% | 33,909@ 9% | 33,695@ 9% | 34,870@ 9% | 35,250@ 9% |
| 3089.25 | 3,051.81 | 3,032.55 | 3,138.30 | 3,172.50 |
| 2% | 2% | 2% | 2% | 2% |

# Cars, vans and related benefits

## Cars

The income tax charge is based on a percentage of the car's price graduated according to the level of the car's carbon dioxide measured in grams per kilometre (g/km). (ITEPA 2003 ss 114–148, 169)

| *$CO_2$ emissions (g/km)* | *% of list price* | | *$CO_2$ emissions (g/km)* | *% of list price* | |
|---|---|---|---|---|---|
| ***2016–17*** | *Petrol* | *Diesel*[1] | ***2017–18*** | *Petrol* | *Diesel*[1] |
| 0–50 | 7%[4] | 10% | **0–50** | 9%[5] | 12% |
| 51–75 | 11% | 14% | **51–75** | 13% | 16% |
| 76–94 | 15% | 18% | **76–94** | 17% | 20% |
| 95–99 | 16% | 19% | **95–99** | 18% | 21% |
| 100–104 | 17% | 20% | **100–104** | 19% | 22% |
| 105–109 | 18% | 21% | **105–109** | 20% | 23% |
| 110–114 | 19% | 22% | **110–114** | 21% | 24% |
| 115–119 | 20% | 23% | **115–119** | 22% | 25% |
| 120–124 | 21% | 24% | **120–124** | 23% | 26% |
| 125–129 | 22% | 25% | **125–129** | 24% | 27% |
| 130–134 | 23% | 26% | **130–134** | 25% | 28% |
| 135–139 | 24% | 27% | **135–139** | 26% | 29% |
| 140–144 | 25% | 28% | **140–144** | 27% | 30% |
| 145–149 | 26% | 29% | **145–149** | 28% | 31% |
| 150–154 | 27% | 30% | **150–154** | 29% | 32% |
| 155–159 | 28% | 31% | **155–159** | 30% | 33% |
| 160–164 | 29% | 32% | **160–164** | 31% | 34% |
| 165–169 | 30% | 33% | **165–169** | 32% | 35% |
| 170–174 | 31% | 34% | **170–174** | 33% | 36% |
| 175–179 | 32% | 35% | **175–179** | 34% | 37% |
| 180–184 | 33% | 36% | **180–184** | 35% | 37% |
| 185–189 | 34% | 37% | **185–189** | 36% | 37% |
| 190–194 | 35% | 37% | **190 or more** | 37% | 37% |
| 195–199 | 36% | 37% | | | |
| 200 or more | 37% | 37% | | | |

| *$CO_2$ emissions (g/km)* | | | *% of list price* | | *$CO_2$ emissions (g/km)* | *% of list price* | |
|---|---|---|---|---|---|---|---|
| ***2012–13*** | ***2013–14*** | ***2014–15*** | *Petrol* | *Diesel*[1] | ***2015–16*** | *Petrol* | *Diesel*[1] |
| 1–75 | 1–75 | 1–75 | 5%[2] | 8% | 0–50 | 5%[3] | 8% |
| 76–99 | 76–94 | N/A | 10% | 13% | 51–75 | 9% | 12% |
| 100–104 | 95–99 | 76–94 | 11% | 14% | 76–94 | 13% | 16% |
| 105–109 | 100–104 | 95–99 | 12% | 15% | 95–99 | 14% | 17% |
| 110–114 | 105–109 | 100–104 | 13% | 16% | 100–104 | 15% | 18% |
| 115–119 | 110–114 | 105–109 | 14% | 17% | 105–109 | 16% | 19% |
| 120–124 | 115–119 | 110–114 | 15% | 18% | 110–114 | 17% | 20% |
| 125–129 | 120–124 | 115–119 | 16% | 19% | 115–119 | 18% | 21% |
| 130–134 | 125–129 | 120–124 | 17% | 20% | 120–124 | 19% | 22% |
| 135–139 | 130–134 | 125–129 | 18% | 21% | 125–129 | 20% | 23% |
| 140–144 | 135–139 | 130–134 | 19% | 22% | 130–134 | 21% | 24% |
| 145–149 | 140–144 | 135–139 | 20% | 23% | 135–139 | 22% | 25% |
| 150–154 | 145–149 | 140–144 | 21% | 24% | 140–144 | 23% | 26% |
| 155–159 | 150–154 | 145–149 | 22% | 25% | 145–149 | 24% | 27% |
| 160–164 | 155–159 | 150–154 | 23% | 26% | 150–154 | 25% | 28% |
| 165–169 | 160–164 | 155–159 | 24% | 27% | 155–159 | 26% | 29% |
| 170–174 | 165–169 | 160–164 | 25% | 28% | 160–164 | 27% | 30% |
| 175–179 | 170–174 | 165–169 | 26% | 29% | 165–169 | 28% | 31% |
| 180–184 | 175–179 | 170–174 | 27% | 30% | 170–174 | 29% | 32% |
| 185–189 | 180–184 | 175–179 | 28% | 31% | 175–179 | 30% | 33% |
| 190–194 | 185–189 | 180–184 | 29% | 32% | 180–184 | 31% | 34% |
| 195–199 | 190–194 | 185–189 | 30% | 33% | 185–189 | 32% | 35% |
| 200–204 | 195–199 | 190–194 | 31% | 34% | 190–194 | 33% | 36% |
| 205–209 | 200–204 | 195–199 | 32% | 35% | 195–199 | 34% | 37% |
| 210–214 | 205–209 | 200–204 | 33% | 35% | 200–204 | 35% | 37% |
| 215–219 | 210–214 | 205–209 | 34% | 35% | 205–209 | 36% | 37% |
| 220 or more | 215 or more | 210 or more | 35% | 35% | 210 or more | 37% | 37% |

1 **Diesel cars:** A 3% supplement applies to diesel cars up to a maximum of 37%.

2 **For 2012–13 to 2014–15:** No benefit applies to cars which are incapable of producing carbon dioxide when driven.

3 **For 2015–16:** The 5% rate applies to cars which are incapable of producing carbon dioxide when driven.

4 **For 2016–17:** The 7% rate applies to cars which are incapable of producing carbon dioxide when driven.
5 **For 2017–18:** The 9% rate applies to cars which are incapable of producing carbon dioxide when driven.
6 **For 2018–19:** The relevant threshold will remain at 95g/km but the percentage applying at that threshold (the threshold percentage) will be increased to 20/23%. The minimum percentage applying if the emissions do not exceed 50g/km will be 13%. For emissions from 51g/km to 75g/km inclusive the rate will be 16%, and for emissions from 76g/km to 94g/km inclusive the rate will be 19%.

## Cars registered after 28 February 2001

For cars registered on or after 1.3.01, the definitive $CO_2$ emissions figure is recorded on the vehicle registration document. For cars first registered between 1.1.98 and 28.2.01, the Vehicle Certification Agency supply relevant information on their website at carfueldata.direct.gov.uk and in their free, twice-yearly edition of the 'New Car Fuel Consumption & Emission Figures' booklet.

## Cars registered on or after 1 January 1998 with no $CO_2$ emission figures

| *Cylinder capacity of car*[2] | *Appropriate percentage*[1] | | | |
|---|---|---|---|---|
| | ***2012–13 to 2014–15*** | ***2015–16*** | ***2016–17*** | ***2017–18*** |
| 1,400cc or less | 15% | 15% | 16% | **18%**[3] |
| Over 1,400cc up to 2,000cc | 25% | 25% | 27% | **29%**[3] |
| Over 2,000cc: | 35% | 37% | 37% | **37%** |
| Cars incapable of producing $CO_2$ when driven | 0% | 5% | 7% | **9%**[3] |

1 **Diesel cars:** A 3% supplement applies to diesel cars up to a maximum of 37%.
2 **No cylinder capacity:** For a car with no cylinder capacity 37% applies.
3 **2018–19:** The percentages will be 20%, 31% and 13% respectively.

**Cars registered before 1.1.98:** For 2015–16 and earlier years tax is charged on 15% of the list price for engines to 1,400cc, 22% for engines of 1,401 to 2,000cc and 32% for engines above 2,000cc. For 2016–17 tax is charged on 16% of the list price for engines to 1,400cc, 27% for engines of 1,401 to 2,000cc and 37% for engines above 2,000cc. For **2017–18** the percentages are 18%, 29% and 37% respectively. For 2018–19 the percentages will be 20%, 31% and 37% respectively. Cars without a cylinder capacity are taxed on 37% (32% before 2016–17) of the list price.

**Automatic cars for disabled drivers:** $CO_2$ figure reduced to equivalent for manual car (ITEPA 2003 s 138).

**Car unavailable for part of year:** Value of the benefit is reduced proportionately (ITEPA 2003 s 143).

**National Insurance:** Also used to calculate the national insurance contributions payable by employers on the benefit of cars they provide for the private use of their employees, see p 111.

The cash equivalent is reduced proportionately where the car is not available for the whole tax year. The amount (as so reduced) is reduced by any payments made by the employee for private use.

**List price of car:**

(1) Includes qualifying accessories, excluding accessories provided after car made available if its list price was less than £100. Accessories designed for use only by disabled people also excluded. From 6 April 2011 accessories do not include certain security enhancements provided to meet the threat to an employee's personal physical security arising from the nature of the employment. Where a car is manufactured so as to be capable of running on road fuel gas, its price is proportionately reduced by so much of that price as is reasonably attributable to it being manufactured in that way. Where a new car is converted to run on road fuel gas, the equipment is not regarded as an accessory. With effect from 6 April 2009 disabled drivers of automatic cars who hold a disabled person's badge can use the list price of an equivalent manual car.

(2) Reduced by capital contributions made by employee up to £5,000.

(3) Classic cars (aged 15 years or more and with a market value of £15,000 or more at end of tax year): substitute market value at end of tax year if higher than adjusted list price. Reduction for capital contributions applies.

(ITEPA 2003 ss 120–132)

## Vans and fuel for vans

(ITEPA 2003 ss 114–119, 154–164, 168, 169A, 170; SI 2016/1174)

| *Van benefit*[1] | *Vans which emit $CO_2$ when driven* | *Vans which do not emit $CO_2$ when driven*[2] |
|---|---|---|
| **2017–18** | **£3,230** | **£646** |
| 2016–17 | £3,170 | £634 |
| 2015–16 | £3,150 | £630 |
| 2014–15 | £3,090 | Nil |
| 2012–13 and 2013–14 | £3,000 | Nil |

1 Vehicle weight up to 3,500kg

2 For 2012–13 to 2014–15 no benefit applies to vans which are incapable of producing $CO_2$ when driven. For 2015–16, 2016–17 and 2017–18, 20% of the van benefit charge for vans which emit $CO_2$ applies. 40% of the charge will apply in 2018–19, 60% in 2019–20, 80% in 2020–21, and 90% in 2021–22, with the rates equalised in 2022–23.

3 No charge applies to employees who have to take their van home and private use is restricted other than for ordinary commuting (insignificant use is disregarded).

| *Van fuel benefit* | |
|---|---|
| **2017–18** | **£610** |
| 2016–17 | £598 |
| 2015–16 | £594 |
| 2014–15 | £581 |
| 2013–14 | £564 |
| 2012–13 | £550 |

The fuel charge applies where the van benefit charge applies (though not where the reduced charge for zero-emission vans applies) and fuel is provided for private use.

## Related benefits

**Parking facilities:** No taxable benefit for work place provision of car or van parking spaces, or parking for bicycles or motorcycles (ITEPA 2003 s 237).

**Cycles and cyclist's safety equipment:** No taxable benefit in respect of the provision to employees of bicycles or cycling safety equipment for travel to and from work (ITEPA 2003 s 244) nor for subsequent transfer to the employee at market value (ITEPA 2003 s 206).

**On-call emergency vehicles:** No tax or NIC charge where emergency service workers have private use of their emergency vehicle when on call (ITEPA 2003 s 248A).

**Bus services:** No taxable benefit in respect of the provision of works buses with a seating capacity of 9 or more provided to employees (or their children) to travel to and from work (ITEPA 2003 s 242).

## Car and motorcycle hire: restricted allowances

(ITTOIA 2005 ss 48–50B; CTA 2009 ss 56–58B; SI 2016/984)

**Hire period from April 2009** (subject to transitional provisions), the disallowance is a flat rate of 15%. This applies only to cars with $CO_2$ emissions exceeding 130g/km (160g/km before 1 April 2013 (corporation tax) or 6 April 2013 (income tax)). **The $CO_2$ emissions threshold will be reduced to 110g/km from 1 April 2018**.

**Hire period before April 2009**, if a car with a retail price when new of more than £12,000 is acquired under a rental lease the maximum allowable deduction in computing trading profits is restricted to:

$$\frac{£12{,}000 + P}{2P} \times R$$

P = retail price of car when new. R = annual rental.

**Capital allowances** see p 30.

## Car fuel: company cars

(ITEPA 2003 ss 149–153; SI 2016/1174)

The same percentage figures on p 80 used to calculate the car benefit charge for the company car, which are directly linked to the car's $CO_2$ emissions, are used to calculate the benefit charge for fuel provided for private motoring. The relevant percentage figure is multiplied by £20,200 for 2012–13, by £21,100 for 2013–14, by £21,700 for 2014–15, by £22,100 for 2015–16, by £22,200 for 2016–17 and by **£22,600 for 2017–18**.

The benefit is reduced to nil if the employee is required to, and does, make good all fuel provided for private use. There is no taxable benefit where the employer only provides fuel for business travel. The charge is proportionately reduced where the employee stops receiving free fuel part way through the tax year, but where free fuel is subsequently provided in the same tax year, the full year's charge is payable. The benefit is proportionately reduced where a car is not available or is incapable of being used for part of a year (being at least 30 days).

| $CO_2$ emissions (g/km) | Petrol | Diesel | $CO_2$ emissions (g/km) | Petrol | Diesel | $CO_2$ emissions (g/km) | Petrol | Diesel |
|---|---|---|---|---|---|---|---|---|
| ***2015–16*** | **£** | **£** | ***2016–17*** | **£** | **£** | ***2017–18*** | **£** | **£** |
| 0–50 | 1,105 | 1,768 | 0–50 | 1,554 | 2,220 | **0–50** | 2,034 | 2,712 |
| 51–75 | 1,989 | 2,652 | 51–75 | 2,442 | 3,108 | **51–75** | 2,938 | 3,616 |
| 76–94 | 2,873 | 3,536 | 76–94 | 3,330 | 3,996 | **76–94** | 3,842 | 4,520 |
| 95–99 | 3,094 | 3,757 | 95–99 | 3,552 | 4,218 | **95–99** | 4,068 | 4,746 |
| 100–104 | 3,315 | 3,978 | 100–104 | 3,774 | 4,440 | **100–104** | 4,294 | 4,972 |
| 105–109 | 3,536 | 4,199 | 105–109 | 3,996 | 4,662 | **105–109** | 4,520 | 5,198 |
| 110–114 | 3,757 | 4,420 | 110–114 | 4,218 | 4,884 | **110–114** | 4,746 | 5,424 |
| 115–119 | 3,978 | 4,641 | 115–119 | 4,440 | 5,106 | **115–119** | 4,972 | 5,650 |
| 120–124 | 4,199 | 4,862 | 120–124 | 4,662 | 5,328 | **120–124** | 5,198 | 5,876 |
| 125–129 | 4,420 | 5,083 | 125–129 | 4,884 | 5,550 | **125–129** | 5,424 | 6,102 |
| 130–134 | 4,641 | 5,304 | 130–134 | 5,106 | 5,772 | **130–134** | 5,650 | 6,328 |
| 135–139 | 4,862 | 5,525 | 135–139 | 5,328 | 5,994 | **135–139** | 5,876 | 6,554 |
| 140–144 | 5,083 | 5,746 | 140–144 | 5,550 | 6,216 | **140–144** | 6,102 | 6,780 |
| 145–149 | 5,304 | 5,967 | 145–149 | 5,772 | 6,438 | **145–149** | 6,328 | 7,006 |
| 150–154 | 5,525 | 6,188 | 150–154 | 5,994 | 6,660 | **150–154** | 6,554 | 7,232 |
| 155–159 | 5,746 | 6,409 | 155–159 | 6,216 | 6,882 | **155–159** | 6,780 | 7,458 |
| 160–164 | 5,967 | 6,630 | 160–164 | 6,438 | 7,104 | **160–164** | 7,006 | 7,684 |
| 165–169 | 6,188 | 6,851 | 165–169 | 6,660 | 7,326 | **165–169** | 7,232 | 7,910 |
| 170–174 | 6,409 | 7,072 | 170–174 | 6,882 | 7,548 | **170–174** | 7,458 | 8,136 |
| 175–179 | 6,630 | 7,293 | 175–179 | 7,104 | 7,770 | **175–179** | 7,684 | 8,362 |
| 180–184 | 6,851 | 7,514 | 180–184 | 7,326 | 7,992 | **180–184** | 7,910 | 8,362 |
| 185–189 | 7,072 | 7,735 | 185–189 | 7,548 | 8,214 | **185–189** | 8,136 | 8,362 |
| 190–194 | 7,293 | 7,956 | 190–194 | 7,770 | 8,214 | **190 or more** | 8,362 | 8,362 |
| 195–199 | 7,514 | 8,177 | 195–199 | 7,992 | 8,214 | | | |
| 200–204 | 7,735 | 8,177 | 200 or more | 8,214 | 8,214 | | | |
| 205–209 | 7,956 | 8,177 | | | | | | |
| 210 or more | 8,177 | 8,177 | | | | | | |

| $CO_2$ emissions (g/km) | Petrol | Diesel | $CO_2$ emissions (g/km) | Petrol | Diesel | $CO_2$ emissions (g/km) | Petrol | Diesel |
|---|---|---|---|---|---|---|---|---|
| ***2012–13*** | **£** | **£** | ***2013–14*** | **£** | **£** | ***2014–15*** | **£** | **£** |
| 1–75 | 1,010 | 1,616 | 1–75 | 1,055 | 1,688 | – | – | – |
| 76–99 | 2,020 | 2,626 | 76–94 | 2,110 | 2,743 | 1–75 | 1,085 | 1,736 |
| 100–104 | 2,222 | 2,828 | 95–99 | 2,321 | 2,954 | 76–94 | 2,387 | 3,038 |
| 105–109 | 2,424 | 3,030 | 100–104 | 2,532 | 3,165 | 95–99 | 2,604 | 3,255 |
| 110–114 | 2,626 | 3,232 | 105–109 | 2,743 | 3,376 | 100–104 | 2,821 | 3,472 |
| 115–119 | 2,828 | 3,434 | 110–114 | 2,954 | 3,587 | 105–109 | 3,038 | 3,689 |
| 120–124 | 3,030 | 3,636 | 115–119 | 3,165 | 3,798 | 110–114 | 3,255 | 3,906 |
| 125–129 | 3,232 | 3,838 | 120–124 | 3,376 | 4,009 | 115–119 | 3,472 | 4,123 |
| 130–134 | 3,434 | 4,040 | 125–129 | 3,587 | 4,220 | 120–124 | 3,689 | 4,340 |
| 135–139 | 3,636 | 4,242 | 130–134 | 3,798 | 4,431 | 125–129 | 3,906 | 4,557 |
| 140–144 | 3,838 | 4,444 | 135–139 | 4,009 | 4,642 | 130–134 | 4,123 | 4,774 |
| 145–149 | 4,040 | 4,646 | 140–144 | 4,220 | 4,853 | 135–139 | 4,340 | 4,991 |
| 150–154 | 4,242 | 4,848 | 145–149 | 4,431 | 5,064 | 140–144 | 4,557 | 5,208 |
| 155–159 | 4,444 | 5,050 | 150–154 | 4,642 | 5,275 | 145–149 | 4,774 | 5,425 |
| 160–164 | 4,646 | 5,252 | 155–159 | 4,853 | 5,486 | 150–154 | 4,991 | 5,642 |
| 165–169 | 4,848 | 5,454 | 160–164 | 5,064 | 5,697 | 155–159 | 5,208 | 5,859 |
| 170–174 | 5,050 | 5,656 | 165–169 | 5,275 | 5,908 | 160–164 | 5,425 | 6,076 |
| 175–179 | 5,252 | 5,858 | 170–174 | 5,486 | 6,119 | 165–169 | 5,642 | 6,293 |
| 180–184 | 5,454 | 6,060 | 175–179 | 5,697 | 6,330 | 170–174 | 5,859 | 6,510 |
| 185–189 | 5,656 | 6,262 | 180–184 | 5,908 | 6,541 | 175–179 | 6,076 | 6,727 |
| 190–194 | 5,858 | 6,464 | 185–189 | 6,119 | 6,752 | 180–184 | 6,293 | 6,944 |
| 195–199 | 6,060 | 6,666 | 190–194 | 6,330 | 6,963 | 185–189 | 6,510 | 7,161 |
| 200–204 | 6,262 | 6,868 | 195–199 | 6,541 | 7,174 | 190–194 | 6,727 | 7,378 |
| 205–209 | 6,464 | 7,070 | 200–204 | 6,752 | 7,385 | 195–199 | 6,944 | 7,595 |
| 210–214 | 6,666 | 7,070 | 205–209 | 6,963 | 7,385 | 200–204 | 7,161 | 7,595 |
| 215–219 | 6,868 | 7,070 | 210–214 | 7,174 | 7,385 | 205–209 | 7,378 | 7,595 |
| 220 or more | 7,070 | 7,070 | 215 or more | 7,385 | 7,385 | 210 or more | 7,595 | 7,595 |

# Mileage allowances

## Advisory fuel rates for company cars

| *Engine size* | *Cost per mile* | | |
|---|---|---|---|
| | *Petrol* | *Diesel* | *LPG* |
| **From 1 September 2017** | | | |
| **1,400cc or less** | **11p** | **–** | **7p** |
| **1,600cc or less** | **–** | **9p** | **–** |
| **1,401–2,000cc** | **13p** | **–** | **8p** |
| **1,601–2,000cc** | **–** | **11p** | **–** |
| **Over 2,000cc** | **21p** | **12p** | **13p** |
| From 1 June 2017–31 August 2017 | | | |
| 1,400cc or less | 11p | – | 7p |
| 1,600cc or less | – | 9p | – |
| 1,401–2,000cc | 14p | – | 9p |
| 1,601–2,000cc | – | 11p | – |
| Over 2,000cc | 21p | 13p | 14p |
| 1 March 2017–31 May 2017 | | | |
| 1,400cc or less | 11p | – | 7p |
| 1,600cc or less | – | 9p | – |
| 1,401–2,000cc | 14p | – | 9p |
| 1,601–2,000cc | – | 11p | – |
| Over 2,000cc | 22p | 13p | 14p |
| 1 December 2016–28 February 2017 | | | |
| 1,400cc or less | 11p | – | 7p |
| 1,600cc or less | – | 9p | – |
| 1,401–2,000cc | 14p | – | 9p |
| 1,601–2,000cc | – | 11p | – |
| Over 2,000cc | 21p | 13p | 13p |
| 1 September 2016–30 November 2016 | | | |
| 1,400cc or less | 11p | – | 7p |
| 1,600cc or less | – | 9p | – |
| 1,401–2,000cc | 13p | – | 9p |
| 1,601–2,000cc | – | 11p | – |
| Over 2,000cc | 20p | 13p | 13p |
| 1 June 2016–31 August 2016 | | | |
| 1,400cc or less | 10p | – | 7p |
| 1,600cc or less | – | 9p | – |
| 1,401–2,000cc | 13p | – | 9p |
| 1,601–2,000cc | – | 10p | – |
| Over 2,000cc | 20p | 12p | 13p |
| 1 March 2016–31 May 2016 | | | |
| 1,400cc or less | 10p | – | 7p |
| 1,600cc or less | – | 8p | – |
| 1,401–2,000cc | 12p | – | 8p |
| 1,601–2,000cc | – | 10p | – |
| Over 2,000cc | 19p | 11p | 13p |
| 1 December 2015–29 February 2016 | | | |
| 1,400cc or less | 11p | – | 7p |
| 1,600cc or less | – | 9p | – |
| 1,401–2,000cc | 13p | – | 9p |
| 1,601–2,000cc | – | 11p | – |
| Over 2,000cc | 20p | 13p | 13p |
| 1 September 2015–30 November 2015 | | | |
| 1,400cc or less | 11p | – | 7p |
| 1,600cc or less | – | 9p | – |
| 1,401–2,000cc | 14p | – | 9p |
| 1,601–2,000cc | – | 11p | – |
| Over 2,000cc | 21p | 13p | 14p |

| *Engine size* | *Cost per mile* | | |
|---|---|---|---|
| | *Petrol* | *Diesel* | *LPG* |
| 1 June 2015–31 August 2015 | | | |
| 1,400cc or less | 12p | – | 8p |
| 1,600cc or less | – | 10p | – |
| 1,401–2,000cc | 14p | – | 9p |
| 1,601–2,000cc | – | 12p | – |
| Over 2,000cc | 21p | 14p | 14p |
| 1 March 2015–31 May 2015 | | | |
| 1,400cc or less | 11p | – | 8p |
| 1,600cc or less | – | 9p | – |
| 1,401–2,000cc | 13p | – | 10p |
| 1,601–2,000cc | – | 11p | – |
| Over 2,000cc | 20p | 14p | 14p |
| 1 December 2014–28 February 2015 | | | |
| 1,400cc or less | 13p | – | 9p |
| 1,600cc or less | – | 11p | – |
| 1,401–2,000cc | 16p | – | 11p |
| 1,601–2,000cc | – | 13p | – |
| Over 2,000cc | 23p | 16p | 16p |
| 1 September 2014–30 November 2014 | | | |
| 1,400cc or less | 14p | – | 9p |
| 1,600cc or less | – | 11p | – |
| 1,401–2,000cc | 16p | – | 11p |
| 1,601–2,000cc | – | 13p | – |
| Over 2,000cc | 24p | 17p | 16p |
| 1 June 2014–31 August 2014 | | | |
| 1,400cc or less | 14p | – | 9p |
| 1,600cc or less | – | 12p | – |
| 1,401–2,000cc | 16p | – | 11p |
| 1,601–2,000cc | – | 14p | – |
| Over 2,000cc | 24p | 17p | 16p |
| 1 March 2014–31 May 2014 | | | |
| 1,400cc or less | 14p | – | 9p |
| 1,600cc or less | – | 12p | – |
| 1,401–2,000cc | 16p | – | 11p |
| 1,601–2,000cc | – | 14p | – |
| Over 2,000cc | 24p | 17p | 17p |
| 1 December 2013–28 February 2014 | | | |
| 1,400cc or less | 14p | – | 9p |
| 1,600cc or less | – | 12p | – |
| 1,401–2,000cc | 16p | – | 11p |
| 1,601–2,000cc | – | 14p | – |
| Over 2,000cc | 24p | 17p | 16p |
| 1 September 2013–30 November 2013 | | | |
| 1,400cc or less | 15p | – | 10p |
| 1,600cc or less | – | 12p | – |
| 1,401–2,000cc | 18p | – | 11p |
| 1,601–2,000cc | – | 15p | – |
| Over 2,000cc | 26p | 18p | 16p |
| 1 June 2013–31 August 2013 | | | |
| 1,400cc or less | 15p | – | 10p |
| 1,600cc or less | – | 12p | – |
| 1,401–2,000cc | 17p | – | 12p |
| 1,601–2,000cc | – | 14p | – |
| Over 2,000cc | 25p | 18p | 18p |

| Engine size | Cost per mile | | |
|---|---|---|---|
| | Petrol | Diesel | LPG |
| 1 March 2013–31 May 2013 | | | |
| 1,400cc or less | 15p | – | 10p |
| 1,600cc or less | – | 13p | – |
| 1,401–2,000cc | 18p | – | 12p |
| 1,601–2,000cc | – | 15p | – |
| Over 2,000cc | 26p | 18p | 18p |

1 Payments at or below these rates are tax and NIC free. The table figures will be accepted for VAT purposes.
2 Other rates may be used if the employer can demonstrate that they are justified.
3 Rates are currently reviewed by HMRC quarterly.

## Authorised mileage rates

| | ***Rate per business mile*** | |
|---|---|---|
| **Cars or vans** | *First 10,000 miles* | *Over 10,000 miles* |
| **2011–12 onwards**[1] | **45p** | **25p** |

1 Where the employer pays less than the authorised rate the employee can claim tax relief for the difference (ITEPA 2003 ss 229–232, 235, 236).

| | ***Rate per business mile*** |
|---|---|
| **Car passengers**<br>Allowance for each fellow passenger carried | |
| **2002–03 onwards** | **5p** |
| **Cycles** | |
| **2002–03 onwards**[1] | **20p** |
| **Motorcycles** | |
| **2002–03 onwards**[1] | **24p** |

1 Where the employer pays less than the authorised rate the employee can claim tax relief for the difference (ITEPA 2003 ss 229–232, 235, 236).

## Travel expenses of members of local authorities

(ITEPA 2003 s 235A)

From April 2016 there is an exemption for qualifying payments made by a local authority in respect of travel expenses incurred by a member on a journey between home and permanent workplace provided the member's home is in the area of the authority or within 20 miles of the boundary of the area. The exemption for mileage payments will be limited to the authorised mileage rates above.

# Employment benefits and expenses payments

Pages 87 to 91 cover some common benefits and expenses payments not detailed separately elsewhere. From 6 April 2016 employees (other than lower-paid ministers of religion) earning at a rate of less than £8,500 per year will pay income tax on their benefits in kind in the same way as other employees earning at a rate of £8,500 or more. Previously all 'lower-paid' employees (ie those whose annual remuneration plus benefits was less than £8,500) were exempted from certain benefits.

## Accommodation, supplies, etc used in employment duties

(ITEPA 2003 s 316)

The provision of accommodation, supplies or services used by employees in performance of employment duties is not taxable provided:

(a) if the benefit is provided on premises occupied by the employer, any private use by the employee (or the employee's family or household) is not significant; or

(b) in any other case, the sole purpose of providing the benefit is to enable the employee to perform those duties, any private use is not significant and the benefit is not an excluded benefit (eg the provision of a motor vehicle, boat or aircraft).

## Amounts which would otherwise be deductible

(ITEPA 2003 ss 289A–289E)

From 6 April 2016 an exemption applies to expenses and benefits paid or reimbursed by the employer where the employee would be due a deduction. The exemption does not apply if the payment or reimbursement is offered in conjunction with a relevant salary sacrifice arrangement.

## Assets given to employees

(ITEPA 2003 ss 203, 204)

If new, tax is chargeable on the cost to the employer (market value in the case of a 'lower-paid' minister of religion, and before 2016–17 in the case of all 'lower-paid' employees). If used, tax is chargeable on the greater of:

(a) market value at the time of transfer; and

(b) where the asset is first applied for the provision of a benefit after 5 April 1980 and a person has been chargeable to tax on its use, market value when first so applied less amounts charged to tax for use up to and including the year of transfer.

## Buses to shops

(SI 2002/205)

The provision of buses for journeys of ten miles or less from the workplace to shops etc on a working day is not taxable.

## Cheap loans

(ITEPA 2003 ss 174–190; SI 2015/411; SI 2017/305)

A taxable benefit arises on employer-related loans to all employees other than 'lower-paid' ministers of religion (previously to directors or employees earning £8,500 or more a year), on the difference between the interest paid and interest payable at the 'official rate' below. There is no tax charge where:

(a) all the employer-related loans (or all loans not qualifying for tax relief) do not exceed £10,000 (£5,000 before 6 April 2014);

(b) all the interest payable is or would be eligible for tax relief; and

(c) the loans are ordinary commercial loans.

The provisions can apply to alternative finance arrangements entered into after 21 March 2006.

The 'official rate' is:

| **From 6 April 2017** | **2.50%** |
|---|---|
| 6 April 2015 to 5 April 2017 | 3.00% |
| 6 April 2014 to 5 April 2015 | 3.25% |
| 6 April 2010 to 5 April 2014 | 4.00% |

The average rate for the tax year is:

| **2017–18** | **2.50%** |
|---|---|
| 2016–17 | 3.00% |
| 2015–16 | 3.00% |
| 2014–15 | 3.25% |
| 2013–14 | 4.00% |
| 2012–13 | 4.00% |

The official rate is set in advance for the whole of the following tax year, subject to review if the typical mortgage rates were to fall sharply during a tax year.

## Childcare provision

(ITEPA 2003 ss 318–318D; CPA 2014; SI 2006/882; SI 2015/537)

No liability arises:

(a) where the premises (which are not wholly or mainly used as a private dwelling) are made available by the employer; or

(b) where the scheme is provided under arrangements with other persons, by one or more of those persons; or

(c) where (a) or (b) does not apply, on the first £55 per week of registered or approved childcare, or where the employee joins the scheme after 5 April 2011, the first £55 (basic rate taxpayers), £28 per week (higher rate taxpayers), £25 per week (additional rate taxpayers, £22 per week before 6 April 2013) of registered or approved childcare.

In April 2017 a 'tax-free childcare' scheme was introduced under which the Government will make a top-up payment of 25% of payments into a childcare account up to a maximum of £8,000 per year (£16,000 for a disabled child). Government support is therefore capped at a maximum of £2,000 each year per qualifying child (£4,000 for a disabled child). A child is a qualifying child until the last day of the week containing 1 September after the child's 11th birthday (16th in the case of a disabled child). There is no liability to income tax or NIC under the scheme. The scheme will be rolled out to all eligible parents by the end of 2017 and replaces those under (b) and (c) above, though existing recipients will continue to receive tax and NIC relief for as long as they remain eligible, provided that their employer continues to operate the scheme.

## Christmas parties and annual functions

(ITEPA 2003 s 264; SI 2003/1361)

Not taxable if cost does not exceed £150 per head per tax year and open to staff generally. Otherwise, fully taxable. Expenditure may be split between more than one function. (Not taxable on 'lower-paid' ministers of religion, and before 2016–17 on all 'lower-paid' employees.)

## Credit tokens

(ITEPA 2003 ss 90–96A, 363)

Where money goods or services are provided to employees through credit tokens, the cost to the employer, less any employee contribution, is taxable on the employee, except if they were used to buy certain non-taxable benefits.

## Cyclists' breakfasts

(SI 2002/205; SI 2012/1808)

**Before 6 April 2013** breakfast provided for employees arriving at the workplace by bicycle in recognition of having cycled to work is not taxable. No limit on number of such breakfasts per year. This exemption is removed from 2013–14 onwards.

## Disabled employees

(ITEPA 2003 ss 246, 247; SI 2002/1596)

The provision of, or payment for, transport for disabled employees for ordinary commuting is tax free. This also applies to the provision of equipment, services or facilities to disabled employees to help them carry out their duties of employment.

## Emergency service vehicles

(ITEPA 2003 s 248A)

There is no tax charge on any benefit arising from use of an emergency vehicle by an employee of an emergency service where private use is prohibited.

## Employees' liability insurance

(ITEPA 2003 s 346)

This is non-taxable.

## Eye tests and corrective appliances

(ITEPA 2003 s 320A)

No liability arises where the provision of tests or special corrective appliances are required under health and safety legislation and are available as required to employees generally.

## Homeworkers

(ITEPA 2003 s 316A)

Employer contributions to additional household costs not taxable where employee works at home. Supporting evidence required if contributions exceed £4 per week (£18 per month for monthly paid employees). Between 6 April 2008 and 5 April 2012 the limit was £3 per week.

## Incidental overnight expenses

(ITEPA 2003 ss 240, 241)

Not taxable where employee stays away from home on business and payment from employer does not exceed:

(a) £5 per night in the UK; or
(b) £10 per night overseas.

## Living accommodation

(ITEPA 2003 ss 97–113)

A taxable benefit (the '*basic charge*') arises on the annual rental value (or actual rent if greater) less any sums made good by the employee. There is an *additional charge* (if the basic charge is not calculated on the full open market rental value) where the cost of accommodation (including costs of any capital improvements less amounts made good by the employee) exceeds £75,000. The additional charge is the excess cost over £75,000 multiplied by the official rate for cheap loans (see above) in force at the start of the tax year less any rent paid by the employee in excess of the basic charge.

For leases of ten years or less entered into on or after 22 April 2009, a lease premium paid is to be treated as if it were rent and spread over the period of the lease accordingly.

The charges are apportioned in the case of multiple occupation or if the property is provided for only part of the year or part is used exclusively for business purposes.

**Exemption:** No taxable benefit arises where living accommodation is provided:

(a) for the proper performance of duties;
(b) by reason that it is customary to do so; or
(c) by reason of special threat to the employee's security.

The above exemptions apply to a full-time working director whose interest in the company does not exceed 5%, otherwise only exemption (c) applies to directors.

## Living expenses

(ITEPA 2003 ss 313–315)

A taxable charge arises on the cost to the employer of the employee's living expenses. For the provision of assets such as furniture, see 'Use of employer's assets' below.

Where the exemption for living accommodation above applies, the tax charge relating to living expenses (including the provision of furniture and items normal for domestic occupation) is restricted to 10% of the employee's net earnings from the related employment less any sums made good by the employee.

Expenditure on alteration and structural repairs which are normally the landlord's responsibility do not give rise to a taxable benefit.

## Long service awards

(ITEPA 2003 s 323; SI 2003/1361)

Not taxable provided the employee has at least 20 years' service and cost to the employer does not exceed £50 for each year of service. No similar award may be made within ten years of such an award.

## Meals

(ITEPA 2003 s 317)

Subsidised or free meals provided for staff generally at the workplace are not taxable. For 2011–12 onwards, however, this relief does not apply if the provision of meals is made under salary sacrifice or flexible remuneration arrangements.

## Medical check-ups, insurance and treatment

(ITEPA 2003 ss 320B, 325; SI 2014/3226; HMRC Employment Income Manual EIM21765)

**Check-ups:**

From 2009–10 onwards one screening and one check-up each year not taxable.

**Insurance:** Premiums paid on behalf of employees (other than 'lower-paid' ministers of religion, and before 2016–17 all 'lower-paid' employees) are taxable unless for treatment outside the UK whilst the employee is performing duties abroad.

**Recommended medical treatment:** From 1 January 2015 any benefit in kind or payment of earnings, up to an annual cap of £500 per employee, is not taxable where an employer meets the cost of certain recommended medical treatment in connection with an employee's return to work after a period of absence due to ill-health or injury.

## Pensions advice

(SI 2002/205; ITEPA 2003 ss 308B, 308C; F(No 2)A 2017 s 3)

Payments provided to employees in respect of advice on pensions (including on general financial and tax issues relating to pensions) are not taxable if the cost is no more than £500 (£150 before 6 April 2017 and restricted to advice on pensions).

From 6 April 2015 payments by employers in respect of independent advice provided to employees in relation to conversions and transfers of pension scheme benefits are exempt.

## Personal expenses

(ITEPA 2003 ss 70–72, 336–341)

Unless covered by specific exemptions, payments to an employee by reason of his employment in respect of expenses or allowances are taxable. Deduction is allowed for expenses the employee is obliged to incur which are:

(a) qualifying travelling expenses (broadly those necessarily incurred other than for ordinary commuting or private travel); or

(b) other amounts incurred wholly, exclusively and necessarily in the performance of employment duties.

## Relocation expenses

(ITEPA 2003 ss 271–289)

Qualifying removal expenses and benefits up to £8,000 per move in connection with job-related residential moves are not taxable. Included are expenses of disposal, acquisition, abortive acquisition, transport of belongings, travelling and subsistence, bridging loans and duplicate expenses (replacement domestic items).

## Salary sacrifice and flexible benefit arrangements

(ITEPA 2003 ss 69A, 69B; FA 2017 s 7, Sch 2)

From 2017–18 the range of benefits that attract income tax and NIC advantages when provided as part of optional remuneration arrangements is limited but savings can still be achieved on employer pension contributions and advice, employer-provided childcare, cycle to work schemes, and ultra-low emission company cars. Any arrangements in place before 6 April 2017 can continue unaffected until 2018 (with a further extension until 2021 for existing longer term agreements covering cars, living accommodation and school fees).

## Scholarships

(ITEPA 2003 ss 211–215)

An employee is taxable on the cost of any scholarship from a trust fund which does not satisfy a 25% distribution test or which is paid because of the employee's employment.

## Subscriptions and fees

(ITEPA 2003 ss 343–345)

Not taxable where paid to professional bodies and the employee has a contractual or professional requirement to be a member of the body.

## Third party gifts

(ITEPA 2003 ss 270, 324; SI 2003/1361)

Gifts during the tax year of goods and non-cash vouchers up to £250 not taxable where provided by a party unconnected with the employer and not for services provided in connection with employment.

## Trivial benefits

(ITEPA 2003 ss 323A–323C)

From 6 April 2016 there is an exemption for qualifying trivial benefits in kind costing less than £50, extending to qualifying benefits provided to former employees. An annual cap of £300 applies to office holders of close companies, and employees who are family members of those office holders.

## Use of employer's assets

(ITEPA 2003 ss 203–206, 242, 244, 319, 320; FA 2005 s 17; FA 2006 ss 60, 61; FA 2017 s 8; HMRC Brief 02/2012)

Tax is chargeable on all employees other than 'lower-paid' ministers of religion (previously all 'lower-paid' employees) on the annual rental value of land and, for other assets, at 20% of the market value when they are first lent or the rental charge to the employer if higher. No taxable benefit arises on:

(a) the loan of a mobile phone for private use. From 6 April 2006 this is restricted to one mobile phone per employee and no longer extends to the employee's family or household but phones first loaned before 6 April 2006 are not affected by the change. HMRC's view from January 2012 is that exemption applies to smartphones with retrospective effect;

(b) the use of works buses (see p 82);

(c) cycles and cycle safety equipment (see p 82);

(d) to 5 April 2006, the loan of computer equipment for private use, provided use is not restricted to directors or senior staff and value of benefit does not exceed £2,500 (computers made available for private use before 6 April 2006 are not affected by the change).

No benefit arises on the subsequent purchase by an employee at market value of computer or cycling equipment previously on loan.

From 2017–18 the benefit is reduced by periods during which the asset is unavailable for private use by the employee or his family/household, or where the asset is shared by two or more employees.

## Vouchers

(ITEPA 2003 ss 73–89, 95, 96, 268–270, 362; FA 2012 Sch 39)

Vouchers are taxable as follows.

| | | |
|---|---|---|
| (a) | Cash vouchers | On amount for which voucher can be exchanged. |
| (b) | Non-cash vouchers | On cost to employer less any contribution from employee (except where used to obtain certain non-taxable benefits). |
| (c) | Luncheon vouchers | Before 6 April 2013 on excess over 15p per working day[1]. |
| (d) | Transport vouchers | On cost to employer less any contribution from employee. |

1 The 15p exemption on luncheon vouchers is repealed from 2013–14 onwards.

# Employment exemption

## Employee-ownership trusts

(ITEPA 2003 ss 312A–312I)

From 1 October 2014 an exemption from income tax applies to qualifying bonus payments of up to £3,600 per tax year made to employees, and qualifying former employees, by a company which is owned directly or indirectly by an employee-ownership trust which meets certain qualifying conditions.

For CGT relief relating to such companies see p 38.

# Employment income

## PAYE and national insurance thresholds

| | 2012–13 | 2013–14 | 2014–15 | 2015–16 | 2016–17 | 2017–18 |
|---|---|---|---|---|---|---|
| | £ | £ | £ | £ | £ | £ |
| Weekly NI | 144/146 | 148/149 | 153 | 155/156 | 155/156 | **157** |
| Weekly PAYE | 156 | 182 | 192 | 204 | 212 | **221** |
| Monthly NI | 624/634 | 641/646 | 663 | 672/676 | 672/676 | **680** |
| Monthly PAYE | 675 | 787 | 833 | 883 | 917 | **958** |

For full list of national insurance rates see p 111.

## PAYE settlement agreements

(SI 2003/2682 Part 6; F(No 2)A 2017 s 6)

These are voluntary agreements between the employer and HMRC under which the employer agrees to meet the tax payable on certain expenses and benefits in kind that are given to his employees. Once an agreement has been signed for a tax year, there is no need to:

- enter the items covered on form P11D (and before 2016–17, form P9D);
- operate PAYE on them, or
- calculate a liability for included items which are liable for Class 1 or Class 1A NICs.

The employer pays Class 1B NICs on the items included in PAYE settlement agreements and on the total amount of tax payable. To be effective for a tax year, an agreement must be signed before 6 July following the end of the year and tax must be paid by 19 October following (or 22 October where paid electronically). They are most suited for payments and benefits provided on an irregular basis, or where benefits are for a group of employees and apportionment is difficult.

From 2018–19, the requirement for employers to agree annually with HMRC which employee expenses and benefits may be included is removed. The intention is that employers will be able to submit their PSA request at the year end, and to make ad hoc requests during the year. This will enable the introduction of a new automated process for employers to apply for a PSA.

## Personal service companies

(ITEPA 2003 ss 48–61; FA 2017 s 6, Sch 1)

These provisions are commonly known under the name 'IR35' and apply where personal services are provided to a client through an intermediary – normally the worker's personal service company. The effect of the legislation is to treat the worker as an employee of the client for working out the 'deemed employment payment'. The computation involves taking into account all payments and benefits, including those paid direct to the worker for a tax year other than by the intermediary for his services. Certain, restricted, allowable expenses, are deducted from 'earnings'. Finally, any payments or benefits received by the worker from the intermediary are deducted. Tax (under PAYE) and NIC is calculated and the amounts due are payable by the worker and his company. From 2013–14 the provisions are extended to office holders.

For public sector engagements from April 2017 the liability to pay the correct employment taxes moves from the worker's own company to the public sector body or agency/third party paying the company, and the amount will be deducted from the amount paid to the company. The normal 5% flat rate deduction from payments for the worker's services cannot be made in computing the deemed employment payment.

## Managed service companies

(ITEPA 2003 ss 61A-61J)

Where an individual provides his services through a managed service company (as defined) all payments made to him by the company are deemed to be employment income and PAYE and NIC have to be applied.

## National minimum wage

(SI 2017/465)

Hourly rate

| *Age of worker* | *apprentice rate*[2] | *Under 18*[1] | *18–20* | *21 or more*[3] | *21–24*[3] |
|---|---|---|---|---|---|
| **From 1 April 2017** | **£3.50** | **£4.05** | **£5.60** | **N/A** | **£7.05** |
| 1.10.16–31.3.17 | £3.40 | £4.00 | £5.55 | N/A | £6.95 |
| 1.4.16–30.9.16 | £3.30 | £3.87 | £5.30 | N/A | £6.70 |
| 1.10.15–5.4.16 | £3.30 | £3.87 | £5.30 | £6.70 | N/A |
| 1.10.14–30.9.15 | £2.73 | £3.79 | £5.13 | £6.50 | N/A |
| 1.10.13–30.9.14 | £2.68 | £3.72 | £5.03 | £6.31 | N/A |
| 1.10.12–30.9.13 | £2.65 | £3.68 | £4.98 | £6.19 | N/A |

1 Applies to all workers under 18 who are no longer of compulsory school age.

2 From 1 October 2010 the apprentice rate applies to apprentices aged under 19 and other apprentices in their first year of apprenticeship.

3 From 1 April 2016 workers age 25 and over are entitled to the national living wage.

## National living wage

(SI 2017/465)

Applies for employees aged 25 and over.

Hourly rate

| *Age of worker* | 25 and over |
|---|---|
| **From 1 April 2017** | **£7.50** |
| 1.4.16–31.3.17 | £7.20 |

## Basis of assessment

(ITEPA 2003 ss 14–41E)

| | ***Services performed*** | | | |
|---|---|---|---|---|
| | *Wholly in UK* | *Partly in UK* | *Partly abroad* | *Wholly abroad* |
| **Persons domiciled in UK** | | | | |
| Non-resident[2] | All | That part | None | None |
| Resident[2] | All | All[1] | All[1] | All[1] |
| **Persons domiciled outside the UK** | | | | |
| *UK employer* | | | | |
| Non-resident | All | That part | None | None |
| Meets requirement for 3-year period of non-residence[3] | All | That part | Remittances | Remittances |
| Resident | All | All[1] | All[1] | All[1] |
| *Foreign employer* | | | | |
| Non-resident | All | That part | None | None |
| Meets requirement for 3-year period of non-residence | All | That part | Remittances | Remittances |
| Resident[4] | All | That part | Remittances | Remittances |

1 Exemption for seafarers if at least half of qualifying period of over 364 days worked abroad (including 183 consecutive days). Deduction extended in April 2011 with retrospective effect to seafarers who are resident for tax purposes in a European Economic Area or European Union State, other than the United Kingdom. (ITEPA 2003 ss 378–385, HMRC Brief 10/2012).

2 A statutory residence test was introduced from 6 April 2013 and ordinary residence was abolished from that date, subject to transitional provisions in certain cases for individuals who were resident but not ordinarily resident in the UK at the end of the tax year 2012–13. Before 6 April 2013 resident but not ordinarily resident taxpayers were taxed broadly on all UK earnings and remittances for duties performed abroad.

3 An employee meets the requirement for a 3-year period of non-residence for a tax year X if he has been non-resident for three consecutive tax years and year X is any of the three years immediately following that spell of non-residence.

4 From 2014–15 an anti-avoidance measure will tax UK resident non-domiciles on an arising basis in respect of certain overseas employment income where separate employment contracts have been artificially arranged to separate the UK and overseas employment to obtain a tax advantage.

## Termination payments

(ITEPA 2003 ss 401–416)

The following lump sum payments are exempt from tax:

(a) Payments in connection with the cessation of employment on the death, injury or disability of the employee.

(b) Payments under tax-exempt pension schemes by way of compensation for loss of employment (or of earnings due to ill-health) or which can properly be regarded as a benefit earned by past service.

(c) Certain payments of terminal grants to members of the armed forces.

(d) Certain benefits under superannuation schemes for civil servants in Commonwealth overseas territories.

(e) Payments in respect of foreign service where the period of foreign service comprises:

   (i) 75% of the whole period of service; or

   (ii) the whole of the last 10 years of service; or

   (iii) where the period of service exceeded 20 years, one-half of that period, including any 10 of the last 20 years.

   Otherwise, a proportion of the payment is exempt, as follows:

$$\frac{\text{length of foreign service}}{\text{length of total service}} \times \text{amount otherwise chargeable}$$

(f) The first £30,000 of genuine ex gratia payments (where there is no 'arrangement' by the employer to make the payment).

(g) Statutory redundancy payments (included in computing £30,000 limit in (*f*) above).

**Note**: It is proposed that foreign service relief will be removed from April 2018.

## Fixed rate expenses

For most classes of industry fixed rate allowances for the upkeep of tools and special clothing have been agreed between HMRC and the trade unions concerned. Alternatively, the individual employee may claim as a deduction his or her actual expenses (ITEPA 2003 s 367). (HMRC Employment Income Manual EIM32712.)

| *Industry* | *Occupation* | | *Deduction* |
|---|---|---|---|
| Agriculture | All workers[1] | | 100 |
| Airlines | | See note 5 below | |
| Aluminium | (*a*) | Continual casting operators, process operators, de-dimplers, driers, drill punchers, dross unloaders, firemen[2], furnace operators and their helpers, leaders, mouldmen, pourers, remelt department labourers, roll flatteners | 140 |
| | (*b*) | Cable hands, case makers, labourers, mates, truck drivers and measurers, storekeepers | 80 |
| | (*c*) | Apprentices | 60 |
| | (*d*) | All other workers[1] | 120 |
| Banks and building societies | Uniformed doormen and messengers | | 60 |
| Brass and copper | Braziers, coppersmiths, finishers, fitters, moulders, turners and all other workers | | 120 |
| Building | (*a*) | Joiners and carpenters | 140 |
| | (*b*) | Cement works, roofing felt and asphalt labourers | 80 |
| | (*c*) | Labourers and navvies | 60 |
| | (*d*) | All other workers | 120 |
| Building materials | (*a*) | Stone masons | 120 |
| | (*b*) | Tilemakers and labourers | 60 |
| | (*c*) | All other workers | 80 |
| Clothing | (*a*) | Lacemakers, hosiery bleachers, dyers, scourers and knitters, knitwear bleachers and dyers | 60 |
| | (*b*) | All other workers | 60 |
| Constructional engineering[3] | (*a*) | Blacksmiths and their strikers, burners, caulkers, chippers, drillers, erectors, fitters, holders up, markers off, platers, riggers, riveters, rivet heaters, scaffolders, sheeters, template workers, turners, welders | 140 |
| | (*b*) | Banksmen, labourers, shop-helpers, slewers, straighteners | 80 |
| | (*c*) | Apprentices and storekeepers | 60 |
| | (*d*) | All other workers | 100 |
| Electrical and electricity supply | (*a*) | Those workers incurring laundry costs only | 60 |
| | (*b*) | All other workers | 120 |
| Engineering (trades ancillary to) | (*a*) | Pattern makers | 140 |
| | (*b*) | Labourers, supervisory and unskilled workers | 80 |
| | (*c*) | Apprentices and storekeepers | 60 |
| | (*d*) | Motor mechanics in garage repair shops | 120 |
| | (*e*) | All other workers | 120 |
| Fire service | Uniformed firefighters and fire officers | | 80 |
| Food | All workers | | 60 |
| Forces personnel | See note 7 below | | |
| Forestry | All workers | | 100 |
| Glass | All workers | | 80 |
| Healthcare staff in the NHS, private hospitals and nursing homes | (*a*) | Ambulance staff on active service | 185 (140 before 6 April 2014) |
| | (*b*) | Nurses and midwives, chiropodists, dental nurses, occupational, speech and other therapists, phlebotomists and radiographers | 125 (100 before 6 April 2014) |
| | (*c*) | Plaster room orderlies, hospital porters, ward clerks, sterile supply workers, hospital domestics, hospital catering staff | 125 (100 before 6 April 2014) |
| | (*d*) | Laboratory staff, pharmacists, pharmacy assistants | 80 (60 before 6 April 2014) |
| | (*e*) | Uniformed ancillary staff: maintenance workers, grounds staff, drivers, parking attendants and security guards, receptionists and other uniformed staff | 80 (60 before 6 April 2014) |
| Heating | (*a*) | Pipe fitters and plumbers | 120 |
| | (*b*) | Coverers, laggers, domestic glaziers, heating engineers and their mates | 120 |
| | (*c*) | All gas workers, all other workers | 100 |
| Iron mining | (*a*) | Fillers, miners and underground workers | 120 |
| | (*b*) | All other workers | 100 |
| Iron and steel | (*a*) | Day labourers, general labourers, stockmen, time keepers, warehouse staff and weighmen | 80 |
| | (*b*) | Apprentices | 60 |
| | (*c*) | All other workers | 140 |
| Leather | (*a*) | Curriers (wet workers), fellmongering workers, tanning operatives (wet) | 80 |
| | (*b*) | All other workers | 60 |

| *Industry* | *Occupation* | | | *Deduction* |
|---|---|---|---|---|
| Particular engineering[4] | (*a*) | Pattern makers | | 140 |
| | (*b*) | Chainmakers, cleaners, galvanisers, tinners and wire drawers in the wire drawing industry, tool-makers in the lock making industry | | 120 |
| | (*c*) | Apprentices and storekeepers | | 60 |
| | (*d*) | All other workers | | 80 |
| Police force | Uniformed police officers (ranks up to and including Chief Inspector) Community Support officers and other police service employees — see note 6 below | | | 140 |
| Precious metals | All workers | | | 100 |
| Printing | (*a*) | Letterpress section — electrical engineers (rotary presses), electrotypers, ink and roller makers, machine minders (rotary), maintenance engineers (rotary presses) and stereotypers | | 140 |
| | (*b*) | Bench hands (periodical and bookbinding section), compositors (letterpress section), readers (letterpress section), telecommunications and electronic section wire room operators, warehousemen (paper box making section) | | 60 |
| | (*c*) | All other workers | | 100 |
| Prisons | Uniformed prison officers | | | 80 |
| Public service | (i) | Dock and inland waterways | | |
| | | (*a*) | Dockers, dredger drivers, hopper steerers | 80 |
| | | (*b*) | All other workers | 60 |
| | (ii) | Public transport | | |
| | | (*a*) | Garage hands (including cleaners) | 80 |
| | | (*b*) | Conductors and drivers | 60 |
| Quarrying | All workers | | | 100 |
| Railways | (See the appropriate category for craftsmen, eg engineers, vehicles etc.) All other workers | | | 100 |
| Seamen | Carpenters | | | |
| | (*a*) | Passenger liners | | 165 |
| | (*b*) | Cargo vessels, tankers, coasters and ferries | | 140 |
| Shipyards | (*a*) | Blacksmiths and their strikers, boilermakers, burners, carpenters, caulkers, drillers, furnacemen (platers), holders up, fitters, platers, plumbers, riveters, sheet iron workers, shipwrights, tubers, welders | | 140 |
| | (*b*) | Labourers | | 80 |
| | (*c*) | Apprentices and storekeepers | | 60 |
| | (*d*) | All other workers | | 100 |
| Textiles and textile printing | (*a*) | Carders, carding engineers, overlookers and technicians in spinning mills | | 120 |
| | (*b*) | All other workers | | 80 |
| Vehicles | (*a*) | Builders, railway vehicle repairers, and railway wagon lifters | | 140 |
| | (*b*) | Railway vehicle painters and letterers, builders' and repairers' assistants | | 80 |
| | (*c*) | All other workers | | 60 |
| Wood & furniture | (*a*) | Carpenters, cabinet makers, joiners, wood carvers and woodcutting machinists | | 140 |
| | (*b*) | Artificial limb makers (other than in wood), organ builders and packing case makers | | 120 |
| | (*c*) | Coopers not providing own tools, labourers, polishers and upholsterers | | 60 |
| | (*d*) | All other workers | | 100 |

1 'All workers' and 'all other workers' refer only to manual workers who have to bear the cost of upkeep of tools and special clothing. They do not extend to other employees such as office staff.

2 'Firemen' means persons engaged to light and maintain furnaces.

3 'Constructional engineering' means engineering undertaken on a construction site, including buildings, shipyards, bridges, roads and other similar operations.

4 'Particular engineering' means engineering undertaken on a commercial basis in a factory or workshop for the purposes of producing components such as wire, springs, nails and locks.

5 A basic flat rate expenses allowance of £1,022 (£850 before 2013–14) applies to all uniformed commercial pilots, co-pilots and other flight deck crew working in the UK (but not stewards/stewardesses). A further £110 (£100 before 2013–14) allowance is allowed for the cost of travel to certain regular specified activities. From 2013–14 stewards/stewardesses may claim basic flat rate expenses of £720.

6 From 2008–09 the allowance for police officers applies to community support officers. Other police service employees who must clean their own uniform can claim a deduction of £60.

7 A flat-rate expenses allowance applies in relation to the laundering of uniforms for naval ratings and other ranks, backdated to 6 April 2008. Negotiations are continuing on a similar allowance for officers. The annual amount is £80 for the Royal Navy and £100 for the Army, RAF and Royal Marines.

8 Correct as at 27 September 2017.

# Apprenticeship levy

(FA 2016 ss 98–121)

From April 2017 an apprenticeship levy applies to UK employers in both the private and public sectors. It is set at a rate of 0.5% of an employer's pay bill and paid through PAYE. Each employer receives an allowance of £15,000 to offset against their levy payment. This means that the levy will only be paid on any pay bill in excess of £3 million. The pay bill is the total of employee earnings subject to Class 1 secondary National Insurance Contributions, as if disregarding the secondary and upper secondary thresholds.

# Investment reliefs

## Community investment tax relief

(ITA 2007 ss 333–382; CTA 2010 ss 218–269)

Investments made by an individual or company in an accredited community development finance institution (CDFI) are eligible for tax relief up to 25%. The investment may be a loan or a subscription for shares or securities. Tax relief may be claimed for the tax year or accounting period in which the investment is made and each of the four subsequent years. Relief for each year is broadly 5% of the invested amount, but from April 2013 any unused balance of the 5% annual relief can be carried forward, although not beyond the 5-year investment period, and only as long as some part of the investment remains within the CDFI. In addition, to comply with European State aid rules, from 1 April 2013 there is a limit on the amounts of relief a company can obtain in any 3-year period — the amount of CITR relief and any de minimis aid from other sources must not exceed €200,000.

## Enterprise investment scheme

(ITA 2007 ss 156–257)

The EIS applies to investments in qualifying unquoted companies trading in the UK. Eligible shares must be held for at least three years from the issue date or commencement of trade if later. The following reliefs apply subject to this and other conditions.

### Relief on investment

| | | |
|---|---|---|
| Maximum investment: | **From 2012–13** | **£1,000,000** |
| | 2008–09 to 2011–12 | £500,000 |
| Minimum investment: | **From 2012–13** | **No minimum** |
| | 1993–94 to 2011–12 | £500 |
| Maximum carry-back to preceding year | **From 2009–10** | **No restriction (subject to annual maximum)** |
| Rate of relief | **From 2011–12** | **30%**[1] |

[1] Given as a deduction against income tax liability.

**Other reliefs** (TCGA 1992 ss 150A–150C, Sch 5B)

(a) A gain on a disposal of shares on which EIS relief has been given and not withdrawn is exempt from capital gains tax.

(b) Deferral relief is available for gains on assets where the disposal proceeds are reinvested in eligible shares in a qualifying company within one year before and three years after the disposal.

(c) A loss on a disposal of shares on which EIS relief has been given may be relieved against income tax or capital gains tax.

## Seed enterprise investment scheme

(ITA 2007 ss 257A–257HG)

From 6 April 2012 SEIS applies to investments in companies with fewer than 25 employees and assets up to £200,000 carrying on or preparing to carry on new business. Eligible shares must be held for at least three years from the issue date. The following reliefs apply subject to this and other conditions.

### Relief on investment

| | | |
|---|---|---|
| Maximum investment: | **From 2012–13** | **£100,000** |
| Maximum carry-back to preceding year | **From 2013–14** | **No restriction (subject to annual maximum)** |
| Rate of relief | **From 2012–13** | **50%**[1] |

[1] Given as a deduction against income tax liability.

**Other reliefs** (TCGA 1992 ss 150E, 150G, Sch 5BB)

(a) A gain on a disposal of shares on which SEIS relief has been given and not withdrawn is exempt from capital gains tax.

(b) Reinvestment relief is available for certain gains on assets where the disposal proceeds are reinvested in SEIS and SEIS relief is claimed (see p 39).

## Social investment tax relief

(ITA 2007 ss 257J–257TE)

Between 6 April 2014 and 5 April 2019 income tax relief is available to both resident and non-UK resident individuals who subscribe for qualifying shares or make qualifying debt investments in a social enterprise which meets the requirements, and who have a UK tax liability against which to set the relief. The investment must be held for a period of three years. The following reliefs apply subject to conditions.

### Relief on investment

| | | |
|---|---|---|
| Maximum investment: | **From 2014–15** | **£1,000,000** |
| Maximum carry-back to preceding year | **From 2015–16** | **No restriction (subject to annual maximum)** |
| Rate of relief | **From 2014–15** | **30%[1]** |

1 Given as a deduction against income tax liability.

**Other reliefs**

(a) A gain on a disposal of shares on which SITR income tax relief has been given and not withdrawn is exempt from capital gains tax where shares held for at least 3 years.

(b) Deferral relief is available for gains arising on assets in the period 6 April 2014 to 5 April 2019 where the disposal proceeds are reinvested in shares or debt investments which also qualify for the SITR income tax relief (see p 39).

## Venture capital trusts

(ITA 2007 ss 258–332)

An individual who subscribes for ordinary shares in a VCT obtains income tax reliefs at the rates in the table below subject to conditions. The shares must be held for at least five years.

### Relief on investment

| | | |
|---|---|---|
| Maximum annual investment: | **From 2004–05** | **£200,000** |
| Rate of relief: | **From 2006–07** | **30%** |

### Other reliefs

(a) Dividends on shares within investment limit exempt from income tax (unless the investor's main purpose is tax avoidance) (ITTOIA 2005 s 709).

(b) Capital gains reliefs (see p 39).

## Urban Regeneration Companies

Relief is available from 1 April 2003 for expenditure incurred by businesses in making contributions to designated Urban Regeneration Companies (ITTOIA 2005 ss 82, 86; CTA 2009 ss 82, 86).

## Individual savings accounts ('ISAs')

(TA 1988 s 333; ITTOIA 2005 ss 694–701; SI 1998/1870; SI 2016/16; SI 2017/186)

Savers can subscribe to an ISA up to the following limits per tax year.

| | 2012–13 | 2013–14 | 6.4.14–30.6.14 | 1.7.14–5.4.15 | 2015–16 | 2016–17 | **2017–18** |
|---|---|---|---|---|---|---|---|
| Overall annual subscription limit | £11,280 | £11,520 | £11,880 | £15,000[1] | £15,240 | £15,240 | **£20,000** |
| Cash limit | £5,640 | £5,760 | £5,940 | £15,000[1] | £15,240 | £15,240 | **£20,000** |

1 From 1 July 2014 ISAs were reformed into a simpler product, the 'New ISA'. All existing ISAs became New ISAs and ISA savers are able to subscribe the full subscription amount to a cash account.

2 The subscription limit applies to each spouse or civil partner. From 2015–16 an additional ISA allowance is available for spouses or civil partners following the death of an ISA saver on or after 3 December 2014, equal to the value of that deceased saver's ISAs.

3 From 6 April 2016 there is the facility to offer a flexible account, whereby withdrawals during the year may be replaced without the replacement counting towards the subscription limit.

4 Shares acquired under a tax-favoured share incentive plan or SAYE option scheme may be transferred to an ISA within 90 days without tax consequences.

5 From a date to be appointed and subject to certain time limits investments retained in an ISA during the administration of a deceased saver's estate will retain their tax-advantaged status.

## Reliefs

(a) Investments under the scheme are free from income tax and capital gains tax. When an investment is transferred to an investor he is deemed to have made a disposal and reacquisition at market value and any notional gain is exempt from capital gains tax.

(b) Withdrawals may be made at any time without loss of tax relief.

## Lifetime ISA

From 6 April 2017 individuals aged between 18 and 40 are able to save up to £4,000 per year into one Lifetime ISA and receive a 25% bonus from the Government at the end of the year. Contributions can continue to be made with the bonus paid up to the age of 50. Funds, including the Government bonus, can be used to buy a first home up to the value of £450,000 at any time from 12 months after opening the account, and can be withdrawn tax-free from age 60 for use in retirement. Withdrawals prior to that will forfeit the Government bonus (plus added interest) and also attract a charge. If an individual has a Help to Buy: ISA he can transfer those savings into the Lifetime ISA in 2017–18, or continue saving into both, or open a Help to Buy: ISA after opening a Lifetime ISA, but he will only be able to use the bonus from one of the ISAs to buy a house.

## Help to Buy: ISAs

Help to Buy: ISAs are available from 1 December 2015 to 30 November 2019 for first-time house buyers. The Government will provide a top-up of 25% of savings up to a maximum monthly savings amount of £200, and the total bonus available will be capped at £3,000 on £12,000 of savings. It is possible to deposit an additional £1,000 when the account is first opened and there is no limit to how long the account may remain open. The interest on the account and the bonus will be tax-free. The bonus will be paid at the time of completion of the purchase of the property provided the property is worth a maximum of £450,000 in London and £250,000 elsewhere in the UK. Accounts are limited to one per person rather than one per property. See above regarding Lifetime ISAs held at the same time as Help to Buy: ISAs.

## Junior individual savings accounts (Junior ISAs)

(ITTOIA 2005 s 695A; SI 2011/1780; SI 2017/186)

The Junior ISA scheme is available to all UK resident children under 18 who do not have a Child Trust Fund account or, from 6 April 2015, to those who wish to transfer a Child Trust Fund account to a Junior ISA. Children are able to have one cash and one stocks and shares Junior ISA at any time.

| | 2013–14 | 6.4.14–30.6.14 | 1.7.14–5.4.15 | 2015–16 | 2016–17 | **2017–18** |
|---|---|---|---|---|---|---|
| Overall annual subscription limit | £3,720 | £3,840 | £4,000 | £4,080 | £4,080 | **£4,128** |

# Miscellaneous reliefs

## Trading allowance and property allowance

(ITTOIA 2005 ss 783A–783AR, 783B–783BQ; F(No 2)A 2017 s 17, Sch 3)

From 6 April 2017 a trading allowance and a property allowance of £1,000 each per year are available to certain individuals. They are not available on income of partners or close company participators, or where rent-a-room relief could be claimed. Where total receipts are less than £1,000, the allowance is given automatically, no tax is payable and the income need not be declared. An election can be made for relief not to apply at all, or for partial relief to apply where receipts exceed £1,000 so that the allowance rather than expenses is deducted from gross receipts.

## Employee shareholder shares

(ITEPA 2003 ss 226A–226D; SI 2013/1755; FA 2017 ss 12–14)

From 1 September 2013 the first £2,000 of the value of shares acquired through the adoption of the 'employee shareholder' employment status is not subject to income tax or national insurance, provided the Employee Shareholder Agreement was entered into before 1 December 2016 (or 2 December 2016 where professional advice was given in relation to the share offer on 23 November 2016 before 1.30pm). For the capital gains tax rules see p 38.

## Foster carers and shared lives carers (Qualifying care)

(ITTOIA 2005 ss 803–828)

Generally, local authority payments to foster carers are not taxable to the extent they do no more than meet the actual costs of caring. In other cases, and for shared lives carers from 6 April 2010:

- where gross receipts do not exceed the 'individual limit' and shared lives care is not being provided to more than three people, the carer is treated as having a nil profit and nil loss for the tax year concerned;
- where gross receipts exceed the 'individual limit' and shared lives care is not being provided to more than three people, the carer can choose to either be taxed on the excess or compute profit or loss using the normal business rules.

The 'individual limit' is made up of a fixed amount of £10,000 per residence for a full tax year plus an amount per adult or child for each week or part week that the individual provides qualifying care. The weekly amounts are £200 for a child under 11 years and £250 for a child of 11 or over and an adult.

## Gift of pre-eminent objects

(FA 2012 Sch 14)

With effect in relation to liabilities for tax years and accounting periods beginning on or after 1 April 2012, individuals who gift pre-eminent objects to the nation will receive a reduction in their UK tax liability of 30% of the value of the object they are donating. The tax reduction can be against income or capital gains tax and can be spread forward across a period of up to five years starting with the tax year in which the object is offered. The gift must be accepted as pre-eminent by the Arts Council under the Cultural Gifts Scheme.

## Landlord's energy-saving allowance

(ITTOIA 2005 ss 312–314; CTA 2009 ss 251–253; SI 2007/831; SI 2007/3278; SI 2008/1520)

***From 6 April 2004 to 5 April 2015*** individual landlords who let residential property and pay income tax could claim a deduction from the property business profits for expenditure in the dwelling-houses let to install:

- loft insulation or cavity wall insulation; or
- (from 7 April 2005) solid wall insulation; or
- (from 6 April 2006) draught-proofing and insulation for hot water systems; or
- (from 6 April 2007) floor insulation.

Expenditure is restricted to £1,500 per building until 5 April 2007 and to £1,500 per dwelling-house from 6 April 2007.

The relief was extended to corporate landlords of residential property for expenditure on or after 8 July 2008.

## Life assurance premium relief

(TA 1988 s 266, Sch 14 para 7; FA 2012 Sch 39)

For premiums due and payable ***before 6 April 2015***, or payable before that date and actually paid before 6 July 2015, relief for premiums paid on qualifying life assurance policies for contracts made before 14 March 1984 is available by deduction of 12.5% from admissible premiums.

## Maintenance payments

(ITTOIA 2005 ss 727, 729; ITA 2007 ss 453–456)

Where either party to the marriage or civil partnership was born before 6 April 1935 tax relief may be claimed by the payer in respect of the lower of:

- the amount of the payments in the year concerned and
- the minimum amount of the married couple's allowance for the year concerned (see p 78).

The relief is restricted to 10% of the relevant amount. The payment must be made to the former/separated spouse or civil partner. It is made gross and is not taxable in the hands of the recipient.

## Rent-a-room relief

(ITTOIA 2005 ss 784–802; SI 2015/1539)

Gross annual receipts from letting furnished accommodation in the only or main home are exempt from tax up to a maximum of £7,500 (£4,250 before 6 April 2016) (provided no other taxable income is derived from a trade, letting or arrangement from which the rent-a-room receipts are derived).

If the gross receipts exceed £7,500 (£4,250 before 6 April 2016), the taxpayer can pay tax on the net receipts after deduction of expenses. Alternatively, the taxpayer can elect to pay tax on the amount by which the gross receipts exceed £7,500, without relief for the actual expenses.

An individual's maximum is halved to £3,750 (£2,125 before 6 April 2016) if during the 'relevant period' for the year (normally the tax year) some other person received income from letting accommodation in that property.

An election can be made to disapply the relief for a particular tax year (for example, if the individual would otherwise make an allowable loss).

# Simplified fixed rate deductions

(ITTOIA 2005 ss 94B–94I)

From 2013–14 individuals carrying on a trade, profession or vocation as self-employed sole traders or in partnership with other individuals can choose certain simplified expenses when calculating their profits for income tax purposes. Conditions apply.

**Vehicle expenditure**

| Kind of vehicle | Rate per business mile |
|---|---|
| Car or goods vehicle | 45p for the first 10,000 miles |
| | 25p after that |
| Motor cycle | 24p |

**Use of home for business purposes**

| Hours worked per month | Amount per month |
|---|---|
| 25 or more | £10 |
| 51 or more | £18 |
| 101 or more | £26 |

**Premises used both as a home and for business**

**Note**: Amount below is the non-business use amount to be deducted from the total expenses claimed. The flat rate includes all household goods and services, food and non-alcoholic drinks and utilities. It does not include mortgage interest, rent of the premises, council tax or rates. A reasonable apportionment of these expenses should be made based on the extent of the private occupation of the premises — HMRC Brief 14/2013.

| Number of occupants | Disallowance amount per month |
|---|---|
| 1 | £350 |
| 2 | £500 |
| 3 or more | £650 |

# Capped income tax reliefs

(ITA 2007 s 24A)

From 2013–14 a limit on previously uncapped income tax reliefs is imposed. The limit is set at the greater of £50,000 or 25% of the individual's adjusted total income for the tax year. The specified reliefs which, taken together, will be limited to the extent that they can be relieved by individuals against general income are:

- Trade loss relief against general income (ITA 2007 s 64)
- Early trade losses relief (ITA 2007 s 72)
- Post-cessation trade relief (ITA 2007 s 96)
- Property loss relief against general income (ITA 2007 s 120)
- Post-cessation property relief (ITA 2007 s 125)
- Employment loss relief against general income (ITA 2007 s 128)
- Former employees deduction for liabilities (ITEPA 2003 s 555)
- Share loss relief on non-Enterprise Investment Scheme / Seed Enterprise Investment Scheme shares (ITA 2007 Pt 4 Ch 6)
- Losses on deeply discounted securities (ITTOIA 2005 ss 446, 454)
- Qualifying loan interest (ITA 2007 Pt 8 Ch 1)

# Pension provision

(FA 2004 ss 149–284, Schs 28–36; F(No 2)A 2017 s 7)

## Tax relief on contributions

**Individual contributions:** An individual may make unlimited contributions and tax relief is available on contributions up to the higher of:

- the full amount of relevant earnings; or
- £3,600 provided the scheme operates tax relief at source,

and subject to the annual allowance.

**Employer contributions:** Employer contributions to registered schemes are deductible for tax purposes, with statutory provision for spreading abnormally large contributions over a period of up to four years. The contributions are not treated as taxable income of the employee, although from 6 April 2013 this relief does not extend to payments for the benefit of family members.

## Annual allowance

Each individual has an annual allowance as set out in the table below. If the annual increase in an individual's rights under all registered schemes exceeds the annual allowance, the excess is chargeable at the individual's marginal rate. The individual is liable for the tax, unless he makes an election for the scheme to pay the charge if it exceeds £2,000. In such cases a consequential adjustment is made to the individual's entitlement to benefits.

| Annual allowance | 2011–12 | 2012–13 | 2013–14 | 2014–15 to 2015–16 | **2016–17 onwards** |
|---|---|---|---|---|---|
| Maximum | £50,000[1] | £50,000[1] | £50,000[1] | £40,000[1, 2] | **£40,000[1, 2]** |
| Minimum[3] | N/A | N/A | N/A | N/A | **£10,000[3]** |

1 From 2011–12 unused allowance can be carried forward three years. For these purposes the annual allowance for 2008–09 to 2010–11 is assumed to be £50,000.

2 Where members make use of flexible access to their money purchase funds from 6 April 2015 the annual allowance is effectively divided between money purchase inputs and defined benefit inputs, resulting in a 'money purchase annual allowance' of £4,000 (£10,000 before 6 April 2017) and an 'alternative annual allowance' that applies to any defined benefit inputs of £36,000 (£30,000 before 6 April 2017). The money purchase annual allowance cannot be increased by amounts brought forward.

3 A tapered reduction in the annual allowance applies from 6 April 2016 for those with an 'adjusted income' (i.e. including pension contributions) over £150,000. The reduction is £1 for every £2 of income over £150,000 and the minimum allowance will be £10,000.

## Taxable benefits

**'Tax-free' lump sum:** The maximum 'tax-free' lump sum that can be paid to a member under a registered scheme is broadly the lower of:

- 25% of the value of the pension rights; and
- 25% of the member's lifetime allowance.

**Lifetime allowance:** Each individual has a lifetime allowance for contributions as set out in the table below. The excess over the lifetime allowance of the benefits crystallising (usually when a pension begins to be paid) is taxable at the following rates:

- 55% if taken as a lump sum;
- 25% in other cases.

Any tax due may be deducted from the individual's benefits.

| Lifetime allowance | 2011–12 | 2012–13 | 2013–14 | 2014–15 to 2015–16 | **2016–17 to 2017–18** |
|---|---|---|---|---|---|
| | £1,800,000 | £1,500,000 | £1,500,000 | £1,250,000 | **£1,000,000** |

**Transitional.** There are transitional provisions for the protection of lump sum and other pension rights accrued before 6 April 2006. Fixed protection also applies to protect pension rights from 6 April 2012, from 6 April 2014 and from 6 April 2016 when the lifetime allowance is decreased. 'Individual protection 2014' and 'individual protection 2016' are also available.

## Age restrictions

**Minimum pension age:** The minimum pension age is 55. A pension cannot be paid before the minimum age except on grounds of ill health. Protection applies to those with existing contractual rights to draw a pension earlier and for members of pre-6 April 2006 approved schemes with early retirement ages. A reduced lifetime allowance will apply in the case of early retirement before minimum pension age except in the case of certain professions such as the police and the armed forces (SI 2005/3451).

# Share schemes

## Share incentive plans ('SIPs')

(TCGA 1992 ss 236A, 238A, Schs 7C, 7D Pt 1; ITEPA 2003 ss 488–515, Sch 2)

### Free share plan

| | | |
|---|---|---|
| **2014–15 onwards** | *annual maximum* | **£3,600** |
| 2000–01 to 2013–14 | *annual maximum* | £3,000 |

### Partnership share plan

| | | |
|---|---|---|
| **2014–15 onwards** | *annual maximum* | **£1,800 or 10% of annual salary if lower** |
| 2003–04 to 2013–14 | *annual maximum* | £1,500 or 10% of annual salary if lower |

### Matching shares

| | | |
|---|---|---|
| **2000–01 onwards** | *Maximum number of shares given by employer to employee for each partnership share bought* | 2 |

Shares are free of tax and NICs if held in the plan for five years. Dividends are tax-free if reinvested in shares (restricted to a maximum of £1,500 per employee per tax year before 6 April 2013). Shares withdrawn from the plan at any time are exempt from capital gains tax and treated as acquired by the employee at their market value at that time.

If shares are withdrawn within between three and five years (with exceptions such as on death, injury, disability, retirement, redundancy, or, from 17 July 2013, certain cash takeovers), liability to income tax and NICs arises on the lower of their value on entering and on leaving the plan. If shares are withdrawn within three years (with similar exceptions), liability is on their value on leaving the plan.

Employer self-certification replaces HMRC approval from 6 April 2014.

## Enterprise management incentives

(TCGA 1992 s 238A, Sch 7D Pt 4; ITEPA 2003 ss 527–541, Sch 5)

Certain independent trading companies with gross assets not exceeding £30 million may grant share options then worth up to £250,000 (£120,000 for options granted before 16 June 2012, £100,000 for options granted before 6 April 2008) to an eligible employee. The total value of shares in respect of which unexercised qualifying options exist must not exceed £3 million. Limited to companies with fewer than 250 full-time equivalent employees for options granted on or after 21 July 2008.

Where the conditions of the scheme are complied with:

(a) There is no charge to tax or NICs when the option is granted provided the option to acquire the shares is not at less than their market values at that date, and there is no charge on exercise providing the option is exercised within ten years.

(b) Capital gains tax will be payable when the shares are sold, though for disposals on or after 6 April 2013, shares acquired through exercising EMI options on or after 6 April 2012 are eligible for capital gains tax entrepreneurs' relief if certain conditions are met.

## Save as you earn (SAYE) share option schemes

(TCGA 1992 s 238A, Sch 7D Pt 2; ITEPA 2003 ss 516–519, Sch 3)

The scheme is linked to a savings arrangement, on which bonuses are exempt from tax, to provide funds for the acquisition of shares when the option is exercised at the end of a three or five-year contract. A five-year contract may offer the option of repayment on the seventh anniversary, although the 7-year savings period is withdrawn with effect from 23 July 2013. Employees who were already saving under existing SAYE contracts before 23 July 2013 were not affected by this change.

### Monthly contributions to SAYE scheme

| | up to 5 April 2014 | **From 6 April 2014** |
|---|---|---|
| *Minimum* | £5–10[1] | **£5–£10**[1] |
| *Maximum* | £250 | **£500** |

[1] The company may choose a minimum savings contribution between £5 and £10.

See the HMRC website (www.gov.uk/government/publications/change-in-bonus-rates-for-save-as-you-earn-saye-share-option-schemes) for the latest bonus rates.

Where the conditions of the scheme are complied with, no income tax charge arises on the employee in respect of:

(a) the grant of an option to acquire shares at a discount of up to 20% of the share price at time of the grant;

(b) the exercise of the option (options must not be exercised before the bonus date subject to exceptions such as on injury, disability, redundancy, retirement, death or, from 17 July 2013, certain cash takeovers); or
(c) any increase in the value of the shares.

Capital gains tax is chargeable on disposal of the shares: the CGT base cost is the consideration given by the employee for both the shares and the option.

Employer self-certification replaces HMRC approval from 6 April 2014.

## Company share option plans ('CSOPs')

(TCGA 1992 s 238A, Sch 7D Pt 3; ITEPA 2003 ss 521–526, Sch 4)

### Limit on value of shares under option held by employee at any one time

| | |
|---|---|
| From 29 April 1996 | **£30,000** |

Scheme shares must be fully paid up, not redeemable and, for options granted before 17 July 2013, not subject to special restrictions. Only full-time directors or qualifying employees may participate in the scheme.

Where the conditions of the scheme are complied with, no tax charge arises on the employee in respect of:
(a) the grant of an option to acquire shares[1];
(b) the exercise of the option[2]; or
(c) any increase in the value of the shares.

Capital gains tax is chargeable on disposal of the shares: the CGT base cost is the consideration given by the employee for both the shares and the option.

Employer self-certification replaces HMRC approval from 6 April 2014.

1 At the time the option is granted the price at which shares can be acquired must not be less than the market value of shares of the same class at that time.

2 The option must be exercised between three and ten years after the grant (or may be exercised less than three years after the grant where the individual ceases to be an employee due to injury, disability, redundancy or retirement, or, from 17 July 2013, where there are certain cash takeovers of constituent companies). For options granted before 9 April 2003, the options had to be exercised between three and ten years after the grant (without exception) and not less than three years after a previous exempt exercise of another option under the same or another approved company share option scheme.

# Tax credits

(TCA 2002)

Tax credits are administered and paid by HMRC, and are non-taxable. Claims must be made after the commencement of the tax year and can be backdated for a maximum of one month (three months before 6 April 2012). Universal credit will replace tax credits. New claimants in some areas started to claim universal credit from October 2013. Existing claimants will be gradually phased onto universal credit, and this is expected to be completed by 2021 (see p 134).

## Child tax credit and working tax credit

| | ***2016–17*** ***Annual amount*** | ***2017–18*** ***Annual amount*** |
|---|---|---|
| **Child tax credit** | £ | **£** |
| Family element[1] | 545 | **545** |
| Child element (for each child or young person)[2] | 2,780 | **2,780** |
| Addition for disabled child or young person | 3,140 | **3,175** |
| Enhancement for severe disabled child or young person | 1,275 | **1,290** |
| **Working tax credit** | £ | **£** |
| Basic element | 1,960 | **1,960** |
| Lone parent and couple element | 2,010 | **2,010** |
| 30-hour element | 810 | **810** |
| Disability element | 2,970 | **3,000** |
| Severe disability element | 1,275 | **1,290** |
| Childcare element – up to 70% of eligible costs | Weekly | **Weekly** |
| – maximum eligible cost for one child | 175 | **175** |
| – maximum eligible cost for two or more children | 300 | **300** |

1 Only one family element per family. It is not payable to those starting a family after 5 April 2017.

2 No child element is payable for third and subsequent children born after 5 April 2017. Does not apply to disabled child element or severely disabled child element and multiple births are protected.

| *Income thresholds and withdrawal rates* | *2016–17* | *2017–18* |
|---|---|---|
| Income threshold for those entitled to CTC and WTC | £6,420 | **£6,420** |
| Withdrawal rate | 41% | **41%** |
| Income threshold for those entitled to CTC only | £16,105 | **£16,105** |
| Income rise disregard | £2,500 | **£2,500** |
| Income fall disregard | £2,500 | **£2,500** |

**Calculation of award.** Tax credits are awarded on an annual basis. They are initially based on the income of the claimant or joint claimants for the preceding tax year and adjusted based on actual income in the tax year in which the credit is claimed. Income broadly includes all taxable income excluding the first £300 of income from pensions, savings, property or foreign assets. If current year's income is greater than the previous year's income by less than £2,500 (£5,000 for 2013–14 to 2015–16, £10,000 for 2012–13), the award is not adjusted. If current year's income is greater than the previous year's income by £2,500 or more (£5,000 for 2013–14 to 2015–16, £10,000 for 2012–13), the award is adjusted to reflect current year's income less £2,500. An income fall disregard of £2,500 applies from 6 April 2012. Thus from 2012–13, where previous year's income exceeds the current year's income by not more than £2,500, the previous year's income will be used, but where the previous year's income exceeds the current year's income by more than £2,500, the current year's income plus £2,500 will be used. In any other case current year's income is used. Where circumstances change during a tax year and different rates apply, the award is recalculated on a proportional, daily basis. Such changes must be notified to HMRC within one month if tax credit entitlement will be reduced as a result.

**Eligibility.** CTC is payable to UK resident single parents and couples responsible for a child or young person. WTC is payable to UK residents who are at least 16 years old and, in the case of single persons, who work at least 16 hours a week. In the case of a couple, from 6 April 2012, they must jointly work at least 24 hours a week and one must work at least 16 hours a week, or where only one of the couple works that person must work for at least 24 hours a week. Additionally, the claimant (or one of them if a couple) must either:

- be at least 25 years old and work at least 30 hours a week; or
- have a dependent child or children; or
- have a mental or physical disability which puts them at a disadvantage in getting a job and have previously been in receipt of some form of disability benefit; or
- from 6 April 2011, be over 60 and work at least 16 hours a week, regardless of whether they have dependent children.

**Renewal claim.** Claims for tax credit must be renewed by 31 July.

# Inheritance tax

## Rates of tax

(IHTA 1984 s 7, Schs 1, 1A; HMRC Inheritance Tax Manual IHTM14593)

### From 15 March 1988 onwards

| | *Rate* |
|---|---|
| **Cumulative gross transfer rate:** | |
| for gross transfers on death over the cumulative chargeable transfer limit | **40%** |
| reduced rate on death | **36%**[1] |
| for gross lifetime transfers over the cumulative chargeable transfer limit | **20%** |
| **Grossing-up net transfer rate** for each £1 over the chargeable transfer limit: | |
| for net transfers on death not bearing own tax | **2/3** |
| for net lifetime transfers | **1/4** |

1 For deaths occurring on or after 6 April 2012 a reduced rate of 36% applies where at least 10% of the net estate is left to charity or registered community amateur sports clubs.

### Nil rate bands[3]

(IHTA 1984 ss 8–8D)

| *Period* | *Limit* | *Period* | *Limit* |
|---|---|---|---|
| | £ | | £ |
| **2009–10 to 2020–21**[2] | 325,000[1] | 1998–99 | 223,000 |
| 2008–09 | 312,000[1] | 1997–98 | 215,000 |
| 2007–08 | 300,000[1] | 1996–97 | 200,000 |
| 2006–07 | 285,000 | 1995–96 | 154,000 |
| 2005–06 | 275,000 | 10.3.92–5.4.95 | 150,000 |
| 2004–05 | 263,000 | 6.4.91–9.3.92 | 140,000 |
| 2003–04 | 255,000 | 1990–91 | 128,000 |
| 2002–03 | 250,000 | 1989–90 | 118,000 |
| 2001–02 | 242,000 | 15.3.88–5.4.89 | 110,000 |
| 2000–01 | 234,000 | 17.3.87–14.3.88 | 90,000 |
| 1999–2000 | 231,000 | 18.3.86–16.3.87 | 71,000 |

1 Any nil-rate band which is unused on a person's death can be transferred to their surviving spouse or civil partner for the purposes of the charge to tax on the death of the survivor on or after 9 October 2007.

2 The nil rate band is frozen at £325,000 until 5 April 2021.

3 An additional **residence nil-rate band** applies when a home is passed on death to direct descendants of the deceased on or after 6 April 2017. **The band is £100,000 in 2017–18** and will increase in stages up to £175,000 in 2020–21. Any unused band is transferable to a spouse or civil partner. There is a tapered withdrawal of the band for estates valued at more than £2 million. It also applies where an individual downsizes from a higher value residence to a lower value one or ceases to own a home on or after 8 July 2015 and assets of equivalent value are passed on death to direct descendants.

## Capital transfer tax nil rate bands

| ***Period*** | ***Limit*** | ***Period*** | ***Limit*** |
|---|---|---|---|
| | **£** | | **£** |
| 6.4.85–17.3.86 | 67,000 | 26.3.80–8.3.82 | 50,000 |
| 13.3.84–5.4.85 | 64,000 | 27.10.77–25.3.80 | 25,000 |
| 15.3.83–12.3.84 | 60,000 | 13.3.75–26.10.77 | 15,000 |
| 9.3.82–14.3.83 | 55,000 | | |

## Estate duty nil rate bands (England, Scotland and Wales)

| ***Period*** | ***Limit*** | ***Period*** | ***Limit*** |
|---|---|---|---|
| | **£** | | **£** |
| 22.3.72–12.3.75 | 15,000 | 9.4.62–3.4.63 | 4,000 |
| 31.3.71–21.3.72 | 12,500 | 30.7.54–8.4.62 | 3,000 |
| 16.4.69–30.3.71 | 10,000 | 10.4.46–29.7.54 | 2,000 |
| 4.4.63–15.4.69 | 5,000 | 16.8.14–9.4.46 | 100 |

## Delivery of accounts: due dates

(IHTA 1984 s 216)

| *Type of transfer* | *Due date* |
|---|---|
| Chargeable lifetime transfers | Later of:<br>(*a*) 12 months after the end of the month in which the transfer took place; and<br>(*b*) three months after the date on which the person delivering the account became liable |
| Relevant property settlements periodic and exit charges | 6 months after end of the month in which the chargeable event occurred. (For chargeable events before 6 April 2014, as for chargeable lifetime transfers, see above)[1] |
| PETs which become chargeable | 12 months after the end of the month in which the transferor died |
| Gifts with reservation chargeable on death | 12 months after the end of the month in which the death occurred |
| Transfers on death | Later of:<br>(*a*) 12 months after the end of the month in which the death occurred; and<br>(*b*) three months after the date on which the personal representatives first act or the person liable first has reason to believe that he is liable to deliver an account |
| National heritage property | 6 months after the end of the month in which the chargeable event occurred |

1 Where higher IHT is payable as a result of IHTA 1984 Sch A1 or the F(No 2)A 2017 domicile changes, the delivery date is the last day of the month following the month of Royal Assent to F(No 2)A 2017 if later than normal due date.

## Delivery of accounts: excepted transfers and estates

(SI 2004/2543; SI 2008/606)

| *Date of transfer or death* | *6 April 2000–5 April 2002* | *6 April 2002–5 April 2003* | *6 April 2003–31 Aug 2006* | *From 1 Sept 2006* |
|---|---|---|---|---|
| *Excepted transfers:* | *Value below* | *Value below* | *Value below* | *Value below* |
| Total chargeable transfers since 6 April | £10,000 | £10,000 | £10,000 | £10,000 |
| Total chargeable transfers during last ten years | £40,000 | £40,000 | £40,000 | £40,000 |
| *Excepted estates:* | | | | |
| Total gross value[1] | £210,000 | £220,000 | (see (*a*) below) | (see (*a*) below) |
| Total gross value of property outside UK | £50,000 | £75,000 | £75,000 | £100,000 |
| Aggregate value of 'specified transfers'[2] | £75,000 | £100,000 | £100,000 | £150,000 |
| Settled property passing on death | – | £100,000 | £100,000 | £150,000 |

For chargeable transfers after 5 April 2007, no account need be delivered where:

(i) the transfer is of cash or quoted shares or securities and the value of the transfer and other chargeable transfers made in the preceding seven years does not exceed the IHT threshold; or

(ii) the value of the transfer and other chargeable transfers made in the preceding seven years does not exceed 80% of the IHT threshold and the value of the transfer does not exceed the net amount of the threshold available to the transferor at the time of the transfer.

For footnotes see the list below.

## Excepted estates

For deaths occurring after 5 April 2004, no account need be delivered where the deceased died domiciled in the UK provided either conditions (a) or (b) below are met, and both conditions (c) and (d) below are met.

(a) the aggregate of the gross value of the estate, and of any 'specified transfers'[2] or 'specified exempt transfers'[3] does not exceed the appropriate IHT threshold[4];

(b) the aggregate of the gross value of the estate, and of any 'specified transfers'[2] or 'specified exempt transfers'[3] does not exceed £1,000,000; for deaths after 28 February 2011 at least part of the estate passes to the person's spouse, civil partner or to a charity; and after deducting from that aggregate figure any exempt spouse, civil partner and charity transfers and total estate liabilities[6], it does not exceed the appropriate IHT threshold[4];

(c) the gross value of settled property or foreign assets do not exceed the limits in the above table; and

(d) there were no chargeable lifetime transfers in the seven years before death other than specified transfers not exceeding the limits in the above table[5].

For deaths occurring after 31 August 2006 and before 6 April 2011, an estate will not be an excepted estate if the provisions for alternatively secured pension funds in IHTA 1984 ss 151A–151C (now repealed) apply by reason of the individual's death.

Where the deceased was never domiciled in the UK, no account need be delivered for deaths after 5 April 2002 provided that:

- the value of the estate in the UK is wholly attributable to cash and quoted shares and securities not exceeding £150,000 (£100,000 before 1 September 2006); and
- for deaths occurring after 31 August 2006 and before 6 April 2011, the provisions for alternatively secured pension funds in IHTA 1984 ss 151A–151C (now repealed) do not apply by reason of the individual's death.

1 See table above — This limit applies to the aggregate gross value of the estate and of 'specified transfers' and 'specified exempt transfers'. For deaths after 28 February 2011 transfers treated as normal expenditure out of income made within 7 years before death and totalling more than £3,000 in any tax year will be treated as chargeable transfers for these purposes.

2 'Specified transfers' are chargeable transfers of cash, quoted shares and securities and, after 6 April 2002, interests in or over land and, after 5 April 2004, personal chattels or corporeal moveable property. For deaths after 28 February 2011 transfers treated as normal expenditure out of income made within 7 years before death and totalling more than £3,000 in any tax year will be treated as chargeable transfers for these purposes.

3 'Specified exempt transfers' are transfers in the seven years before death between spouses or civil partners, gifts to charity, political parties or housing associations, transfers to maintenance funds for historical buildings, etc or to employee trusts.

4 For deaths after 5 April 2010 the IHT threshold for these purposes is increased by 100% where—

(a) the deceased is a surviving spouse or civil partner;

(b) a claim has been made for the transfer of the unused nil-rate band of their deceased spouse or civil partner;

(c) all of the first deceased spouse's or civil partner's nil-rate band was unused; and

(d) the first deceased met certain other criteria similar to those listed above for excepted estates.

5 For deaths after 28 February 2011 transfers treated as normal expenditure out of income made within 7 years before death and totalling more than £3,000 in any tax year will be treated as chargeable transfers for these purposes.

6 For deaths on or after 1 April 2014 total estate liabilities do not include those which are not discharged on or after death out of the estate in money or money's worth, or those which are prevented by any other provision in IHTA 1984 from being taken into account, or those attributable to financing the acquisition of, or maintenance or enhancement of the value of, excluded property.

## Excepted settlements

No account need be delivered of property comprised in an excepted settlement (i.e. one with no qualifying interest in possession) where a chargeable event occurs after 5 April 2007 and cash not exceeding £1,000 is the only property comprised in the settlement. Other conditions to be fulfilled are that, the settlor has not provided further property, the trustees are UK resident throughout the settlement's existence and there are no related settlements.

# Reliefs

The following is a summary of the main reliefs and exemptions under the Inheritance Tax Act 1984 (Parts II and V). The legislation should be referred to for conditions and exceptions.

**Agricultural property**

| | |
|---|---|
| Transfer with vacant possession (or right to obtain it within 12 months); transfer on or after 1 September 1995, of land let (or treated as let) on or after that date. | 100% of agricultural value |
| Any other case. | 50% of agricultural value |

*Note:* The 100% relief is extended in limited circumstances by Concession F17.

**Annual gifts** £3,000

**Business property**

| | | | |
|---|---|---|---|
| Unincorporated business. | 100% | | |
| Unquoted shares (including shares in AIM or USM companies) (held for 2 years or more).[1] | 100% | Controlling holding in fully quoted companies. | 50% |
| Unquoted securities which alone, or together with other such securities and unquoted shares, give the transferor control of the company (held for 2 years or more).[1] | 100% | Land, buildings, machinery or plant used in business of company or partnership. | 50% |
| Settled property used in life tenant's business. | 100% | | |

[1] Tax charges arising and transfers occurring after 5 April 1996. 10 March 1992–5 April 1996 minority holding of shares or securities of up to 25% in unquoted or USM company qualified for 50% relief; larger holdings qualified for 100% relief.

**Charities, gifts to** Exempt

From 1 April 2002, Community Amateur Sports Clubs are treated as charities.

**Marriage/civil partnership gifts**

| | | |
|---|---|---|
| Made by: | parent | £5,000 |
| | remoter ancestor | £2,500 |
| | party to marriage/civil partnership | £2,500 |
| | other person | £1,000 |

**National purposes**

Property given or bequeathed to bodies listed in IHTA 1984 Sch 3. Exempt

**Political parties, gifts to** Exempt

**Potentially exempt transfers**

Exempt if made 7 or more years before the date of death. Except for gifts with reservation etc, they include:

- (a) transfers by individuals to other individuals or certain trusts for the disabled;
- (b) transfers after 21 March 2006 by individuals to a bereaved minor's trust on the coming to an end of an immediate post-death interest;
- (c) transfers before 22 March 2006 by individuals to accumulation and maintenance trusts;
- (d) transfers by individuals into interest in possession trusts in which, for transfers after 21 March 2006, the beneficiary has a disabled person's interest; and
- (e) certain transfers on the termination or disposal of an individual's beneficial interest in possession in settled property (in restricted circumstances following FA 2006).

| | |
|---|---|
| **Quick succession relief** | |
| Estate increased by chargeable transfer followed by death within 5 years. | |
| Death within 1st year. | 100% |
| Each additional year: decreased by | 20% |
| **Small gifts to same person** | £250 |
| **Spouses/civil partners with separate domicile (one not being in the UK)** | |
| Total exemption. | £325,000[1] |

[1] For transfers of value before 6 April 2013 the total exemption was £55,000. From 6 April 2013 the limit is increased to the level of the prevailing IHT nil-rate band (see p 109). For transfers of value made on or after 6 April 2013 individuals can elect to be treated as domiciled in the UK if, at any time on or after 6 April 2013 and during the period of 7 years ending with the date on which the election is made, they have a UK-domiciled spouse or civil partner. The election may be made in some cases where the UK-domiciled individual had died. Personal representatives may make an election on behalf of a deceased person in certain circumstances. Other conditions apply.

**Tapering relief**

The value of the estate on death is taxed as the top slice of cumulative transfers in the 7 years before death. Transfers on or within 7 years of death are taxed on their value at the date of the gift on the death rate scale, but using the scale in force at the date of death, subject to the following taper:

| *Years between gift and death* | *Percentage of full charge at death rates* |
|---|---|
| 0–3 | 100 |
| 3–4 | 80 |
| 4–5 | 60 |
| 5–6 | 40 |
| 6–7 | 20 |

**Penalties** see p 17.

# National insurance contributions

(SI 2001/1004)

## From 6 April 2017

| **Class 1 contributions**[1] | | | |
|---|---|---|---|
| **Earnings limits and threshold** | Weekly £ | Monthly £ | Yearly £ |
| Lower earnings limit | 113 | 490 | 5,876 |
| Primary threshold | 157 | 680 | 8,164 |
| Secondary threshold | 157 | 680 | 8,164 |
| Upper secondary threshold[3, 4] | 866 | 3,750 | 45,000 |
| Upper earnings limit | 866 | 3,750 | 45,000 |
| **Rates** | | | |
| **Employees' contributions** | | | |
| *Weekly earnings:* | £157.01–£866 | 12% | |
| | Over £866 | 2% | |
| **Employers' contributions**[3, 4] | | | |
| *Weekly earnings:* | Over £157[3, 4] | 13.8% | |
| **Women at reduced rate** | | | |
| **Employees' contributions** | | | |
| *Weekly earnings:* | £157.01–£866 | 5.85% | |
| | Over £866 | 2% | |
| **Employers' contributions** | | | |
| *Weekly earnings:* | Over £157 | 13.8% | |
| **Employment allowance**[2] | | **£3,000** | |
| **Class 1A and Class 1B contributions** | | 13.8% | |

1 Employees' rates are nil for children under 16 and those over state pensionable age but employers' contributions are still payable. Employees' NICs are not payable on earnings up to the primary threshold, employers' NICs are not payable on earnings up to the secondary threshold.

2 An employment allowance of £3,000 per year (£2,000 from 6 April 2014 to 5 April 2016) applies for businesses, charities and CASCs to be offset against their employer Class 1 secondary NICs. The allowance is claimed as part of the normal payroll process through RTI. Only one company in a group may claim. There are some excluded employers such as certain employers of domestic staff, public authorities and those which carry out functions wholly or mainly of a public nature. From 6 April 2015 the allowance was extended to employers of care and support workers where the duties of employment relate to the employer's personal, family or household affairs. From 6 April 2016 the allowance is no longer available to companies whose only employee is the director.

3 From 6 April 2015 employers with employees under the age of 21 are no longer required to pay Class 1 secondary NICs on earnings up to the upper secondary threshold for those employees.

4 From 6 April 2016 employers with apprentices under the age of 25 are longer required to pay Class 1 secondary NICs on earnings up to the upper secondary threshold for those employees.

# 6 April 2016–5 April 2017

| **Class 1 contributions**[1] | | | |
|---|---|---|---|
| **Earnings limits and threshold** | Weekly £ | Monthly £ | Yearly £ |
| Lower earnings limit | 112 | 486 | 5,824 |
| Primary threshold | 155 | 672 | 8,060 |
| Secondary threshold | 156 | 676 | 8,112 |
| Upper secondary threshold[3, 4] | 827 | 3,583 | 43,000 |
| Upper earnings limit | 827 | 3,583 | 43,000 |
| **Rates**[5] | | | |
| **Employees' contributions** | | | |
| *Weekly earnings:* | £155.01–£827 | 12% | |
| | Over £827 | 2% | |
| **Employers' contributions**[3, 4] | | | |
| *Weekly earnings:* | Over £156[3, 4] | 13.8% | |
| **Women at reduced rate** | | | |
| **Employees' contributions** | | | |
| *Weekly earnings:* | £155.01–£827 | 5.85% | |
| | Over £827 | 2% | |
| **Employers' contributions** | | | |
| *Weekly earnings:* | Over £156 | 13.8% | |
| **Employment allowance**[2] | | **£3,000** | |
| **Class 1A and Class 1B contributions** | | 13.8% | |

1 Employees' rates are nil for children under 16 and those over state pensionable age but employers' contributions are still payable. Employees' NICs are not payable on earnings up to the primary threshold, employers' NICs are not payable on earnings up to the secondary threshold.

2 An employment allowance of £3,000 per year (£2,000 from 6 April 2014 to 5 April 2016) applies for businesses, charities and CASCs to be offset against their employer Class 1 secondary NICs. The allowance is claimed as part of the normal payroll process through RTI. Only one company in a group may claim. There are some excluded employers such as certain employers of domestic staff, public authorities and those which carry out functions wholly or mainly of a public nature. From 6 April 2015 the allowance was extended to employers of care and support workers where the duties of employment relate to the employer's personal, family or household affairs. From 6 April 2016 the allowance is no longer available to companies whose only employee is the director.

3 From 6 April 2015 employers with employees under the age of 21 are no longer required to pay Class 1 secondary NICs on earnings up to the upper secondary threshold for those employees.

4 From 6 April 2016 employers with apprentices under the age of 25 are longer required to pay Class 1 secondary NICs on earnings up to the upper secondary threshold for those employees.

5 Contracting out is no longer possible from 6 April 2016 as the single-tier state pension was introduced.

# 6 April 2015–5 April 2016

| ***Class 1 contributions***[1] | | | | |
|---|---|---|---|---|
| Earnings limits and threshold | | Weekly £ | Monthly £ | Yearly £ |
| Lower earnings limit | | 112 | 486 | 5,824 |
| Primary threshold | | 155 | 672 | 8,060 |
| Secondary threshold | | 156 | 676 | 8,112 |
| Upper secondary threshold[5] | | 815 | 3,532 | 42,385 |
| Upper earnings limit | | 815 | 3,532 | 42,385 |
| Upper accruals point | | 770 | 3,337 | 40,040 |
| | | **Not contracted out** | **Contracted out** *Salary-related schemes*[3] | |
| **Employees' contributions** | | | | |
| *Weekly earnings:* | £155.01–770 | 12% | 10.6% | |
| | £770.01–£815 | 12% | 12% | |
| | Over £815 | 2% | 2% | |
| | – rebate £112–£155 | | 1.4%[2, 3] | |
| **Employers' contributions**[4, 5] | | | | |
| *Weekly earnings:* | £156.01–£770[5] | 13.8% | 10.4% | |
| | Over £770[5] | 13.8% | 13.8% | |
| | – rebate £112–£156 | | 3.4%[2, 3] | |
| **Women at reduced rate** | | | | |
| **Employees' contributions** | | | | |
| *Weekly earnings:* | £155.01–£815 | 5.85% | | |
| | Over £815 | 2% | | |
| **Employers' contributions** | Normal employers' contributions apply as above | | | |
| **Employment allowance**[4] | | **£2,000** | | |
| **Class 1A and Class 1B contributions** | | 13.8% | | |

1 Employees' rates are nil for children under 16 and those over state pensionable age but employers' contributions are still payable. Employees' NICs are not payable on earnings up to the primary threshold, employers' NICs are not payable on earnings up to the secondary threshold.

2 The rebate is given on earnings between the lower earnings limit and the primary threshold for employees, and between the lower earnings limit and the secondary threshold for employers. The rebate for employees is given to employers to the extent that insufficient contributions have been paid by the employee for offset.

3 From 2012 the rebates for defined benefit schemes (salary-related schemes) are 3.4% for employers and 1.4% for employees. Contracting out on a defined contribution basis (money purchase schemes) is abolished from 6 April 2012. Contracting out via a personal pension plan is also not possible from 6 April 2012.

4 From 6 April 2014 an employment allowance of £2,000 per year applies for businesses, charities and CASCs to be offset against their employer Class 1 secondary NICs. The allowance is claimed as part of the normal payroll process through RTI. Only one company in a group may claim. There are some excluded employers such as certain employers of domestic staff, public authorities and those which carry out functions wholly or mainly of a public nature. From 6 April 2015 the allowance is extended to employers of care and support workers where the duties of employment relate to the employer's personal, family or household affairs.

5 From 6 April 2015 employers with employees under the age of 21 are no longer required to pay Class 1 secondary NICs on earnings up to the upper secondary threshold for those employees.

# 6 April 2014–5 April 2015

| *Class 1 contributions*[1] | | | | |
|---|---|---|---|---|
| Earnings limits and threshold | | Weekly £ | Monthly £ | Yearly £ |
| Lower earnings limit | | 111 | 481 | 5,772 |
| Secondary threshold | | 153 | 663 | 7,956 |
| Primary threshold | | 153 | 663 | 7,956 |
| Upper earnings limit | | 805 | 3,489 | 41,865 |
| Upper accruals point | | 770 | 3,337 | 40,040 |
| | | **Not contracted out** | **Contracted out** *Salary-related schemes*[3] | |
| **Employees' contributions** | | | | |
| *Weekly earnings:* | £153.01–770 | 12% | 10.6% | |
| | £770.01–£805 | 12% | 12% | |
| | Over £805 | 2% | 2% | |
| | – rebate £111–£153 | | 1.4%[2, 3] | |
| **Employers' contributions**[4] | | | | |
| *Weekly earnings:* | £153.01–£770 | 13.8% | 10.4% | |
| | Over £770 | 13.8% | 13.8% | |
| | – rebate £111–£153 | | 3.4%[2, 3] | |
| **Women at reduced rate** | | | | |
| **Employees' contributions** | | | | |
| *Weekly earnings:* | £153.01–£805 | 5.85% | | |
| | Over £805 | 2% | | |
| **Employers' contributions** | Normal employers' contributions apply as above | | | |
| **Employment allowance**[4] | | **£2,000** | | |
| **Class 1A and Class 1B contributions** | | 13.8% | | |

1 Employees' rates are nil for children under 16 and those over state pensionable age but employers' contributions are still payable. Employees' NICs are not payable on earnings up to the primary threshold, employers' NICs are not payable on earnings up to the secondary threshold. The primary and secondary thresholds are the same in 2014–15.

2 The rebate is given on earnings between the lower earnings limit and the primary threshold for employees, and between the lower earnings limit and the secondary threshold for employers. The rebate for employees is given to employers to the extent that insufficient contributions have been paid by the employee for offset.

3 From 2012 the rebates for defined benefit schemes (salary-related schemes) are 3.4% for employers and 1.4% for employees. Contracting out on a defined contribution basis (money purchase schemes) is abolished from 6 April 2012. Contracting out via a personal pension plan is also not possible from 6 April 2012. Contracting out via defined benefit schemes will no longer be possible from 6 April 2016 when the single-tier state pension is introduced.

4 From 6 April 2014 an employment allowance of £2,000 per year applies for businesses, charities and CASCs to be offset against their employer Class 1 secondary NICs. The allowance is claimed as part of the normal payroll process through RTI. Only one company in a group may claim. There are some excluded employers such as domestic employers, public authorities and those which carry out functions wholly or mainly of a public nature.

# 6 April 2013–5 April 2014

| | | | | |
|---|---|---|---|---|
| ***Class 1 contributions*[1]** | | | | |
| Earnings limits and threshold | | Weekly £ | Monthly £ | Yearly £ |
| Lower earnings limit | | 109 | 473 | 5,668 |
| Secondary threshold[3] | | 148 | 641 | 7,696 |
| Primary threshold[3] | | 149 | 646 | 7,755 |
| Upper earnings limit | | 797 | 3,454 | 41,450 |
| Upper accruals point | | 770 | 3,337 | 40,040 |
| | | **Not contracted out** | **Contracted out** *Salary-related schemes*[5] | |
| **Employees' contributions** | | | | |
| *Weekly earnings:* | £149.01–770 | 12% | 10.6% | |
| | £770.01–£797 | 12% | 12% | |
| | Over £797 | 2% | 2% | |
| | – rebate £109–£149 | | 1.4%[2, 5] | |
| **Employers' contributions**[4] | | | | |
| *Weekly earnings:* | £148.01–£770 | 13.8% | 10.4% | |
| | Over £770 | 13.8% | 13.8% | |
| | – rebate £109–£148 | | 3.4%[2, 5] | |
| **Women at reduced rate** | | | | |
| **Employees' contributions** | | | | |
| *Weekly earnings:* | £149.01–£797 | 5.85% | | |
| | Over £797 | 2% | | |
| **Employers' contributions** | Normal employers' contributions apply as above | | | |
| **Class 1A and Class 1B contributions** | | 13.8% | | |

1 Employees' rates are nil for children under 16 and those over state pensionable age but employers' contributions are still payable. Employees' NICs are not payable on earnings up to the primary threshold, employers' NICs are not payable on earnings up to the secondary threshold.

2 The rebate is given on earnings between the lower earnings limit and the primary threshold for employees, and between the lower earnings limit and the secondary threshold for employers. The rebate for employees is given to employers to the extent that insufficient contributions have been paid by the employee for offset.

3 From 6 April 2011 the primary threshold applies for employees' contributions and the secondary threshold applies for employers' contributions.

4 An employer NIC 'holiday' applies to new businesses started in certain regions between 22 June 2010 and 5 September 2013. Between 6 September 2010 and 5 September 2013 the businesses may qualify for a deduction of up to £5,000 of their employer Class 1 contributions for each of the first ten employees hired in the first year of business.

5 From 2012 the rebates for defined benefit schemes (salary-related schemes) are 3.4% for employers and 1.4% for employees. Contracting out on a defined contribution basis (money purchase schemes) is abolished from 6 April 2012. Contracting out via a personal pension plan is also not possible from 6 April 2012.

# 6 April 2012–5 April 2013

| ***Class 1 contributions***[1] | | | | |
|---|---|---|---|---|
| Earnings limits and threshold | | Weekly £ | Monthly £ | Yearly £ |
| Lower earnings limit | | 107 | 464 | 5,564 |
| Secondary threshold[3] | | 144 | 624 | 7,488 |
| Primary threshold[3] | | 146 | 634 | 7,605 |
| Upper earnings limit | | 817 | 3,540 | 42,475 |
| Upper accruals point | | 770 | 3,337 | 40,040 |
| | | **Not contracted out** | **Contracted out** *Salary-related schemes*[5] | |
| **Employees' contributions** | | | | |
| *Weekly earnings:* | £146.01–770 | 12% | 10.6% | |
| | £770.01–£817 | 12% | 12% | |
| | Over £817 | 2% | 2% | |
| | – rebate £107–£146 | | 1.4%[2, 5] | |
| **Employers' contributions**[4] | | | | |
| *Weekly earnings:* | £144.01–£770 | 13.8% | 10.4% | |
| | Over £770 | 13.8% | 13.8% | |
| | – rebate £107–£144 | | 3.4%[2, 5] | |
| **Women at reduced rate** | | | | |
| **Employees' contributions** | | | | |
| *Weekly earnings:* | £146.01–£817 | 5.85% | | |
| | Over £817 | 2% | | |
| **Employers' contributions** | Normal employers' contributions apply as above | | | |
| **Class 1A and Class 1B contributions** | | 13.8% | | |

1 Employees' rates are nil for children under 16 and those over state pensionable age but employers' contributions are still payable. Employees' NICs are not payable on earnings up to the primary threshold, employers' NICs are not payable on earnings up to the secondary threshold.

2 The rebate is given on earnings between the lower earnings limit and the primary threshold for employees, and between the lower earnings limit and the secondary threshold for employers. The rebate for employees is given to employers to the extent that insufficient contributions have been paid by the employee for offset.

3 From 6 April 2011 the primary threshold applies for employees' contributions and the secondary threshold applies for employers' contributions.

4 An employer NIC 'holiday' applies to new businesses started in certain regions between 22 June 2010 and 5 September 2013. Between 6 September 2010 and 5 September 2013 the businesses may qualify for a deduction of up to £5,000 of their employer Class 1 contributions for each of the first ten employees hired in the first year of business.

5 From 2012 the rebates for defined benefit schemes (salary-related schemes) are reduced to 3.4% for employers and 1.4% for employees. Contracting out on a defined contribution basis (money purchase schemes) is abolished from 6 April 2012. Contracting out via a personal pension plan is also not possible from 6 April 2012.

# Class 2, 3 and 4 contributions

| | **2017–18** | **2016–17** | **2015–16** |
|---|---|---|---|
| **Class 2** (self-employed)[1] | | | |
| Flat rate—per week | **£2.85** | £2.80 | £2.80 |
| Share fishermen—per week | **£3.50** | £3.45 | £3.45 |
| Volunteer development workers—per week | **£5.65** | £5.60 | £5.60 |
| Small profits threshold—per year[4] | **£6,025** | £5,965 | £5,965 |
| **Class 3** (voluntary contributions) | | | |
| Flat rate—per week | **£14.25** | £14.10 | £14.10 |
| **Class 4** (self-employed)[1] | | | |
| Lower annual profits limit | **£8,164** | £8,060 | £8,060 |
| Upper annual profits limit | **£45,000** | £43,000 | £42,385 |
| Rate between lower and upper limits | **9%** | 9% | 9% |
| Rate on profits above upper limit | **2%** | 2% | 2% |
| **Maximum contributions** | | | |
| Class 1 or Class 1/Class 2[2] | **£4,509.24** | £4,273.92 | £4,197.60 |
| – plus rate on earnings above upper limit | **2%** | 2% | 2% |
| Class 4 limiting amount[3] | **£3,466.29** | £3,293.00 | £3,237.65 |
| – plus rate on profits above upper limit | **2%** | 2% | 2% |

1 Not payable if pensionable age is reached by the beginning of the tax year. Class 2 will be abolished from April 2018.

2 Where an earner has more than one employment (including self-employment), liability for Class 1 or Class 1 and Class 2 contributions cannot exceed a maximum amount equal to 53 employees' Class 1 contributions at the maximum standard rate, plus 2% on earnings over the individual's upper earnings limit (which varies depending on individual circumstances).

3 Where Class 4 contributions are payable in addition to Class 1 and/or Class 2 contributions, liability for Class 4 contributions cannot exceed such an amount as, when added to the Class 1/Class 2 contributions payable (after applying the maximum if appropriate), equals the limiting amount. The limiting amount is the maximum Class 4 contributions payable (including 2% on earnings over the upper profit limit) plus 53 Class 2 contributions. Before 2015–16, if a contributor expected to exceed this amount he could apply for deferment of Class 4 contributions for the year in question. Deferment had no effect on the 2% payable on earnings over the upper profit limit, which was still payable. Collection of Class 2 contributions via self-assessment means deferment is no longer necessary.

4 Following the reform of the collection of Class 2, from 2015–16 the small earnings exception arrangements are no longer necessary. Liability for Class 2 contributions will be determined by whether the self-employed earner's Class 4 NICs profits (rather than earnings) declared at the year end exceed a set threshold, the small profits threshold.

| | **2014–15** | **2013–14** | **2012–13** |
|---|---|---|---|
| **Class 2** (self-employed)[1] | | | |
| Flat rate—per week | £2.75 | £2.70 | £2.65 |
| Share fishermen—per week | £3.40 | £3.35 | £3.30 |
| Volunteer development workers—per week | £5.55 | £5.45 | £5.35 |
| Small earnings exception—per year | £5,885 | £5,725 | £5,595 |
| **Class 3** (voluntary contributions) | | | |
| Flat rate—per week | £13.90 | £13.55 | £13.25 |
| **Class 4** (self-employed)[1] | | | |
| Lower annual profits limit | £7,956 | £7,755 | £7,605 |
| Upper annual profits limit | £41,865 | £41,450 | £42,475 |
| Rate between lower and upper limits | 9% | 9% | 9% |
| Rate on profits above upper limit | 2% | 2% | 2% |
| **Maximum contributions** | | | |
| Class 1 or Class 1/Class 2[2] | £4,146.72 | £4,121.28 | £4,267.56 |
| – plus rate on earnings above upper limit | 2% | 2% | 2% |
| Class 4 limiting amount[3] | £3,197.56 | £3,175.65 | £3,278.75 |
| – plus rate on profits above upper limit | 2% | 2% | 2% |

1 Not payable if pensionable age is reached by the beginning of the tax year.

2 Where an earner has more than one employment (including self-employment), liability for Class 1 or Class 1 and Class 2 contributions cannot exceed a maximum amount equal to 53 employees' Class 1 contributions at the maximum standard rate, plus 2% on earnings over the individual's upper earnings limit (which varies depending on individual circumstances).

3 Where Class 4 contributions are payable in addition to Class 1 and/or Class 2 contributions, liability for Class 4 contributions cannot exceed such an amount as, when added to the Class 1/Class 2 contributions payable (after applying the maximum if appropriate), equals the limiting amount. The limiting amount is the maximum Class 4 contributions payable (including 2% on earnings over the upper profit limit) plus 53 Class 2 contributions. If a contributor expects to exceed this amount he may apply for deferment of Class 4 contributions for the year in question. Deferment has no effect on the 2% payable on earnings over the

upper profit limit, which is still payable.

## Class 3A contributions

(SSCBA 1992 ss 14A-14C; SI 2014/3240)

Class 3A contributions were introduced for an 18-month period from 12 October 2015 to 5 April 2017 as a state pension top up and payment will allow existing pensioners, and those entitled to a state pension and reaching state pension age before 6 April 2016, the opportunity to gain additional state pension. The measure is in addition to the existing Class 3 voluntary contributions (see p 117). The rates set out below show the contribution needed for £1 per week of additional state pension, according to age. Class 3A contributions cannot provide more than £25 per week additional pension.

| Age[1] on payment date[2] (October 2015 to April 2017) | Rate for each additional pension unit of £1 per week | Age[1] on payment date[2] (October 2015 to April 2017) | Rate for each additional pension unit of £1 per week |
|---|---|---|---|
| 62 (women only) | **£956** | 82 | **£484** |
| 63 (women only) | **£934** | 83 | **£454** |
| 64 (women only) | **£913** | 84 | **£424** |
| 65 | **£890** | 85 | **£394** |
| 66 | **£871** | 86 | **£366** |
| 67 | **£847** | 87 | **£339** |
| 68 | **£827** | 88 | **£314** |
| 69 | **£801** | 89 | **£291** |
| 70 | **£779** | 90 | **£270** |
| 71 | **£761** | 91 | **£251** |
| 72 | **£738** | 92 | **£232** |
| 73 | **£719** | 93 | **£216** |
| 74 | **£694** | 94 | **£200** |
| 75 | **£674** | 95 | **£185** |
| 76 | **£646** | 96 | **£172** |
| 77 | **£625** | 97 | **£159** |
| 78 | **£596** | 98 | **£148** |
| 79 | **£574** | 99 | **£137** |
| 80 | **£544** | 100 | **£127** |
| 81 | **£514** | | |

1 If a person pays a contribution before reaching state pension age the amount of contribution needed to obtain a unit of additional pension is the amount he would have needed to pay if on the date of payment he had reached state pension age.

2 The date of payment is the date the contribution is received by HMRC.

# Employers' contributions: benefits in kind

**Class 1A** NICs are payable by employers on most taxable benefits in kind, excluding benefits:

(1) included in a PAYE settlement agreement;
(2) provided to 'lower-paid' ministers of religion, and before 6 April 2016 all 'lower-paid' employees (including benefits in kind and expenses payments);
(3) otherwise not required to be included on a P11D;
(4) on which Class 1 NICs were due;
(5) which were covered by a dispensation before 6 April 2016 (see below).

From 6 April 2016 the dispensations regime is abolished and replaced with a new exemption for paid or reimbursed amounts that would otherwise be deductible. Also from 6 April 2016 employees (other than lower-paid ministers of religion) earning at a rate of less than £8,500 per year pay income tax on their benefits in kind in the same way as other employees earning at a rate of £8,500 or more.

**Class 1B** contributions are payable by employers by reference to the value of any items included in a PAYE settlement agreement (PSA) which would otherwise be earnings for Class 1 or Class 1A, including the amount of tax paid. Income tax and Class 1B contributions on a PSA are payable by 19 October after the end of the tax year to which the PSA relates (or 22 October if paid electronically).

## Common benefits subject to Class 1 and Class 1A NICs (CWG5 2017)

| *Benefit* | | *NICs Class* | *PAYE or P11D* |
|---|---|---|---|
| Assets transferred to employees but not readily convertible assets | | 1A | P11D |
| Assets placed at employee's disposal for mixed business and private use | | 1A | P11D |
| Car fuel supplied for private motoring in company car | | 1A | P11D |
| Car/van fuel supplied for private motoring in privately owned car/van | – supplied using company credit card, garage account, agency card or employer's own fuel pump | 1A | P11D |
| | – any other circumstances | 1 | P11D |
| Cars available for private use | | 1A | P11D |
| Car parking facilities other than at or near place of work or as part of business travel | | 1A | P11D |
| Car parking fees paid for or reimbursed to employee other than at or near place of work or as part of business travel | | 1 | P11D |
| Childcare where employer contracts with provider and either the value exceeds the permitted maximum or the qualifying conditions are not met | | 1A | P11D |
| Childcare where employee reimbursed or additional salary provided to meet cost | | 1 | PAYE |
| Christmas boxes | – cash | 1 | PAYE |
| | – goods | 1A | P11D |
| Clothing and uniforms | | | |
| – cash payment to employee for clothing that can be worn at any time | | 1 | PAYE or P11D[1] |
| – clothing provided by employer that can be worn at any time | | 1A | P11D |
| Council tax, unless employee provided with living accommodation which is not a benefit | | 1 | P11D |
| Credit and charge cards – personal expenses on employer's card | | 1 | P11D |
| Entertaining staff — expenses/ allowances | – employer contract with provider | 1A | P11D |
| | – employee contract with provider | 1 | PAYE or P11D[1] |
| Expenses not covered by an exemption— any profit element in payment | | 1 | P11D[4] |
| Food, groceries, farm produce | – employer contract with provider | 1A | P11D |
| | – employee contract with provider | 1 | PAYE or P11D[1] |
| Goods transferred to employee | – employer contract with provider | 1A | P11D |
| | – employee contract with provider | 1 | PAYE or P11D[1] |
| Holidays | – employer contract with provider | 1A | P11D |
| | – employee contract with provider, or holiday vouchers | 1 | PAYE or P11D[1] |
| Income tax paid but not deducted from employee, or paid on notional payments not borne by employee within 90 days of receipt of each notional payment | | 1 | P11D |
| Insurance premiums for pensions etc on employee's death or retirement, employee contract with provider | | 1 | PAYE or P11D[1] |
| Living accommodation (beneficial) | | 1A | P11D |
| Loans | – non-qualifying | 1A | P11D |
| | – written off | 1 | P11D |

| *Benefit* | | *NICs Class* | *PAYE or P11D* |
|---|---|---|---|
| Meals vouchers (other than 15p a day of value before 6 April 2013) | | 1 | P11D |
| Meals provided other than at canteen or at business premises open to all staff on a reasonable scale where all employees may obtain free or subsidised meals not provided in connection with salary sacrifice or flexible remuneration arrangements | | 1A | P11D |
| Medical, dental insurance or treatment provided in the UK by employer | – employer contract with provider | 1A | P11D |
| | – employee contract with provider | 1 | PAYE or P11D[1] |
| Mobile phone[5] — cost of private calls, employee contract with provider | | 1 | PAYE or P11D[1] |
| Personal bills | | 1 | PAYE or P11D[1] |
| Readily convertible assets[2] | | 1 | PAYE |
| Relocation payments | – qualifying over £8,000 | 1A | P11D |
| | – non-qualifying benefits or qualifying expenses paid after relevant day | 1A | P11D |
| | – non-qualifying expenses | 1 | P11D |
| Round sum allowances (not identified as business expense) | | 1 | P11D |
| Scholarships awarded to students because of parent's employment or payment of school fees | – employer contract with provider | 1A | P11D |
| | – employee contract with provider | 1 | PAYE or P11D[1] |
| Social functions unless ITEPA 2003 s 264 satisfied | | 1A | P11D |
| Sporting or recreational facilities unless ITEPA 2003 s 261 satisfied | | 1A | P11D |
| Subscriptions, professional and fees not allowable as tax deduction | – employer contract with provider | 1A | P11D |
| | – employee contract with provider | 1 | PAYE or P11D[1] |
| Telephones | – employer contract with provider, unless private use is insignificant or employee reimburses cost of all private calls | 1A | P11D |
| | – employee contract with provider, unless used exclusively for business. If mixed use, not applicable to business calls if supported by evidence | 1 | PAYE or P11D[1] |
| Training payments | – employer contract with provider, unless work-related or encouraged by employer | 1A | P11D |
| | – employee contract with provider, unless work-related or encouraged by employer | 1 | PAYE or P11D[1] |
| Vans available for commuting and other private use | | 1A[3] | P11D |
| Van fuel provided for use in van available for commuting and other private use | | 1A[3] | P11D |
| Vouchers (other than exceptions for childcare, meals, etc) | | 1 | P11D |

1 Payments by employer to provider should be entered on P11D. Reimbursements to the employee are subject to PAYE.

2 See detailed information in HMRC booklet CWG2(2017) para 5.13.1.

3 No Class 1A due if van is available mainly for employee's business travel and commuting and other private use is insignificant.

4 Specific and distinct business expenses within the payments should be recorded in appropriate section of P11D.

5 No limit to number of mobile phones which employer can contract to provide NIC free solely for business with insignificant private use. Only one mobile per employee NIC free for private use where employer contracts. No mobile phone may be provided NICs free to a member of an employee's family or household.

# Overseas

## Average rates of exchange

| *Average for year ending* | ***31.03.15*** | ***31.12.15*** | ***31.03.16*** | ***31.12.16*** | ***31.03.17*** |
|---|---|---|---|---|---|
| **Abu Dhabi** (Dirham) | 5.941769 | 5.617715 | 5.545785 | 5.056488 | 4.870015 |
| **Afghanistan** (Afghani) | Not quoted | Not quoted | Not quoted | Not quoted | Not quoted |
| **Albania** (Lek) | 177.562875 | 192.233831 | 190.5769 | 170.723375 | 165.255417 |
| **Algeria** (Dinar) | 135.184926 | 153.017646 | 156.345498 | 150.356917 | 145.760208 |
| **Angola** (Readj Kwanza) | 161.431601 | 179.568367 | 194.43726 | 223.259667 | 219.334167 |
| **Antigua** (EC$) | 4.368359 | 4.130179 | 4.076723 | 3.716987 | 3.579938 |
| **Argentina** (Peso) | 13.518555 | 14.037548 | 15.815366 | 20.039292 | 19.813125 |
| **Armenia** (Dram) | 680.756376 | 730.6634 | 725.102419 | 661.087208 | 635.039167 |
| **Aruba** (Florin) | 2.895548 | 2.737471 | 2.70257 | 2.464473 | 2.37361 |
| **Australia** (A$) | 1.844671 | 2.034292 | 2.048381 | 1.852649 | 1.766681 |
| **Austria** (Euro) | 1.270009 | 1.377437 | 1.368138 | 1.240784 | 1.2077 |
| **Azerbaijan** (New Manat) | 1.290865 | 1.535137 | 1.776242 | 2.182317 | 2.166667 |
| **Bahamas** ($ pegged to US$) | 1.598652 | 1.530538 | 1.508298 | 1.376045 | 1.327506 |
| **Bahrain** (Dinar) | 0.609907 | 0.576827 | 0.569447 | 0.519127 | 0.499965 |
| **Bangladesh** (Taka) | 125.427223 | 119.104992 | 117.868189 | 108.051708 | 104.331667 |
| **Barbados** (BD$) | 3.23580 | 3.059387 | 3.019789 | 2.753181 | 2.651663 |
| **Belarus** (Rouble) | 18,178.92469 | 24,079.84737 | 25,925.56886 | 2.57286 | 2.54075 |
| **Belgium** (Euro) | 1.270009 | 1.377437 | 1.368138 | 1.240784 | 1.2077 |
| **Belize** (Dollar) | 3.232967 | 3.058137 | 3.018125 | 2.753017 | 2.654854 |
| **Benin** (CFA Franc) | 832.173132 | 901.980046 | 897.121292 | 814.319917 | 791.886667 |
| **Bermuda** ($ pegged to US$) | 1.598652 | 1.530538 | 1.508298 | 1.376045 | 1.327506 |
| **Bhutan** (Ngultrum) | 98.809869 | 98.143187 | 98.517936 | 92.449 | 89.215625 |
| **Bolivia** (Boliviano) | 11.179465 | 10.557679 | 10.412043 | 9.505183 | 9.170683 |
| **Bosnia-Herzegovina** (Marka) | 2.482128 | 2.690275 | 2.674975 | 2.428067 | 2.361131 |
| **Botswana** (Pula) | 14.754930 | 15.4398 | 15.818653 | 15.039908 | 14.237492 |
| **Brazil** (Real) | 3.949423 | 5.076827 | 5.396725 | 4.854893 | 4.433554 |
| **Brunei** ($) | 2.076375 | 2.09915 | 2.091509 | 3.408618 | 3.34355 |
| **Bulgaria** (Lev) | 2.481734 | 2.690038 | 2.675091 | 2.428196 | 2.361273 |
| **Burkina Faso** (CFA Franc) | 832.173132 | 901.980046 | 897.121292 | 814.319917 | 791.886667 |
| **Burundi** (Franc) | 2,513.098240 | 2,394.192352 | 2,366.003657 | 2,222.357583 | 2,181.28875 |
| **Cambodia** (Riel) | 6,531.265625 | 6,216.972687 | 6,125.978626 | 5,330.036625 | 5,123.295 |
| **Cameroon Republic** (CFA Franc) | 832.173132 | 901.980046 | 897.121292 | 814.319917 | 791.886667 |
| **Canada** (Can$) | 1.831271 | 1.951654 | 1.975398 | 1.817877 | 1.730748 |
| **Cape Verde Islands** (Escudo) | 138.240394 | 151.846646 | 151.102058 | 136.919417 | 133.193333 |
| **Cayman Islands** (CI$) | 1.326696 | 1.254344 | 1.238113 | 1.128863 | 1.087065 |
| **Central African** (CFA Franc) | 832.173132 | 901.980046 | 897.121292 | 814.319917 | 791.886667 |
| **Chad** (CFA Franc) | 832.173132 | 901.980046 | 897.121292 | 814.319917 | 791.886667 |
| **Chile** (Peso) | 946.055778 | 996.370454 | 1,011.773945 | 937.166708 | 886.574792 |
| **China** (Renminbi Yuan) | 9.926634 | 9.505037 | 9.582777 | 9.098112 | 8.870269 |
| **Colombia** (Peso) | 3,371.950846 | 4,164.852829 | 4,393.427606 | 4,207.046542 | 3,943.479375 |
| **Comoros** (Franc) | 611.577542 | 675.780462 | 672.839977 | 610.738583 | 593.913958 |
| **Congo Brazzaville** (CFA Franc) | 832.173132 | 901.980046 | 897.121292 | 814.319917 | 791.886667 |
| **Congo Dem Rep** (Zaire) (Congolese Franc) | 1,491.183525 | 1,413.383087 | 1,388.737494 | 1,217.051375 | 1,272.947917 |
| **Costa Rica** (Colon) | 876.715363 | 816.970533 | 805.544166 | 745.827167 | 724.224375 |
| **Cote d'Ivoire** (CFA Franc) | 832.173132 | 901.980046 | 897.121292 | 814.319917 | 791.886667 |
| **Croatia** (Kuna) | 9.697926 | 10.465646 | 10.388589 | 9.354187 | 9.058758 |
| **Cuba** (Peso) | 1.617905 | 1.529537 | 1.509685 | 1.376575 | 1.325902 |
| **Cyprus** (Euro) | 1.270009 | 1.377437 | 1.368138 | 1.240784 | 1.2077 |
| **Czech Republic** (Koruna) | 35.001730 | 37.533369 | 37.128996 | 33.553167 | 32.624567 |
| **Denmark** (Krone) | 9.463411 | 10.270454 | 10.204585 | 9.239276 | 8.985713 |
| **Djibouti** (Franc) | 287.467869 | 273.048819 | 268.334328 | 244.655458 | 235.63375 |
| **Dominica** (EC$) | 4.368359 | 4.130179 | 4.076723 | 3.716987 | 3.579938 |
| **Dominican Republic** (Peso) | 70.785615 | 68.710954 | 68.159266 | 63.174 | 61.189167 |

| *Average for year ending* | ***31.03.15*** | ***31.12.15*** | ***31.03.16*** | ***31.12.16*** | ***31.03.17*** |
|---|---|---|---|---|---|
| **Dubai** (Dirham) | 5.941769 | 5.617715 | 5.545785 | 5.056488 | 4.870015 |
| **Ecuador** (US$) | 1.598652 | 1.530538 | 1.508298 | 1.376045 | 1.327506 |
| **Egypt** (£) | 11.629050 | 11.751173 | 11.760721 | 12.756667 | 15.525625 |
| **El Salvador** (Colon) | 14.144994 | 13.285217 | 13.119923 | 12.041875 | 11.59625 |
| **Equatorial Guinea** (CFA Franc) | 832.173132 | 901.980046 | 897.121292 | 814.319917 | 791.886667 |
| **Eritrea** (Nakfa) | 24.205738 | 22.964285 | 22.643617 | 20.6435 | 19.882083 |
| **Estonia** (Euro) | 1.270009 | 1.377437 | 1.368138 | 1.240784 | 1.2077 |
| **Ethiopia** (Birr) | 32.199032 | 31.626637 | 31.528464 | 29.935083 | 29.262083 |
| **European Community** (Euro) | 1.270009 | 1.377437 | 1.368138 | 1.240784 | 1.2077 |
| **Fiji Islands** (F$) | 3.089850 | 3.194563 | 3.197892 | 2.88288 | 2.758275 |
| **Finland** (Euro) | 1.270009 | 1.377437 | 1.368138 | 1.240784 | 1.2077 |
| **France** (Euro) | 1.270009 | 1.377437 | 1.368138 | 1.240784 | 1.2077 |
| **French Polynesia** (CFP franc) | 151.415111 | 164.117132 | 162.612789 | 148.136792 | 144.055417 |
| **Gabon** (CFA franc) | 832.173132 | 901.980046 | 897.121292 | 814.319917 | 791.886667 |
| **Gambia** (Dalasi) | 66.209526 | 63.07811 | 60.858828 | 57.703958 | 57.026875 |
| **Georgia** (Lari) | 2.949080 | 3.452683 | 3.548008 | 3.206053 | 3.165079 |
| **Germany** (Euro) | 1.270009 | 1.377437 | 1.368138 | 1.240784 | 1.2077 |
| **Ghana** (Cedi) | 5.235273 | 5.764697 | 5.877119 | 5.395412 | 5.328192 |
| **Greece** (Euro) | 1.270009 | 1.377437 | 1.368138 | 1.240784 | 1.2077 |
| **Grenada/Wind. Isles** (EC$) | 4.368359 | 4.130179 | 4.076723 | 3.716987 | 3.579938 |
| **Guatemala** (Quetzal) | 12.468307 | 11.709317 | 11.568525 | 10.486725 | 10.041267 |
| **Guinea Bissau** (CFA Franc) | 832.173132 | 901.980046 | 897.121292 | 814.319917 | 791.886667 |
| **Guinea Republic** (Franc) | 11,212.558170 | 11,314.51788 | 11,360.92819 | 9,424.586583 | 9,557.783333 |
| **Guyana** (G$) | 331.443521 | 306.632931 | 303.457213 | 285.108708 | 274.8625 |
| **Haiti** (Gourde) | 73.930236 | 77.008237 | 80.510608 | 86.077125 | 85.69875 |
| **Honduras** (Lempira) | 33.571838 | 33.223748 | 33.305926 | 31.304417 | 30.48125 |
| **Hong Kong** (HK$) | 12.547017 | 11.861838 | 11.694423 | 10.676933 | 10.296783 |
| **Hungary** (Forint) | 392.366607 | 426.207017 | 424.226477 | 386.828917 | 375.333958 |
| **Iceland** (Krona) | 194.715648 | 201.548187 | 197.546906 | 168.441917 | 156.928542 |
| **India** (Rupee) | 98.809869 | 98.143187 | 98.517936 | 92.449 | 89.215625 |
| **Indonesia** (Rupiah) | 19,449.24370 | 20,435.62194 | 20,451.65261 | 18,335.22346 | 17,584.31896 |
| **Iran** (Rial) | Not quoted | Not quoted | Not quoted | Not quoted | Not quoted |
| **Iraq** (Dinar) | 1,876.876603 | 1,792.199458 | 1,768.418649 | 1,616.382625 | 1,567.59125 |
| **Ireland** (Euro) | 1.270009 | 1.377437 | 1.368138 | 1.240784 | 1.2077 |
| **Israel** (Shekel) | 5.932238 | 5.9466 | 5.851666 | 5.285135 | 5.057563 |
| **Italy** (Euro) | 1.270009 | 1.377437 | 1.368138 | 1.240784 | 1.2077 |
| **Jamaica** (J$) | 182.027048 | 178.569379 | 178.29906 | 171.248417 | 167.475417 |
| **Japan** (Yen) | 176.516505 | 185.254427 | 181.381545 | 150.168417 | 144.307083 |
| **Jordan** (Dinar) | 1.145896 | 1.084179 | 1.070389 | 0.976191 | 0.940108 |
| **Kazakhstan** (Tenge) | 295.638825 | 335.87236 | 391.130298 | 469.985917 | 443.701458 |
| **Kenya** (Shilling) | 143.896907 | 149.915017 | 151.6759 | 139.787417 | 135.004375 |
| **Korea North** (Won) | Not quoted | Not quoted | Not quoted | Not quoted | Not quoted |
| **Korea South** (Won) | 1,712.111742 | 1,730.683523 | 1,741.725521 | 1,598.662625 | 1,529.039792 |
| **Kuwait** (Dinar) | 0.464909 | 0.460042 | 0.456362 | 0.415885 | 0.401694 |
| **Kyrgyz Republic** (Som) | 89.656744 | 98.008696 | 101.800558 | 96.609792 | 91.083333 |
| **Laos** (New Kip) | 13,016.24603 | 12,428.74771 | 12,280.30938 | 11,193.88567 | 10,799.85042 |
| **Latvia** (Euro from 1.1.14, previously Lat) | 1.270009 | 1.377437 | 1.368138 | 1.240784 | 1.2077 |
| **Lebanon** (£) | 2,443.963980 | 2,306.354808 | 2,276.813075 | 2,076.391292 | 1,999.26 |
| **Lesotho** (Loti) | 18.3761 | 19.398063 | 20.590709 | 20.421333 | 18.895 |
| **Liberia** ($ pegged to US$) | 1.598652 | 1.530538 | 1.508298 | 1.385863 | 1.327506 |
| **Libya** (Dinar) | 1.997203 | 2.058446 | 2.055243 | 1.873744 | 1.82859 |
| **Lithuania** (Euro from 1.1.15, Litas) | 3.685982 | 1.377437 | 1.368138 | 1.240784 | 1.2077 |
| **Luxembourg** (Euro) | 1.270009 | 1.377437 | 1.368138 | 1.240784 | 1.2077 |
| **Macao** (Pataca) | 12.920921 | 12.210492 | 12.057558 | 11.001733 | 10.592617 |
| **Macedonia** (Denar) | 77.971421 | 84.479937 | 84.124579 | 76.4425 | 74.335625 |
| **Madagascar** (Malagasy Ariary) | 4,165.129490 | 4,731.082538 | 4,825.506009 | 4,370.964 | 4,223.932083 |
| **Malawi** (Kwacha) | 686.484492 | 756.899462 | 838.537291 | 975.086042 | 944.816875 |
| **Malaysia** (Ringgit) | 5.399236 | 5.965808 | 6.092072 | 5.660823 | 5.525885 |
| **Maldive Islands** (Rufiyaa) | 24.855546 | 23.28051 | 22.968374 | 21.074542 | 20.336667 |

| *Average for year ending* | ***31.03.15*** | ***31.12.15*** | ***31.03.16*** | ***31.12.16*** | ***31.03.17*** |
|---|---|---|---|---|---|
| **Mali Republic** (CFA Franc) | 832.173132 | 901.980046 | 897.121292 | 814.319917 | 791.886667 |
| **Malta** (Euro) | 1.270009 | 1.377437 | 1.368138 | 1.240784 | 1.2077 |
| **Mauritania** (Ouguiya) | 473.639950 | 474.054502 | 484.156051 | 481.10375 | 471.101667 |
| **Mauritius** (Rupee) | 50.568207 | 53.560142 | 53.80344 | 48.857917 | 47.026042 |
| **Mexico** (Peso) | 22.087078 | 24.245179 | 24.979304 | 25.431792 | 25.433958 |
| **Moldova** (Leu) | 24.067980 | 28.5733 | 29.115332 | 27.330792 | 26.318958 |
| **Mongolia** (Tugrik) | 3,003.960344 | 3,005.484631 | 2,993.241942 | 2,891.671958 | 2,935.9775 |
| **Montserrat** (EC$) | 4.368359 | 4.130179 | 4.076723 | 3.716987 | 3.579938 |
| **Morocco** (Dirham) | 14.039213 | 14.878727 | 14.798226 | 13.476167 | 13.060625 |
| **Mozambique** (Metical) | 51.399896 | 59.6656 | 64.096872 | 83.258833 | 87.956667 |
| **Myanmar (Burma)** (Kyat) | 1,602.103403 | 1,764.693746 | 1,824.413732 | 1,693.940542 | 1,659.734167 |
| **Nepal** (Rupee) | 158.123055 | 156.951923 | 157.621228 | 147.969542 | 142.607917 |
| **Netherlands** (Euro) | 1.270009 | 1.377437 | 1.368138 | 1.240784 | 1.2077 |
| **New Caledonia** (CFP Franc) | 151.415111 | 164.117132 | 162.612789 | 148.136792 | 144.055417 |
| **New Zealand** (NZ$) | 1.993251 | 2.19244 | 2.222953 | 1.984533 | 1.881252 |
| **Nicaragua** (Gold Cordoba) | 42.398398 | 41.637015 | 41.574764 | 39.258144 | 38.249977 |
| **Niger Republic** (CFA Franc) | 832.173132 | 901.980046 | 897.121292 | 814.319917 | 791.886667 |
| **Nigeria** (Naira) | 277.120103 | 302.439854 | 300.565604 | 347.059917 | 372.817917 |
| **Norway** (Krone) | 10.747198 | 12.315446 | 12.468953 | 11.563583 | 11.078125 |
| **Oman** (Rial Omani) | 0.622811 | 0.588877 | 0.581332 | 0.53006 | 0.510533 |
| **Pakistan** (Rupee) | 162.236948 | 156.988858 | 156.175647 | 144.189208 | 138.893542 |
| **Panama** (Balboa) | 1.617934 | 1.52966 | 1.509849 | 1.376654 | 1.325902 |
| **Papua New Guinea** (Kina) | 4.172923 | 4.215304 | 4.309964 | 4.301563 | 4.192831 |
| **Paraguay** (Guarani) | 7,289.729365 | 7,928.098338 | 8,196.462577 | 7,789.234917 | 7,464.89875 |
| **Peru** (New Sol) | 4.666884 | 4.853837 | 4.932809 | 4.635137 | 4.4238 |
| **Philippines** (Peso) | 71.664084 | 69.615546 | 69.612753 | 65.009792 | 63.514375 |
| **Poland** (Zloty) | 5.316865 | 5.755385 | 5.76733 | 5.402822 | 5.256254 |
| **Portugal** (Euro) | 1.270009 | 1.377437 | 1.368138 | 1.240784 | 1.2077 |
| **Qatar** (Riyal) | 5.890167 | 5.568679 | 5.497479 | 5.01264 | 4.82779 |
| **Romania** (Leu) | 5.625182 | 6.111275 | 6.092487 | 5.575248 | 5.422944 |
| **Russia** (Rouble-Market) | 71.37214 | 93.04131 | 96.035998 | 92.835625 | 84.216875 |
| **Rwanda** (R Franc) | 1,110.898894 | 1,090.582458 | 1,099.592742 | 1,075.026417 | 1,056.958125 |
| **Saotome & Principe** (Dobra) | 29,958.59048 | 32,675.8499 | 32,924.74188 | 27,787.62243 | 26,963.36918 |
| **Saudi Arabia** (Riyal) | 6.070709 | 5.741169 | 5.656204 | 5.160259 | 4.978908 |
| **Senegal** (CFA Franc) | 832.173132 | 901.980046 | 897.121292 | 814.319917 | 791.886667 |
| **Serbia** (Dinar) | 150.396971 | 165.901383 | 165.383875 | 152.777667 | 148.926458 |
| **Seychelles** (Rupee) | 21.147042 | 20.428638 | 19.969996 | 18.33075 | 17.704583 |
| **Sierra Leone** (Leone) | 7,017.841884 | 6,589.731404 | 6,440.172736 | 6,389.390333 | 7,017.53375 |
| **Singapore** (S$) | 2.078003 | 2.101794 | 2.090721 | 1.896978 | 1.834148 |
| **Slovakia** (Euro) | 1.270009 | 1.377437 | 1.368138 | 1.240784 | 1.2077 |
| **Slovenia** (Euro) | 1.270009 | 1.377437 | 1.368138 | 1.240784 | 1.2077 |
| **Solomon Islands** (SI$) | 11.983561 | 12.023992 | 12.003711 | 10.874433 | 10.367517 |
| **Somali Republic** (Schilling) | 1,321.721605 | 1,008.076813 | 962.529826 | 819.771 | 776.039167 |
| **South Africa** (Rand) | 17.834982 | 19.440012 | 20.614979 | 20.428208 | 18.90375 |
| **Spain** (Euro) | 1.270009 | 1.377437 | 1.368138 | 1.240784 | 1.2077 |
| **Sri Lanka** (Rupee) | 211.766992 | 207.593 | 209.096951 | 200.72675 | 195.195625 |
| **St Christopher & Nevis** (EC$) | 4.368359 | 4.130179 | 4.076723 | 3.716987 | 3.579938 |
| **St Lucia** (EC$) | 4.368359 | 4.130179 | 4.076723 | 3.716987 | 3.579938 |
| **St Vincent** (EC$) | 4.368359 | 4.130179 | 4.076723 | 3.716987 | 3.579938 |
| **Sudan Republic** (£) | 9.163836 | 9.192113 | 9.130853 | 8.427427 | 8.224729 |
| **Surinam** (Dollar) | 5.329569 | 5.140081 | 5.329725 | 8.26306 | 9.132498 |
| **Swaziland** (Lilangeni) | 17.807253 | 19.40616 | 20.59096 | 20.421575 | 18.895 |
| **Sweden** (Krona) | 11.712365 | 12.883544 | 12.771428 | 11.667417 | 11.421667 |
| **Switzerland** (Franc) | 1.501175 | 1.475871 | 1.467847 | 1.35263 | 1.3093 |
| **Syria** (Pound) | Not quoted | Not quoted | Not quoted | Not quoted | Not quoted |
| **Taiwan** (New T$) | 49.464353 | 48.575563 | 48.42813 | 44.499375 | 42.342708 |
| **Tajikistan** (Somoni) | Not quoted | Not quoted | Not quoted | Not quoted | Not quoted |
| **Tanzania** (Schilling) | 2,750.949825 | 3,102.657985 | 3,196.90593 | 3,009.647958 | 2,909.941875 |
| **Thailand** (Baht) | 52.555153 | 52.388969 | 52.675466 | 48.517458 | 46.692083 |
| **Togo Republic** (CFA Franc) | 832.173132 | 901.980046 | 897.121292 | 814.319917 | 791.886667 |
| **Tonga Islands** (Pa'Anga) | 1.844671 | 2.034292 | 2.048381 | 1.852649 | 1.766681 |
| **Trinidad and Tobago** (TT$) | 10.316169 | 9.722429 | 9.641411 | 9.113027 | 8.867246 |

| *Average for year ending* | ***31.03.15*** | ***31.12.15*** | ***31.03.16*** | ***31.12.16*** | ***31.03.17*** |
|---|---|---|---|---|---|
| **Tunisia** (Dinar) | 2.852901 | 2.993625 | 2.990621 | 2.921115 | 2.901442 |
| **Turkey** (Lira) | 3.609650 | 4.146825 | 4.244572 | 4.076891 | 4.175619 |
| **Turkmenistan** (New Manat) | 4.788902 | 5.252937 | 5.229315 | 4.821745 | 4.644727 |
| **Uganda** (New Schilling) | 4,327.11030 | 4,932.62775 | 5,057.432026 | 4,676.453958 | 4,556.602917 |
| **Ukraine** (Hryvnia) | 23.276661 | 33.122208 | 34.492042 | 34.921333 | 34.161667 |
| **United Arab Emirates** (Dirham) | 5.941769 | 5.617715 | 5.545785 | 5.056488 | 4.870015 |
| **Uruguay** (Peso Uruguayo) | 38.430992 | 41.565002 | 43.36413 | 41.794083 | 39.41375 |
| **USA** (US$) | 1.598652 | 1.530538 | 1.508298 | 1.376045 | 1.327506 |
| **Uzbekistan** (Sum) | 3,809.483059 | 3,916.370296 | 4,000.185779 | 4,039.4335 | 4,029.228958 |
| **Vanuatu** (Vatu) | 160.865048 | 163.768017 | 164.816234 | 152.664458 | 146.318125 |
| **Venezuela** (Bolivar Fuerte) | 15.849496 | 9.803137 | 9.514275 | 12.311973 | 13.1331 |
| **Vietnam** (Dong) | 34,369.76326 | 33,476.88722 | 33,402.43577 | 30,756.86363 | 29,726.64333 |
| **Wallis & Futuna Islands** (CFP Franc) | 151.415111 | 164.117132 | 162.612789 | 148.136792 | 144.055417 |
| **Western Samoa** (Tala) | 3.823928 | 3.894758 | 3.880187 | 3.509119 | 3.351075 |
| **Yemen (Republic of)** (Rial) | 347.809490 | 328.824262 | 324.63136 | 329.298792 | 329.275 |
| **Zambia** (Kwacha) | 10.324705 | 13.051338 | 14.447917 | 14.221917 | 13.219792 |
| **Zimbabwe** (Dollar) | 605.873298 | 553.889392 | 546.427136 | 498.20875 | 479.838958 |

# Rates of exchange on year-end dates

| | ***31.03.15*** | ***31.12.15*** | ***31.03.16*** | ***31.12.16*** | ***31.03.17*** |
|---|---|---|---|---|---|
| **Australia** (A$) | 1.9432 | 2.034 | 1.8684 | 1.7065 | 1.6279 |
| **Canada** (Can$) | 1.8801 | 2.0599 | 1.8591 | 1.6571 | 1.6605 |
| **Denmark** (Krone) | 10.3261 | 10.14 | 9.397 | 8.7108 | 8.6547 |
| **European Community** (Euro) | 1.3822 | 1.3592 | 1.2613 | 1.1715 | 1.1637 |
| **Hong Kong** (HK$) | 11.5094 | 11.49 | 11.14 | 9.5802 | 9.7076 |
| **Japan** (Yen) | 178.02 | 178.84 | 161.54 | 144.12 | 139.03 |
| **Norway** (Krone) | 11.9637 | 13.08 | 11.88 | 10.63 | 10.66 |
| **South Africa** (Rand) | 17.9865 | 23.07 | 21.13 | 16.89 | 16.03 |
| **Sweden** (Krona) | 12.8024 | 12.49 | 11.65 | 11.22 | 11.12 |
| **Switzerland** (Franc) | 1.4419 | 1.4688 | 1.3764 | 1.2559 | 1.2444 |
| **USA** (US$) | 1.4845 | 1.4833 | 1.4373 | 1.2357 | 1.2493 |

Note: The material on pp 121–124 is reproduced from information provided by HMRC and is Crown copyright. The rates for 31.12.16 and 31.3.17 are correct at 27 April 2017.

# Double taxation agreements (including protocols and regulations)

## Agreements in force covering taxes on income and capital gains

| ***Country*** | ***SI/SR & O*** |
|---|---|
| Albania | **2013/3145** |
| Algeria | **2015/1888** |
| Antigua & Barbuda | **1947/2865** |
| | 1968/1096 |
| Argentina | **1997/1777** |
| Armenia[1] | **2011/2722** |
| Australia | **2003/3199** |
| Austria | **1970/1947** |
| | 1979/117 |
| | 1994/768 |
| | 2010/2688 |
| Azerbaijan[1] | **1995/762** |
| Bahrain | **2012/3075** |
| Bangladesh | **1980/708** |
| Barbados | **2012/3076** |
| Belarus[1] | **1986/224** |
| Belgium | **1987/2053** |
| | 2010/2979 |
| Belize | **1947/2866** |
| | 1968/573 |
| | 1973/2097 |
| Bolivia | **1995/2707** |
| Bosnia Herzegovina[2] | **1981/1815** |
| Botswana | **2006/1925** |
| British Virgin Islands | **2009/3013** |
| Brunei | **1950/1977** |
| | 1968/306 |
| | 1973/2098 |
| | 2013/3146 |
| Bulgaria | **2015/1890** |
| Canada | **1980/709** |
| | 1980/1528 |
| | 1985/1996 |
| | 2003/2619 |
| | 2014/3274 |
| | 2015/2011 |
| Cayman Islands | **2010/2973** |
| Chile | **2003/3200** |
| China[4] | **2011/2724** |
| | 2013/3142 |
| Croatia[2] | **2015/1889** |
| Cyprus | **1975/425** |
| | 1980/1529 |
| Czech Republic[3] | **1991/2876** |
| Denmark | **1980/1960** |
| | 1991/2877 |
| | 1996/3165 |
| Egypt | **1980/1091** |
| Estonia[1] | **1994/3207** |
| Ethiopia | **2011/2725** |
| Falkland Islands | **1997/2985** |
| Faroes | **2007/3469** |
| Fiji | **1976/1342** |
| Finland | **1970/153** |
| | 1973/1327 |
| | 1980/710 |
| | 1985/1997 |
| | 1991/2878 |
| | 1996/3166 |

| ***Country*** | ***SI/SR & O*** |
|---|---|
| France | **2009/226** |
| Gambia | **1980/1963** |
| Georgia[1] | **2004/3325** |
| | 2010/2972 |
| Germany | 1967/25 |
| | 1971/874 |
| | **2010/2975**[5] |
| | 2014/1874 |
| Ghana | **1993/1800** |
| Greece | **1954/142** |
| Grenada | **1949/361** |
| | 1968/1867 |
| Guernsey | **1952/1215** |
| | 1994/3209 |
| | 2009/3011 |
| | 2015/2008 |
| | 2016/750 |
| Guyana | **1992/3207** |
| Hong Kong | **2010/2974** |
| Hungary | **2011/2726**[6] |
| Iceland | **2014/1879** |
| India | **1993/1801** |
| | 2013/3147 |
| Indonesia | **1994/769** |
| Irish Republic | **1976/2151** |
| | 1976/2152 |
| | 1995/764 |
| | 1998/3151 |
| Isle of Man | **1955/1205** |
| | 1991/2880 |
| | 1994/3208 |
| | 2009/228 |
| | 2016/749 |
| Israel | **1963/616** |
| | 1971/391 |
| Italy | **1990/2590** |
| Ivory Coast | **1987/169** |
| Jamaica | **1973/1329** |
| Japan | **2006/1924** |
| | 2014/1881 |
| Jersey | **1952/1216** |
| | 1994/3210 |
| | 2009/3012 |
| | 2015/2009 |
| | 2016/752 |
| Jordan | **2001/3924** |
| Kazakhstan[1] | **1994/3211** |
| | 1998/2567 |
| Kenya | **1977/1299** |
| Kiribati (and Tuvalu) | **1950/750** |
| | 1968/309 |
| | 1974/1271 |
| Korea (South) | **1996/3168** |
| Kosovo[2] | **2015/2007** |
| Kuwait | **1999/2036** |
| Kyrgyzstan[1] | |
| Latvia[1] | **1996/3167** |
| Lesotho | **1997/2986** |
| Liechtenstein | **2012/3077** |

| ***Country*** | ***SI/SR & O*** |
|---|---|
| Libya | **2010/243** |
| Lithuania[1] | **2001/3925** |
| | 2002/2847 |
| Luxembourg | **1968/1100** |
| | 1980/567 |
| | 1984/364 |
| | 2010/237 |
| Macedonia[2] | **2007/2127** |
| Malawi | **1956/619** |
| | 1964/1401 |
| | 1968/1101 |
| | 1979/302 |
| Malaysia | **1997/2987** |
| | 2010/2971 |
| Malta | **1995/763** |
| Mauritius | **1981/1121** |
| | 1987/467 |
| | 2003/2620 |
| | 2011/2442 |
| Mexico | **1994/3212** |
| | 2010/2686 |
| Moldova[1] | **2008/1795** |
| Mongolia | **1996/2598** |
| Montenegro[2] | **1981/1815** |
| Montserrat | **1947/2869** |
| | 1968/576 |
| | 2011/1083 |
| Morocco | **1991/2881** |
| Myanmar (Burma) | **1952/751** |
| Namibia | **1962/2352** |
| | 1962/2788 |
| | 1967/1489 |
| | 1967/1490 |
| Netherlands | **2009/227** |
| | 2013/3143 |
| New Zealand | **1984/365** |
| | 2004/1274 |
| | 2008/1793 |
| Nigeria | **1987/2057** |
| Norway | **2013/3144** |
| Oman | **1998/2568** |
| | 2010/2687 |
| Pakistan | **1987/2058** |
| Panama | **2013/3149** |
| Papua New Guinea | **1991/2882** |
| Philippines | **1978/184** |
| Poland | **2006/3323** |
| Portugal | **1969/599** |
| Qatar | **2010/241** |
| | 2011/1684 |

| ***Country*** | ***SI/SR & O*** |
|---|---|
| Romania | **1977/57** |
| Russian Federation[1] | **1994/3213** |
| St Kitts and Nevis | **1947/2872** |
| Saudi Arabia | **2008/1770** |
| Senegal | **2015/1892** |
| Serbia[2] | **1981/1815** |
| Sierra Leone | **1947/2873** |
| | 1968/1104 |
| Singapore | **1997/2988** |
| | 2010/2685 |
| | 2012/3078 |
| Slovak Republic[3] | **1991/2876** |
| Slovenia[2] | **2008/1796** |
| Solomon Islands | **1950/748** |
| | 1968/574 |
| | 1974/1270 |
| South Africa | **2002/3138** |
| | 2011/2441 |
| Spain | **2013/3152** |
| Sri Lanka | **1980/713** |
| Sudan | **1977/1719** |
| Swaziland | **1969/380** |
| Sweden | **2015/1891** |
| Switzerland | **1978/1408** |
| | 1982/714 |
| | 1994/3215 |
| | 2007/3465 |
| | 2010/2689 |
| | 2012/3079 |
| Taiwan | **2002/3137** |
| Tajikistan[1] | **2014/3275** |
| Thailand | **1981/1546** |
| Trinidad and Tobago | **1983/1903** |
| Tunisia | **1984/133** |
| Turkey | **1988/932** |
| Turkmenistan[1] | **2016/1217** |
| Tuvalu (and Kiribati) | **1950/750** |
| | 1968/309 |
| | 1974/1271 |
| Uganda | **1993/1802** |
| Ukraine | **1993/1803** |
| Ukraine[1] | **1993/1803** |
| Uruguay | **2016/753** |
| USA | **2002/2848** |
| Uzbekistan[1] | **1994/770** |
| Venezuela | **1996/2599** |
| Vietnam | **1994/3216** |
| Zambia | **2014/1876** |
| Zimbabwe | **1982/1842** |

1 Following dissolution of the USSR, new agreements are now in force with Armenia, Azerbaijan, Estonia, Georgia, Kazakhstan, Latvia, Lithuania, Moldova, the Russian Federation, Tajikistan, Turkmenistan, Ukraine and Uzbekistan. *SI 1986/224* (former USSR agreement) is treated as continuing to apply to Belarus until coming into force of the agreement signed on 26 September 2017. The UK did not apply the terms of the convention in the case of residents of Tajikistan for profits arising on or after 1 April 2014 (corporation tax) and for income and gains arising on or after 6 April 2014 (income and capital gains tax). The former USSR agreement was similarly treated as continuing to apply by the UK until 31 March 2002 for Armenia, Georgia, Kyrgyzstan, Moldova and Lithuania (none of which considered itself bound by that convention) but as ceasing so to apply after that date (but new treaties now in force with Armenia, Lithuania, Moldova and Georgia). (SP 4/01). A new agreement was signed with Kyrgyzstan on 13 June 2017 but is not yet in force.

2 *SI 1981/1815* (former Yugoslavia agreement) treated as remaining in force between the UK and, respectively, Bosnia-Herzegovina, Croatia and Serbia and Montenegro until superseded by new agreements. (SP 3/04.) The agreement was also treated as applying to Kosovo. New Croatia agreement came into force on 19 November 2015. New Kosovo agreement came into force on 16 December 2015.

3 *SI 1991/2876* (former Czechoslovakia agreement) treated as remaining in force between the UK and, respectively, Czech Republic and Slovak Republic. (SP 5/93.)

4 Hong Kong Special Administrative Region has its own agreement.

5 Treaty replaces 1967/25 with effect from 1 January 2011 or 6 April 2011 depending on type of income. However, where a resident of Germany was, before 30 December 2010, in receipt of a UK pension (including State Pension) or annuity relievable under Article X of prior treaty 1967/25, the individual may elect for the terms of the prior treaty to continue to apply to the pension or annuity.

## Tax information exchange agreements in force

| ***Country*** | ***SI*** | ***Country*** | ***SI*** |
|---|---|---|---|
| Anguilla | **2010/2677** | Isle of Man | **2009/228** |
| Antigua and Barbuda | **2011/1075** | Jersey | **2009/3012** |
| Aruba | **2011/2435** | Liberia | **2011/2434** |
| Bahamas | **2010/2684** | Liechtenstein | **2010/2678** |
| Belize | **2011/1685** | Macao | **2015/801** |
| Bermuda | **2008/1789** | Monaco | **2015/804** |
| British Virgin Islands | **2009/3013** | San Marino | **2011/1688** |
| Curaçao, Sint Maarten and BES Islands (formerly the Netherlands Antilles) | **2011/2433** | St Christopher and Nevis | **2011/1077** |
| Dominica | **2011/1686** | St Lucia | **2011/1076** |
| Gibraltar | **2010/2680** | St Vincent and Grenadines | **2011/1078** |
| Grenada | **2011/1687** | Turks and Caicos Islands | **2010/2679** |
| Guernsey | **2009/3011** | Uruguay | **2014/1358** |

## Tax information exchange agreements signed but not in force

| | | |
|---|---|---|
| Marshall Islands | Jersey Exchange of Letters[1] | British Virgin Islands Exchange of Letters[1] |
| Brazil | Guernsey Exchange of Letters[1] | Turks and Caicos Islands Exchange of Letters[1] |
| Bermuda Exchange of Letters[1] | Gibraltar Exchange of Letters[1] | Anguilla Exchange of Letters[1] |

1 These will amend the existing tax information exchange agreements.

## Tax information exchange agreements in force — EU savings directives

| ***Country*** | ***SI*** | ***Country*** | ***SI*** |
|---|---|---|---|
| Aruba | **2005/1458** | Isle of Man | **2005/1263** |
| British Virgin Islands | **2005/1457** | Jersey | **2005/1261** |
| Gibraltar | **2006/1453** | Montserrat | **2005/1459** |
| Guernsey | **2005/1262** | former Netherlands Antilles (now known as Curaçao, Sint Maarten and BES Islands) | **2005/1460** |

## International agreements in force to improve tax compliance

| | |
|---|---|
| Isle of Man, Guernsey, Jersey, Gibraltar | **2014/520** |
| USA | **2015/878** |

## Agreements in force covering shipping and air transport profits

| *Country* | *SI/SR & O* | *Country* | *SI/SR & O* |
|---|---|---|---|
| Algeria (air) | **2015/1888** | Iran (air) | **1960/2419** |
| Armenia (USSR air)* | **1974/1269** | Kyrgyzstan (USSR air)* | **1974/1269** |
| Belarus (USSR air)* | **1974/1269** | Lebanon | **1964/278** |
| Brazil | **1968/572** | Moldova (USSR air)* | **1974/1269** |
| Cameroon (air) | **1982/1841** | Saudi Arabia (air) | **1994/767** |
| China (air) | **1981/1119** | Tajikistan (USSR air)* | **1974/1269** |
| Congo Democratic Republic | **1977/1298** | Turkmenistan (USSR air)* | **1974/1269** |
| Ethiopia (air) | **1977/1297** | | |
| Georgia (USSR air)* | **1974/1269** | | |
| Hong Kong (air) | **1998/2566** | | |
| (shipping) | **2000/3248** | | |

* HMRC have confirmed that this Arrangement will be treated in the same way as the Convention covering income and capital gains (SI 1986/224). See note 1 p 126.

## Agreements in force covering estates, inheritances and gifts

| | | | |
|---|---|---|---|
| France* | **1963/1319** | Pakistan* | **1957/1522** |
| India* | **1956/998** | South Africa | **1979/576** |
| Ireland | **1978/1107** | Sweden | **1981/840** |
| Italy* | **1968/304** | | 1989/986 |
| Netherlands | **1980/706** | Switzerland | **1994/3214** |
| | 1996/730 | USA | **1979/1454** |

* Agreements pre-date UK inheritance tax/capital transfer tax.

# Overseas income – basis of assessment

(ITTOIA 2005 Pt 8; ITEPA 2003 ss 573–576A, 642, 642A; ITA 2007 ss 809A–809Z10; FA 2017 Sch 3; F(No 2)A 2017 s 29, Sch 8)

| | Professions, trades, etc | Pensions | Other income |
|---|---|---|---|
| Non-residents | Exempt | Exempt | Exempt |
| Residents | | | |
| (1) **Foreign domicile**[2] | Remittance | Remittance | Remittance |
| (2) **UK domicile** | Arising | 100%[1] | Arising |

1 90% arising basis before 6 April 2017. Pensions paid by the governments of the Federal Republic of Germany, Austria, and from 6 April 2016 the Netherlands, to certain victims of WW2 persecution are exempt.

2 Where from 6 April 2008, an individual not domiciled (or, before 6 April 2013, not ordinarily resident) in the UK who has overseas income (or, for non-domiciles only, gains) in excess of £2,000 claims the remittance basis, he will not qualify for personal allowances or the capital gains tax annual exemption. The claim for remittance basis must be made annually. If the individual is not UK domiciled (or before 6 April 2013, not ordinarily resident) in a year and has been resident in the UK for at least seven out of the last nine tax years and has overseas income or gains in excess of £2,000, there is an additional charge of £30,000. From 6 April 2015 this charge is £60,000 for non-domiciles who have been UK resident for at least twelve tax years in the previous fourteen (£50,000 from 6 April 2012 to 5 April 2015), and, before 6 April 2017, £90,000 for non-domiciles who have been UK resident for at least seventeen tax years in the previous twenty. From April 2017 an individual who has been resident in the UK for more than 15 of the last 20 tax years will be deemed UK-domiciled for tax purposes and hence the £90,000 charge will no longer apply. It is also no longer possible for an individual born in the UK to parents who are UK-domiciled to claim non-domicile status if they leave but then return and take up residency in the UK.

3 A statutory residence test is introduced from 6 April 2013 and ordinary residence is abolished from that date, subject to transitional provisions in certain cases for individuals who were resident but not ordinarily resident in the UK at the end of the tax year 2012–13. Before 6 April 2013 UK-domiciled taxpayers who were not ordinarily resident were taxed on the remittance basis.

**Employment income liability of non-resident employees** see p 92.

# Tax-free (FOTRA) securities

(FA 1996 s 154; FA 1998 s 161; ITTOIA 2005 ss 713, 714; CTA 2009 s 1279)

Interest on all government stock is exempt from tax where the beneficial owner is not resident in the UK. Except in the case of 3½% War Loan 1952 or after, the exemption does not apply where the securities are held for the purposes of a trade or business carried on in the UK.

# Social security benefits

## Taxable state benefits

| | **Weekly 10.4.17** | **Total 2017–18 (52 weeks)** | **Weekly 11.4.16** | **Total 2016–17 (52 weeks)** |
|---|---|---|---|---|
| | **£** | **£** | **£** | **£** |
| **Bereavement benefits — deaths before 6 April 2017**[1] | | | | |
| Bereavement allowance: standard rate | **113.70** | **5,912** | 112.55 | 5,852 |
| Widowed parent's allowance | **113.70** | **5,912** | 112.55 | 5,852 |
| **Carer's allowance** | **62.70** | **3,260** | 62.10 | 3,229 |
| – Adult dependency increase[7] | **36.90** | **1,918** | 36.55 | 1,900 |
| **Employment and support allowance**[6] | | | | |
| –under 25 | **57.90** | **–** | 57.90 | – |
| –25 or over | **73.10** | **–** | 73.10 | – |
| **Incapacity benefit**[6] | | | | |
| Long-term (after 52 weeks) | **106.40** | **5,532** | 105.35 | 5,478 |
| – Adult dependency increase | **61.80** | **3,213** | 61.20 | 3,182 |
| – Age increase: higher rate | **11.25** | **585** | 11.15 | 579 |
| lower rate | **6.25** | **325** | 6.20 | 322 |
| Short term | | | | |
| – Under pension age: higher rate | **95.00** | **–** | 94.05 | – |
| – Adult dependency increase | **48.15** | **–** | 47.65 | – |
| – Over pension age: higher rate | **106.40** | **–** | 105.35 | – |
| – Adult dependency increase | **59.50** | **–** | 58.90 | – |
| **Industrial death benefit**[2] | | | | |
| Widow's pension: higher rate | **122.30** | **6,359** | 119.30 | 6,203 |
| lower rate | **36.69** | **1,907** | 35.79 | 1,861 |
| Widower's pension | **122.30** | **6,359** | 119.30 | 6,203 |
| **Invalidity allowance**[3] | | | | |
| Higher rate | **21.70** | **1,128** | 21.50 | 1,118 |
| Middle rate | **14.00** | **728** | 13.90 | 722 |
| Lower rate | **7.00** | **364** | 6.95 | 361 |
| **Jobseeker's allowance**[4] | | | | |
| Single: under 25 | **57.90** | **–** | 57.90 | – |
| 25 or over | **73.10** | **–** | 73.10 | – |
| Couple: both under 18 | **57.90** | **–** | 57.90 | – |
| both under 18 higher rate | **87.50** | **–** | 87.50 | – |
| one under 18, one under 25 | **57.90** | **–** | 57.90 | – |
| one under 18, one 25 or over | **73.10** | **–** | 73.10 | – |
| both 18 or over | **114.85** | **–** | 114.85 | – |
| **State pension — retired before 6 April 2016** | | | | |
| Single person (Category A or B) | **122.30** | **6,359** | 119.30 | 6,203 |
| Single person (Category B lower) based on spouse's or civil partner's insurance | **73.30** | **3,811** | 71.50 | 3,718 |
| Adult dependency increase[7] | **66.35** | **3,450** | 65.70 | 3,416 |
| Non-contributory pension | | | | |
| – single (Category C (higher) or Category D) | **73.30** | **3,811** | 71.50 | 3,718 |
| – single (Category C (lower)) | **–** | **–** | – | – |
| Age addition (over 80) (each) | **0.25** | **13** | 0.25 | 13 |
| **State pension — retired after 5 April 2016** | | | | |
| Rate | **159.55** | **8,296** | 155.65 | 8,093 |
| **Statutory adoption pay** | | | | |
| Rate[5] | **140.98** | **–** | 139.58 | – |
| Earnings threshold | **113.00** | **–** | 112.00 | – |
| **Statutory maternity pay** | | | | |
| Rate[5] | **140.98** | **–** | 139.58 | – |
| Earnings threshold | **113.00** | **–** | 112.00 | – |

| | *Weekly 10.4.17* | *Total 2017–18 (52 weeks)* | *Weekly 11.4.16* | *Total 2016–17 (52 weeks)* |
|---|---|---|---|---|
| | **£** | **£** | **£** | **£** |
| **Statutory paternity pay** | | | | |
| Rate[5] | **140.98** | **–** | 139.58 | – |
| Earnings threshold | **113.00** | **–** | 112.00 | – |
| **Statutory shared parental pay** | | | | |
| Rate[5,10] | **140.98** | **–** | 139.58 | – |
| Earnings threshold | **113.00** | **–** | 112.00 | – |
| **Statutory sick pay** | | | | |
| Rate | **89.35** | **–** | 88.45 | – |
| Earnings threshold | **113.00** | **–** | 112.00 | – |

1 Paid to widows, widowers and the civil partner of the deceased for up to 52 weeks. For deaths on or after 6 April 2017 bereavement support payments replace bereavement benefits and are non-taxable.

2 For deaths before 11 April 1988 only.

3 When paid with retirement pensions. See note below on non-taxable benefits on p 134.

4 Where the allowance exceeds the amount shown above, the excess is not taxable.

5 The allowance is 90% of average weekly earnings if less than the above amount. In the first six weeks the rate of SMP and SAP is 90% of average weekly earnings even if higher than the standard rate.

6 Employment and support allowance replaces incapacity benefits for new claimants on or after 27 October 2008. Only contributory employment and support allowance is taxable. Income related allowance is not taxable.

7 Not available to new retirees or new carer's allowance claimants from 6 April 2010. To be withdrawn completely on 5 April 2020.

8 **A cap is placed on the total amount of benefit** that most people aged 16 to 64 can receive. The cap applies to the total amount that the people in a household receive from certain benefits. From 7 November 2016, the cap is £384.61 a week or £442.30 in Greater London (previously, £500 nationwide) for couples (with or without children living with them), and for single parents whose children live with them, and £257.69 a week or £296.34 in Greater London (previously, £350 nationwide) for single adults who do not have children, or whose children do not live with them. See www.gov.uk/benefit-cap.

9 **Universal credit** is being phased in gradually from 29 April 2013 and will be completed by 2021. It replaces some of the benefits above. For current rates see table of non-taxable benefits on p 135. See www.gov.uk/universal-credit.

10 Statutory shared parental pay (ShPP) is available for eligible parents (the mother and her partner) whose baby is due on or after 5 April 2015 or where a child is placed for adoption (the parental equivalents are the primary and secondary adopter) on or after the same date.

# Non-taxable state benefits

| *Weekly rates from* | | | **10.4.17** | **11.4.16** |
|---|---|---|---|---|
| | | | **£** | **£** |
| **Attendance allowance** | | | | |
| Higher rate (day and night) | | | **83.10** | 82.30 |
| Lower rate (day or night) | | | **55.65** | 55.10 |
| **Child benefit**[3] | | | | |
| Eldest child | | | **20.70** | 20.70 |
| Each subsequent child | | | **13.70** | 13.70 |
| **Child dependency addition** | | | | |
| Paid with state pension; widowed mother's/parent's allowance; short-term incapacity benefit - higher rate or over state pension age; long-term incapacity benefit; carer's allowance; severe disablement unemployability supplement | | | **11.35** | 11.35 |
| **Disability living allowance**[2] | | | | |
| Care component | higher rate | | **83.10** | 82.30 |
| | middle rate | | **55.65** | 55.10 |
| | lower rate | | **22.00** | 21.80 |
| Mobility component | higher rate | | **58.00** | 57.45 |
| | lower rate | | **22.00** | 21.80 |
| **Personal independence payment**[2] | | | | |
| Daily living component | enhanced rate | | **83.10** | 82.30 |
| | standard rate | | **55.65** | 55.10 |
| Mobility component | enhanced rate | | **58.00** | 57.45 |
| | standard rate | | **22.00** | 21.80 |
| **Guardian's allowance** | | | **16.70** | 16.55 |
| **Incapacity benefit (short-term)**[1] | | | | |
| Under pension age – lower rate (first 28 weeks) | | | **80.25** | 79.45 |
| – Adult dependency increase | | | **48.15** | 47.65 |
| Over pension age – lower rate (first 28 weeks) | | | **102.10** | 101.10 |
| – Adult dependency increase | | | **59.50** | 58.90 |
| **Maternity allowance (where SMP not available)** | | | | |
| Standard rate | | | **140.98** | 139.58 |
| MA threshold | | | **30.00** | 30.00 |
| **Severe disablement allowance**[7] | | | | |
| Basic rate | | | **75.40** | 74.65 |
| Age-related addition | | higher rate | **11.25** | 11.15 |
| | | middle rate | **6.25** | 6.20 |
| | | lower rate | **6.25** | 6.20 |
| – Adult dependency increase | | | **37.10** | 36.75 |

***See next page for universal credit amounts***

| *Amount payable per assessment period[5] in:* | | **2017–18** | **2016–17** |
|---|---|---|---|
| | | **£** | **£** |
| **Universal credit[5]** | | | |
| **Universal credit amounts** | | | |
| Standard allowance | single under 25 | **251.77** | 251.77 |
| | single 25 or over | **317.82** | 317.82 |
| | joint claimants both under 25 | **395.20** | 395.20 |
| | joint claimants either 25 or over | **498.89** | 498.89 |
| Child element[6] | first child | **277.08** | 277.08 |
| | second/ subsequent child | **231.67** | 231.67 |
| Disabled child additions | lower rate addition | **126.11** | 126.11 |
| | higher rate addition | **372.30** | 367.92 |
| Limited capability for work element | | **126.11** | 126.11 |
| Limited capability for work and work-related activity element | | **318.76** | 315.60 |
| Carer element | | **151.89** | 150.39 |
| Childcare cost element | maximum for one child | **646.35** | 646.35 |
| | maximum for two or more children | **1,108.04** | 1,108.04 |
| **Non-dependants' housing cost contributions** | | **70.06** | 69.37 |
| **Work allowances** | | | |
| Higher work allowance (no housing element) | single, no dependent children | **Nil** | Nil |
| | single, one or more children | **397.00** | 397.00 |
| | single, limited capability for work | **397.00** | 397.00 |
| | joint claimant, no dependent children | **Nil** | Nil |
| | joint claimant, one or more children | **397.00** | 397.00 |
| | joint claimant, limited capability for work | **397.00** | 397.00 |
| Lower work allowance | single, no dependent children | **Nil** | Nil |
| | single, one or more children | **192.00** | 192.00 |
| | single, limited capability for work | **192.00** | 192.00 |
| | joint claimant, no dependent children | **Nil** | Nil |
| | joint claimant, one or more children | **192.00** | 192.00 |
| | joint claimant, limited capability for work | **192.00** | 192.00 |

1 Incapacity benefit replaced invalidity allowance from April 1995. The benefits are taxable except those paid in the first 28 weeks of incapacity and those paid to persons already receiving invalidity benefit on 13 April 1995 so long as they remain incapable of work.

2 Personal Independence Payment (PIP) started to replace Disability Living Allowance (DLA) for new claims by eligible people aged 16 to 64 from 8 April 2013. PIP will be introduced in stages over a number of years for existing DLA claimants.

3 See note on p 77 regarding the income tax charge arising to certain child benefit claimants from 7 January 2013.

4 **A cap is placed on the total amount of benefit** that most people aged 16 to 64 can receive. The cap applies to the total amount that the people in a household receive from certain benefits. From 7 November 2016, the cap is £384.61 a week or £442.30 in Greater London (previously, £500 nationwide) for couples (with or without children living with them), and for single parents whose children live with them, and £257.69 a week or £296.34 in Greater London (previously, £350 nationwide) for single adults who do not have children, or whose children do not live with them. See www.gov.uk/benefit-cap.

5 **Universal credit** is being phased in gradually from 29 April 2013 and will be completed by 2021. It replaces some of the benefits listed in the above tables. An assessment period is a calendar month from effective date of claim. See www.gov.uk/universal-credit.

6 The child element of universal credit is no longer awarded for third and subsequent children born after 6 April 2017. This also applies to families claiming universal credit for the first time after April 2017. The restriction does not apply to disabled children and multiple births.

7 Severe disablement allowance has been replaced with employment and support allowance except for those who reached retirement age before 6 April 2014.

***See next page for* Other non-taxable benefits**

| | 2017–18 | 2017–18 | 2016–17 | 2016–17 |
|---|---|---|---|---|
| **Bereavement support payments — deaths on or after 6 April 2017**[1] | **First payment** | **Monthly** | | |
| | **£** | **£** | | |
| With children under 20 in full-time education | **3,500** | **350**[1] | — | — |
| Without children under 20 in full-time education | **2,500** | **100**[1] | — | — |

1 Paid to widows, widowers and the civil partner of the deceased. For deaths on or after 6 April 2017 bereavement support payments replace taxable bereavement benefits. Monthly payments paid for up to 18 months.

## Other non-taxable benefits include:

Bereavement payment (lump sum £2,000)
Back to Work bonus
Child tax credit (see Tax Credits, p 103)
Christmas bonus (with retirement pension)
Cold weather payments
Housing benefit (income related)
Income support (income related)
Industrial injuries disablement pension
Pension credit
Pneumoconiosis, byssinosis and miscellaneous disease benefits
Social fund payments
Vaccine damage (lump sum)
War pensions
Winter fuel payment
Working tax credit (see Tax Credits, p 103)

# Stamp taxes

## Stamp duty land tax

(FA 2003 Schs 2A–9)

Stamp duty land tax applies to contracts entered into (or varied) after 10 July 2003 and completed after 30 November 2003 and to leases granted after that date (FA 2003 ss 55, 56, Sch 5). With effect from 22 July 2004, it also applies to the transfer of an interest in land into, or out of, a partnership and to the acquisition of an interest in a partnership where the partnership property includes an interest in land. With effect from 19 July 2006, it applies to transfers of partnership interests only where the sole or main activity of the partnership is investing or dealing in interests in land. Stamp duty land tax does not apply in Scotland to transactions with an effective date on or after 1 April 2015, from which date Scottish land and buildings transaction tax applies (see table below), subject to transitional provisions in particular in relation to contracts entered into on or before 1 May 2012. The power to raise stamp duty land tax has been devolved to the Welsh Government from April 2018 (see table below).

| ***Land transactions*** | | | | | |
|---|---|---|---|---|---|
| | ***Residential property***[5] | ***Rate*** | ***Higher rate applying to certain purchases***[7] | ***Non-residential or mixed property*** | ***Rate*** |
| **Effective date** | **From 1.4.16** | | | **From 17.3.16** | |
| | On band of consideration[2] | | | On band of consideration[2] | |
| | **Up to £125,000** | **Nil** | **3%** | **Up to £150,000** | **Nil** |
| | **£125,001–£250,000** | **2%** | **5%** | **£150,001–£250,000** | **2%** |
| | **£250,001–£925,000** | **5%** | **8%** | **£250,001 or more** | **5%** |
| | **£925,001–£1,500,000** | **10%** | **13%** | | |
| | **£1,500,001 or more** | **12%** | **15%** | | |
| | On total consideration[1] | | | | |
| Non-natural persons[1,6] | **£500,001 or more** | **15%** | | | |
| Effective date | 4.12.14–31.3.16 | | | 4.12.14–16.3.16 | |
| | On band of consideration[2] | | | On total consideration[1] | |
| | Up to £125,000 | Nil | | Up to £150,000 | Nil |
| | £125,001–£250,000 | 2% | | £150,001–£250,000 | 1% |
| | £250,001–£925,000 | 5% | | £250,001–£500,000 | 3% |
| | £925,001–£1,500,000 | 10% | | £500,001 or more | 4% |
| | £1,500,001 or more | 12% | | | |
| | On total consideration[1] | | | | |
| Non-natural persons[1,6] | £500,001 or more | 15% | | | |
| Effective date | 20.3.14–3.12.14 | | | 20.3.14–3.12.14 | |
| | On total consideration[1] | | | On total consideration[1] | |
| | Up to £125,000 | Nil | | Up to £150,000 | Nil |
| | £125,001–£250,000 | 1% | | £150,001–£250,000 | 1% |
| | £250,001–£500,000 | 3% | | £250,001–£500,000 | 3% |
| | £500,001–£1,000,000 | 4% | | £500,001 or more | 4% |
| | £1,000,001–£2,000,000 | 5% | | | |
| | £2,000,001 or more | 7% | | | |
| Non-natural persons[1,6] | £500,001 or more | 15% | | | |

| ***Land transactions*** | | | | |
|---|---|---|---|---|
| | ***Residential property***[5] | ***Rate*** | ***Non-residential or mixed property*** | ***Rate*** |
| Effective date | 22.3.12–19.3.14 | | 22.3.12–19.3.14 | |
| | On total consideration[1] | | On total consideration[1] | |
| | Up to £125,000 | Nil | Up to £150,000 | Nil |
| | £125,001–£250,000 | 1% | £150,001–£250,000 | 1% |
| | £250,001–£500,000 | 3% | £250,001–£500,000 | 3% |
| | £500,001–£1,000,000 | 4% | £500,001 or more | 4% |
| | £1,000,001–£2,000,000 | 5% | | |
| | £2,000,001 or more | 7% | | |
| Non-natural persons[1,6] | £2,000,001 or more | 15% | | |
| Effective date | 6.4.11–21.3.12[2, 3] | | 6.4.11–21.3.12[2] | |
| | On total consideration[1] | | On total consideration[1] | |
| | Up to £125,000 | Nil | Up to £150,000 | Nil |
| | £125,001–£250,000 | 1% | £150,001–£250,000 | 1% |
| | £250,001–£500,000 | 3% | £250,001–£500,000 | 3% |
| | £500,001–£1,000,000 | 4% | £500,001 or more | 4% |
| | £1,000,001 or more | 5% | | |
| **Lease rentals** | *On net present value of rent over term of lease (applying a discount rate of 3.5%)*[4] | | | |
| Effective date | ***Residential property*** | ***Rate*** | ***Non-residential or mixed property*** | ***Rate*** |
| **From 17.3.16** | **Up to £125,000** | **Nil** | **Up to £150,000** | **Nil** |
| | **£125,001 or more** | **1%** | **£150,001–£5,000,000** | **1%** |
| | | | **£5,000,001 or more** | **2%** |
| 1.1.10–16.3.16 | Up to £125,000 | Nil | Up to £150,000 | Nil |
| | £125,001 or more | 1% | £150,001 or more | 1% |

**Premiums**
The same tax is payable for a premium granted as for a land transaction. Special rules applied before 17 March 2016 to a premium in respect of non-residential property where the rent exceeds £1,000 a year. For transactions before 12 March 2008, the rules applied to all property where the rent exceeded £600 a year.

1 Rates apply to the full consideration, not only to that in excess of the previous band.

2 Rates are charged on the portion of the consideration that falls within each rate band. Where the change from calculations based on total consideration to those based on band of consideration took place for residential property from 4 December 2014, and for non-residential property from 16 March 2016, in certain circumstances the taxpayer could elect for the new rules not to apply.

3 For residential property, purchases by first-time buyers between 25 March 2010 and 24 March 2012 inclusive attracted a nil rate of SDLT for purchase consideration up to £250,000.

4 Rates apply to the amount of npv in the slice, not the whole value.

5 With effect from 19 July 2011, where a purchaser (or a connected person) of residential property acquires more than one dwelling from the same vendor (or a connected person) and makes a claim, the rate of SDLT will be calculated based on the mean consideration for each property, subject to a minimum rate of 1%. For leases granted on or after 26 March 2015 relief may be claimed in respect of superior interests in dwellings subject to a long lease, where the transaction is the lease element of a "lease and leaseback" funding arrangement entered into by a housing association or other qualifying body.

6 From 21 March 2012 a 15% rate applies to certain non-natural persons (ie companies, partnerships with at least one company member, and collective investment schemes) acquiring a residential property where consideration exceeds a specified threshold, which is £2,000,000 from 21 March 2012 to 19 March 2014, and £500,000 from 20 March 2014. Relief is available for certain acquisitions so that the charge is at the lower percentage. See p 65 for the annual tax on enveloped dwellings and capital gains tax charge which also apply to such properties.

7 From 1 April 2016 (for contracts exchanged after 25 November 2015) a higher rate applies broadly to purchases of additional residential property by individuals, and to purchases of residential property by companies and trusts other than bare trusts and interest in possession trusts. It does not apply to purchases of property under £40,000 or to purchases of caravans, mobile homes and houseboats. If there is a period of overlap in ownership of a main residence, a refund of the higher rate can be obtained if the previous main residence is sold within 36 months following the purchase of the new.

## Exemptions and reliefs

No SDLT (or, where relevant, stamp duty) is chargeable on:

(1) transfers to charities for use for charitable purposes.
(2) transfers to bodies established for national purposes.
(3) gifts inter vivos.
(4) certain transfers on divorce or dissolution of a civil partnership.
(5) transfers of property to beneficiaries under a will or an intestacy.
(6) land transfers within groups of companies.
(7) land transferred in exchange for shares on company reconstruction and acquisitions.
(8) certain transfers to or leases granted by registered providers of social housing. (Although the relief is repealed for the old stamp duty rules for instruments executed on or after 6 April 2013, it still applies to stamp duty land tax).
(9) sale and leaseback and lease and leaseback arrangements involving commercial and residential property.
(10) certain acquisitions of residential property by house building companies or property traders from personal representatives, or when people move into a new dwelling or a chain of transactions break down, or by employers involving employee relocations.
(11) for transactions with an effective date before 6 April 2013, transfers on sale of residential property for a consideration of up to £150,000 in disadvantaged parts of the UK. This also applied to leases broadly, on rent where the relevant rental value did not exceed £150,000 and to premiums not exceeding £150,000. No claims can be made after 5 May 2014.
(12) from 1 October 2007 until 30 September 2012 for new zero carbon homes (including flats) with a purchase price of up to £500,000, there was no SDLT charged. Where the purchase price was in excess of £500,000, the SDLT liability on the purchase price was reduced by £15,000.
(13) from 25 March 2010 until 24 March 2012 purchases of residential property by first-time buyers for consideration of more than £125,000 but not more than £250,000 (see p 138).
(14) demutualisation of building societies and insurance companies.
(15) incorporation of limited liability partnerships.
(16) transfers of land between public bodies under a statutory reorganisation.
(17) compulsory purchase of land facilitating redevelopment.
(18) land transactions in compliance with planning obligations enforceable against the vendor and made within five years of the obligation where the purchaser is one of certain public authorities.
(19) transfers by a local constituency association in consequence of a reorganisation of parliamentary constituencies.
(20) purchases or leases of certain diplomatic or consular premises or headquarters premises of certain international organisations.
(21) from 15 September 2016, transfer of properties into an authorised PAIF or CoACS within an initial period if conditions are met.

Relief from SDLT may also apply on:

(a) right to buy transactions, shared ownership leases and rent to loan transactions.
(b) alternative property finance schemes.
(c) exercise of collective rights by leaseholders.
(d) crofting community right to buy.
(e) certain arrangements relating to land transactions involving public or educational bodies.
(f) acquisitions of interests in land by certain National Health Service bodies.

# Land and buildings transaction tax (Scotland)

(Land and Buildings Transaction Tax (Scotland) Act 2013; Land and Buildings Transaction Tax (Amendment) (Scotland) Act 2016; SSI 2015/126; SSI 2017/233)

Land and buildings transaction tax applies in Scotland instead of stamp duty land tax from 1 April 2015.

| **Land transactions** | | | | |
|---|---|---|---|---|
| **Effective date** | ***Residential property*** | **Rate**[2] | ***Non-residential or mixed property*** | **Rate**[2] |
| | On band of consideration[1] | | On band of consideration[1] | |
| **From 1.4.15** | **Up to £145,000** | **Nil** | **Up to £150,000** | **Nil** |
| | **£145,001–£250,000** | **2%** | **£150,001–£350,000** | **3%** |
| | **£250,001–£325,000** | **5%** | **£350,001 or more** | **4.5%** |
| | **£325,001–£750,000** | **10%** | | |
| | **£750,001 or more** | **12%** | | |
| **Lease rentals**<br>LBTT is applied to non-residential leases. Residential leases are generally exempt from LBTT with the exception of certain long leases which are qualifying leases. Where a lease is chargeable the amount of tax payable is 1% of the amount of net present value of the rent above £150,000. Licences to occupy property are exempt interests, except licences that are of a description prescribed under Land and Buildings Transaction Tax (Scotland) Act 2013 s 53(1). | | | | |
| **Premiums**<br>The same tax is payable for a premium granted as for a land transaction, subject to the exemption for residential leases other than qualifying leases (see above). Special rules apply to a premium in respect of non-residential property where the rent exceeds £1,000 a year. | | | | |

1 Rates are charged on the portion of the consideration that falls within each rate band.

2 For land transactions with an effective date on or after 1 April 2016, unless missives were concluded before 28 January 2016, an additional amount of tax equal to 3% of the relevant consideration applies broadly to transactions which consist of or include the acquisition of an additional dwelling by individuals and trusts over which the beneficiary has substantial rights, and to purchases of a dwelling by certain businesses, companies and other trusts. It does not apply to purchases of property under £40,000. If there is a period of overlap in ownership of a main residence, a refund of the higher rate can be obtained if the previous main residence is sold within 18 months following the purchase of the new. From 30 June 2017 relief is available in certain circumstances when two buyers jointly buy a new dwelling and previously lived together as a married couple, civil partners or cohabitants in a dwelling owned by either one of them solely.

## Exemptions and reliefs

There are various exemptions and reliefs from LBTT, all of which currently apply to SDLT (see p 139).

# Land transaction tax (Wales)

(Land Transaction Tax and Anti-avoidance of Devolved Taxes (Wales) Act 2017; WSI 2017/953)

Land transaction tax applies in Wales instead of stamp duty land tax from 1 April 2018.

| **Land transactions** | | | | | |
|---|---|---|---|---|---|
| **Effective date** | ***Residential property*** | **Rate** | ***Higher rate applying to certain purchases***[2] | ***Non-residential or mixed property*** | **Rate** |
| | On band of consideration[1] | | | On band of consideration[1] | |
| From 1.4.18 | Up to £150,000 | Nil | 3% | Up to £150,000 | Nil |
| | £150,001–£250,000 | 2.5% | 5.5% | £150,001–£250,000 | 1% |
| | £250,001–£400,000 | 5% | 8% | £250,001–£1,000,000 | 5% |
| | £400,001–£750,000 | 7.5% | 10.5% | £1,000,001 or more | 6% |
| | £750,001–£1,500,000 | 10% | 13% | | |
| | £1,500,001 or more | 12% | 15% | | |
| **Lease rentals**<br>LTT is applied to non-residential leases and the amount of tax payable is 1% of the amount of net present value of the rent between £150,000 and £2m, and 2% above £2m. | | | | | |

| Premiums |
|---|
| The same tax is payable for a premium granted as for a land transaction. |

1 Rates are charged on the portion of the consideration that falls within each rate band.

2 A higher rate applies broadly to purchases of additional residential property by individuals, and to purchases of residential property by companies and trusts other than bare trusts and interest in possession trusts. It does not apply to purchases of property under £40,000. If there is a period of overlap in ownership of a main residence, a refund of the higher rate can be obtained if the previous main residence is sold within 36 months following the purchase of the new.

# Stamp duty

(FA 1986 Part III; FA 1999 Sch 13)

For contracts entered into (or varied) after 10 July 2003 and completed after 30 November 2003 and for leases granted after that date, stamp duty is abolished for all transfers other than stocks and marketable securities, and interests in partnerships. From 22 July 2004 stamp duty is also abolished for certain partnership transactions involving an interest in land. From those dates, transfers of land are subject to stamp duty land tax (see p 137).

| Shares, etc | |
|---|---|
| Shares put into depository receipts or put into duty free clearance systems[5] | 1.5% |
| Purchase of own shares by company | 0.5% |
| Transfers of stock or marketable securities | 0.5% |
| Takeovers, mergers, demergers, schemes of reconstruction and amalgamation (except where no real change of ownership) | 0.5% |

1 Stamp duty is rounded to the next multiple of £5.

2 For instruments executed after 11 March 2008 stamp duty is not chargeable where the amount or value of the consideration is less than £1,000.

3 From April 2014 transfers of interests in exchange traded funds will be exempt from stamp duty and stamp duty reserve tax.

4 From 28 April 2014 no stamp duty or stamp duty reserve tax is due on trades in 'recognised growth markets' such as the Alternative Investment Market and the ISDX Growth Market.

5 For options entered into on or after 25 November 2015 and exercised on or after 16 March 2016, where UK securities are deposited with a depositary receipt issuer or clearance service following the exercise of an option, the transfer will be chargeable to stamp duty or stamp duty reserve tax (SDRT) at 1.5% of the higher of the market value or the option strike price at the date the instrument is executed (for stamp duty) or the date of transfer (for SDRT).

## Fixed duties

| | |
|---|---|
| Instruments affecting land transactions | £5 |

From 13 March 2008 fixed duties are generally abolished other than as above. The £5 rate applies to instruments effected from 1 October 1999.

# Stamp Duty Reserve Tax (SDRT)

(FA 1986 Part IV)

| | |
|---|---|
| Agreements to transfer chargeable securities for money or money's worth (eg renounceable letters of allotment)[1] | 0.5% |
| Chargeable securities put into a clearance service[2] or converted into depositary receipts where the transfer is not an integral part of an issue of share capital[4,7] | 1.5% |
| Dealings of units in unit trusts and shares in open-ended investment companies before 30 March 2014[3] | 0.5% |
| Transfers of foreign currency bearer shares and agreements to transfer sterling or foreign currency convertible or equity-related loan stock issued by UK companies | 0.5% |

1 If the transaction is completed by a duly stamped instrument within six years from the date on which the charge is imposed, the SDRT will be cancelled or repaid.

2 Where the operator of a clearance service elects to collect and account for SDRT on the normal rate of 0.5% on dealing within the system the higher SDRT charge of 1.5% does not apply.

3 From 6 April 2001 transfers of units in a unit trust and surrenders of shares in open-ended investment companies are exempt when held within individual pension accounts. From 30 March 2014 the exemption applies to all transfers of units in a unit trust and all surrenders of shares in open-ended investment companies, although the charge will remain on non pro-rata in specie redemptions.

4 Following the cases of HSBC Holdings plc and the Bank of New York Mellon Corporation v HMRC and HSBC Holdings plc and Vidacos Nominees Limited v Commissioners for HMRC, SDRT of 1.5% is no longer applicable on issues of UK shares to depositary receipt issuers and clearance services. Claims for repayment of SDRT may be made.

[5] From April 2014 transfers of interests in exchange traded funds will be exempt from stamp duty and stamp duty reserve tax.

[6] From 28 April 2014 no stamp duty or stamp duty reserve tax is due on trades in 'recognised growth markets' such as the Alternative Investment Market and the ISDX Growth Market.

[7] For options entered into on or after 25 November 2015 and exercised on or after 16 March 2016, where UK securities are deposited with a depositary receipt issuer or clearance service following the exercise of an option, the transfer will be chargeable to stamp duty or stamp duty reserve tax (SDRT) at 1.5% of the higher of the market value or the option strike price at the date the instrument is executed (for stamp duty) or the date of transfer (for SDRT).

## Interest on unpaid tax

**Stamp duty land tax. *From 26 September 2005*:** Interest runs from the end of 30 days after the effective date of transaction (normally completion), or the date of a disqualifying event, until the tax is paid. In the case of a deferred payment, interest runs from the date the payment is due until the tax is paid. A penalty carries interest from the date determined until the date of payment. There are proposals to reduce the payment window to 14 days from 2018–19.

**Stamp duty. *For instruments executed from 1 October 1999*:** Interest runs from the end of 30 days after the date the instrument is executed until the tax is paid. Amounts less than £25 are not charged.

**Stamp duty reserve tax. *From 1 January 2015*:** The harmonised interest regime applies, see p 4.

*Before 1 January 2015*: Interest was charged from 14 days after the transaction date for exchange transactions and otherwise from seven days after the end of the month of the transaction. Amounts less than £25 were not charged.

*Rates:* see pp 4, 5.

**Land and buildings transaction tax. *From 1 April 2015*:** Interest runs broadly from the filing date of the return and is charged at the same rate as under the harmonised interest regime but paid to Revenue Scotland — see p 4.

## Repayment supplement / Interest on overpaid tax

**Stamp duty land tax. *From 26 September 2005*:** Interest is added to repayments of overpaid stamp duty land tax and runs from the date tax was paid or an amount was lodged with HMRC, or the date a penalty was made, to the date the order for repayment is issued.

**Stamp duty. *For instruments executed from 1 October 1999*:** Interest is added to repayments of overpaid stamp duty and runs from 30 days after the date the instrument is executed or the date of payment if later. Amounts less than £25 are not paid.

**Stamp duty reserve tax. *From 1 January 2015*:** The harmonised interest regime applies, see p 4.

*Before 1 January 2015*: Interest was paid from the date the tax was paid to the date the order for repayment was issued.

*Rates:* see pp 4, 6.

**Land and buildings transaction tax. *From 1 April 2015*:** Interest runs from the date the tax, penalty or interest was paid or an amount was lodged with Revenue Scotland, to the date repayment is made. It is paid at the same rate as under the harmonised interest regime but by Revenue Scotland — see p 4.

# Penalties

| *Offence* | *Penalty* |
|---|---|
| **Stamp duty land tax and stamp duty reserve tax** | |
| Inaccuracy in return or other document (FA 2007 Sch 24). | See **Penalties — modernised penalty regime** on p 10 |
| Inaccuracy in return or other document as a result of third party providing incorrect (or withholding) information (FA 2007 Sch 24). | See **Penalties — modernised penalty regime** on p 10 |
| Failure to notify HMRC of an error in an assessment (within 30 days) (FA 2007 Sch 24). | See **Penalties — modernised penalty regime** on p 10 |
| Failure to comply with HMRC investigatory powers with effect from 1 April 2010 (FA 2008 Sch 36). | (*a*) Initial penalty of £300;<br>(*b*) if failure/obstruction continues, a further penalty of up to £60 per day;<br>(*c*) if failure/obstruction continues after penalty under (*a*) imposed, a tax-related amount determined by the Upper Tribunal. |
| Provision of inaccurate information or document when complying with an information notice with effect from 1 April 2010 (FA 2008 Sch 36). | Up to £3,000 per inaccuracy. |
| **Stamp duty reserve tax – for charges due and payable from 1 January 2015** | |
| Failure to make returns on time (FA 2009 Sch 55) | See **Penalties — modernised penalty regime** on p 10 |
| Failure to make payments on time (FA 2009 Sch 56) | See **Penalties — modernised penalty regime** on p 10 |
| **Stamp duty – for instruments executed from 1 October 1999** | |
| Failure to present instrument for stamping within 30 days after execution (or the day in which it is first received in the UK if executed outside the UK) (Stamp Act 1891 s 15B; SI 1999/2537). (Extended to instruments executed from 24 July 2002 for transfers of UK land and buildings, wherever executed (FA 2002 s 114)). From 1 October 2014 HMRC guidance to penalty amounts applies. | Documents submitted late for stamping **on or after 1 October 2014**:<br>If presented within one year after the end of the 30-day period: 10% of the unpaid duty capped at £300.<br>If presented more than one year after the end of the 30-day period but not more than two years after: 20% of the amount of unpaid duty.<br>If presented more than two years after the end of the 30-day period: 30% of the unpaid duty.<br>For delays of one year or more, penalty rate may be higher if there is evidence that the failure to submit documents was deliberate.<br>Before 1 October 2014:<br>If presented within one year after the end of the 30-day period: the lower of £300 or the amount of the unpaid duty.<br>If presented more than one year after the end of the 30-day period: the greater of £300 or the amount of unpaid duty. |
| **Stamp duty land tax – contracts completed after 30 November 2003** | |
| Failure to deliver a land transaction return by the filing date (FA 2003 Sch 10 paras 3, 4). | £100 if return delivered within three months of filing date, otherwise £200. If not delivered within 12 months, penalty up to amount of tax chargeable. |
| Failure to comply with notice to deliver return within specified period (FA 2003 Sch 10 para 5). | Up to £60 for each day on which the failure continues after notification. |
| Failure to keep and preserve records under FA 2003 Sch 10 para 9 or Sch 11 para 4 (FA 2003 Sch 10 para 11, Sch 11 para 6). | Up to £3,000 unless the information is provided by other documentary evidence. |
| Failure (From 1 August 2005) to disclose certain SDLT proposals or arrangements (TMA 1970 s 98C; SI 2005/1868; SI 2005/1869; SI 2010/2743). | (*a*) Up to £600 per day during 'initial period' (but tribunal can determine a higher penalty up to £1 million);<br>(*b*) further penalty up to £600 per day while failure continues.<br>Both the initial penalty in (*a*) above and the secondary penalty in (*b*) above can be increased up to £5,000 per day that failure continues from 10 days after the order is made. |
| Failure (From 1 August 2005) to provide prescribed information relating to disclosure certain SDLT proposals or arrangements (TMA 1970 s 98C; SI 2005/1868; SI 2005/1869; SI 2010/2743). | (*a*) Initial penalty up to £5,000;<br>(*b*) further penalty up to £600 per day while failure continues. This can be increased up to £5,000 per day after a tribunal has issued a disclosure order. |

| *Offence* | *Penalty* |
|---|---|
| Failure (From 1 August 2005) to provide scheme reference number relating to certain SDLT proposals or arrangements (TMA 1970 s 98C; SI 2005/1868; SI 2005/1869; SI 2010/2743); | (*a*) Penalty of £100 in respect of each scheme to which the failure relates; |
| for second failure, occurring within three years from the date on which the first failure began; | (*b*) penalty of £500 in respect of each scheme to which the failure relates; |
| for subsequent failures, occurring within three years from the date on which the previous failure began. | (*c*) penalty of £1,000 in respect of each scheme to which the failure relates. |
| **Land and buildings transaction tax from 1 April 2015** | |
| Inaccuracy in return or document (RSTPA 2014 ss 182, 183) | Careless inaccuracy — maximum 30% of tax lost<br>Deliberate inaccuracy — maximum 100% of tax lost |
| Failure to make returns on time (RSTPA 2014 ss 160–163) | The penalty rates applying are as for stamp duty reserve tax **Penalties — modernised penalty regime** on p 10, though reductions for disclosure differ. Penalties are payable to Revenue Scotland. |
| Failure to make payments on time (RSTPA 2014 s 169) | The penalty rates applying are as for stamp duty reserve tax **Penalties — modernised penalty regime** on p 10, though for some types of payment penalty is due as soon as tax is late. Penalties are payable to Revenue Scotland. |
| ***Stamp duty reserve tax replaced provisions*** | |
| Failure to notify HMRC and pay tax (TMA 1970 s 93, SI 1986/1711 as applied in practice by HMRC; see under 'Penalties and appeals —stamp duty reserve tax' on HMRC website). | *If notified within one year of the payment deadline: the lower of £100 or the amount of the unpaid duty.*<br>*If notified more than one year after the payment deadline: £100 plus up to the amount of unpaid duty, subject to a reduction for mitigating factors*<br>***Replaced by penalties under FA 2009 Schs 55 and 56 from 1 January 2015.*** |

# Value added tax

## Rates

(VATA 1994 s 2)

| | *From 4.1.11* | | *1.1.10–3.1.11* | | *1.12.08–31.12.09* | |
|---|---|---|---|---|---|---|
| | *Rate* | *VAT fraction* | *Rate* | *VAT Fraction* | *Rate* | *VAT Fraction* |
| **Standard rate** | **20%** | **1/6** | 17.5% | 7/47 | 15.0% | 3/23 |
| **Reduced rate** (see p 154) | **5.0%** | **1/21** | 5.0% | 1/21 | 5.0% | 1/21 |
| **Flat-rate scheme for farmers** | **4.0%**[1] | | 4.0%[1] | | 4.0%[1] | |

1 Flat rate addition to sale price
2 From April 2019 an assignment of a percentage of VAT receipts attributable to Scotland will be made to the Scottish Parliament.

## Registration limits

### UK taxable supplies

(VATA 1994 Sch 1 para 1, Sch 1A para 1; SI 2017/290)

A person who is UK-established (from 1 December 2012[3], previously both UK and non-UK established persons) and makes taxable supplies is liable to be registered:

(a) at the end of any month, or
(b) at any time, if:

| | *(a) turnover in the past year*[1] *(b) turnover in the next 30 days*[2] *exceeds:* | *Unless, in the case of (a), turnover for next year not expected to exceed:* |
|---|---|---|
| **1.4.17 onwards** | **£85,000** | **£83,000** |
| 1.4.16–31.3.17 | £83,000 | £81,000 |
| 1.4.15–31.3.16 | £82,000 | £80,000 |
| 1.4.14–31.3.15 | £81,000 | £79,000 |
| 1.4.13–31.3.14 | £79,000 | £77,000 |
| 1.4.12–31.3.13 | £77,000 | £75,000 |

1 The value of taxable supplies in the year then ending.
2 If there are reasonable grounds for believing the value of taxable supplies will exceed limit.
3 For supplies made on or after 1 December 2012 non-UK established businesses are required to register for VAT regardless of the value of taxable supplies made in the UK.

### Supplies from other EC countries ('distance selling')

(VATA 1994 Sch 2)

A business person in another EC country not registered or liable to be registered in the UK is liable to be registered on any day if, in the period beginning with 1 January in that year, the value of supplies by that person to non-taxable persons in the UK exceeds:

| | |
|---|---|
| **1.1.93 onwards** | **£70,000** |

## Acquisitions from other EC countries

(VATA 1994 Sch 3; SI 2017/290)

A person not registered or liable to be registered under the above rules is liable to be registered:

(a) at the end of any month if, in the period beginning with 1 January in that year, the value of taxable goods acquired by that person for business purposes (or for non-business purposes if a public body, charity, club, etc) from suppliers in other EC countries exceeds the following limits; or

(b) at any time, if there are reasonable grounds for believing the value of such acquisitions in the next 30 days will exceed the following limits:

| **1.4.17 onwards** | **£85,000** |
|---|---|
| 1.4.16–31.3.17 | £83,000 |
| 1.4.15–31.3.16 | £82,000 |
| 1.4.14–31.3.15 | £81,000 |
| 1.4.13–31.3.14 | £79,000 |
| 1.4.12–31.3.13 | £77,000 |

# Deregistration limits

## UK taxable supplies

(VATA 1994 Sch 1 para 4; SI 2017/290)

A registered taxable person who is UK-established (from 1 December 2012[1], previously both UK and non-UK established persons) ceases to be liable to be registered if, at any time, HMRC are satisfied that the value of taxable supplies in the year then beginning will not exceed:

| **1.4.17 onwards** | **£83,000** |
|---|---|
| 1.4.16–31.3.17 | £81,000 |
| 1.4.15–31.3.16 | £80,000 |
| 1.4.14–31.3.15 | £79,000 |
| 1.4.13–31.3.14 | £77,000 |
| 1.4.12–31.3.13 | £75,000 |
| Unless the reason for not exceeding the limit during that year is that the person will cease making taxable supplies or suspend making taxable supplies for 30 days or more. | |

1 For supplies made on or after 1 December 2012 non-UK established businesses are required to register for VAT regardless of the value of taxable supplies made in the UK.

## Supplies from other EC countries ('distance selling')

(VATA 1994 Sch 2)

A person registered under these provisions ceases to be liable to be registered if, at any time:

(a) relevant supplies in year ended 31 December last before that time did not exceed following limit; and
(b) HMRC are satisfied that value of relevant supplies in year immediately following that year will not exceed following limit:

| **1.1.93 onwards** | **£70,000** |
|---|---|

## Acquisitions from other EC countries

(VATA 1994 Sch 3; SI 2017/290)

A person registered under these provisions ceases to be liable to be registered if, at any time:

(a) relevant acquisitions in year ended 31 December last before that time did not exceed the following limits; and
(b) HMRC are satisfied that value of relevant acquisitions in year immediately following that year will not exceed the following limits:

| **1.4.17 onwards** | **£85,000** |
|---|---|
| 1.4.16–31.3.17 | £83,000 |
| 1.4.15–31.3.16 | £82,000 |
| 1.4.14–31.3.15 | £81,000 |
| 1.4.13–31.3.14 | £79,000 |
| 1.4.12–31.3.13 | £77,000 |

# Annual accounting scheme

(SI 1995/2518 regs 49–55)

A business may, subject to conditions, complete one VAT return a year. Quarterly or monthly interim payments to be made.

| | *Can join if taxable supplies in next year not expected to exceed:* | *Must leave at end of accounting year if taxable supplies exceeded:* |
|---|---|---|
| **1.4.06 onwards** | **£1,350,000** | **£1,600,000** |

# Cash accounting scheme

(SI 1995/2518 regs 56–65)

A business may, subject to conditions, account for and pay VAT on the basis of cash paid and received. It can join the scheme at any time as follows.

| | *Can join if taxable supplies in next year not expected to exceed:* | *Must leave at end of VAT period if taxable supplies in previous year exceed:* | *Unless turnover for next year not expected to exceed:* |
|---|---|---|---|
| **1.4.07 onwards** | **£1,350,000** | **£1,600,000** | **£1,350,000** |

# Flat-rate scheme for small businesses

(SI 1995/2518 regs 55A–55V; SI 2017/295)

A business which expects its taxable supplies in the next year to be no more than £150,000 can opt to join a flat-rate scheme. The appropriate percentage below is applied to total turnover generated, including exempt income, to calculate net VAT due. Once in the scheme a business may continue to use it until its total business income exceeds £230,000, and if income does exceed this limit, the business can still remain in the scheme if the income in the following year is estimated not to exceed £191,500.

**From 1 April 2017 a 16.5% rate applies to a 'limited cost trader'**, that is a trader whose VAT-inclusive expenditure on goods used for business purposes (excluding capital expenditure, food and drink for consumption by the business or its employees, and certain vehicles, vehicle parts and fuel) is less than 2% of turnover, or greater than 2% of turnover but less than £1,000 per year. Any trader which is not a limited cost trader continues to use the flat rate based on the categories of business detailed below.

| *Category of business* | *Appropriate %* | |
|---|---|---|
| | ***From 4.1.11*** | ***1.1.10–3.1.11*** |
| Accountancy or book-keeping | **14.5** | 13 |
| Advertising | **11** | 10 |
| Agricultural services | **11** | 10 |
| Any other activity not listed elsewhere | **12** | 10.5 |
| Architect | **14.5** | 13 |
| Boarding or care of animals | **12** | 10.5 |
| Business services that are not listed elsewhere | **12** | 10.5 |
| Catering services, including restaurants and takeaways | **12.5** | 11 |
| Civil and structural engineer or surveyor | **14.5** | 13 |
| Computer and IT consultancy or data processing | **14.5** | 13 |
| Computer repair services | **10.5** | 9.5 |
| Dealing in waste or scrap | **10.5** | 9.5 |
| Entertainment or journalism | **12.5** | 11 |
| Estate agency and property management services | **12** | 10.5 |
| Farming or agriculture that is not listed elsewhere | **6.5** | 6 |
| Film, radio, television or video production | **13** | 11.5 |
| Financial services | **13.5** | 12 |
| Forestry or fishing | **10.5** | 9.5 |
| General building or construction services | **9.5** | 8.5 |
| Hairdressing or other beauty treatment services | **13** | 11.5 |
| Hiring or renting goods | **9.5** | 8.5 |
| Hotel or accommodation | **10.5** | 9.5 |
| Investigation or security | **12** | 10.5 |
| Labour-only building or construction services[1] | **14.5** | 13 |
| Laundry or dry-cleaning services | **12** | 10.5 |
| Lawyer or legal services | **14.5** | 13 |
| Library, archive, museum or other cultural activity | **9.5** | 8.5 |
| Management consultancy | **14** | 12.5 |
| Manufacturing fabricated metal products | **10.5** | 9.5 |
| Manufacturing food | **9** | 8 |

| Category of business | Appropriate % | |
|---|---|---|
| | **From 4.1.11** | **1.1.10–3.1.11** |
| Manufacturing that is not listed elsewhere | **9.5** | 8.5 |
| Manufacturing yarn, textiles or clothing | **9** | 8 |
| Membership organisation | **8** | 7 |
| Mining or quarrying | **10** | 9 |
| Packaging | **9** | 8 |
| Photography | **11** | 10 |
| Post Offices | **5** | 4.5 |
| Printing | **8.5** | 7.5 |
| Publishing | **11** | 10 |
| Pubs | **6.5** | 6 |
| Real estate activity not listed elsewhere | **14** | 12.5 |
| Repairing personal or household goods | **10** | 9 |
| Repairing vehicles | **8.5** | 7.5 |
| Retailing food, confectionery, tobacco, newspapers or children's clothing | **4** | 3.5 |
| Retailing pharmaceuticals, medical goods, cosmetics or toiletries | **8** | 7 |
| Retailing that is not listed elsewhere | **7.5** | 6.5 |
| Retailing vehicles or fuel | **6.5** | 6 |
| Secretarial services | **13** | 11.5 |
| Social work | **11** | 10 |
| Sport or recreation | **8.5** | 7.5 |
| Transport or storage, couriers, freight, removals and taxis | **10** | 9 |
| Travel agency | **10.5** | 9.5 |
| Veterinary medicine | **11** | 10 |
| Wholesaling agricultural products | **8** | 7 |
| Wholesaling food | **7.5** | 6.5 |
| Wholesaling that is not listed elsewhere | **8.5** | 7.5 |

1 That is, services where value of materials supplied is less than 10% of turnover of such services; any other services are 'general building or construction services'.

## Partial exemption

(SI 1995/2518 regs 106–107)

A registered person who makes taxable and exempt supplies is partly exempt and may not be able to deduct (or reclaim) all his input tax. Where, however, input tax attributable to exempt supplies in a prescribed accounting period or tax year is within the de minimis limits below, all such input tax is attributable to taxable supplies and recoverable (subject to the normal rules).

| | |
|---|---|
| De minimis limits | £625 per month on average and 50% of all input tax for the period concerned |

# Capital goods scheme

(SI 1995/2518 regs 112–116)

## Input tax adjustment following change in taxable use of capital goods

| *Item* | *Value* | *Adjustment period* |
|---|---|---|
| Computer equipment | £50,000 or more | Five years |
| Ships, boats or other vessels[1] | £50,000 or more | Five years |
| Aircraft[1] | £50,000 or more | Five years |
| Land and buildings | £250,000 or more[2] | Ten years (for adjustment periods commenced before 1 January 2011, five years where interest had less than ten years to run on acquisition) |

1 Applies for goods acquired on or after 1 January 2011.

2 Figure reduced to £1 where owner ('O') of item or a person to whom O has granted an interest in that item:
(a) uses that item to make a grant falling within VATA 1994 Sch 9 Group 1 Item 1(ka) (self-storage facilities excluded from exemption);
(b) decides, no later than 31 March 2013, to treat the item as a capital item; and
(c) makes a written record to that effect, specifying the date of the decision.

Adjustment formula where adjustment period begins on or after 1 January 2011

$$\frac{\text{Total VAT on item}}{\text{Length of adjustment period}} \times \text{adjustment percentage}$$

The adjustment percentage is the percentage change in the extent to which the item is used (or treated as used) in making taxable supplies between the first interval in the adjustment period & a subsequent interval. (The first interval generally ends on the last day of the tax year in which the input tax was incurred.) For goods acquired on or after 1.1.11 total VAT includes any non-business VAT & the extent to which a capital item is used for business purposes must be determined when ascertaining taxable use for each subsequent interval.

# Zero-rated supplies

A zero-rated supply is a taxable supply, but the rate of tax is nil (VATA 1994 Sch 8).

Group 1 – Food
Group 2 – Sewerage services and water
Group 3 – Books etc
Group 4 – Talking books for the blind and disabled and wireless sets for the blind
Group 5 – Construction of buildings etc
Group 6 – Protected buildings
Group 7 – International services
Group 8 – Transport
Group 9 – Caravans and houseboats
Group 10 – Gold
Group 11 – Bank notes
Group 12 – Drugs, medicines, aids for the disabled etc
Group 13 – Imports, exports etc
Group 15 – Charities etc
Group 16 – Clothing and footwear
Group 18 – European Research Infrastructure Consortia (from 1 January 2013)
Group 19 – Women's sanitary products (from a date to be appointed)

# Reduced rate supplies

(VATA 1994 Sch 7A)

Group 1 – Domestic fuel and power
Group 2 – Installation of energy-saving materials
Group 3 – Grant-funded installation of heating equipment or security goods or connection of a gas supply
Group 4 – Women's sanitary products (to be reduced to zero-rated from a date to be appointed)
Group 5 – Children's car seats and bases
Group 6 – Residential conversions
Group 7 – Residential renovations and alterations
Group 8 – Contraceptive products (from 1 July 2006)
Group 9 – Welfare advice or information (from 1 July 2006)
Group 10 – Installation of mobility aids for the elderly (from 1 July 2007)
Group 11 – Smoking cessation products (from 1 July 2007)
Group 12 – Caravans (from 6 April 2013)
Group 13 – Cable-suspended transport systems (from 1 April 2013)

# Exempt supplies

(VATA 1994 Sch 9)

Group 1 – Land

Group 2 – Insurance

Group 3 – Postal services

Group 4 – Betting, gaming, dutiable machine games and lotteries

Group 5 – Finance

Group 6 – Education

Group 7 – Health and welfare

Group 8 – Burial and cremation

Group 9 – Subscriptions to trade unions, professional and other public interest bodies

Group 10 – Sport, sports competitions and physical education

Group 11 – Works of art etc

Group 12 – Fund-raising events by charities and other qualifying bodies

Group 13 – Cultural services etc

Group 14 – Supplies of goods where input tax cannot be recovered

Group 15 – Investment gold

Group 16 – Supplies of services by groups involving cost sharing (from 17 July 2012)

# EC Sales Lists

(SI 1995/2518 regs 2, 21–23)

All VAT-registered businesses in the UK must provide HMRC with details of goods and services supplied to a VAT-registered customer in another EU country. The requirement for returns is as follows:

| Supplies of | | Frequency |
|---|---|---|
| Goods | Supplies of goods are in excess of £35,000 (£70,000 before 1 January 2012) in any of the current or last four quarters | Monthly |
| Goods | Supplies of goods are below £35,000 (£70,000 before 1 January 2012) per quarter in the current and previous four quarters | Quarterly on 31 March, 30 June, 30 September and 31 December |
| Services supplied to a business where the place of supply is where the customer belongs | | Quarterly as above |
| Goods and services where a business is required to submit monthly lists for goods | | Monthly for all supplies, or monthly for goods and quarterly for services |
| Goods or services supplied by a business completing annual VAT returns | Total annual taxable turnover does not exceed £145,000; annual value of supplies to other EU countries not more than £11,000 (and do not include *New Means of Transport*) | On application — annual on agreed due date |
| Goods only supplied | Total annual taxable turnover does not exceed the VAT registration threshold plus £25,500; annual value of supplies to other EU countries not more than £11,000 (and do not include *New Means of Transport*) | On application — annual in simple format on agreed due date |

The due date for returns is 21 days after the end of the period if submitted online and 14 days after the end of the period if submitted on paper.

| Country | Code |
|---|---|
| Austria[10] | AT |
| Belgium | BE |
| Bulgaria | BG |
| Croatia[13] | HR |
| Cyprus[9] | CY |
| Czech Republic | CZ |
| Denmark[2] | DK |
| Estonia | EE |
| Finland[3] | FI |
| France[4] | FR |
| Germany[5] | DE |
| Greece[11] | EL |
| Hungary | HU |
| Ireland | IE |
| Italy[6] | IT |
| Latvia | LV |
| Lithuania | LT |
| Luxembourg | LU |
| Malta | MT |
| Netherlands[12] | NL |
| Poland | PL |
| Portugal[7] | PT |
| Romania | RO |
| Slovak Republic | SK |
| Slovenia | SI |
| Spain[8] | ES |
| Sweden | SE |

1 Countries not listed in the table above are not part of the EU VAT area and so sales to those countries should not be included on the EC sales list. The following are not part of the EU VAT area; Andorra, The Channel Islands, Gibraltar, Mount Athos, San Marino, and Vatican City. The UK and the Isle of Man are part of the EU VAT area, but sales to these should not be included on the list.

2 Does not include the Faroe Islands and Greenland.

3 Does not include Aland Islands.

4 Includes Monaco; excludes Martinique, Guadeloupe, Reunion, St Pierre & Miquelon, and French Guiana.

5 Does not include Businqen and Isle of Heligoland.
6 Does not include communes of Livigno and Campione d'Italia and the Italian waters of Lake Lugano.
7 Includes the Azores and Madeira.
8 Includes the Balearic Islands but excludes Ceuta, Melilla, and the Canary Islands.
9 Includes British sovereign base areas of Akrotiri and Dhekelia, but excludes those areas in United Nations buffer zone and to the north of that where the Republic of Cyprus does not have effective control.
10 Includes Jungholz and Mittelberg.
11 Excludes Mount Athos.
12 Excludes Antilles (now Curaçao, Sint Maarten and BES Islands).
13 Croatia joined the EU on 1 July 2013. Supplies of goods, or services subject to the reverse charge, to a VAT registered customer in Croatia, must be included in the ESL.

# Intrastat

(SI 1992/2790)

All VAT-registered businesses in the UK must complete boxes 8 and 9 on the VAT return showing the total value of goods supplied to and acquired from other EC member states respectively. Businesses with a total value of such supplies (dispatches) or acquisitions (arrivals) exceeding a threshold must make supplementary declarations containing further information each month. Thresholds are set for each calendar year and recent thresholds are shown below. If a person's dispatches or arrivals in the previous calendar year exceeded the current year's threshold, supplementary declarations must be made for the full current year. If the cumulative total of dispatches or arrivals in a year exceeds that calendar year's threshold, supplementary declarations must be made for the rest of the year, starting in the month in which the threshold is exceeded. Additional delivery terms information must be provided on the supplementary declaration only if the annual value of arrivals or dispatches exceeds the delivery terms threshold, and the information must be submitted from the start of the next calendar year. If the delivery terms threshold for arrivals is exceeded, but not that for dispatches, delivery terms must be provided for arrivals only, and vice versa. From April 2012 declarations must be submitted electronically and will be due 21 days after the end of the month in which there is EU trade to declare.

| Year | Supplies (dispatches) threshold per calendar year | Acquisitions (arrivals) threshold per calendar year | Delivery terms threshold per calendar year |
|---|---|---|---|
| **From 1.1.15** | **£250,000** | **£1,500,000** | **£24,000,000** |
| 1.1.14–31.12.14 | £250,000 | £1,200,000 | £24,000,000 |
| 1.1.10–31.12.13 | £250,000 | £600,000 | £16,000,000 |

Some of the EU country codes and the areas included for intrastat purposes differ from those used for EC sales list purposes. The intrastat codes are as follows.

| *Country* | *Code* |
|---|---|
| Austria | AT |
| Belgium | BE |
| Bulgaria | BG |
| Croatia[12] | HR |
| Cyprus[9] | CY |
| Czech Republic | CZ |
| Denmark[2] | DK |
| Estonia | EE |
| Finland[3] | FI |
| France[4] | FR |
| Germany[5] | DE |
| Greece[10] | GR |
| Hungary | HU |
| Ireland | IE |
| Italy[6] | IT |
| Latvia | LV |
| Lithuania | LT |
| Luxembourg | LU |
| Malta | MT |
| Netherlands | NL |
| Poland | PL |
| Portugal[7] | PT |
| Romania | RO |
| Slovak Republic | SK |
| Slovenia | SI |
| Spain[8] | ES |
| Sweden | SE |
| United Kingdom[11] | GB |

1 Andorra and Liechtenstein are both outside the customs territory (and therefore the statistical territory) of the EU.
2 Does not include the Faroe Islands.

[3] Includes Aland Islands.
[4] Includes Monaco, but excludes all French Overseas departments and territories. Martinique, Guadeloupe, Reunion, Mayotte, and French Guiana are part of the statistical territory of France but because customs documentation is still required for exports to, or imports from, these territories HMRC continue to collect trade statistics from that documentation and it must not be declared on the intrastat.
[5] Includes Isle of Heligoland but excludes Busingen.
[6] Does not include communes of Livigno and Campione d'Italia, the Italian waters of Lake Lugano and the Vatican. Livigno is part of the statistical territory of Italy but because customs documentation is still required for exports to, or imports from, this territory HMRC continue to collect trade statistics from that documentation and it must not be declared on the intrastat.
[7] Includes the Azores and Madeira.
[8] Includes the Balearic Islands but excludes Ceuta, Melilla, and the Canary Islands. The Canary Islands are part of the statistical territory of Spain but because customs documentation is still required for exports to, or imports from, these territories HMRC continue to collect trade statistics from that documentation and it must not be declared on the intrastat.
[9] Includes UK sovereign base areas but excludes Northern Cyprus.
[10] Includes Mount Athos.
[11] Includes the Isle of Man and the Channel Islands but excludes Gibraltar.
[12] Croatia joined the EU on 1 July 2013. Dispatches and arrivals to/from Croatia should be included from this date.

# VAT Mini One Stop Shop (VAT MOSS)

(VATA 1994 Sch 4A paras 15, 16; SI 2014/2726; HMRC Brief 46/2014)

From 1 January 2015 the place of supply for business-to-consumer (B2C) supplies of broadcasting, telecommunications and e-services (digital services) is determined by the location of the consumer. The changes affect all businesses that supply digital services to consumers (ie private individuals), whether or not they are registered for UK VAT, because there are no registration limits for digital service supplies made to consumers outside the UK. Any business supplying digital services to a consumer in another member state therefore has to charge VAT on the supply in that member state and register for VAT in that member state. Supplies of digital services to businesses only (including the self-employed) are not affected by the changes.

To avoid having to register for VAT in every EU member state where digital services are supplied, a business may opt to use the VAT Mini One Stop Shop online service (VAT MOSS). Using the VAT MOSS online service means a business can submit a single calendar quarterly VAT MOSS return and payment covering all its EU digital service supplies. If the business registers for the VAT MOSS online service in the UK, HMRC will send an electronic copy of the appropriate part of the VAT MOSS return, and the related VAT payment, to each relevant member state's tax authority.

# Car fuel

(VATA 1994 ss 56, 57, Schs 4, 6; FA 2013 Sch 38)

Where an employer pays mileage allowances, he may use the advisory fuel rates on p 85 to calculate the input VAT to reclaim on the fuel element. Receipts must still be retained.

VAT-inclusive scale figures can be used to assess VAT due on fuel provided at no cost (from 11 December 2012, previously at below cost) for private journeys by registered traders or their employees, where the fuel has been provided from business resources. The figures represent the tax-inclusive value of the fuel supplied to each individual and relate to return periods beginning on the dates shown. If the trader or employer opts to use the scale figures he must use them for all supplies of fuel for private use made for no consideration in the prescribed accounting period. From 17 July 2013, the scale charge may also be used as an alternative to accounting for VAT on the required open market value where the fuel is supplied for a consideration below that value.

| | *12 months* £ | *3 months* £ | *1 month* £ |
|---|---|---|---|
| **From 1 May 2017:** $CO_2$ band | | | |
| **120 or below** | 563 | 140 | 46 |
| **125** | 842 | 211 | 70 |
| **130** | 901 | 224 | 74 |
| **135** | 955 | 238 | 79 |
| **140** | 1,013 | 252 | 84 |
| **145** | 1,068 | 267 | 88 |
| **150** | 1,126 | 281 | 93 |
| **155** | 1,180 | 295 | 98 |
| **160** | 1,239 | 309 | 102 |
| **165** | 1,293 | 323 | 107 |
| **170** | 1,351 | 337 | 111 |
| **175** | 1,405 | 351 | 116 |
| **180** | 1,464 | 365 | 121 |
| **185** | 1,518 | 379 | 125 |
| **190** | 1,577 | 393 | 131 |
| **195** | 1,631 | 408 | 136 |
| **200** | 1,689 | 422 | 140 |
| **205** | 1,743 | 436 | 145 |
| **210** | 1,802 | 449 | 149 |
| **215** | 1,856 | 463 | 154 |
| **220** | 1,914 | 478 | 159 |
| **225 or above** | 1,969 | 492 | 163 |

| | *12 months* £ | *3 months* £ | *1 month* £ |
|---|---|---|---|
| **1 May 2016–30 April 2017:** $CO_2$ band | | | |
| **120 or below** | 467 | 116 | 38 |
| **125** | 699 | 175 | 58 |
| **130** | 747 | 186 | 61 |
| **135** | 792 | 197 | 65 |
| **140** | 841 | 209 | 69 |
| **145** | 886 | 221 | 73 |
| **150** | 934 | 233 | 77 |
| **155** | 979 | 245 | 81 |
| **160** | 1,028 | 256 | 85 |
| **165** | 1,073 | 268 | 89 |
| **170** | 1,121 | 279 | 92 |
| **175** | 1,166 | 291 | 96 |
| **180** | 1,214 | 303 | 101 |
| **185** | 1,259 | 314 | 104 |
| **190** | 1,308 | 326 | 108 |
| **195** | 1,353 | 338 | 112 |
| **200** | 1,401 | 350 | 116 |
| **205** | 1,446 | 362 | 120 |
| **210** | 1,495 | 373 | 123 |
| **215** | 1,540 | 384 | 128 |
| **220** | 1,588 | 396 | 132 |
| **225 or above** | 1,633 | 408 | 135 |

| | *12 months* £ | *3 months* £ | *1 month* £ |
|---|---|---|---|
| **1 May 2015–30 April 2016:** $CO_2$ band | | | |
| **120 or below** | 536 | 133 | 44 |
| **125** | 802 | 200 | 66 |
| **130** | 857 | 213 | 70 |
| **135** | 909 | 227 | 75 |
| **140** | 965 | 240 | 80 |
| **145** | 1,016 | 254 | 84 |
| **150** | 1,072 | 267 | 88 |
| **155** | 1,123 | 281 | 93 |
| **160** | 1,179 | 294 | 97 |
| **165** | 1,231 | 308 | 102 |
| **170** | 1,286 | 320 | 106 |
| **175** | 1,338 | 334 | 111 |
| **180** | 1,393 | 347 | 115 |
| **185** | 1,445 | 361 | 119 |
| **190** | 1,501 | 374 | 124 |
| **195** | 1,552 | 388 | 129 |
| **200** | 1,608 | 401 | 133 |
| **205** | 1,660 | 415 | 138 |
| **210** | 1,715 | 428 | 142 |
| **215** | 1,767 | 441 | 146 |
| **220** | 1,822 | 455 | 151 |
| **225 or above** | 1,874 | 468 | 155 |

| | *12 months* £ | *3 months* £ | *1 month* £ |
|---|---|---|---|
| **1 May 2014–30 April 2015:** $CO_2$ band | | | |
| **120 or below** | 627 | 156 | 52 |
| **125** | 939 | 234 | 78 |
| **130** | 1,004 | 251 | 83 |
| **135** | 1,064 | 266 | 88 |
| **140** | 1,129 | 282 | 94 |
| **145** | 1,190 | 297 | 99 |
| **150** | 1,255 | 313 | 104 |
| **155** | 1,315 | 328 | 109 |
| **160** | 1,381 | 345 | 115 |
| **165** | 1,441 | 360 | 120 |
| **170** | 1,506 | 376 | 125 |
| **175** | 1,567 | 391 | 130 |
| **180** | 1,632 | 408 | 136 |
| **185** | 1,692 | 423 | 141 |
| **190** | 1,757 | 439 | 146 |
| **195** | 1,818 | 454 | 151 |
| **200** | 1,883 | 470 | 156 |
| **205** | 1,943 | 485 | 161 |
| **210** | 2,008 | 502 | 167 |
| **215** | 2,069 | 517 | 172 |
| **220** | 2,134 | 533 | 177 |
| **225 or above** | 2,194 | 548 | 182 |

| | *12 months* £ | *3 months* £ | *1 month* £ |
|---|---|---|---|
| **1 May 2013–30 April 2014:** $CO_2$ band | | | |
| **120 or below** | 675 | 168 | 56 |
| **125** | 1,010 | 253 | 84 |
| **130** | 1,080 | 269 | 89 |
| **135** | 1,145 | 286 | 95 |
| **140** | 1,215 | 303 | 101 |
| **145** | 1,280 | 320 | 106 |
| **150** | 1,350 | 337 | 112 |
| **155** | 1,415 | 354 | 118 |
| **160** | 1,485 | 371 | 123 |
| **165** | 1,550 | 388 | 129 |
| **170** | 1,620 | 404 | 134 |
| **175** | 1,685 | 421 | 140 |
| **180** | 1,755 | 438 | 146 |
| **185** | 1,820 | 455 | 151 |
| **190** | 1,890 | 472 | 157 |
| **195** | 1,955 | 489 | 163 |
| **200** | 2,025 | 506 | 168 |
| **205** | 2,090 | 523 | 174 |
| **210** | 2,160 | 539 | 179 |
| **215** | 2,225 | 556 | 185 |
| **220** | 2,295 | 573 | 191 |
| **225 or above** | 2,360 | 590 | 196 |

| | *12 months* £ | *3 months* £ | *1 month* £ |
|---|---|---|---|
| **1 May 2012–30 April 2013:** $CO_2$ band | | | |
| **120 or below** | 665 | 166 | 55 |
| **125** | 1,000 | 250 | 83 |
| **130** | 1,065 | 266 | 88 |
| **135** | 1,135 | 283 | 94 |
| **140** | 1,200 | 300 | 100 |
| **145** | 1,270 | 316 | 105 |
| **150** | 1,335 | 333 | 111 |
| **155** | 1,400 | 350 | 116 |
| **160** | 1,470 | 366 | 122 |
| **165** | 1,535 | 383 | 127 |
| **170** | 1,600 | 400 | 133 |
| **175** | 1,670 | 416 | 138 |
| **180** | 1,735 | 433 | 144 |
| **185** | 1,800 | 450 | 150 |
| **190** | 1,870 | 467 | 155 |
| **195** | 1,935 | 483 | 161 |
| **200** | 2,000 | 500 | 166 |
| **205** | 2,070 | 517 | 172 |
| **210** | 2,135 | 533 | 177 |
| **215** | 2,200 | 550 | 183 |
| **220** | 2,270 | 567 | 189 |
| **225 or above** | 2,335 | 583 | 194 |

# Interest and penalties

## Default interest

(VATA 1994 s 74)

Interest runs on the amount of any VAT assessed (or paid late by voluntary disclosure):

- from the reckonable date (normally the latest date on which a return is required for the period in question);
- until the date of payment (although in practice it runs to the date shown on the notice of assessment or notice of voluntary disclosure if paid within 30 days of that date).

The period of interest cannot commence more than three years before the date of assessment or payment.

The rates of interest are as follows:

| *Period* | *Rate* |
|---|---|
| **from 23 August 2016** | **2.75%** |
| 29 September 2009–22 August 2016 | 3.00% |
| 24 March 2009–28 September 2009 | 2.50% |
| 27 January 2009–23 March 2009 | 3.50% |
| 6 January 2009–26 January 2009 | 4.50% |

## Interest on VAT overpaid in cases of official error

(VATA 1994 s 78)

Where VAT has been overpaid or underclaimed due to an error by HMRC, then on a claim HMRC must pay interest:

- from the date they receive payment (or authorise a repayment) for the return period in question;
- until the date on which they authorise payment of the amount on which interest is due.

This provision does not require HMRC to pay interest on an amount on which repayment supplement is due.

The rates of interest are as follows:

| *Period* | *Rate* |
|---|---|
| **from 29 September 2009** | **0.50%** |
| 27 January 2009–28 September 2009 | 0.00% |
| 6 January 2009–26 January 2009 | 1.00% |

## Repayment supplement – VAT

(VATA 1994 s 79)

Where a person is entitled to a repayment the payment due is increased by a supplement of the greater of:

(i) 5% of that amount; or
(ii) £50.

The supplement will only be paid if:

(a) the return or claim is received by HMRC not later than the last day on which it is required to be made;
(b) HMRC do not issue a written instruction making the refund within the relevant period; and
(c) the amount shown on the return or claim does not exceed the amount due by more than 5% of that amount or £250, whichever is the greater.

The 'relevant period' is 30 days beginning with the receipt of the return or claim or, if later, the day after the last day of the VAT period to which the return or claim relates.

## Penalties and surcharges

| *Offence* | *Penalty* |
|---|---|
| Inaccuracy in return or other document (FA 2007 Sch 24)[1]. | See **Penalties — modernised penalty regime** on p 10. |
| Failure to notify obligation to register for VAT, change in supplies made by person exempted from registration, acquisition affecting exemption, acquisition of goods from another member state and unauthorised issue of an invoice (FA 2008 Sch 41). | See **Penalties — modernised penalty regime** on p 10. |
| Inaccuracy in return or other document as a result of third party providing incorrect (or withholding) information (FA 2007 Sch 24). | See **Penalties — modernised penalty regime** on p 10. |
| Failure to inform HMRC of an error in an assessment within 30 days of the date of the assessment (FA 2007 Sch 24). | See **Penalties — modernised penalty regime** on p 10. |
| Failure to comply with HMRC investigatory powers with effect from 1 April 2009 (FA 2008 Sch 36). | (*a*) Initial penalty of £300;<br>(*b*) if failure/obstruction continues, a further penalty of up to £60 per day;<br>(*c*) if failure/obstruction continues after penalty under (*a*) imposed, a tax-related amount determined by the Upper Tribunal. |
| Provision of inaccurate information or document when complying with an information notice (FA 2008 Sch 36). | Up to £3,000 per inaccuracy. |
| Failure to submit a return electronically if required to do so by SI 1995/2518 reg 25 for prescribed accounting periods starting on or after 1 April 2012. Before 1 April 2012, failure of a *specified person* to make a *specified return* using an electronic return system for prescribed accounting periods ending on or after 31 March 2011 (SI 1995/2518 reg 25A). 'Specified person' was broadly a person registered for VAT on or after 1 April 2010, or one registered before that date who at 31 December 2009 or any later date has an annual VAT exclusive turnover of £100,000 or more. Penalty will only apply to prescribed accounting periods ending on or after 31 March 2013 where the person is required to make an electronic return only as a result of the removal of the turnover test from 1 April 2012. | Annual VAT exclusive turnover of:<br>£22,800,001 or more — £400<br>£5,600,001 to £22,800,000 — £300<br>£100,001 to £5,600,000 — £200<br>£100,000 or under — £100 |
| Failure to submit return or pay VAT due within time limit (where a return is late but the VAT is paid on time or no VAT is due, a default is recorded but no surcharge arises) (VATA 1994 s 59)[2].<br>Failure to pay tax due under the payment on account scheme on time (VATA 1994 s 59A). | The greater of £30 and a specified percentage of outstanding VAT for period, depending on number of defaults in surcharge period: first default in period 2%, second default 5%, third default 10%, fourth and further defaults 15%. (Surcharge assessments are not issued for sums of less than £400 unless the rate of the surcharge is 10% or more.)<br>**Due to be replaced by penalties under FA 2009 Schs 55 and 56 from a date to be appointed.** |
| Issuing incorrect certificate stating that certain supplies fall to be zero-rated or taxed at the reduced rate (VATA 1994 s 62). | Difference between tax actually charged and tax which should have been charged. |
| Material inaccuracy in EC sales statement (VATA 1994 s 65). | £100 for each material inaccuracy in two-year penalty period (which commences following notice of second material inaccuracy). |
| Failure to submit an EC sales statement (VATA 1994 s 66). | Greater of £50 or a daily penalty (maximum 100 days) £5 for the first, £10 for the second, £15 for the third or subsequent failure in the default period. |
| Breach of walking possession agreement (VATA 1994 s 68). | 50% of VAT due or amount recoverable. |
| Failure to preserve records for prescribed period (VATA 1994 ss 69, 69B). | £500. |
| Failure to preserve records specified in HMRC direction (VATA 1994 ss 69, 69B). | £200 for each day of failure (maximum 30 days). |
| Breaches of regulatory provisions, including failure to notify cessation of liability or entitlement to be registered, failure to keep records and non-compliance with any regulations made under VATA 1994 (VATA 1994 s 69). | Greater of £50 and a daily penalty (maximum 100 days) of a specified amount depending on number of failures in preceding two years: £5* per day if no previous failures; £10* per day if one previous failure; £15* per day if two or more previous failures. |
| Where failure consists of not paying VAT or not making a return in the required time. | *1/6, 1/3 and 1/2 of 1% of the VAT due respectively, if greater. |

| *Offence* | *Penalty* |
|---|---|
| Breaches of regulatory provisions involving failure to pay VAT or submit return by due date (VATA 1994 s 69). | Greater of £50 and a daily penalty (for no more than 100 days) of a specified amount depending on number of failures in preceding two years: greater of £5 and 1/6 % of VAT due if no previous failures; greater of £10 and 1/3% of VAT due if one previous failure; greater of £15 and 1/2% of VAT due if two or more previous failures. |
| Failure to comply with the requirements of the investment gold scheme (VATA 1994 s 69A). | 17.5% of the value of transactions concerned. |
| Import VAT (FA 2003 ss 24–41): | |
| – failures relating to non-compliance | maximum penalty of £2,500 |
| – evasion. | maximum penalty equal to VAT sought to be evaded. |
| Evasion of VAT: conduct involving dishonesty (VATA 1994 ss 60, 61). Does not apply to acts or omissions relating to an inaccuracy in a document or failure to notify HMRC of an under-assessment (to which penalties under FA 2007 Sch 24 apply). | Amount of tax evaded or sought to be evaded (subject to mitigation). |
| Transactions connected with fraudulent evasion of VAT (VATA 1994 ss 69C–69E; F(No 2)A 2017 s 68). | 30% of potential lost VAT. |
| *Failure to notify the use of a designated avoidance scheme (VATA 1994 Sch 11A paras 10, 11).* | *15% of the tax avoided (applies to businesses with supplies of £600,000 or more).* ***To be replaced from 1 January 2018, see below***. |
| *Failure to disclose certain schemes within 30 days of the due date or the first return affected (VATA 1994 Sch 11A paras 10, 11).* | *£5,000 (applies to businesses with supplies exceeding £10 million).* ***To be replaced from 1 January 2018, see below***. |
| Failure from 1 January 2018 to notify details of, or notify use of, a notifiable proposal which enables a person to obtain a tax advantage within 31 days of the making of the proposal (F(No 2)A 2017 Sch 17). | Penalty up to £600 per day in 'initial period'<br>A continuing penalty not exceeding £600 for each day on which the failure continues after imposition of initial penalty<br>(but a tribunal can determine a higher penalty up to £1 million). |
| Failure from 1 January 2018 to provide HMRC with the reference number and related information in relation to notifiable arrangements above (F(No 2)A 2017 Sch 17). | Penalty not exceeding £5,000 in respect of each scheme to which the failure relates<br>For second failure within three years of first, penalty not exceeding £7,500 in respect of each scheme<br>For subsequent failures within three years of previous, penalty not exceeding £10,000 in respect of each scheme. |

1 In relation to VAT MOSS returns, a penalty under FA 2007 Sch 24 only applies when the recipient of the supply is in the UK. If an inaccuracy on a UK return relates to a supply to a recipient in another member state, there is no penalty under UK legislation, but a penalty may apply in that other member state in which the recipient is located. If an inaccuracy on (say) a French VAT return relates to a supply to a recipient in the UK, there could be a penalty under UK legislation.

2 In relation to VAT MOSS returns, a penalty for a late return or late payment could be charged by each member state in which the supplies are deemed to be made.

# Index

**D**



**E**

## F



## G



## H



## I